Dear John,

Thank you for all
your support and encouragement.
There is a little of you
in this book.

Tony

11/24/98

Legal Positivism in American Jurisprudence

This book is both a work of intellectual history and a contribution to legal philosophy. It represents a serious and philosophically sophisticated guide to modern American legal theory, demonstrating that legal positivism has been a misunderstood and underappreciated perspective throughout most of twentieth-century American legal thought.

Having traced the roots of positivism through the first half of the twentieth century, Anthony J. Sebok argues that it was "hijacked" during the Warren Court by conservative legal scholars who were moral skeptics, and this created the impression that positivism is necessarily hostile to moral principles in the law. The author rejects the view that one must adopt some version of natural law theory in order to recognize moral principles in the law. On the contrary, once one corrects for the mistakes of formalism and postwar legal process, one is left with a theory of legal positivism that takes moral principles seriously while avoiding the pitfalls of natural law.

The broad scope of this book ensures that it will be read by philosophers of law, historians of law, historians of American intellectual life, and those in political science concerned with public law and administration.

Anthony J. Sebok is a professor of law at Brooklyn Law School.

Cambridge Studies in Philosophy and Law

GENERAL EDITOR: Gerald Postema
(University of North Carolina at Chapel Hill)

ADVISORY BOARD

Jules Coleman (Yale Law School)
Antony Duff (University of Stirling)
David Lyons (Boston University)
Neil MacCormick (University of Edinburgh)
Stephen Munzer (UCLA Law School)
Phillip Pettit (The Australian National University)
Joseph Raz (University of Oxford)
Jeremy Waldron (Columbia Law School)

Legal Positivism in American Jurisprudence

ANTHONY J. SEBOK

CAMBRIDGE
UNIVERSITY PRESS

PUBLISHED BY THE PRESS SYNDICATE OF THE UNIVERSITY OF CAMBRIDGE
The Pitt Building, Trumpington Street, Cambridge CB2 1RP, United Kingdom

CAMBRIDGE UNIVERSITY PRESS
The Edinburgh Building, Cambridge CB2 2RU, UK   http://www.cup.cam.ac.uk
40 West 20th Street, New York, NY 10011-4211, USA   http://www.cup.org
10 Stamford Road, Oakleigh, Melbourne 3166, Australia

© Cambridge University Press 1998

First published 1998

Printed in the United States of America

Typeset in Palatino 10/12 pt, QuarkXPress™ [CS]

*A catalog record for this book is available from
the British Library.*

Library of Congress Cataloging-in-Publication Data
Sebok, Anthony James (date)
Legal positivism in American jurisprudence /
Anthony Sebok.
p.   cm. – (Cambridge studies in philosophy and law)
ISBN 0-521-48041-8 (hb)
1. Legal positivism.   2. Law – United States – Philosophy.
I. Title.   II. Series.
K331.S43   1998
340'.112 – dc21   97-52780
CIP

ISBN 0 521 48041 8 hardback

To my parents

Contents

Contents

Acknowledgments

This book draws its inspiration from three great teachers. The first, Joseph Raz, introduced me to legal positivism and helped me to see its rigorous virtues. The second, Walter Murphy, challenged my commitment to legal positivism by teaching me that the U.S. Constitution is based upon moral concepts that are difficult if not impossible to capture in the language of law. The third, Jules Coleman, helped me to reconcile my interests in legal positivism and the U.S. Constitution by insisting that positivists can take moral language seriously. Even though I disagree with each of my former teachers at one point or another in this book, it was through their example and encouragement that I gradually built my argument. This book reflects the influence that each has had upon me. Like a point discovered through triangulation, I have found my own true position by carefully measuring my distance from all three of them.

As with many first books, this work is a map of my graduate education. The path formed across the years reveals that at each turn I was irresistibly pulled back to the same questions. From the start of my training in political theory at Oxford I have been fascinated by the ambiguous status of law in liberal democracy. Given that liberalism presupposes disagreement among sincere participants in the common practice of government, how was a liberal to view the role of the judge? No less than anyone else, the judge knows, in advance, that there is a good chance that he or she will sincerely disagree with some of the practical judgments of those empowered to make the law. Yet the judge knows too that liberalism requires the rule of law, which forbids anyone to change the law after it has been duly made, except as the law itself requires. What then was the responsibility of the judge who wanted to be faithful to justice? What honor or nobility could there be in a job in which one was required not only to watch, but to help, the state to do what one knows is wrong? And yet, I felt strongly that law is an extraordinary and rich form of practical reasoning, and that the power of law came from the fact that it asks the judge to efface him- or herself. To adjudicate is to promote justice by being an instrument of the law. Sometimes the law's normative universe matches the judge's own picture of justice; many times it does not. Sometimes the law asks the judge to fill in gaps where the law itself is silent on a question that sounds in justice. Regardless of which of these moments the judge finds him- or herself, in each of them he or she is being asked to suppress a part of his or her own judgment about justice itself in order to perform a job crucial to the success of liberal democracy.

As I learned more about legal positivism, I became convinced that it could explain how legal reasoning helps judges perform the difficult job that has been asked of them by liberal democracies like the United States and England. But even as I grew more convinced of the value of positivism to modern liberal thought, I became increasingly aware of the view, held by many who study the U.S. Constitution, that positivism supports a peculiar view of legal reasoning associated with the theories of original intent and "judicial restraint." Much of my time studying public law at Princeton and legal theory at Yale Law School was dedicated to challenging the assumption that positivism is a theory of law for judicial conservatives. I am very grateful to all of my teachers at both these schools for tolerating my almost obsessive interest in questioning the "conservative positivist" paradigm.

The one thing for which my graduate studies did not prepare me, and for which my teachers should feel no responsibility, is the amount of historical research I ultimately had to do to write this book. Shortly after I decided to write about the importance of legal positivism to modern American law, I realized that the burden fell on me to prove that the conventional picture of positivism held by lawyers and political scientists was a mistake. The best way to prove that the views to which scholars had heretofore attached the label "positivism" were in fact inimical to positivism was to show how the misimpression had been created. My research therefore took me back to Fuller's conflation of realism and positivism in the middle of the twentieth century, which then took me back to the realists' own attack on analytic jurisprudence. By the time I had done my "preparatory" research for my dissertation, I had discovered that English positivism had come to the United States through the doctrine we now call formalism; that it was the focus of much of the realists's jurisprudential criticism; and that positivism reemerged, changed and much improved, in the writings of the legal process school.

This story of the evolution of American positivism startled me and seemed important. I realized that it was a story that had never been told, partly because the sources did not directly address themselves to the question of positivism. It is for these reasons that I decided to lead the reader through the same process of discovery that I experienced when I first worked through the materials. I apologize in advance for the unusual structure of my historical argument. Not only am I not a professional historian, and therefore untrained in the difficult task of writing intellectual history, but the subject matter itself forced me to adopt an awkward expository style. Because much of what we know about nineteenth-century formalism is based upon what its critics have said about it, and it is my contention that those critics have misunderstood formalism's positivist core, I have had to reconstruct the history of positivism by first telling the story of its misrepresentation. The most difficult part of this project, and the part that may confound legal historians the most, is the relative absence of any positivists actually speaking for themselves until the history reaches the middle of the twentieth century. The reason for this is simple: Given the lack of materials available to me, I found it useful first to build a picture based on what formalism's critics *believed* they were attacking, and only then to ask whether, and to what extent, the legal theory at the heart of that picture looked anything like positivism. To conclude that the formalists were not positivists because they did not say they were positivists would be to mistake silence for absence. Nonetheless, I recognize that my method may strike some as less rigorous than what one might expect of a legal historian: I plead guilty to that charge. This is the work of a legal theorist who found that he could not do legal theory without doing legal history.

Parts of my argument have been published in articles in the *Michigan Law Review* and the *Southern California Law Review*. I have significantly revised my ideas since these articles were published, and the process of working with the editors of these journals has helped me refine and improve my arguments. I am grateful to the editors of these journals for allowing me to publish with them and for their careful and thoughtful criticisms. I am also grateful for their permission to use sections from my original articles in this book.

Many people have supported and aided me through the course of this project. I was lucky to receive a lot of advice over the past ten years. I probably made a great mistake by not following the advice of others more carefully. But even when I did not follow their suggestions, I was always grateful for the patience and time of the following friends, teachers, and colleagues. Many thanks to Bruce Ackerman, Larry Alexander, Akhil Amar, Mark Brandon, Hon. Guido Calabresi, David Carlson, Randall Costa, Michael Dorf, David Dorsey, Neil Duxbury, David Dyzenhaus, Chris Eisgruber, Julie Faber, Judy Failer, Jim Fanto, Stephen Feldman, Owen Fiss, Jim Fleming, Robert George, Amy Guttman, Les Green, Abner Greene, Tom Grey, Randy Hahn, Cheryl Hall, Gil Harmon, Susan Herman, Dean Tony Kronman, Bailey Kuklin, Arthur Jacobson, Marianne Lado, Sheldon Leader, Brian Leiter, Tim Lytton, Gary Minda, Wayne Moore, William Reynolds, Michel Rosenfeld, Alan Ryan, Larry Sager, Fred Schauer, Amos Shapira, Scott Shapiro, Paul Shupack, Brian Tamanaha, Ruti Teitel, Paul Vogt, Spencer Weber Waller, Dean Harry Wellington, G. Edward White, Steven Winter, and Ben Zipursky. I would like to thank the two deans who supported my research at Brooklyn Law School, Hon. David Trager and Dean Joan Wexler. Sara Robbins, the head librarian of Brooklyn Law School, made this project much less painful than it could have been by making it easy for me to use our library's resources. I have been lucky to have the help of an extraordinary group of research assistants: Peter Bucklin (BLS '95), Margaret Foley (BLS '99), Tom Uhl (BLS '96), and David Gordon. Finally I would like to thank two people who have been engaged in conversation with me about legal theory ever since we met in graduate school: John Goldberg and Eldon Soifer. Each has confirmed for me the simple truth that the greatest reward of philosophy is friendship.

Chapter 1

Why Study Legal Positivism?

1.1. LEGAL POSITIVISM'S CHECKERED PAST

The past forty years have not been kind to legal positivism. Ever since H.L.A. Hart's famous debate with Lon Fuller over the charge that German legal positivists were partly responsible for the rise of Adolf Hitler, positivism has often been the target of frequent attacks by American lawyers.[1] Its critics have tried, at various times, to connect positivism with a diverse and jointly inconsistent group of theories, such as legal formalism,[2] legal realism,[3] and originalism.[4] Furthermore, since the 1960s, legal positivism has been associated almost entirely with politically conservative forces in the United States, especially with an approach to constitutional interpretation known during the 1970s as "judicial restraint."[5] Given the

[1] H.L.A. Hart, *Positivism and the Separation of Law and Morals*, 71 *Harv. L. Rev.* 593, 595 (1958) (citing Gustav Radbruch, *Die Erneuerung der Rechts*, 2 *Die Wandlung* 8 [Germany 1947]; Gustav Radbruch, *Gesetzliches Unrecht und Ubergesetzliches Recht*, 1 *Suddeutsche Juristen-Zeitung* 105 [Germany 1946]); Lon Fuller, *Positivism and Fidelity to Law – A Reply to Professor Hart*, 71 *Harv. L. Rev.* 630 (1958); and see Wolfgang Friedmann, *Legal Theory* 416 (3d ed. 1953) (Austin's positivist theory of sovereignty "enabled the rising national State [sic] to assert its authority undisturbed by juristic doubts").

[2] See Duncan Kennedy, *Legal Formality*, 2 *J. Legal Stud.* 351, 362 n19 (1972); William Nelson, *The Impact of the Antislavery Movement Upon Styles of Judicial Reasoning in Nineteenth Century America*, 87 *Harv. L. Rev.* 513 (1974).

[3] See, for example, Lon Fuller, *The Law in Quest of Itself* 47 (1960); John Dickinson, *Legal Rules: Their Function in the Process of Decision*, 79 *U. Pa. L. Rev.* 833 (1931); Charles Miltner, *Law and Morals*, 10 *Notre Dame Lawyer* 1 (1934); Hermann Kantorowicz, *Some Rationalism About Realism*, 43 *Yale L. J.* 1240 (1934); Rufus Harris, *Idealism Emergent in Jurisprudence*, 10 *Tul. L. Rev.* 169 (1936); Philip Mechem, *The Jurisprudence of Despair*, 21 *Iowa L. Rev.* 669 (1936).

[4] See Suzanna Sherry, *The Ninth Amendment: Righting an Unwritten Constitution*, 64 *Chicago-Kent L. Rev.* 1001, 1009 (1990); James Wilson, *Contrasts of Power: The Constitutional Opinions of Judges Scalia, Bork, Posner, and Winter*, 40 *U. Miami L. Rev.* 1171, 1172 (1986).

[5] See, for example, Ronald Dworkin, *Taking Rights Seriously* 131–2 (1977). Positivism's conservative reputation in America is especially ironic, given that Jeremy

1

various contexts in which the term *positivist* has been used, it is clear that in recent years it has become a pejorative in modern American legal circles.[6]

The first task of this book is to set out a historical account of the transformation of legal positivism in American jurisprudence. The method is somewhat inductive: The argument begins with the observation that, although scholars today treat legal positivism as a major – if not the major – jurisprudence in the United States, no such theory was discussed by name in legal literature before the late 1920s. The first half of this book argues that although legal positivism did not properly emerge as a major theory of law in America until Fuller's attack in 1940, positivism had been playing a major role in shaping American jurisprudence since the late nineteenth century. The fact that the term *legal positivism* was rarely used before 1940, and probably never used before 1927, does not mean that the theoretical content of legal positivism was not abroad before that date. I will show that legal positivism played its part in jurisprudential debate under other names – *noms de guerre,* so to speak. In fact, two other historical schools of jurisprudence present themselves as the "aliases" that concealed prewar positivism's influence: formalism and "analytic jurisprudence." The former has a credible claim to a family resemblance with positivism because by the 1930s many of the critics of formalism were using the expression *positivism* interchangeably with *formalism.* Analytic jurisprudence has a credible claim because the authors to whom Fuller (and later Dworkin) refer when discussing positivism are Thomas Hobbes,

---

Bentham and H.L.A. Hart, positivism's chief spokespersons in England in the nineteenth and twentieth centuries, were also outspoken liberal reformers of the law. See, for example, H.L.A. Hart, *Law, Liberty and Morality* (1963) (responding to the *Report of the Committee on Homosexual Offenses and Prostitution,* Cmd. no. 247 [1957] ["The Wolfenden Report"] and Lord Devlin's criticisms thereof); Hart, *Positivism and the Separation of Law and Morals* at 594–6 (Bentham was one of "the most earnest thinkers in England about legal and social problems and [among] the architects of great reforms").

6 See Frederick Schauer, *Positivism as Pariah,* in *The Autonomy of Law: Essays in Legal Positivism* (Robert George, ed., 1996); Frederick Schauer, *Constitutional Positivism,* 25 *Conn. L. Rev.* 797, 798 (1993) (positivism "until recently" viewed as "simultaneously irrelevant and pernicious"); Robert Summers, *Legal Philosophy Today – An Introduction,* in *Essays in Legal Philosophy* 16 (Robert Summers, ed., 1970) (the use of the term *positivism* "is now radically ambiguous and dominantly pejorative"); see also James Boyle, *Thomas Hobbes and the Invented Tradition of Positivism: Reflections on Language, Power, and Essentialism,* 135 *U. Pa. L. Rev.* 383 (1987); William Eskridge, *Metaprocedure,* 98 *Yale L. J.* 945, 964 (1989).

John Austin, and Jeremy Bentham. In the nineteenth and early twentieth centuries, these theorists were generally seen as the founders of analytic jurisprudence.

It would be convenient and reasonable to conclude that both pre-1940 schools of thought – formalism and analytic jurisprudence – were compatible facets of the same concatenation of theoretical commitments. In fact, I suggest that a useful way to redefine formalism would be to see it as a subspecies of positivism and hence consistent with the commitments of Austin and Bentham. By extension, therefore, the rise of legal realism in the early twentieth century was in no small part an attack on some of the basic elements of legal positivism. The points of conflict between legal realism and formalism are quite familiar to the student of jurisprudence. What is less familiar, and what Chapter 2 sets out to illustrate, is a similar set of contrasts between Austin and Bentham and the realists.

Classical legal positivism was developed in England by Austin and Bentham and brought to the United States through the writings of Langdell and Beale, who were influenced by the English positivists. In Chapter 3 I argue that Langdell and Beale were interpreted by the realists as having erected a much more complex rule of recognition than Austin's. According to the realists, the formalists defined law as a deductive science of rules. The rule of recognition that follows from this definition, I argue, forces onto the formalist a picture of law with all of the vices of natural law and none of its virtues: Law is seen as a set of requirements whose validity exists independent of the will of any legal actor or sovereign, or correspondence with practical moral reasoning. Thus, by 1930, American legal positivism, as portrayed by the realists in the form of formalism, had taken on a shape quite different from that of its English original. If formalism were committed to supernatural principles of law that existed independent of human authority, it would have been at loggerheads with the "sources thesis" of classical legal positivism. In fact, the realists had attributed to formalism a theory of law that resembled Blackstonian natural law. American formalism may have been guilty of many sins, but natural law is not one of them. By picturing the formalist as committed to pure deduction, the realists created a "straw man" that aided their more general program of arguing for rule and fact skepticism in law. Had they attacked the sort of rules Austin's sovereign might command, they would have had a more difficult time than they had proving that legal rules are not instantiations of perfectly coherent, internally consistent rules that were not written but simply "there," in the nature of things.[7]

In Chapter 4 I argue that those associated with the form of positivism called formalism attempted to mount a counterattack against realism. If they had given the impression that they believed that law was a system of deductive rules, they conceded, then this view was properly criticized by realism. But, they continued, realism's solution – skepticism about whether rules can constrain at all – was itself an extreme view. So, they argued, law can still be defined as a system of rules, but only as a system of rules that channel discretion. Otherwise, these opponents of realism argued, we are left with no reliable mechanism by which the sovereign can control future behavior. If the law is mostly indeterminate, its usefulness to society disappears. This counterargument to realism was the foundation of the legal process school, and later Herbert Wechsler's theory of neutral principles. Its logic is simple: Unless a legal rule can, at some level, constrain the preferences of the law applier, there is no point in talking about the rule of recognition, because legal rules appear and disappear with each new judgment by a legal actor.

In Chapter 5 I explain why legal process did not flourish after it appeared as an alternative to realism. I draw attention to the fact that, while on the one hand the legal process school represented a healthy repudiation of whatever formalist tendencies had been attributed to positivism, on the other hand, contingent historical reasons led the legal process school to saddle itself with a variety of other liabilities. Some members of the legal process school, after correctly identifying the role of rules in defining law, next adopted a theory of adjudication that produced interpretations of the rules of federal jurisdiction and constitutional civil rights that, in retrospect, have proven to be incorrect. I argue that there are two distinct movements within the legal process school: The first, defined by Hart and Sacks, laid the foundation for the kind of positivism I think is defensible and is not an obvious ally of political conser-

---

[7] To its credit, Critical Legal Studies has taken on the harder task of trying to show that rules uttered by human sovereigns (such as legislatures and agencies) are fundamentally incoherent and cannot live up to the standard of the liberal rule of law that such regimes set for themselves. See, for example, Kennedy, *Legal Formality*, at 351.

vatism; the second, defined by Wechsler, Bickel, and Bork, came later and twisted Hart and Sacks's theory of law into a conservative theory of adjudication. The later legal process scholars' criticisms of the Warren Court's interpretation of the Constitution were based on a misconception about the degree to which the legal norms of the Constitution could identify moral concepts and command judges to apply them. Wechsler, especially, made the mistake of believing that for legal rules to constrain judges, the rules had to be as value-neutral as possible. In fact, I argue that the later legal process scholars relied on a controversial form of moral skepticism. They assumed that legal norms cannot command judges to enforce moral principles because it is unclear whether moral principles have any cognizable existence. Not even Austinian positivism required such a crabbed interpretation of legal norms.

I conclude Chapter 5 by arguing that it was not a coincidence that the political consequence of the later legal process scholars' "narrow" interpretation of constitutional norms was to buttress the conservative movement that formed in reaction to the Warren Court's perceived activism in the areas of civil rights and the right to privacy. The later legal process scholars' misapplication of Hart and Sacks to the Warren Court was informed, I argue, by a rejection of the Court's liberal, reformist politics as well as by a sincere attempt to develop the jurisprudence of legal process. Although it is difficult to prove, I suggest that part of what drove the later legal process scholars to develop their theory of rules as they did was that their final model produced political results of which they approved. By the end of the 1960s, positivism had taken on a new image in American jurisprudence. It was now a theory that championed the idea that law was a system of authoritative rules *and* that championed a particular method to determine the content of those rules. In fact, as I show, Justice William H. Rehnquist and Judge Robert H. Bork's theory of adjudication is based on a peculiar mixture of original intent and moral skepticism. The fact that the opponents of the Warren Court were positivists was, in the eyes of the Warren Court's defenders, conflated with the fact that these same opponents were using a particular theory of adjudication to attack the Court. I argue that when the liberal response to the legal process school began, liberals mistakenly assumed that in order to rebut the later legal process scholars' theory of adjudication, one had to do away with the fundamental tenets of legal positivism as well. I argue that the liberal critics picked exactly the wrong aspect of legal process to reject. The liberal critics built into their alternative theory of fundamental rights the assumption that legal norms cannot fully or completely specify moral principles for law appliers to enforce. Unlike the later legal process scholars with whom they shared this assumption, however, most of the liberals were not moral skeptics. The liberal legal theory that resulted from the rejection of the legal process school insisted that all law (especially constitutions) have moral content; if they could not find that content in the law, they would find it in "unwritten law." Thus, in their rush to avoid the moral skepticism of Wechsler, Bork, and Bickel, the liberal critics rejected an essential positivist tenet, the separation of law and morality, and ultimately, I argue, embraced a version of natural law (what I call in Chapter 6 *epistemic natural law*).

In Chapter 6 I consider the various methods by which a fundamental rights theorist might evade the charge that he or she is an epistemic natural lawyer; all of them fail, I argue, because of the insatiable nature of moral reasoning. Because moral reasoning is unlike other forms of practical reasoning, it cannot be cabined by any other form of practical reasoning. Thus, sophisticated attempts to show that positive law can authorize the application of moral reasoning collapse into the simpler forms of epistemic natural law that these more sophisticated versions were designed to cure. I conclude the chapter by arguing that the fundamental rights school's adoption of an approach as problematic as epistemic natural law was unnecessary.

In Chapter 7 I review attempts by recent legal positivists to explain how a legal system can fully and adequately describe moral principles for application by law appliers without collapsing into natural law. I compare Jules Coleman's arguments for "incorporationist" positivism with Joseph Raz's and Frederick Schauer's arguments for "nonincorporationist" positivism. Incorporationism says that moral principles may be part of a positivist rule of recognition. I argue that when the rule of recognition is viewed as a device through which the power to interpret is constrained, positivism can explain how morality can be both incorporated and cabined by law. I conclude by suggesting that incorporationism – modified according to my suggestions – looks like the form of positivism that legal process would have become had it not been "hijacked" by skeptical conservatives in the 1960s.

1.2. SYMPATHY FOR THE DEVIL:
LEGAL POSITIVISM AND CREON

It is a peculiarly American belief that positivism is somehow inherently conservative.[8] In this book I argue that it is a mistake to think that legal positivism, which grounds the definition of law on the analytical separability of law and morality, offers reliable shelter to any political camp. This book began as a study of the American myth that legal positivism is inherently conservative. In its final form, this book not only tells the story of a jurisprudential myth but also defends legal positivism by demonstrating that positivism has played a positive role in the development of modern American jurisprudence. Furthermore, I argue that although the essential tenets of positivism have often been endorsed throughout the past century by lawyers with primarily conservative agendas, positivism's association with conservatism was the result of historical contingency, and not theoretical necessity.

One of the enduring examples of legal positivism's alleged conservatism is Creon the tyrant in the play *Antigone*. In Sophocles' tragedy, Antigone, the daughter of Oedipus, is condemned to die by Creon, who has just become king, because she disobeyed a law that forbade the burial of her brother, Polynices. Creon had made the burial of Polynices a capital offense because Polynices betrayed Thebes. Antigone openly disobeyed the law because her religious beliefs obliged her to bury her brother, regardless of the Theban law. Despite the fact that Antigone is his own niece, that his son is engaged to marry her, and that the people of Thebes beg for her life, Creon insists on enforcing the law. By the time Creon relents, Antigone and Creon's son have committed suicide, with Creon's wife soon to follow. The play ends with Creon's acknowledging his mistake and regretting his inflexibility.

Antigone clearly celebrates a certain vision of civil disobedience, and in the modern era it has come to symbolize the struggle between justice and authority. In Jean Anhouilh's 1944 Paris production, Antigone was identified with the French resistance, and in Bertolt Brecht's 1948 production, Creon was clearly identified with Hitler.[9] Among American legal scholars, the conflict between

---

[8]   Hart, *Positivism and the Separation of Law and Morals*, at 594–5.
[9]   Bernard Knox, *Introduction*, in Sophocles, *The Three Theban Plays* 36 (Robert Fagles, trans., 1982).

Antigone and Creon has also taken on a certain character. Creon has come to be seen as a symbol of legal positivism, and the awful consequences of his legal reasoning have been held up as proof of legal positivism's inherent bias toward injustice.[10] Robert Cover, by calling Antigone an "archetype for civil disobedience," clearly suggested that Creon was an archetype too, but he added that Creon was a disappointingly "one-dimensional" symbol for legal positivism.[11] Cover noted that because Creon both made and applied the law of Thebes, his legal role was not like that of a judge in a modern legal system.[12] According to Cover, Creon did not visibly wrestle with his conscience in the play because Creon *qua* legislator wanted the same thing that Creon *qua* judge wanted. Cover suggested that Melville's Captain Vere from *Billy Budd* was a better symbol of positivism because Melville explicitly described Vere's process of self-rationalization, through which he convinced himself and the other members of the courtmartial that they were obliged by their uniforms to sentence to death a man they believed to be "innocent before God" yet guilty in the eyes of the law.[13] Cover thought that because he had only one role, that of adjudicator, Vere experienced a form of "cognitive dissonance" between his desire for justice and the state's desire for injustice that Creon, in his unidimensional state, escaped.[14]

According to Martha Nussbaum, Creon's unidimensionality is a vital element of *Antigone*. Nussbaum offered a Hegelian interpretation, arguing that Sophocles constructed Antigone and Creon as complementary opposites, each representing a portion of practical reasoning.[15] Neither Antigone nor Creon is just because each "is somehow defective in vision . . . [and] has omitted recognitions, denied claims, called situations by names that are not their most rele-

---

[10] See, for example, Richard Posner, *The Problems of Jurisprudence* 400 (1990) (Agamemnon and Creon were the first legal positivists); David Luban, *Legal Storytelling: Difference Made Legal: The Court and Dr. King*, 87 Mich. L. Rev. 2152, 2160 (1989) (comparing the racist court that convicted Martin Luther King to Creon); Robin West, *Jurisprudence as Narrative: An Aesthetic Analysis of Modern Legal Theory*, 60 N.Y.U. L. Rev. 145, 200 (1985) (contrasting Antigone's "tragic" natural law with Creon's positivism).

[11] Robert Cover, *Justice Accused* 1 (1975).

[12] Ibid., at 2.

[13] Ibid., at 2 (quoting Herman Melville, *Billy Budd* [Hayford & Sealts, eds., 1962]).

[14] Cover, *Justice Accused*, at 6–7. Cover specifically adopted Vere as a symbol of the dilemma that northern antebellum judges faced in the fugitive slave cases.

[15] Martha C. Nussbaum, *The Fragility of Goodness* 52 (1986).

vant or truest names."[16] Nussbaum's choice of metaphor suggests that, like Oedipus, Antigone and Creon are *tragic* heroes because they are blind in one way and yet insightful in another.[17]

Nussbaum's picture of Creon, which presents his character as carefully and deliberately drawn by Sophocles, conflicts with Cover's picture, which presents Creon as a crudely drawn afterthought compared with Antigone. I will argue that Nussbaum is right and that the value of positivism is that it can explain to us why Creon is a better judge than Vere. I will argue that Creon's unidimensionality makes sense only in the context of the fact that he acts as both law maker and law applier. As I will show, Creon is a tyrant not because he was a bad judge but because he was a bad king. This simple distinction lies at the center of my modest defense of positivism. As we will see, most critics of positivism do not object to how positivist judges perform their judicial duties; what they object to is that positivist judges refuse also to take on the duties of the sovereign, or when they do take on the sovereign role, it turns out that what may have made them good judges has little to do with whether they are good at making law.

Creon performs a number of adjudicative acts and a number of sovereign acts in the course of *Antigone*. As the play opens, he adjudicates the question of whether Thebes will allow Polynices, the

---

[16] Nussbaum, *The Fragility of Goodness,* at 52. Nussbaum nonetheless believed that Antigone makes the better decision, but she emphatically denied that the fact that Antigone's choice is just necessarily implies that Antigone is just. Nussbaum, *The Fragility of Goodness,* at 52 n7.

[17] In *Oedipus at Colonus,* Creon, who is attempting to force Oedipus to return to Thebes against his will, taunts Oedipus by reminding him of his parricide and incest. Oedipus acknowledges his sin and points out the difference between him and Creon: "One thing I do know: *you* [Creon] know what you do." Sophocles, *Oedipus at Colonus* 126 (line 1132) (David Grene, trans., 1991). Oedipus' characterization is correct. Throughout all three plays of the Oedipus Cycle, Creon's unjust acts are rarely the result of factual error or misapprehension (unlike Oedipus'). In *Oedipus Rex,* Creon counsels Oedipus to be more deliberative in his decision making. See, for example, Sophocles, *Oedipus the King* 189 (line 607) (Robert Fagles, trans., 1982) ("Hear me out, then judge me on the facts"). In fact, when Oedipus unjustly accuses Creon of treason and condemns him to death, Creon says to him:

> If you detect that I . . .
> have plotted anything, arrest me,
> execute me. Not on the strength of one vote,
> two in this case, mine as well as yours.
> *But don't convict me on sheer unverified surmise.*

Sophocles, *Oedipus the King* 193 (line 684) (Robert Fagles, trans., 1982) (emphasis added). When Creon unjustly condemns Antigone to death, the only thing about Creon's practical reasoning that is not flawed is his fact finding: Everything he accused Antigone of was true and based on either her words or witnesses.

9

traitor, to be buried. Although he adjudicates this question in his capacity as king of Thebes, he is not making the law in this matter; rather, he is interpreting a relatively rich body of "customary" public law that governed such questions. As Nussbaum noted, in the Greek city-state, although "corpses of enemies may be returned to their kin for honorable burial, traitors are not given this much consideration."[18] That is why Hegel argued that Creon was not in the wrong, because he in fact represented the "moral force" of the city's public law.[19] Nussbaum concluded that "Creon is within custom and justified . . . insofar as he shows dishonor to the corpse and forbids it burial in or near the city."[20]

Nussbaum noted that Creon was obliged, as Polynices' uncle, to bury him. Therefore, an audience in ancient Greece would have expected Creon to be caught between two powerful and equally valid demands. The audience would have expected Antigone to have experienced exactly the same tension but to have resolved it in the opposite way from the way Creon did. And yet neither Creon nor

---

[18] Nussbaum, *The Fragility of Goodness,* at 55. It must be stressed that Polynices was a traitor to Thebes, not just a leader in a civil war. Polynices, who had shared the kingship with his brother Eteocles after Oedipus gave up the crown, was expelled from the city by Eteocles. Polynices had every reason to feel wronged by his brother, especially because he was the elder of the two. But Polynices' next step was utterly unwarranted. He went to Argos, married into the royal family, and raised an army to take Thebes on behalf of Argos. See Sophocles, *Oedipus at Colonus* (lines 415–20). Polynices boasts that his captain Capaneus has vowed to "burn the city of Thebes into the ground." Sophocles, *Oedipus at Colonus* 138 (line 1508) (David Grene, trans., 1991).

[19] See Bernard Knox, *Introduction,* in Sophocles, *The Three Theban Plays* 41 (Robert Fagles, trans., 1982) (quoting Hegel); and see A. C. Bradley, *Hegel's Theory of Tragedy,* in *Hegel on Tragedy* 367 (A. and H. Paolucci, eds., 1975).

[20] Nussbaum, *The Fragility of Goodness,* at 55 n14. Nussbaum raised a complication about the law of the burial of traitors. Nussbaum noted that although customary law forbade the burial of Polynices "in or near the city," the law would not have required that Creon forbid the burial of Polynices *anywhere else.* Ibid., at 55 n14. Nussbaum cited sources that "Athenian traitors, though forbidden burial in Attic territory, were frequently buried by their kin in Megara." Ibid., at 55 n14 (citing G. Perrota, *Sofocle* [1935]). Creon's proclamation forbade any citizen of Thebes from burying or mourning Polynices. If Creon intended to control what Thebans did outside Thebes or felt in their own hearts, then this application of customary law would have been both historically incorrect and practically absurd. But as Nussbaum pointed out, these outer limits of Creon's ruling were not tested by Antigone: She attempted to provide Polynices with a public burial (with full honors) where he fell, right by the city. Ibid., at 55 n14. To the extent that the purpose or point of Creon's ruling was to deny Polynices "honor" in Thebes (see *Antigone,* lines 222–8), then Creon's ruling was consistent with the customary law cited by Nussbaum, and Antigone's intent – to honor Polynices – was clearly in violation of customary law.

Antigone displays any sign of being aware of competing demands in their deliberations. Nussbaum endorsed Hegel's argument that Sophocles purposefully confounded the expectations of his audience in order to illustrate vividly the inadequacy of Creon and Antigone's perspectives and the importance of dialectic and synthesis in ethical conduct.[21] Nussbaum was clearly right that Creon's utter disinterest in his familial obligations reveals something important about Sophocles' dramatic strategy. But at what level should the missing (family) obligation have entered into Creon's practical reasoning? As one branch of Theban law that was in conflict with another, putting Creon in the position of a judge who must choose between two conflicting precedents? Or rather as one form of obligation (moral) in conflict with another (legal)? I think that Hegel's and Nussbaum's readings of *Antigone* are consistent only with the latter option. Hegel thought that the tragedy of *Antigone* was produced by the failure of Creon and Antigone to resolve the tension between civil law and moral obligation. Nussbaum agreed with Hegel that Sophocles' audience would have immediately understood that Creon and Antigone were working from two utterly separate spheres.[22]

For the Hegel/Nussbaum perspective to make sense, Creon's moral obligation *qua* uncle (to bury Polynices) must be seen as separate and independent from his legal obligation *qua* sovereign (to prevent the burial of Polynices in Thebes). The Hegel/Nussbaum "separate spheres" perspective is supported in another part of the Theban Plays trilogy. In *Oedipus at Colonus* (which was written after *Antigone* but describes events that take place before *Antigone*), the question of burial is raised again, this time in the context of Oedipus' death. At the beginning of *Oedipus at Colonus*, Oedipus, who

---

[21] Nussbaum, *The Fragility of Goodness*, at 67 (citing G.W.F. Hegel, *The Philosophy of Fine Art* [P. B. Osmaston, trans., 1920]).

[22] Nussbaum doubted Hegel's conclusion that Sophocles intended to suggest that although the antagonists in *Antigone* could not resolve the tension between the spheres of law and morality, Athens had resolved this tension.

> Certainly [Sophocles would have liked to have made] the proud claim that Periclean Athens [had] developed a civic order that incorporat[ed] and respect[ed] the claims of "unwritten laws" of religious obligation. But it is one thing to say that the state will in general respect these claims, and quite another to say, with Hegel, that the very possibility of conflict or tension between *different spheres of value* will be altogether eliminated.

Nussbaum, *The Fragility of Goodness*, at 68 (quoting Thucydides) (emphasis added).

had been expelled from Thebes by his two sons, arrives in Athens begging for hospitality.[23] While in Athens, he is told by Ismene, his younger daughter, who has followed him from Thebes, that Eteocles and Polynices have begun to feud. He is also told that there had been a prophecy that the city which buries Oedipus will win the next war between Thebes and Athens.[24] This prophecy explains much of the action that occurs in the play. It explains why Creon (acting on behalf of Eteocles) and Polynices come to Athens to win back Oedipus' favor. It even explains, or at least adds a new dimension to, the reason why Theseus, king of Athens, treats Oedipus so well in Athens.[25] In the midst of the many emotionally charged accusations hurled between Oedipus, Creon, Theseus, and Polynices, Sophocles reveals, through Ismene, as almost an aside, a shocking fact about the limits of the Theban civil law. As soon as Ismene tells Oedipus that both his sons are seeking to win Oedipus' favor in order to preserve Thebes in the prophesied Athenian war, Oedipus asks whether either son, as king, would bury him *in* Thebes were he to return. Ismene's answer is swift and unambiguous:

> OEDIPUS: Will they let the shadowing dust of Thebes lie on me?
> ISMENE: No, for the guilt of family bloodletting debars it, father.[26]

---

[23] At the end of *Oedipus Rex*, when Oedipus begged to be exiled from Thebes, Creon told him that exile was up to the gods. Creon and Oedipus' two sons, Eteocles and Polynices, who ruled Thebes together, decided to allow Oedipus to stay in Thebes. Sometime after Eteocles and Polynices took over the throne (but before they began to fight with each other), they exiled Oedipus.

[24] See *Oedipus at Colonus*, at lines 420–30 and lines 660–90.

[25] It is only *after* Oedipus convinces Theseus that it is in Athens's national interest to bury him that Theseus fully welcomes Oedipus:

> Such kindness – who could reject such a man?
> First, in any case, Oedipus is our ally:
> by mutual rights we owe him hospitality.
> What's more, he has come to beg our gods for help
> and render no small benefit to our country
> in return, to me as well.
> So in respect his claims, I'll never reject
> the gifts he offers, no, I will settle him
> in our land, a fellow-citizen with full rights.

Sophocles, *Oedipus at Colonus* 323 (lines 716–24) (Robert Fagles, trans., 1982).

[26] Sophocles, *Oedipus at Colonus* 98 (lines 453–4) (David Grene, trans., 1991). Of course, Oedipus' crime was both a violation of Theban law and an affront to the gods. It is possible that killing one's father *and* killing the king of Thebes (which is what Oedipus did) is worse than killing one's brother *and* killing the king of Thebes (which is what Polynices did), but it is hard to imagine the Theban law of burial turning on such a subtle point.

Ismene says that Eteocles plans to settle Oedipus in the frontier *between* Thebes and Athens, so that after he dies Thebes can keep the body out of Athenian hands.[27] Interestingly, Oedipus seems willing to go along with the first part of Eteocles' plan (to dwell outside of Thebes), but he is driven away by the second half of the plan (to be denied a Theban burial).[28]

The reason this scene bears upon Creon in *Antigone* is that one must wonder why Creon, who was Eteocles' envoy in *Oedipus at Colonus,* did not simply promise Oedipus burial in Thebes. Given what was at stake (Thebes's survival) it would seem that the Theban government would have had every reason to compromise on the location of Oedipus' grave. And yet, as Ismene makes clear, burying Oedipus in Thebes was simply not an option available to Creon or Eteocles. Creon's unwillingness to offer burial in Thebes cannot be explained as a product of sheer stubbornness or tyranny, which is how his prohibition of Polynices' burial in *Antigone* is often explained. I say this not because Creon's character is that much better in this play than in *Antigone*: In *Oedipus at Colonus,* Creon is presented as a man who will do anything (even kidnap a man's daughter) in order to gain control over Oedipus. *And yet he does not promise to bury Oedipus in Thebes.* The only explanation for this, which is evidenced by Ismene's incredulous reaction to Oedipus' suggestion that he be buried in Thebes if he returned, even as a prisoner, is that a promise by Creon to bury Oedipus in Thebes would have been patently unbelievable, because Creon would have been making a promise on behalf of Eteocles to do something that Oedipus knew no sovereign could do under color of law.

Even when it would have served the state's national interest *and* his personal moral obligations, Eteocles could not ignore the city's customary law and bury his own kin in Thebes. It is not surprising that Creon, who had far less interest in burying Polynices, felt constrained by the same law. I therefore agree with Hegel and Nussbaum that Creon applied Theban law to the question of Polynices

---

[27] See Sophocles, *Oedipus at Colonus,* at lines 443–8.

[28] After Ismene tells Oedipus that Eteocles wants him to return but will not let him reenter the city, Oedipus merely asks if he would nonetheless be buried in Thebes if he returned under Eteocles' conditions. When Ismene reminds Oedipus that burial in Thebes is forbidden by law, Oedipus then explodes in a rage and says, "then they will never get me in their clutches – never!" Sophocles, *Oedipus at Colonus* 307 (line 453) (Robert Fagles, trans., 1982). It must be noted that even Ismene, who cannot be accused of any ulterior motivation, finds her father's wish to be buried in Thebes absurd. Furthermore, Oedipus' refusal to accept burial outside of Thebes had the consequence, in effect, of handing Thebes over to Athens.

correctly. At the beginning of *Antigone* Creon is presented to the audience as a good judge. By the end of the play, of course, Creon is a broken man: Although he changes his mind about both Polynices' burial and Antigone's execution, he cannot prevent the death of everyone he holds dear. Under the Hegel/Nussbaum reading, the reason Creon comes to a tragic end is that his moral sensibility is as weak as his legal sensibility was strong. While Creon could not have changed Theban law and allowed the burial of Polynices in Thebes, he did not have to make burying Polynices a capital offense.[29] Making the burial of Polynices a capital offense, which was one of Creon's first acts of law making, demonstrated Creon's lack of moral (and political) judgment. Furthermore, once he had applied the law he made, he was not bound to follow through with the sentence he imposed. A hallmark of all sovereigns is their capacity to pardon. The power to pardon is a uniquely executive function. While no one finds it odd that the U.S. Constitution gives the president the power to pardon, it seems almost unimaginable that the power to pardon would be granted to the Supreme Court.[30] By failing to pardon Antigone, as both his son Haemon and the Chorus beg him to do, Creon compounds his bad legislative judgment with bad executive judgment.

[29]   As Nussbaum noted, Creon could have also permitted Polynices to have been moved away from Thebes by his family. Nussbaum, *The Fragility of Goodness*, at 55 n14. It is not clear what Creon's decision to bury Polynices at the end of the play is supposed to symbolize. Sophocles may have been mocking Creon's legalistic nature yet again, because the play suggests that Creon's decision to bury Polynices *before* he frees Antigone may have actually contributed to his son's and wife's deaths. The text leaves open the possibility that had Creon gone first to Antigone, he could have reached her before she killed herself. Pardoning Antigone, which the Chorus told him to do first, would not be the reversal of a prior adjudicative act, but a prior executive decision. See *Antigone,* at lines 1175–80. Furthermore, the fact that the death of Creon's family occurs *after* he buries Polynices suggests that Creon's tragedy was not rooted in his judicial decision.

[30]   U.S. Const., Art. II, sec. 2 (1). By pardoning Antigone, Creon would not be using his judicial power to make an executive decision, which was one of the things that concerned Lon Fuller in his parable *The Case of the Speluncean Explorers.* In *The Speluncean Explorers,* the Newgarth Supreme Court had to decide whether its murder statute applied to a group of men trapped in a cave who killed and ate a colleague. Chief Justice Truepenny argued that the Court should hold that the law applied to the defendants but that the Court should also, in its decision, ask the executive to pardon the men. Lon Fuller, *The Case of the Speluncean Explorers,* 62 *Harv. L. Rev.* 616, 619 (1949). For a recent decision in which a judge arguably exercised the executive power to pardon, see *United States of America v. Lynch,* 1997 WL 12808 (S.D.N.Y.), in which the judge, as fact finder, refused to convict a Catholic bishop and monk whose religious convictions led them to violate the Freedom of Access to Clinic Entrances Act of 1994 even though "the circumstances would otherwise be sufficient to convict." *Lynch,* 1997 WL 12808 at *3–*4.

The Chorus argues to Creon that, like a ship, a city is buffeted by forces beyond its control.[31] As Nussbaum noted, Sophocles suggests that the good legislator, like a good captain, must navigate between "indefeasible obligations"; the metaphor of the ship used by the Chorus leads us "to think, then, of the central moral conflict of the play and to see it as one not easily defeasible by the art of even the best legislator."[32] In the face of irreconcilable demands, the good legislator (and executive) must learn to "yield" like a tree whose branches are caught by the overflowing banks of a swiftly flowing stream, or a helmsman who "gives with the winds and currents."[33] Nussbaum called the sovereign virtue described in *Antigone* a combination of "practical wisdom and supple flexibility."[34] Creon displays his lack of practical wisdom when he tries to resolve the conflict between the law of Thebes and religious law by invoking the death penalty; he displays his lack of flexibility by refusing to pardon Antigone after she broke the law of Thebes.[35] At a deeper level, the reason why Creon is a bad king is that he lacks the capacity to balance his own will with that of others. He does not understand that the good sovereign cannot conflate himself with his office:

> CREON: Must I rule the land by someone else's judgment rather than my own?
> HAEMON: There is no city possessed by one man only.
> CREON: Is not the city thought to be the ruler's?
> HAEMON: You would be a fine dictator of a desert.[36]

---

[31] Sophocles, *Antigone*, at lines 584–93.

[32] Nussbaum, *The Fragility of Goodness*, at 74.

[33] See Nussbaum, *The Fragility of Goodness,* at 79–80 (citing Sophocles, *Antigone*, at lines 711–20).

[34] Nussbaum, *The Fragility of Goodness,* at 80.

[35] It is ironic that Creon's tragic end was caused by his unwillingness to bend. At the end of *Oedipus the King,* Creon's final words to Oedipus are: "Do not seek to be master of everything, for the things you mastered did not follow you throughout your life." Sophocles, *Oedipus Rex* 76 (lines 1521–3) (David Grene, trans., 1991).

[36] Sophocles, *Antigone* 189–90 (lines 796–801) (David Grene, trans., 1991). Again, it is interesting to note the irony in Haemon's words to Creon: Creon says essentially the same to Oedipus.

> CREON: Suppose you do not understand [the truth]?
> OEDIPUS: But yet – I must be ruler.
> CREON: Not if you rule badly.
> OEDIPUS: O city, my city!
> CREON: I too have some share in the city; it is not yours alone.

Sophocles, *Oedipus Rex* 38 (lines 627–30) (David Grene, trans., 1991).

Creon does not understand the concept of sovereignty. This is because, as Nussbaum pointed out, Creon cannot understand the idea of a complex good. For Creon, a "final good must itself be single or simple; it must not contain conflicts or oppositions within itself."[37] Creon cannot imagine conflict over ultimate values as anything but painful and frustrating. Given Sophocles' view that sovereignty is a constant process of mediation between irreconcilable spheres, it is not surprising that Creon is such a bad king in *Antigone*.[38]

Creon's failings as a king are separate from and unrelated to his limited success as a judge. There is no necessary relationship between Creon's accurate reading of Theban customary law and his failure either to make good laws or exercise mercy. Nussbaum should not be read as having suggested that Creon's tragic unidimensionality is a necessary consequence of his being a good judge. On the other hand, Creon's short career as judge and king illustrates the differences between adjudication and sovereignty that lie at the heart of legal positivism. Creon's approach to the question of the treatment of Polynices' body under Theban law reflects the core elements of nineteenth-century "classical" legal positivism that I will discuss in detail in this book. Creon's appeal to customary law reflects what the classical positivist calls the "sources thesis." The idea that Theban customary law was an indefeasible reason for action to Creon *qua* king (as opposed to Creon *qua* kinsman) reflects what the classical positivist calls the "command theory of law." Finally, the recognition that there may be a distinct sphere of law and another distinct sphere of morality that place obligations upon an individual in a given episode of practical reasoning reflects what the classical legal positivist calls the "separability thesis." And yet, for all that Creon may have been a good judge, tragedy still flowed from his actions. That is because, as the legal positivist emphasizes, there is no necessary relationship between being a good judge and being a good sovereign. The legal positivist does not need to dis-

---

[37] Nussbaum, *The Fragility of Goodness,* at 60.

[38] Even though Creon is only a minor character in *Oedipus Rex,* Sophocles allows the audience to hear Creon predict in *Antigone* exactly what kind of king he will turn out to be. Early in *Oedipus Rex,* Oedipus unjustly accuses Creon of conspiring to usurp the throne. Because Oedipus is unmoved by evidence, Creon tries to prove by deduction that he is not interested in becoming king of Thebes: "I was not born with such a frantic yearning to be a king . . . if I were the king myself, I must do much that went against the grain." Sophocles, *Oedipus Rex* 36 (lines 587–92) (David Grene, trans., 1991).

tance himself from Creon, but the positivist should be eager to point out that the effort to vilify Creon's positivism is fundamentally misguided. The critic of legal positivism is wrong in two ways: The tragedy of Antigone was not "caused" by Creon's positivism, and the tragedy of Antigone could not have been averted by focusing on Creon's theory of law. There is nothing tragic in *Antigone* in the fact that Theban law was judged by a legal positivist. The source of tragedy in *Antigone* – that Thebes had bad laws that were applied without mercy – is not something that debate about legal philosophy can cure.

It is precisely because Creon plays two distinct roles – one well and one poorly – that he is a fitting symbol for legal positivism.[39] As I will argue in this book, legal positivism tries to understand law as a system of variably constrained discretion. The positivist recognizes that the law sometimes requires the judge to exercise significant amounts of discretion but distinguishes judicial discretion from sovereign power by tethering the delegation of judicial discretion to the law itself. I will argue that classical positivists did not understand the importance of describing the role that judicial discretion plays in an adequate theory of law, and that the failure by late-nineteenth-century American legal positivists to appreciate the importance of discretion led to the problems we now associate with Langdellian formalism. I will also argue that Henry Hart and Albert Sacks's *The Legal Process* set out, for the first time, a positivist theory of law that could explain how different legal actors could exercise varying degrees of legislative and executive power without giving up on the distinction between adjudication and sovereignty. I will conclude the book by considering how modern American theories of legal positivism defend drawing a distinction between Creon's two roles when the law seems to ask the adjudicator to behave like

---

[39] Cover was wrong to prefer Vere to Creon for two reasons. First, Vere did not obviously see himself in a legislative capacity. Second, Vere, unlike Creon, did not make law, but the law he applied (the Articles of War of 1749) was not obviously unjust. The tragedy of *Billy Budd* flowed, in part, from Vere's illegal application of the Mutiny Act. See Melville, *Billy Budd*, at 110–11 and Richard Weisberg, *How Judges Speak: Some Lessons on Adjudication in* Billy Budd, Sailor *with an Application to Justice Rehnquist*, 57 N.Y.U. L. Rev. 1, 19–31 (1982) (listing numerous procedural and substantive law errors made by Vere that Melville clearly would have known were mistakes when he wrote the book). Cover's mistake goes to the heart of his comparison of Vere with the northern judges. Whereas Billy Budd reached a tragic end because of the mistaken application of a (reasonably) just law, the fugitive slaves of whom Cover wrote reached tragic ends because of the correct application of an unjust law.

a sovereign so often that it seems that the disjunction between the good judge and the good king has been eliminated by command of the law itself.

I believe that the modern American critics of legal positivism are working with a confused and ultimately incoherent picture of positivism, one developed by conservatives to help achieve certain political ends. This book is a first step in an effort to develop a form of positivism that is not only robust and defensible but also more attractive in its political goals to a broader range of scholars and lawyers than earlier forms of American positivism. Showing how different strands of legal positivism were emphasized by its leading critics at different times is therefore a critical part of my argument. Not only has the generally accepted meaning and point of positivism changed over the past century, but that change can be explained through the theoretical and political needs of the three dominant theories of the twentieth century: legal realism, legal process, and fundamental rights. In order to defend my theory of positivism, I must first show how and *why* positivism got transformed into the conservative theory that repulsed so many liberals in the 1960s and 1970s.

The example of Creon's positivism provides a dramatically condensed picture of the argument of this book: that the history of legal positivism has been one in which a relatively thin theory of law, based on Austin's insights, has been systematically portrayed by various forces as possessing more theoretical baggage than it was ever meant to carry. From formalism to the legal process school to the fundamental rights school, positivism has suffered at the hands of its foes and its alleged friends. This story of misrepresentation would be nothing more than a historical curiosity if it were not the case that it teaches us two important lessons. First, this book is designed to help lay the foundation for a skeptical review of the most recent arguments for the fundamental rights school, because to some extent, those arguments are based on a successful attack on a conservative theory of adjudication that has, erroneously, been taken to be legal positivism itself. Whatever the political attractiveness of the fundamental rights school's goals, its own theory of adjudication should not be accepted by us simply because it is better than the later legal process scholars' own failed theory of adjudication.

Second, this book provides reasons to believe that something could be learned from the fact that legal positivism has been built up from its thin theoretical frame often, but never to its advantage.

Thus, it may help support Jules Coleman's argument that a successful theory of law can perform only so much work in jurisprudence. In the essay *Negative and Positive Positivism*, he argued that legal positivism may be seen as a "semantic" theory of law, as a theory about the truthfulness of the argument that the rule of recognition identifies authoritative legal statements.[40] He argued that positivism should not be seen as an "epistemic" theory of law – that is, as restricting or determining the content of the rule of recognition. Ultimately, I disagree with Coleman's insight, although not in its entirety. I will argue that the thin theory of positivism must limit the content of the rule of recognition, but only to prevent the collapse of the rule of recognition and moral reasoning but not to exclude moral concepts.[41] Thus, I believe that American positivism can grow into a mature and attractive theory, one that respects the autonomy of law but rejects moral skepticism.

[40] See Coleman, *Negative and Positive Positivism*, 11 J. Legal Stud. 139 (1982), reprinted in J. Coleman, *Markets, Morals, and the Law* (1988).
[41] My argument follows the spirit but not the letter of Kent Greenawalt's observation that modern legal positivism is "thin" enough to fit comfortably within the leading legal traditions of the United States. See Kent Greenawalt, *Too Thin and Too Rich: Distinguishing Features of Legal Positivism*, in *The Autonomy of Law: Essays in Legal Positivism* (Robert George, ed., 1996).

Chapter 2

Positivism and Formalism

2.1. CLASSICAL LEGAL POSITIVISM AND CLASSICAL COMMON LAW THEORY

The best place to begin any discussion of legal positivism and American jurisprudence is 1940, which is when Lon Fuller accused legal realism of being merely a subspecies of positivism. Fuller thought that legal realism and legal positivism were part of the same jurisprudential family tree. He thought that legal realism was a modern American modification to the legal positivism of Jeremy Bentham and John Austin:

> We may say of modern positivistic theories that they diverge . . . [One view] which may be called the "realist" view is represented by numerous American writers . . . These men represent that direction of legal positivism which seeks to anchor itself in some datum of nature, which considers that the law's quest for itself can end successfully only if it terminates in some tangible reality.[1]

It is clear that the association of realism with positivism was supposed to weaken realism, and this suggests that positivism was perceived as quite unpopular among Fuller's intended audience. Fuller represented a tendency among American natural law theorists to conflate legal realism and legal positivism. It seemed quite natural to Fuller to attribute the rise of fascism to the European embrace of positivism: "[Legal positivism] played an important part . . . in bringing Germany and Spain to the disasters which engulfed

---

[1] Lon Fuller, *The Law in Quest of Itself* 47 (1940); see also Martin P. Golding, *Jurisprudence and Legal Philosophy in Twentieth Century America – Major Themes and Developments*, 36 J. Legal Educ. 441, 475–7 (1986).

those countries."[2] Fuller's comments gave support to others who were mounting a campaign to connect legal realism and fascism. For example, after Fuller linked legal realism and legal positivism, natural lawyers in American Catholic law schools cited his arguments with approval. Francis Lucey, a major figure in the Neo-Scholastic movement at Georgetown, completed Fuller's equation by adopting the connection between legal positivism and legal realism,[3] and then linked legal realism to totalitarianism: "Realism is being tried out today in Germany and Russia. . . . There is not a single tenet of realism that these dictatorships do not cherish, adhere to, and try to apply."[4] Natural lawyers were not the only theorists who drew a connection between legal positivism and totalitarianism. F. A. Hayek argued in 1960 that, because the command theory of law at the center of positivism legitimized the removal of all constraints on the state and dismissed the idea of the "rule of law" as a metaphysical superstition, positivists prepared the way for fascism and communism.[5]

Curiously, in 1940 many other theorists thought that legal realism and legal positivism were opposite approaches to law and were in direct conflict. H. E. Yntema, a prominent realist, observed in 1941 that Fuller's 1940 lecture represented a basic misunderstanding of legal realism:

> The classification of American legal realism in the category of positivism along with Austin, Kelsen, etc., is so superficial as to border on the perverse. As the author [Fuller] truly states, the typical interest of a genuine legal positivist is in logic and form, while the interest of the legal realists in these aspects of law is in a degree incidental to their interest in the . . . substance of the law.[6]

---

[2] Fuller, *Law in Quest of Itself*, at 122; but see Ingo Muller, *Hitler's Justice: The Courts of the Third Reich* 220–2 (1991) (disputing the equation of positivism and fascism).

[3] Realism is "only a further development and refinement" of nineteenth-century legal positivism." Francis E. Lucey, *Natural Law and American Legal Realism: Their Respective Contributions to a Theory of Law in a Democratic Society*, 30 Geo. L. J. 494, 494–5.

[4] Lucey, *Natural Law and American Legal Realism*, at 523–4; see also Brendan F. Brown, *Natural Law and the Law-Making Function in American Jurisprudence*, 15 *Notre Dame Lawyer* 9 (1939); Paul L. Gregg, *The Pragmatism of Mr. Justice Holmes*, 31 Geo. L. J. 262 (1943); Ben W. Palmer, *Holmes, Hobbes, and Hitler*, 31 A.B.A. J. 569 (1945).

[5] See Friedrich Hayek, *The Constitution of Liberty* 236–46 (1960).

[6] Hessel E. Yntema, *Jurisprudence on Parade*, 39 Mich. L. Rev. 1154, 1164 (1941).

After World War II, younger realists – apparently unpersuaded by the claims made by Fuller and others – continued to assert the incompatibility of legal realism and legal positivism. For example, Lasswell and McDougal's magisterial textbook on "policy science" was very critical of positivism, which was described as "more a science of logical derivation of syntactic forms than an empirical science" like sociological jurisprudence or legal realism.[7] In their view, positivism's emphasis on rules results in the creation of a "maze of mystical theories to explain . . . law."[8] Similarly, Reisman and Schreiber's textbook presented legal positivism as a rigid system lacking the flexibility of legal realism.[9] Moreover, realists defined themselves through their opposition to legal positivism. Reisman and Schreiber noted how important the attack on legal positivism was to the development of realists like Walter Cook and Karl Llewellyn.[10]

It may be supposed that the conflicts between legal realism and legal positivism were emphasized by realists only, because in their own minds they felt a need to distinguish themselves from the earlier English theorists of positivism. Yet there were many critics of legal realism who did not agree with Fuller's formulation and instead understood legal realism and legal positivism to be two rival and incompatible theories of law. In 1958, Edgar Bodenheimer, a longtime critic of realism, observed, "[A]nalytical positivism and legal realism constitute basic approaches to the science of jurisprudence which are customarily regarded as representing sharply antithetical viewpoints with respect to the nature of law and the method of its application in judicial practice."[11] Roscoe Pound distinguished analytical jurisprudence, which is what many early theorists called legal positivism, from realism in his treatise on jurisprudence. Pound drew the following contrast: "As the analytical jurist insisted on the pure fact of law, the new realist seeks the pure fact of fact."[12]

The realists (and some anti-realists) believed that realism was defined, in part, by its rejection of analytical jurisprudence, whereas

---

[7] Harold D. Lasswell and Myres S. McDougal, 1 *Jurisprudence for a Free Society: Studies in Law, Science, and Policy* 8 (1992).

[8] Lasswell and McDougal, *Jurisprudence for a Free Society*, at 10.

[9] W. Michael Reisman and Aaron M. Schreiber, *Jurisprudence* 269–307 (1987).

[10] Reisman and Schreiber, *Jurisprudence*, at 449.

[11] Edgar Bodenheimer, *Analytical Positivism, Legal Realism, and the Future of Legal Method*, 44 *Va. L. Rev.* 356, 365 (1958).

[12] Roscoe Pound, 1 *Jurisprudence* 258 (1959).

Fuller believed that realism was defined, in part, by its embrace of English positivism. If nineteenth-century analytic jurisprudence was in fact nineteenth-century legal positivism (and we shall see that it was), then either Fuller or the realists were very confused about the relationship between realism and legal positivism. Positivism could not be a form of realism if realism were built on the repudiation of positivism. As will be shown, the solution to this jurisprudential riddle is that positivism overlapped partially with realism and partially with analytical jurisprudence, the theory realism rejected. But for now, the one interesting feature of the debate to observe is the point of agreement between the realists and Fuller – namely, that positivism was a bad thing. Therefore, the realists tried to establish the argument for realism by identifying those aspects of traditional (nonrealist) legal scholarship that were rooted in analytical jurisprudence, while Fuller tried to establish the case against realism by identifying those aspects of realism that were rooted in the very same nineteenth-century positivism it attacked.

This book begins, therefore, at a curious point in American jurisprudence. In the early twentieth century, every leading legal theorist – from Fuller to Frank – could agree to only one thing: Legal positivism was wrong. I hope to show in the final chapter of this book why legal positivism may in fact be an adequate theory of law. In this chapter, however, I will show that, regardless of whether positivism is in fact wrong, it could not be wrong for the reasons generally accepted by legal scholars in the early twentieth century. Before we can get to a defense of positivism, we must first see how its rejection was based on an incomplete and somewhat bizarre interpretation of classical positivism.

Classical positivism is the theory of law developed in England by Jeremy Bentham and John Austin which formed the foundation for any subsequent theory that can be characterized as "positivist." Few modern positivists look upon classical positivism uncritically; in fact, much of the most important work of H.L.A. Hart was dedicated to exposing the errors of classical positivism.[13] Nonetheless, classical positivism set out the parameters, or minimal content, of any positivist theory of law. We must use classical positivism as a baseline in order to determine just how far afield Fuller or the realists went in their use of the term *positivism*. Bentham and Austin

---

[13]   See H.L.A. Hart, *The Concept of Law* 18–78 (2d ed., 1994).

wrote in reaction to Blackstone's theory of the common law, which had become the dominant theory of English law before the nineteenth century.[14] Blackstone's theory of law, which set for itself the task of explaining the source and authority of judge-made law, was held to be inadequate by Bentham and Austin not only because it failed to explain statutory law but also because it failed, in their eyes, even to explain the authority of common law. Classical common law theory, as Blackstone's approach is now known,[15] was based on three claims that, although never carefully laid out, were implicit in various arguments that had emerged by 1800.[16]

The first and most famous principle was the idea that the source of common law is custom: that "the only method of proving, that this or that maxim is a rule of the common law, is by showing that it hath been always the custom to observe it."[17] Furthermore, the authority for common law was bound up in its source: "[I]n our law the goodness of a custom depends upon its having been used time out of mind; or, in the solemnity of our legal phrase, time whereof the memory of man runneth not to the contrary. This it is that gives it its weight and authority."[18] The legitimacy of the common law rested upon its continued application, which in turn required continued acceptance – not only by lawyers, but also by society. Thus, "a crucial element in eighteenth-century attitudes to [law] . . . drew upon Hale's influential statement of the special strengths of the common law, which on account of its 'long experience and use,' had successfully 'wrought out' the 'errors, distempers or iniquities of men or times.'"[19]

The second principle was that the common law was rational and was "fraught with the accumulated wisdom of the ages."[20] Accord-

---

[14]   This is not to say that Bentham and Austin were in complete agreement; in fact, Austin disagreed with Bentham's critique of judge-made law. See Wilfrid E. Rumble, *The Legal Positivism of John Austin and the Realist Movement in American Jurisprudence*, 66 *Cornell L. Rev.* 986, 1019 n180 (1981).

[15]   See Gerald J. Postema, *Bentham and the Common Law Tradition* 3 n1 (1986) (hereafter *Bentham*).

[16]   See Matthew Hale, *A History of the Common Law* (Charles Gray, ed., 1971, originally published 1713).

[17]   William Blackstone, 1 *Commentaries on the Law of England* 68 (1767) (hereafter *Commentaries*).

[18]   Ibid., at 67.

[19]   David Lieberman, *Province of Legislation Determined* 44 (1989) (quoting Hale, *History of the Common Law of England*).

[20]   Blackstone, quoted in Postema, *Bentham,* at 63. The common law possessed "a kind of superhuman wisdom reflected in the collective work of the common law

ing to classical common law theory, common law was not just the accumulation of custom, it was coincident with natural law: "the principles and axioms of law, which are general propositions, flowing from abstracted reason."[21] This is why Blackstone argued that, where a judicial decision was "contrary to reason," a judge ought to declare "that it was not law; that is, that it is not the established custom of the realm."[22] Therefore, although it would be correct to say that Blackstone was not deferential to precedent, it would be wrong to conclude that he thought that judges, when overturning past decisions, were making new law.[23] Where a judge overturns precedent, argued Blackstone, he does not "pretend to make a new law but to vindicate the old one from misrepresentation."[24] The common law method was the means by which the judge guarded natural law against "misrepresentation" by either the sovereign or other judges. Thus, natural law and decisional law were one and the same: "In the common law system no very clear distinction exists between saying that a particular solution to a problem is in accordance with the law, and saying that it is the rational, or fair, or just solution."[25] As Robert Cover has wryly observed, "[I]t was Blackstone's blessing and curse to almost uniformly find coincidence of common law and natural law."[26] It was a blessing because classical common law could base the authority of judges on the law itself: They were "living oracles of the law" who discovered (and did not create) the common law.[27] A judge was "a representative of a collective wisdom greater than his own."[28] A judgment, "though

judges throughout the centuries but impossible for any single person to possess." Roger Cotterrell, *The Politics of Jurisprudence* 24 (1989).

[21] Blackstone, 3 *Commentaries*, at 379; and see Daniel J. Boorstin, *The Mysterious Science of Law* 122–3 (1941) and Lieberman, *Province of Justice Determined*, at 44.

[22] Blackstone, 1 *Commentaries*, at 69–70.

[23] As Albert Alschuler noted, many modern lawyers have wrongly assumed that Blackstone's "declaratory theory" of adjudication entailed slavish deference to precedent. Albert Alschuler, *Rediscovering Blackstone*, 145 *U. Pa. L. Rev.* 1, 37 (1996).

[24] Blackstone, 1 *Commentaries*, at 70.

[25] A.W.B. Simpson, *The Common Law and Legal Theory*, in *Oxford Essays in Legal Theory* 2d Series 79 (A.W.B. Simpson, ed., 1973).

[26] Robert Cover, *Justice Accused* 15 (1975).

[27] Blackstone, 1 *Commentaries*, at 69.

[28] Cotterrell, *Politics of Jurisprudence*, at 25. According to Hale, a judicial opinion was "less than a law, yet [was] greater evidence than the opinion of any private person." Matthew Hale, quoted in Henri Levy-Ullmann, *The English Legal Tradition* 56 (M. Mitchell, trans., 1935).

pronounced or awarded by the judges, is not their determination or sentence, but the determination or sentence of *the law*."[29]

If, as Blackstone argued, the "opinion of the judge" was not the "same thing" as "*the* law" itself, then the law found by the judges had to have its own independent source of validity, and for the classical common law theorist that source was the law's rationality.[30] For Blackstone, the law was "an independent realm of logic and . . . a system of interdependent definitions."[31] However, the judge was not only *an* interpreter of the law for the community, "but a particularly authoritative spokesman."[32] Lawyers were uniquely equipped to interpret common law because the law reflected a special type of reason that was steeped in custom: "[T]he common law itself is nothing else . . . but [the] artificial perfection of reason gotten by long study, observation, and experience, and not of every man's natural reason."[33]

When Blackstone used the term *reason*, he meant "artificial" reason – a term rooted in the common law and first articulated by Coke. Artificial reason is "neither deductive nor inductive . . . [but] analogical, arguing from particular case to particular case, reflecting 'upon the likenesses and dissimilarities of particular instances either actual or hypothetical, particular to particular.'"[34] For Coke, there was something unique about legal interpretation that could be gained only by careful study and training. Thus, even though kings were properly empowered to issue commands, they were not equipped to interpret their own common law, which, after all, they did not author.[35] Despite Blackstone's acceptance of the "absolute despotic power" of Parliament to create positive law, he remained steadfast in the classical common law belief that lawmakers would be able to make far better law if they were trained as lawyers in arti-

---

[29] Blackstone, 3 *Commentaries*, at 396.

[30] Blackstone, 1 *Commentaries*, at 71.

[31] Boorstin, *The Mysterious Science of Law*, at 123.

[32] Cotterrell, *Politics of Jurisprudence*, at 25.

[33] Edward Coke, 1 *Institutes of the Laws of England* 1 (J. H. Thomas, ed., 1836; reprinted 1986) (originally published 1628).

[34] Postema, *Bentham*, at 31 (quoting R. Stone, *Ratiocination not Rationalization*, 74 *Mind* 463, 481 [1965]).

[35] "The King said, that he thought the law was founded upon reason, and that he and others had reason, as well as the Judges: to which it was answered by me, and true it was, that God had endowed his Majesty with excellent science, and great endowments of nature; but his Majesty was not learned in the laws of his realm of England, and causes which concern the life, or inheritance, or goods, or fortunes of his subjects, are not to be decided by natural reason but by artificial reason and judgement by law. . . ." Prohibitions Del Roy, 6 Coke Rep. 280, 282 (1608).

ficial reason.[36] In fact, for the classical common law theorist, Parliament's supremacy, because it was the product of customary law, was itself based in artificial reason.[37] By relying on a distinction between natural and artificial reason, common law theorists like Blackstone were able to justify the status quo without resorting to more positivist theories of sovereignty like Hobbes's.[38]

As critics later observed, the coincidence between classical common law theory and natural law was a curse because it allowed judges to rationalize fundamentally conservative judicial practices.[39] When Blackstone referred to "nature" in natural law, he meant both abstract reason and the "world of experience."[40] As Boorstin noted, "[I]n many cases the *Commentaries* stated a rule of law in such a manner as to make it appear that the law was merely recognizing a physical fact," when in reality it was entrenching an

---

[36]   See James Sedgwick, *Remarks Critical and Miscellaneous on the Commentaries of Sir William Blackstone* 126 (1800). Blackstone marveled at the fact that "there should be no other state of life, no other occupation, art or science, in which some method of instruction is not looked upon as requisite, except only the science of legislation." Blackstone, 1 *Commentaries*, at 9. Similarly, Sir Matthew Hale expressed the classical common law point of view when he argued that as a result of their training in natural reason, "schoolmen and moral philosophers" made the worst judges. Sir Matthew Hale, *Reflections by the Lrd. Chiefe Justice Hale on Mr. Hobbes His Dialogue on the Laws*, in W. Holdsworth, 1 *A History of English Law* 503 (7th ed., 1956).

[37]   "As Parliament's supremacy in law creation was affirmed, common law thought treated the authority to enact statutes as, itself, grounded in common law." Cotterrell, *Politics of Jurisprudence*, at 31.

[38]   Hobbes criticized classical common law theory's idea of artificial reason on the grounds that there "is no Reason in Earthly Creatures, but Humane Reason." Thomas Hobbes, *A Dialogue between a Philosopher and a Student of Common Law* 55 (Joseph Cropsey, ed., 1971). Hobbes argued that without the façade of artificial reason to hide behind, judges needed an additional reason to claim authority. Hobbes set out his suggestion for such a reason in *Leviathan*. Because law is the command of the sovereign, it is the reason of the sovereign which governs the interpretation of the law. When a judge (acting under the authority of the sovereign) interprets a law, this interpretation must be consonant with the expressed will of the sovereign. Therefore, the judge must use natural reason (e.g., the reason the sovereign used in creating the law) to interpret the law in a fashion consonant with the sovereign's will. Thomas Hobbes, *Leviathan*, at 317, 321–6 (C. B. MacPherson, ed., 1968). This break between Hobbes and Coke anticipates the break between classical common law theory and the classical positivism of Austin and Bentham.

[39]   See, for example, Jeremy Bentham, *A Comment on the Commentaries and a Fragment on Government* 404–13 (J. H. Burns and H.L.A. Hart, eds., 1970); C. K. Allen, *Law in the Making* 427–8 (5th ed., 1951); Ernest Barker, *Essays in Government* 129 (2d ed., 1951); Frederick Pollock, *A Plea for Historical Interpretation*, 34 *Law Q. Rev.* 163, 165 (1923); Paul Lucas, Ex Parte *Sir William Blackstone, 'Plagiarist': A Note on Blackstone and Natural Law*, 7 *Am. J. Legal Hist.* 142, 149–56 (1963).

[40]   Boorstin, *The Mysterious Science of Law*, at 128.

ancient act of judicial discretion.[41] Although Blackstone spoke of "absolute rights," these rights played almost no role in his theory of natural law.[42] Absolute rights existed in the state of nature, but they were limited in the state of political society whenever "necessary and expedient for the general advantage of the public."[43] Furthermore, natural law could not provide a guide to the particular choices made by a legal system about the scope and content of its subject's legal rights. Most positive law concerned "things in themselves indifferent" to natural law, and even where the subject of the law touched on natural law, "the particular circumstances and mode of doing it become right or wrong as the laws of the land shall direct."[44] Natural *law* placed a constraint on when and how natural *rights* were to be limited by the state, and natural law was ultimately discovered through artificial reason.[45]

Blackstone's impulse to prove the identity of law and reason sometimes pulled him in different directions, and when that happened, he constructed elaborate theoretical escape hatches to avoid choosing between the two.[46] So, for example, when confronted with the fact that English common law had changed radically from its customary roots, Blackstone answered with the theory of legal fictions, which explained how "minute contrivances" adapted ancient forms of law "to all the most useful purposes of remedial justice."[47] Slavery posed an even more difficult challenge to classical common law theory. Even though Blackstone wrote that slavery was "repugnant to reason, and the principles of natural law,"[48] Lord Mansfield, following Blackstone, nonetheless said in *Somerset's Case* that "the state of slavery is of such a nature that it is incapable of being intro-

---

[41] Ibid.

[42] See Blackstone, 1 *Commentaries,* at 124, 128–38 (there are three "absolute rights, . . . vested in [men] by immutable laws of nature": personal security, personal liberty, and private property).

[43] Ibid., at 125.

[44] Ibid., at 55.

[45] See Alschuler, *Rediscovering Blackstone,* at 30 ("When human law limited natural rights for corrupt, arbitrary or otherwise inadequate reasons, this law was not binding" [citations omitted]).

[46] "Blackstone's eagerness to prove the identity of law and fact was as great as his eagerness to show that legal fictions perfected the logical symmetry of the law." Boorstin, *The Mysterious Science of Law,* at 135.

[47] Blackstone, 3 *Commentaries,* at 268.

[48] Blackstone, 1 *Commentaries,* at 423.

duced on any reasons . . . [except] positive law."[49] The artificial reason of law placed a limit on how slavery could become part of a legal system (it could not be found in its common law) but not on whether it could become part of a legal system (England could recognize it through positive law). Classical common law theory placed the work of judges, not natural rights, at the center of natural law and hence generated a theory that was potentially anti-reformist.[50]

The third principle was that the law was not susceptible to being expressed as a rule or set of rules – that is, in a form that could be set down in any specificity and used to guide future action. As Simpson has noted, "[I]t is a feature of the common law system that there is no way of settling the correct text or formulation of the rules, so it is inherently impossible to state so much as a single rule. . . ."[51] The interweaving of the principles of the common law with its social base prevents its codification: "[A]ll . . . are doctrines that are not set down in any written statute or ordinance, but depend merely upon immemorial usage . . . for their support."[52] The indeterminate nature of the law implied a necessary hostility to law created by the sovereign's will. While it remained theoretically possible that a sovereign could create new law, the logic of classical common law theory suggested that laws produced by the sovereign's will would often be unreasonable, unfair, or jointly incoherent. Because law promulgated by the sovereign is a product of will

---

[49]   Cover, *Justice Accused,* at 17, citing 1 Lofft's Rep. 1 (1772). Blackstone and Mansfield were quite close and reinforced each other's approach to common law. See Alschuler, *Rediscovering Blackstone,* at 41.

[50]   If "the law is the repository of . . . tradition and the arena in which it publicly unfolds, radical challenge to it cannot get off the ground." Postema, *Bentham,* at 76. While Postema noted the Hegelian resonances in classical common law theory (see, for example, his discussion of the similarity between classical common law theory and Hegel's arguments in *The Phenomenology of Spirit* in Postema, *Bentham,* at 76), there are also modern resonances with contemporary conservative legal arguments. See, for example, Richard A. Posner, *What Has Pragmatism to Offer Law?*, 63 *S. Cal. L. Rev.* 1653 (1990); Charles Fried, *The Artificial Reason of the Law or: What Lawyers Know,* 60 *Texas L. Rev.* 35 (1981). One cannot also but help notice an interesting parallel between classical common law theory's conception of artificial reason and neopragmatist legal theory. See, for example, Richard Rorty, *The Banality of Pragmatism and the Poetry of Justice,* 63 *S. Cal. L. Rev.* 1811 (1990); Thomas C. Grey, *Hear the Other Side: Wallace Stevens and Pragmatist Legal Theory,* 63 *S. Cal. L. Rev.* 1569 (1990); Thomas C. Grey, *Holmes and Legal Pragmatism,* 41 *Stan. L. Rev.* 787 (1989).

[51]   Simpson, *The Common Law and Legal Theory,* at 94.

[52]   Blackstone, 1 *Commentaries,* at 68.

rather than the product of reason, all such law lacks any guarantee that the legislation will not be arbitrary.[53] Blackstone was deeply skeptical of legislation, calling it an "evil" that demolished the symmetry of the common law.[54]

Classical positivism developed in reaction to classical common law theory. If we look at Bentham and Austin's arguments against Blackstone, we see that they focused on the three features described previously and proposed a set of principles that would replace them. The following represents a general description of the principles proposed by Bentham and Austin. This list is not likely to be precise or exhaustive, but it should give us a starting point. It is compiled from H.L.A. Hart's discussion of classical positivism as well as from other sources.[55]

The first principle was the separability thesis – that there is no necessary connection between law and morals. Bentham attacked Blackstone's use of natural law to explain the authority of common law. The appeal to natural law was not only an appeal to an unprovable "chimera," but it also allowed each law applier to inject his or her own morality into the law. Bentham wrote:

> When a man disapproves of a mode of conduct considered independently of any actual System of Jurisprudence he says there is a Law of Nature against it. . . . If he cannot tell why he disapproves of it he begins talking of a Rules of Right, a Fitness of Things, a Moral Sense or some other imaginary standard which howsoever varied in description, is from first to last nothing but his own private opinion in disguise.[56]

Thus, as Postema pointed out, for Bentham, law could serve its primary tasks only if its authority could be established without

---

[53] See Postema, *Bentham,* at 16; and see ibid. at 15 ("Coke and Blackstone regarded parliamentary legislation as the sole, or at least major, cause of all that was confused, incoherent, and unjust in the law of England").

[54] Blackstone, 1 *Commentaries,* at 10–11; see also Lieberman, *Province of Legislation Determined,* at 60–2 (on Blackstone's criticisms of Parliament).

[55] See H.L.A. Hart, *Positivism and the Separation of Law and Morals, 71 Harv. L. Rev.* 593, 594–606 (1958); Hart, *Concept of Law,* at 18–78; Jules L. Coleman and Jeffrie G. Murphy, *Philosophy of Law,* 19–33 (2d ed., 1990). It should be pointed out that all these works discuss positivism in terms of their reaction, to some extent, to the theories of John Austin. See John Austin, *The Province of Jurisprudence Determined* (H.L.A. Hart, ed., 1954) (hereafter *Province*); John Austin, *Lectures on Jurisprudence or the Philosophy of Positive Law* (5th ed., R. Campbell, ed., 1885) (hereafter *Lectures*).

[56] Postema, *Bentham,* at 269 (quoting Bentham Manuscripts in the University College London Library).

recourse to moral, historical, or theological sources.[57] Similarly, Austin stressed that jurisprudence does not involve any ethical evaluation of positive law: "The science of jurisprudence . . . is concerned with positive laws, or with laws strictly so called, as considered without regard to their goodness or badness."[58] For Austin, the "goodness" of a law was a function of relative, not absolute, value, because a law's value could be judged by a variety of standards.[59]

The second principle was the "command theory of law" – that law was an expression of human will. Bentham criticized classical common law theory for proposing norms so vague that "[the] law is to be extracted by every man who can fancy that he is able: by each man perhaps a different law. . . ."[60] According to classical positivism, law consisted of general propositions, not principles. Bentham believed that a law must be reducible to a command that one person might give another. A command must have a positive form:

> [A law must be] conceived mostly in general, and always in determinate words – expressive of the will of some person or persons, to whom, on the occasion, and in relation to the subject in question, whether by habit or express engagement, the members of the community to which it is addressed are disposed to pay obedience.[61]

In contrast, Austin was not as sure as Bentham that a law had to be reducible to a verbal form. He recognized that some intelligible commands could be merely expressive: "A command is distinguished from other significations of desire, not by the style in which the desire is signified, but by the power and purpose of the party commanding to inflict an evil or pain in case the desire be disregarded."[62] What distinguished some authoritative commands as law, Austin believed, was that legal commands not only are accompanied by sanctions but are *general* (e.g., directed toward a class of the public).[63]

The third principle was the "sources thesis" – that every valid legal norm was promulgated by the legal system's sovereign, and

---

[57] Postema, *Bentham*, at 315.

[58] Austin, *Province*, at 126; see also Cotterrell, *Politics of Jurisprudence*, at 57 ("it seemed obvious to [Austin] that the starting point for the science of law must be a clear analytical separation of law and morality").

[59] Austin, *Province*, at 128–9.

[60] Jeremy Bentham, *Of Laws in General* 192 (H.L.A. Hart, ed., 1970).

[61] Jeremy Bentham, *Chrestomathia*, in 8 *The Works of Jeremy Bentham* 94 (Bowring, ed., 1838–43).

[62] See Austin, *Province*, at 14.

[63] See Cotterrell, *Politics of Jurisprudence*, at 60.

that the norm's authority could be traced to that sovereign. According to Bentham, "the authenticity of a law is a question exterior to, and independent of, that of its content," and one therefore had to know by whom and in what manner a norm was promulgated in order to determine its status as law.[64] Furthermore, Bentham argued, valid laws possessed a very specific pedigree: They were promulgated by the legal system's "sovereign." Bentham was convinced that every legal system had a sovereign, including democracies, where the sovereign was the entire citizenry.[65] The sovereign was the one supreme, absolute, and unlimited legislative power that every legal system necessarily possessed. Austin built upon the sources thesis as set out by Bentham and refined the definition of the sovereign. According to Austin, the sovereign was identifiable by two characteristics: habitual obedience from the bulk of the population, and habitual noncompliance with the commands of any other human superior.[66] The key point for Austin, as for Bentham, was to discover the unique source of legal norms in a given legal system.[67]

2.2. CLASSICAL LEGAL POSITIVISM AND SOCIOLOGICAL POSITIVISM

A curious feature of American jurisprudence in the early twentieth century is that the expression "legal positivism" did not appear in its legal scholarship. As mentioned previously, its first notable presence in the general debate occurred in Fuller's lectures in 1940. Nonetheless, Fuller did not pick the expression out of mid-air. He borrowed it from a discourse that, although obscure, was already in motion.

The occasion of the earliest use of the expression *positivism* in modern American legal theory itself presents a problem. When Pound first used the expression in 1912, he did not use it as we would today (even assuming the most expansive or flexible use of the term). In the survey essay *The Scope and Purpose of Sociological Ju-*

---

[64] Postema, *Bentham,* at 313 (quoting Bentham Manuscripts in the University College London Library).

[65] See Jeremy Bentham, *Constitutional Code,* in 9 *The Works of Jeremy Bentham* 10, 46 (Bowring, ed., 1838–43).

[66] See Austin, *Province,* at 193–4.

[67] For Austin, who was most concerned with modern constitutional democracies, the source of law lay with that body of people which has ultimate authority to alter the state's constitution (the population at large). Austin, *Province,* at 250–1.

risprudence, Pound traced the development of sociological jurisprudence – an early antiformalist theory and Pound's own contribution to legal theory – and listed four stages in its development: the positivist stage, the biological stage, the psychological stage, and the "stage of unification."[68] Pound used *positivism* in the sense found in traditional sociology, where the term was shorthand for the tradition associated with Auguste Comte. Comte's sociological positivism was based on his conviction that social life could be analyzed and reformed through the careful use of the mathematical techniques of measurement and analysis.[69] In the late nineteenth century, positivistic sociology had become associated with deterministic social theories positing that some set of forces – economic or otherwise – governed the histories of societies.

Pound's decision to call those legal theories that borrowed from sociological determinism "positivist" is understandable but fraught with potentially confusing consequences. In fact, what Pound referred to as positivism did not really resemble classical legal positivism at all:

> [Positivist theory] calls for a search for a body of rules governing legal developments to which law must and will conform, do what we may. Whatever exists in law exists because of the operation of these rules. The operation of these same rules will change it and will change it in accordance to fixed and definite rules in every way comparable to those which determine the events of nature. . . . "[The theory] treat[s] social forces as though they were mills of the gods which men could at most learn to describe, but which they might not presume to organize and control."[70]

Positivism, as Pound used the term in 1912, did not reflect the separability thesis, the command theory, or the sources thesis. Pound's use of the term indicated that he was criticizing Comtean (sociological) positivism rather than legal positivism. To understand pre-

---

[68]   Roscoe Pound, *The Scope and Purpose of Sociological Jurisprudence* 25 *Harv. L. Rev.* 489, 491, 495, 503, 509 (1912); and see Roscoe Pound, *The Scope and Purpose of Sociological Jurisprudence*, 25 *Harv. L. Rev* 140 (1911); Roscoe Pound, *The Scope and Purpose of Sociological Jurisprudence*, 24 *Harv. L. Rev.* 591 (1911) (three parts).

[69]   As one commentator explains, for Comte, "uniform organization of the totality of human knowledge was indispensable to pave the way for a fully-fledged science known as 'sociology,' which alone would make it possible to transform collective life." Leszek Kolakowski, *Positivist Philosophy* 63 (1972).

[70]   Pound, *Scope and Purpose of Sociological Jurisprudence,* at 492–3 (quoting from Albion W. Small, *General Sociology* 84 [1905]).

cisely what Pound was attacking, it is necessary to consider briefly these two versions of positivism.

Initially, they share an epistemology: Both are rooted in empiricism. Bentham was influenced by Hobbes and shared Hobbes's suspicion of idealism in both metaphysics and ethics. Thus, Bentham's rejection of natural rights as "nonsense on stilts"[71] was motivated by his rejection of ethical values that were not grounded in something measurable like utility. Similarly, Comte concerned himself with the "investigation of facts rather than transcendental illusions."[72] The Comtean positivist pursued a "method of observed facts handled with the use of hypothesis but refrain[ed] from any conclusions about the substantive nature of reality."[73] Second, both saw themselves as system builders within their own respective domains. Bentham believed that his scientific approach to jurisprudence laid the foundation "for the plan of the complete body of laws . . . grounded on natural and universal principles."[74] Similarly, Comte's scientific sociology portrayed all human behavior as the product of the operation of "invariant physical laws" that reflected a system of predictable social laws in which there was no free will.[75]

Notwithstanding the similarities between Bentham and Comte's positivism (the bulk of which is attributable to the rise of rationalism throughout Europe), Bentham treated the relationship between science and society very differently from Comte. To begin with, Bentham did not attempt to build a system that would explain all of social life, just the social institution of law. It is important to understand the significance of Bentham's limited focus. Not only was Bentham self-consciously modest in his system building, but he also rejected the Comtean idea that *all* of social life was determined by fixed universal principles. Bentham's commitment to utilitarianism depended on the possibility of individuals' changing their social conditions, instead of being ruled by them.[76] While Bentham did not develop a philosophical theory of free will, he did not base

[71] Jeremy Bentham, *Anarchial Fallacies,* in 2 *The Works of Jeremy Bentham* 501 (Bowring, ed., 1838–43).

[72] Herbert Marcuse, *Reason and Revolution: Hegel and the Rise of Social Theory* 341 (2d ed., 1954).

[73] Roland N. Stromberg, *European Intellectual History Since 1789* 112 (3d ed., 1981).

[74] Bentham, *Of Laws in General,* at 232.

[75] Marcuse, *Reason and Revolution,* at 344 (quoting Comte, *Cours de Philosophie Positive*).

[76] "The general object which all laws have, or ought to have, in common, is to augment the total happiness of the community. . . ." Jeremy Bentham, *An Introduc-*

his theory on its rejection.[77] Comte's scientific positivism, on the other hand, was thoroughgoing and conservative.[78] While Comte spoke of the advancement of society, this advancement would come about as a result of progress that was independent of men's political choices or their social theories; rather, like Hegel, Comte posited that man had passed through a series of stages of development.[79] European society was, at the time of Comte's writing, in the positivist stage, which, as noted previously, was dominated by scientific reasoning.[80] Comte's conception of progress through stages was not incompatible with his conservatism; as Marcuse has noted, Comte's emphasis on classification and systematization allowed him to prophesize that the social order would be improved by the action of impartial laws rather than the acts of men.[81] Thus man could perhaps understand but not control the immutable forces of social change; and social scientists, who could guide but not change the development of society, were far more like Blackstone's oracles than Bentham's legislators.[82]

It is possible that the conflation of Bentham and Comte's positivisms by Pound and others in the early part of the twentieth century helped fuel the perception that legal positivism relied upon moral relativism.[83] Despite their common empiricist roots, only

---

tion to the Principles of Morals and Legislation 158 (H.L.A. Hart and J. H. Burns, eds., 1970).

[77] In one sense, Bentham's entire theory must be built upon free will: By basing the calculus of pleasure upon that pleasure sought by each individual, he argues that all acts are an effort of the will to achieve pleasure and avoid pain: "Let a man's motive be ill-will; call it even malice, envy, cruelty; it is still a kind of pleasure that is his motive . . . while it lasts . . . it is as good as any other that is not more intense." Ibid., at 100 n.e. Ultimately, his system supposed that an individual, when free of the shackles that force obedience, was a "rationally self-directed individual, prudently adjust[ing] his actions and plans to the realities of his environment, *but always thinking and judging for himself.*" Postema, *Bentham,* at 167 (emphasis added).

[78] "Rarely in the past has any philosophy urged itself forward with so strong and so overt a recommendation that it be utilized for the maintenance of prevailing authority. . . ." Marcuse, *Reason and Revolution,* at 345. Marcuse noted that Comte shared with de Maistre the belief that reason was incapable of altering society. Marcuse, *Reason and Revolution,* at 344.

[79] Shlomo Avineri, *Hegel's Theory of the Modern State* 223 (1972); Stromberg, *European Intellectual History,* at 86.

[80] Stromberg, *European Intellectual History,* at 134.

[81] Marcuse, *Reason and Revolution,* at 348.

[82] Stromberg, *European Intellectual History,* at 115.

[83] As noted previously, Fuller collapsed realism into positivism. For Fuller, the most salient feature of a legal theory was whether it conceived of law in scientific or moral terms; and accordingly he concluded that "positivism was the only theory of

Comte was a moral relativist. Because, for Comte, the principles that underlay society could be discovered only through observation, the mores of society were a function of the amount of knowledge that society possessed.[84] Hence the irrelevancy of human social or political action: Moral progress, being a function of the growth of human technical and cultural knowledge, was hostage to the material evolution of society. As a result, although Comte did not quite equate the "is" with the "ought," he thought that societies would be swept toward social betterment regardless of their own self-conscious attempts to control history: "'[S]ocial movement is necessarily subject to invariant physical laws, instead of being governed by some kind of will.'"[85] Comte's worldview did not need the language of rights, because men did not, as in Locke, master nature through economic activity but rather were mastered by the natural laws of economics. Thus Comte decoupled science from social reform and linked it to social conservatism.[86] This linkage would reach its apogee in the United States during the vogue of Herbert Spencer and his disciples, where the combination of the Comtean systematizing impulse and Darwinian theories of evolution gave rise to the concept of Social Darwinism.[87]

Bentham had a much more complex relationship to relativism in morals than Comte. Bentham also called for a separation of law and

law that could claim to be 'scientific' in an Age of Science." Lon L. Fuller, *Positivism and Fidelity to Law – A Reply to Professor Hart*, 71 Harv. L. Rev. 630, 659 (1958). Fuller thought it was obvious that scientific jurisprudence must be committed to moral relativism. Fuller, *Law in Quest of Itself*, at 87–91.

[84] Marcuse, *Reason and Revolution*, at 353–5.

[85] Ibid., at 344 (quoting Comte, *Cours de Philosophie Positive*).

[86] Mirroring, of course, Marx's scientific social thought, except that Marx's deeper understanding of the relationship to culture and the economy led Marx to conclude exactly the opposite – that radical resistance was a natural consequence of the material evolution of society. See Marcuse, *Reason and Revolution*, at 356, Stromberg *European Intellectual History*, at 149–50, and Karl Marx, *Letter to P. V. Annenkov*, reprinted as *Society and Economy in History* in *The Marx-Engels Reader* 137–8 (Robert C. Tucker, ed., 1978).

[87] See Neil Duxbury, *Patterns of American Jurisprudence* 25–7 (1995). Like Comtean positivists, Social Darwinists were skeptical of the extent to which people could control the direction of society: "Swayed by evolutionary economics, late nineteenth-century American public figures and policy-makers were on the whole convinced that the economy was fated to rise and fall at regular intervals in accordance with the natural laws of the market." Duxbury, *Patterns*, at 25–7 (citing Sidney Fine, *Laissez-faire and the General Welfare State: A Study of Conflict in American Thought 1865–1901* [1956]).

morals and based that call, like Comte, on his rejection of meta-physical idealism and especially his rejection of the language of rights. But Bentham, as we saw previously, imagined that his empiricism would lead to reform, and he never intended that utilitarianism be used as a justification for political or moral conservatism.[88] Bentham's relentless application of the principle of utility introduced a critical element into his social theory that was utterly lacking in Comte. For Comte, because we can understand the universal laws of society only in a relative fashion, social improvement is likely to be misguided, and the only thing social scientists can do with any accuracy is understand social evolution that has already occurred. In contrast, Bentham subjected all law to the principle of utility (of which he was sure) and criticized that which he found lacking; hence his many proposals for reform. For Bentham, it was clear that the "is" could not be confused with the "ought."[89]

It may be useful to consider why Pound and others conflated Comtean sociological positivism and classical legal positivism. One possible reason is historical: Comte's positivism was in vogue in Europe just as Austin's lectures on jurisprudence were re-published.[90] Another possible reason is that the confusion was inevitable because classical legal positivism, being a "scientific" theory, was received as yet another form of evolutionary theory. Although it is difficult to appreciate today, the impact of evolutionary thinking on nineteenth-century American thought was so profound that it is likely that any "scientific" theory of society was assumed to be

---

[88]   Bentham rejected classical common law theory in part because of its reactionary implications: He noted in Blackstone a "complacency" that confused what is and what ought to be. Jeremy Bentham, *A Fragment on Government* 18 (H.L.A. Hart and J. H. Burns, eds., 1988).

[89]   As Postema noted, there is a conflict in Bentham's writings "between the demand for stability and certainty of law and the need for flexibility in adjudication." Still, though he was "[k]eenly aware of the utility, indeed necessity, of relatively fixed general rules for social conduct, Bentham nevertheless regarded the principle of utility as the sole and sovereign rational decision principle." Postema, *Bentham*, at 147. The relevant distinction then, is, in Bentham's words, between "'submission in behaviour which is the mother of peace; [and to] submission of *judgement* which is the mother of stupidity.'" Jeremy Bentham, *A Comment on the Commentaries* (emphasis added), quoted in Postema, *Bentham*, at 319.

[90]   Stromberg, *European Intellectual History*, at 116. Austin's Lectures on Jurisprudence were republished in 1862, and received a much warmer welcome than the first edition published thirty years earlier. James Herget, *American Jurisprudence, 1870–1970* 16 (1990).

related to Social Darwinism in some way.[91] Any connection to Social Darwinism, however tenuous, would have immediately placed Bentham and Austin in the middle of Comtean sociological positivism, for Herbert Spencer's work paralleled Comte's.[92] Like Comte, Spencer synthesized every type of scientific endeavor under the banner of scientific empiricism,[93] and, like Comte's, Spencer's vision of the universe was evolutionary and amoral: Progress consisted of allowing the universal laws of nature to work, which would result (if left free of governmental meddling) in the ultimate improvement of society.[94] However, by the 1880s many American lawyers and social scientists had developed scientific theories of law and society that rejected the prevailing Social Darwinist world-view.[95] As Bentham and Austin had done in England, reform-minded intellectuals divorced the passive conception of the universe as composed of unalterable rules from the methodology of modern science. Thus it became possible for thinkers such as Lester Ward to reassert the importance of human will in the shaping of society and to describe the strong relationship between social theory and social evolution.[96] Thus, there were reformers who rejected the

[91] "'Probably no philosopher ever had such a vogue as Spencer had from 1870 to 1890.'" Stromberg, *European Intellectual History*, at 135 (quoting Henry Holt, Spencer's American publisher). It is difficult to overstate Spencer's importance to the intellectual development of the latter half of the nineteenth century. As Hofstadter noted, Holmes "hardly exaggerated" when he stated that aside from Spencer, he doubted if "'any writer of English except Darwin has done so much to affect our whole way of thinking about the universe.'. . . In the three decades after the Civil War it was impossible to be active in any field of intellectual work without mastering Spencer." Richard Hofstadter, *Social Darwinism in American Thought*, at 31–3, quoting Oliver Wendell Holmes, 1 *Holmes-Pollock Letters* 57–8 (M. Howe, ed., 1941).

[92] Indeed, Spencer had been called "the British Comte." See Stromberg, *European Intellectual History*, at 135.

[93] Stromberg, *European Intellectual History*, at 135.

[94] Hofstadter, *Social Darwinism in American Thought*, at 43–4.

[95] "With no thought of being Positivists, the reformers of the eighties and nineties had faith in the capacity of social science to translate ethics into action." Arthur Mann, *Yankee Reformers in the Urban Age: Social Reform in Boston 1880–1900* (1954; reprinted 1974). See also Ibid. at 126–44 (discussing Frank Parsons, who wrote a number of legal treatises and who criticized the "passive determinism" of Herbert Spencer).

[96] Hofstadter, *Social Darwinism in American Thought*, at 66–84. See also Hofstadter, *Social Darwinism in American Thought*, at 156–60 (describing the rejection of the biological model). Lester Frank Ward, author of the first comprehensive sociological treatise in the United States, followed Comte and Spencer in assuming that the laws of the universe at large were also applicable to human societies. Yet his theory of social systems, as reflected in his books *Dynamic Sociology* (1883) and *Pure Sociology* (1903), was entirely different from those of either Comte or Spencer, in that it re-

conservatism of Comte and Spencer but retained their empiricism. Their break with Social Darwinism was not much noticed, and despite the logical possibility of a social science independent of Comte's positivism, it is perfectly understandable why Pound would have assumed that all positivist social theory, whether Benthamite or Spencerian, was ultimately Comtean.[97] It is likely that Pound's references to Comtean positivism made it only more difficult for legal theorists to identify properly the influence of classical legal positivism in early-twentieth-century America.

2.3. CLASSICAL LEGAL POSITIVISM AND LEGAL FORMALISM

Classical legal positivism was properly raised and discussed during a 1931 debate between Hessel Yntema (a realist) and Morris Cohen (an antirealist) over Holmes's legacy. In *Justice Holmes and the Nature of Law*, Morris Cohen argued that Holmes's "idealist" thought was being abused by realist scholars.[98] He argued that one group of "extremists" had wrongly associated Holmes with "positivism," which Cohen defined as "view[ing] the law exclusively as uniformities of existing behavior, in total disregard of any ideals as to what should be."[99]

Yntema's response to Morris Cohen contained a lengthy and detailed defense of the realists' adoption of Holmes. Yntema wanted to keep the connection between Holmes and realism, but discard positivism. He suggested that Morris Cohen confused *positivism*, which was not part of the realist position, with *empiricism*, which

flected a pragmatic bias through its emphasis on the importance of purposive action in human mental development. See Hofstadter, *Social Darwinism in American Thought*, at 52–3.

[97] "[T]he four sociologists who with propriety may be regarded as the chief modern founders of their subject – Montesquieu, Comte, Spencer and Ward – all approached legal phenomena from different angles but all nevertheless put forward conclusions which are to-day an essential part of a sound sociological legal theory." Huntington Cairns, *Law and the Social Sciences* 146 (1935; reprinted 1969, with a forword by Roscoe Pound).

[98] "The danger today is not that [Holmes's ideas] will be ignored, but that their rich content will be impoverished by being harnessed to some ism. . . . Thus contemporary irrationalists frequently support their case by his dictum 'experience not logic is the life of the law.'" Morris R. Cohen, *Justice Holmes and the Nature of Law*, 31 Colum. L. Rev. 352, 356 (1931).

[99] M. Cohen, *Holmes and the Nature of Law*, at 360.

was an important tool of the realists.[100] Yntema agreed with Cohen's definition of positivism, but he simply denied that he or
Holmes was a positivist.[101] He thought that Cohen had the right description of positivism but erred in linking it with realism. The linkage, as Yntema would say ten years later, was "so superficial as to
border on the perverse."[102]

The history of the definition of positivism employed by Cohen is
quite interesting. Cohen introduced this particular definition in a
1927 article entitled *Positivism and the Limits of Idealism in the Law*. In
that essay Cohen tried to contrast two opposed, yet mutually dependent approaches to jurisprudence: idealism and positivism. The
idealist realized that "it is impossible to engage in [legal reasoning]
without exercising one's views as to what the policy of the law
should be."[103] The positivist believed that "the jurist can dispense
with any consideration as to what the law ought to be."[104] Positivism "arises from the fiction that the law is a complete and closed
system, and that judges and juries are mere automata to record its
will or phonographs to pronounce its provisions."[105]

The adoption of Cohen's definition of positivism by Yntema (despite his other differences with Cohen) is interesting for a number
of reasons. First, Cohen's 1927 definition captured most of the elements of classical positivism. Its two-pronged test for positivism – the separation of law and morals and the idea of law as a system of authoritative rules – looks a lot like what Fuller attacked in
1940. Second, Yntema responded to Cohen's attempt to associate realism with positivism by denying the association and not by denying the accuracy of Cohen's definition of positivism. Both Yntema
and Morris Cohen agreed that positivism endorsed the view that a
judge can "attain perfect consistency" and that the law can be a
"complete and closed system." This view of positivism was, with-

---

[100] "It is just possible that Cohen has thus confused the 'positivism' of continental jurisprudence and empirical legal science, without noticing their totally different
backgrounds and objectives." Hessel E. Yntema, *The Rational Basis of Legal Science*, 31
Colum. L. Rev. 925, 946 n62 (1931) (hereafter *Rational Basis*).

[101] Ibid., at 946 n62.

[102] Ibid., at 1164.

[103] Morris R. Cohen, *Positivism and the Limits of Idealism in the Law*, 27 *Colum. L.
Rev.* 237, 238 (1927) (hereafter *Positivism*).

[104] M. Cohen, *Positivism*, at 238.

[105] Ibid., at 238.

out a doubt, how realists defined analytical jurisprudence. Further, Yntema did not reject Cohen's assertion that positivism endorsed the separation of law and morals and the authoritative nature of legal rules. Although there was a lot of disagreement between Yntema and Cohen over the extent to which realism shared in positivism's moral relativism, they agreed that positivism endorsed some form of moral relativism in law because it was committed to the separation of law and morals and to the autonomy of legal reasoning. What Yntema resisted was Morris Cohen's suggestion that realism was a form of positivism. Notwithstanding Yntema's efforts, Cohen's equation of realism and positivism would reemerge as the core notion behind Fuller's attack on legal positivism in 1940.[106] In the 1960s, both aspects of Cohen's definition of positivism were at the center of the debate between H.L.A. Hart and Ronald Dworkin.

Morris Cohen's discussion of what was clearly an American form of classical legal positivism is significant not so much for what it said but because it represents the first time the term *positivism* was attached to the position identified by Cohen. It is my contention that classical legal positivism was actually quite familiar to legal scholars in early-twentieth-century America, but that Bentham and Austin were discussed on this side of the Atlantic under other names that are not immediately recognized by our modern ears. We know the definition of positivism that antirealists and realists agreed upon: "the fiction that the law is a complete and closed system, and that judges and juries are mere automata to record its will."[107] We know that both the realist and the antirealist disavowed positivism because of its relationship to analytical jurisprudence. These clues point to the idea that the basic elements of legal positivism – the separability thesis, the command theory of law, and the sources thesis – could be found hidden within those late-nineteenth-century theories of law associated with the idea that law is a complete and closed system. Thus, even though the *positivism* may not have been used before 1931 or 1912, it was in substance, if not in name, the jurisprudential heart of that central late-nineteenth-century American school of thought: analytical jurispru-

---

[106] See, for example, Fuller, *Law in Quest of Itself.*
[107] M. Cohen, *Positivism*, at 238.

dence.[108] If I am correct about the relation between positivism and late-nineteenth-century American jurisprudence, then what historians today call "legal formalism" is basically a version of legal positivism, and the attack by the realists on late-nineteenth-century American formalism was really an attack on the fundamentals of positivism.[109]

One way of discovering the degree to which legal positivism is related to formalism is to look at the roots of both theories. In the case of classical legal positivism, the roots are easy to find. As we saw previously, most basic histories of legal positivism explain that its origins lay in Bentham and Austin.[110] As we will see later, both of these figures – especially Austin – were closely associated with the theory of law we today call formalism. A casual review of the literature of the period indicates that scholars of every jurisprudential persuasion drew a connection between English positivism and late-nineteenth-century formalism. Pound, for example, in his criticisms of formalism, equated "mechanical jurisprudence" with analytical jurisprudence, which he equated with nineteenth-century English jurisprudence.[111] In his attack on realism, Fuller identified Hobbes and Austin as the sources of positivism and linked Austin and his followers to the "analytical jurists" of late-nineteenth-century formalism.[112] Even those who disagreed with Fuller's conflation of

---

[108]   Were it not for the equation of analytical jurisprudence and positivism in the late nineteenth century, there would have been no need for Samuel Shuman to begin his 1963 textbook on legal positivism with the following protest:

> One of the obstacles to an understanding of the inadequacies of analytical jurisprudence and legal positivism is the all-too-common confusion of these two very different aspects of legal philosophy. Indeed, it would probably be fair to say that the two are more frequently confused than distinguished, and hence accused of each other's sins and of defects which may be properly attributable to one, but not necessarily both.

Samuel Shuman, *Legal Positivism* 11 (1963) (citing Wolfgang Friedmann, *Legal Theory* 163 [3rd ed., 1953] ["The analytical lawyer is a positivist"]). While I agree with Shuman that, by 1963, modern positivism was distinguishable from analytical jurisprudence, I disagree with Shuman to the extent that he meant to suggest there was much difference between classical legal positivism and nineteenth-century analytical jurisprudence.

[109]   Morton J. Horwitz, *The Transformation of American Law, 1870–1960* 254 (1977).

[110]   See, for example, Keekok Lee, *The Positivist Science of Law* 16–17 (1989); Postema, *Bentham*; H.L.A. Hart, *Essays on Bentham* (1982); Hart, *Concept of Law*, at 124–47; Fuller, *Law in Quest of Itself*, at 22–8.

[111]   See, for example, Pound, *Scope and Purpose of Sociological Jurisprudence*, at 609 (referring to the "analytical school, which revived the imperative theory").

[112]   See Fuller, *Law in Quest of Itself*, at 30–1.

positivism and realism mimicked his adoption of Pound's terminology and his association of Austin with formalism. Llewellyn claimed that: "[F]or the nineteenth century schools I am content to accept one of Pound's summaries. . . . With regard to the analytical jurists, Pound stresses their interest in a body of established precepts whereby a definite legal result is supposed to be fitted to a definite set of facts."[113] Jerome Frank discovered in Austin the origins of two basic formalist "myths": that "every law is a command" from an identifiable human sovereign, and that the law can be made into "an all-sufficient code." Frank observed that the latter "myth" provided the support for the former:

> [T]here appears to be more than chance in this combination of the advocacy of an exhaustive code and the espousal of the command theory of law. That every law is a command becomes a more plausible assumption when law takes on the form of a seemingly complete body of enacted statutes.[114]

As we shall explore in the next chapter, the conflation of English positivism and formalism was an important theoretical tactic to the realists because it strengthened their case against the status quo. Realists like Kessler saw a close relationship between the repudiation of analytical jurisprudence and the growth of realism:

> Legal realism, as it called itself, has tremendously influenced the way of thinking of modern lawyers about the role of law in our society. Its criticism of analytical jurisprudence has made us realize that preoccupation with efforts at making the law consistent and predictable (at a high level of abstraction) may afford an easy escape from a more important task: namely, of constantly testing out the desirability, efficiency and fairness of inherited legal rules and institutions. . . .[115]

Similarly, Albert Kocourek, who called Austin "one of the founders of analytic jurisprudence," observed how the realists defined themselves through their repudiation of the "Austin century": "[Realism] combatted the idea that legal systems are closed logical structures. . . . In a word, the judge is not a mere automaton, but has a

---

[113] Karl Llewellyn, *A Realistic Jurisprudence – The Next Step*, 30 Colum. L. Rev. 27 (1930). See also Friedrich Kessler, *Natural Law, Justice and Democracy – Some Reflections on Three Types of Thinking About Law and Justice*, 19 Tul. L. Rev. 32, 50 (1944) (equating nineteenth-century legal positivism and the "emerging new school of thought within the legal profession: the school of analytical jurisprudence").
[114] Jerome Frank, *Law and the Modern Mind* 208 (6th ed., 1948).
[115] Kessler, *Natural Law, Justice and Democracy*, at 52.

creative role in the application of law."[116] For example, Frank's criticism of Austin paralleled his critiques of the leading formalists Christopher Columbus Langdell and Joseph Beale. According to Frank, they too believed that law was a closed system, and they believed, like Austin, that legal systems were posited by an authority, and that the individual act of adjudication was a matter of discovering a previously unseen element of a preexisting structure. For Frank, the defining characteristic shared by positivism and formalism and the one that set them apart from realism was their belief in a transcendent legal order. It is striking, in fact, how much the realist picture of Austin looked like his picture of Langdell and Beale.[117] Austin, it therefore turns out, was the father of formalism and the original enemy of legal realism.[118]

The mere fact that legal theorists used the same terminology to describe English positivists and American formalists is not, by itself, enough evidence for us to conclude that formalism was a form of classical positivism. We should be able to find the elements of classical positivism in the various descriptions of formalism that connected theorists like Langdell and Beale with Austin and Bentham. In fact, early-twentieth-century critiques of formalism very specifically identified and described the central tenets of positivism discussed earlier in this chapter. For example, Pound's critique of

---

[116] Albert Kocourek, *The Century of Analytic Jurisprudence Since John Austin*, in 2 *Law: A Century of Progress: Public Law and Jurisprudence 1835–1935*, 216–17, 221 (1937) ("the Austin century witnessed the rise and development of analytic jurisprudence. . ."). Kocourek distinguished between the European "freie Rechtsfindung" ("free adjudication") movement and American realism, although he insisted that the latter was the "distinct inheritor" of the former. For purposes of this argument, I have chosen to treat Kocourek's statements about the European and American movements interchangeably.

[117] Rumble has noted the connection between American formalism and English positivism: "Despite important differences between Austin and Langdell, they were, in a sense, spiritually closer to each other than either was to the realists. Both men presumed that principles exist which provide a complete map of the law. They assumed that law has an underlying unity of doctrine that can be measured by the right kind of approach. As such their position sharply contrasts with the views of the legal realists." Rumble, *The Legal Positivism of John Austin and the Realist Movement in American Jurisprudence*, at 1004 n87.

[118] Modern realists, who have been surrounded by discussions of legal positivism since the 1950s, have abandoned Pound's category of analytical jurists and, through the common link of Austin, directly equated legal positivism with that which the realists opposed. See, for example, Lasswell and McDougal, 1 *Jurisprudence for a Free Society*, at 53; see also William P. LaPiana, *Logic and Experience: The Origin of Modern American Legal Education* 77 (1994).

"analytic jurisprudence" targeted two of the three central elements of classical positivism:

> [T]he analytical method . . . has had two serious ill consequences: (1) It led in the nineteenth century to what Jhering called a jurisprudence of conceptions, in which new situations were always to be met by deduction from traditional fixed conceptions, and criticism of the premises of legal reasoning with reference to the ends to be served was neglected. (2) The imperative theory of law – the theory of law as no more than a conscious product of human will – has tended to lead lawmakers, both legislative and judicial, to overlook the need of squaring the rules . . . with the demands of reason and the exigencies of human conduct . [119]

The criticism that analytical jurisprudence "neglects" the ends of law was simply a reprise of the separability thesis, and the attribution of the "imperative" theory of law to analytical jurisprudence simply recapitulates the command theory. Pound brought Bentham and Austin together with the American formalists by linking these elements of positivism with the "jurisprudence of conceptions." The latter expression was, for Pound and the realists, code for Langdell and Beale. But if the antiformalists were rejecting Austin or Bentham, then, in the mind of Pound, they must also have been rejecting classical positivism. The elements of classical positivism – the separability thesis, the command theory, and the sources thesis – when combined, constituted formalism itself. Accordingly, the rejection of Austin implies that classical positivism entailed a concept of law as a uniform system, as a "self-contained legal science," and, as a complete system, free of gaps.

We may conclude, therefore, that many early-twentieth-century theorists equated formalism with classical positivism. Although the historical argument for the equation seems convincing, the equation is a little hard to accept from the positivist side of the equation. By connecting Austin and Bentham to Langdell and Beale, scholars like Pound and Bodenheimer associated positivism with a set of claims that Bentham and Austin would never have endorsed. For

---

[119] Pound, *Jurisprudence*, at 92–3. According to Bodenheimer, in Pound's view, "the quintessence of the analytical approach to the law consists in a belief in the autonomous and self-contained character of legal science, joined with a conviction that it is possible to decide legal issues coming before the courts almost completely by the logical processes of deductive reasoning from given principles and established norms of the positive legal system." Bodenheimer, *Analytical Positivism, Legal Realism, and the Future of Legal Method*, at 365–6.

example, after Pound correctly identified the command theory of law with Austin, he jumped to the conclusion that Austin believed that law is a "science in which legal conceptions are carried out logically even at a sacrifice of the ends of law."[120] It is not obvious why Pound conflated the command theory with the claim that legal conclusions could be logically deduced from *a priori* premises.

The poor fit between classical positivism and Pound's picture of formalism is revealed once we remember that the realists rejected positivism in the early twentieth century for reasons that were utterly inconsistent with Fuller's reasons for rejecting positivism only twenty years later. Pound and Bodenheimer, because of their equation of Austin with formalism, attacked the command theory. The early-twentieth-century attack on formalism did not focus on the separability thesis at all, and only very tangentially on the sources thesis – and for good reason, because both of these claims were compatible with the progressive jurisprudence of Pound and the realists who followed him. Yet in 1940 Fuller shifted the entire critique of positivism from the command theory (which modern positivists like H.L.A. Hart would themselves attempt to repudiate) to the separability thesis and the sources thesis.

The Fullerian critique has become so pervasive that few theorists today recognize the inconsistency between Pound's antiformalist/anticlassical positivist critique and Fuller's antirealist/antipositivist critique. One might explain this inconsistency by suggesting that Fuller had a hidden agenda that skewed his picture of positivism, or one might argue that Pound simply misunderstood the relationship between classical positivism and formalism. I reject the former explanation (Fuller was a scrupulously honest theorist) and embrace – in a modified form – the second explanation. To understand why the postwar picture of positivism varied so much with the prewar picture, we must look at how Pound and the realists framed their main opponent, formalism.

If English positivism had less in common with formalism than theorists like Pound believed, then one conclusion that might be drawn is that the early-twentieth-century critics of classical positivism were wrong to have equated positivism with formalism. I wish to argue a different claim, however, by running the entailment backward. I will argue that Pound was right to equate formalism

---

[120] Pound, *Jurisprudence*, at 91–2.

with classical positivism, but wrong to have attributed to formalism some of the conclusions that classical positivism would clearly have rejected. Thus, I want to use what we know about classical positivism to revise certain deeply held beliefs about formalism that are based more in myth than reality. In the next chapter I will thus argue that the picture of formalism commonly deployed by its critics mischaracterized its relationship with logic and natural law. We will see that American formalism was not deeply inconsistent with English positivism because formalists did not really embrace some of the more bizarre views on legal reasoning and law that their critics attributed to analytical jurisprudence.

Chapter 3

The Varieties of Formalism

3.1. DOES LEGAL FORMALISM EXIST?

The first step in my argument is to show that, as a historical matter, legal positivism was represented in the United States by the theory of law we now call formalism. I have defined positivism (partially through its historical origins in Bentham and Austin), and I have proven that it operated as a placeholder for formalism in jurisprudential argument at the turn of the century, but I have not yet defined formalism. In this chapter I shall define formalism, but I shall do so in a particularly indirect way. It is naturally crucial to my argument that I construct, as I did with positivism, a relatively precise set of conditions that distinguish formalism as a theory of law, and it is even more crucial for my argument that this list overlaps – more or less – the three conditions I attributed to positivism in Chapter 2. I cannot simply list the elements of legal formalism as I did with positivism because unlike positivism, formalism was not codified by a set of theorists as focused or confident as Bentham and Austin. As we shall see later, although there is little doubt as to the identity of formalism's chief architects (namely Langdell and Beale), they were not nearly as self-conscious about their roles as the founders of a movement as were Bentham and Austin. Hence, no formalist left behind a document as foundational as either Bentham's *Of the Laws in General* or Austin's *Province.*

Unlike with positivism, I do not face the difficulty of trying to find evidence that lawyers actually used the term *formalism.* There is such a wealth of scholarship on the influence of formalism on American law that to observe that American law has, at various periods of our history, been "formalist" is to state something so common as to border on the banal.[1] The difficulty I face is that *formalism* is used in such different – almost inconsistent – ways that it may be the case that the very ubiquity of formalism proves that it does not really stand for anything at all. An illustration of this problem can be found in the treatment of Chief Justice Lemuel Shaw by two thoughtful legal historians, Robert Cover and William Nelson. In *Justice Accused*, Cover characterized Shaw as trapped on the formalist side of the "moral/formal" dilemma. Like Justice Joseph Story, Shaw was widely reviled by abolitionists for his narrow obedience to the language of the Fugitive Slave Clause of the U.S. Constitution. As Cover noted, "Story and Lemuel Shaw were as close to confirmed opponents of slavery as existed on the bench ... [yet they] not only perceived their primary obligation, as judges, to the Constitution, but they also affirmed the general principles of impersonal, neutral construction ... even in the face of their own moral beliefs."[2] In the infamous *Sims* case, Shaw upheld the constitutionality of the Fugitive Slave Act of 1850 and rejected any collateral attack under Massachusetts law on the forcible return of Thomas Sims to the South where his fugitive status would be judged under southern law.[3] Cover found a special poignancy in Shaw's approach to the law in this decision:

> I would tender a guess that Shaw's singular act that so captured the imagination of the abolitionists – the bowing beneath federally imposed chains surrounding the courthouse for the *Sims* case – was also an act fraught with symbolic import for Shaw himself. The chains were not of his making. He would have preferred that they not be necessary; but they were there, and his only choice was between accepting the yoke of office or resigning it. The sense of overwhelming and external compulsion, the subjugation of deep personal instinct to social necessity, was symbolized by the Justice's acceptance of these chains.[4]

Of course, Cover must have known of Shaw's legacy as an activist judge in *private* law; for example, Shaw's rejection of strict liability in favor of the fault principle in *Brown v. Kendall* reflected

---

[1] Morton J. Horwitz, *The Transformation of American Law, 1870–1960* (1992) (hereafter *Transformation II*), at 9–31.
[2] Robert Cover, *Justice Accused* 171 (1975).
[3] Ibid., at 176–7.
[4] Ibid., at 250.

a bold and original judicial temperament.[5] Nonetheless, Cover concluded that the *Sims* case epitomized Shaw's "retreat to formalism."[6]

The moral/formal dilemma forced judges to choose between two sets of values: Morality demanded that fugitive slaves remain North, whereas the Fugitive Slave Clause and federal law required that alleged fugitives be tried in the South.[7] According to Cover, judges who opted for the formal side of the equation (and almost all did) rationalized their decisions by resorting to three strategies. First, they could "elevate the formal stakes" by choosing "the highest of possible justifications for the principle of formalism relied upon."[8] Cover argued that Shaw did this by beginning his decisions with the premise that without the Fugitive Slave Clause, the Constitution would never have been ratified.[9] Second, judges could "retreat to a mechanistic formalism." This maneuver was the one we mostly closely associate with legal formalism, and the one that Cover attributed most frequently to Shaw.[10] According to Cover, Shaw's legal reasoning was "mechanistic" because he wrote as if the legal result in the *Sims* case was compelled by precedent or legislative intent and ignored the fact that "like all legal issues of complexity, [it] was amenable to a broad range of solutions with a concomitant broad area for potential introduction of morality."[11] The final strategy employed by the formalist was the "ascription of responsibility elsewhere."[12] By focusing on the legal principle of separation of powers, Shaw was able to "externaliz[e] responsibility for unwanted consequences" by blaming Congress or the framers of the Constitution.[13] In other words, Shaw-the-judge had to construct

---

[5]   60 Mass. 292 (1850) (holding that plaintiff must prove negligence for the purpose of imposing liability for direct accidental injury); see also G. Edward White, *Tort Law in America* 15 (1985) and Peck, *Negligence and Liability without Fault in Tort Law* 54 (1970).

[6]   Cover, *Justice Accused,* at 251.

[7]   See Anthony J. Sebok, *Judging the Fugitive Slave Acts,* 100 Yale L.J. 1835, 1837–9 (1991).

[8]   Cover, *Justice Accused,* at 199.

[9]   Ibid., at 265–6.

[10]   Ibid., at 234.

[11]   Ibid., at 233.

[12]   Ibid., at 236.

[13]   Ibid.

a very narrow role for adjudication in order to prevent total cognitive dissonance with Shaw-the-abolitionist.[14]

Cover's analysis of the judicial response to the fugitive slave cases in the North is thorough and persuasive. Nonetheless, there is something curious about Cover's "discovery" of a deep vein of extreme formalism in so many important judges of the early nineteenth century. As Cover himself noted, scholars since Llewellyn had characterized the early nineteenth century as a period of *antiformalism*.[15] Cover agreed with Morton Horwitz's thesis that the antebellum period was marked by an "instrumental" approach to adjudication, which Llewellyn had called the "Grand Style" of legal reasoning.[16] According to the view propounded by Llewellyn and Horwitz, instrumentalism is a pragmatic, policy-oriented approach to adjudication in which judges are driven by "considerations of policy or 'convenience,' [and] the functional needs of society."[17] Instrumentalism, in short, is the opposite of formalism.

Although Cover did not think that Llewellyn and Horwitz were wrong about the distinction between instrumentalism and formalism, he was concerned that their model of formalism had been applied too crudely: "[Judicial] appeals to formalism may be not only the product of an 'age.'. . . Thus, in slavery . . . the 1840's and 1850's were not a golden age of free-wheeling policy jurisprudence, but an

---

[14] Of all the judges Cover discussed, Shaw seemed to affect him most deeply. He began his book by trying to connect Shaw to Melville's literary creation Captain Vere in *Billy Budd* (Shaw was Melville's father-in-law). Cover recalled that the abolitionist newspapers of Boston accused Shaw of being Pilate, where Sims the fugitive was Christ, and he suggested that Melville may have seen Shaw's motivations as more complex than the newspapers understood:

> Melville, in his last artistic act, may have been paying his respect to the soul of his departed father-in-law to whom he dedicated in more conventional fashion his first novel [*Typee*]. If so, Melville, as least, saw the soul of Shaw as intertwined with the complex interaction of crucifixion forgiveness and salvation. Such theological symbolism would be unlikely without the more earthly concomitant of guilt, remorse, and justification.

Ibid., at 252.

[15] Ibid., at 200; see also Karl Llewellyn, *The Common Law Tradition: Deciding Appeals* 155 (1960).

[16] Cover, *Justice Accused*, at 200 (citing Morton J. Horwitz, *The Emergence of the Instrumental Conception of American Law, 1780–1820*, 5 *Persp. in Am. Hist.* 285, 287 [1971]).

[17] Robert W. Gordon, *The Case for (and Against) Harvard*, 93 *Mich. L. Rev.* 1231, 1252–3 (1995) (reviewing William P. LaPiana, *Logic and Experience: The Origins of American Legal Education* [1994]).

age of the retreat to formalism."[18] I do not think that Cover was contradicting Horwitz's thesis when he tried to prove that Shaw was a formalist in the slave cases. It is likely that Horwitz and Cover understood the term *formalism* in the same way and that he and Cover were simply studying different parts of Shaw's judicial practice – Horwitz was focusing on Shaw's commercial law decisions and Cover focused on the slave cases. There is a problem, however, when we next encounter William Nelson's application of the term *formalism*. Nelson – who was self-consciously working within the Horwitz/Llewellyn model – examined the same slave law decisions as Cover and concluded that Shaw and other northern judges had been unable to protect fugitive slaves not because they were formalists but because they were not formalist enough.

To Nelson, Shaw's decisions were based on entirely instrumental, antiformalist grounds, that is, an "overriding concern with the preservation of the Union."[19] The appeal to natural law arguments on behalf of the slaves (the rejection of which by Shaw led Cover to label Shaw a "formalist") were themselves perceived by Shaw to be formalist in that they posited fixed and binding rules that would trump policy arguments. Thus, according to Nelson, judges like Shaw treated the slave cases with the same instrumentalist creativity that they applied to common law cases involving property: They focused on "the promotion of economic growth by deciding specific cases in a 'manner most conducive to the general prosperity of commerce.'"[20] Shaw and the other northern judges "rested their case upon instrumentalist arguments about what was politically wise

---

[18]   Cover, *Justice Accused*, at 200.

[19]   William Nelson, *The Impact of the Antislavery Movement Upon Styles of Judicial Reasoning in Nineteenth Century America*, 87 Harv. L. Rev. 513, 540 (1974) (hereafter *The Impact of the Antislavery Movement*).

[20]   Ibid., at 514 (quoting *Thurston v. Koch*, 23 F. Cas. 1183, 1186 [No. 14,016] [C.C.D. Pa. 1805]). For Nelson, early-nineteenth-century instrumentalism was perfectly symbolized by *Charles River Bridge v. Warren Bridge*, 36 U.S. (11 Pet.) 420 (1837), *aff'g* 24 Mass. (7 Pick.) 344 (1829), in which, as in "innumerable contemporary cases, the judges chose to modify rules to promote development rather than to have stable and predictable rules." Nelson, *Impact of the Anti-Slavery Movement*, at 519. *Charles River Bridge* also played an important role in Horwitz's discussion of instrumentalism: he used it to prove how, under instrumental reasoning, "conventional notions of property rights began to give way under the pressures of economic development." Morton J. Horwitz, *The Transformation of American Law, 1780–1860* 132 (1977) (hereafter *Transformation I*). Clearly, Nelson agreed with the Horwitz/Llewellyn model both as to its definitions and its dates, as did Cover. Nelson and Cover simply had diametrically opposed views as to whether the slave law instantiated formalism or instrumentalism.

and economically expedient, whereas opponents of slavery made essentially moralistic arguments about the law of God and the rights of man."[21] Far from being the source of Shaw's analysis, Nelson concluded that formalism arose in reaction to the instrumental judicial style of *Latimer's Case* and *Sims's Case*:

> As a result of the association of instrumentalism with proslavery forces before the war and the political defeat of those forces during the 1860's, instrumentalism became discredited as a style of judicial reasoning, thereby creating a void that had to be filled. That void, as will appear, was ultimately filled by American formalism, which . . . enabled judges to avoid engaging in the sort of utilitarian and political reasoning that had been commonplace to instrumentalism.[22]

Recall that for Cover, Shaw was a formalist because he mechanistically applied positive federal law and refused to acknowledge his own political and moral judgments in his role as a judge in the slave cases. For Nelson, Shaw was *not* a formalist because he exercised political will and refused to acknowledge the necessary and logical demands of natural law embedded in the Constitution. For Cover, the will-less judge was a formalist because for Cover, the opposite of political willfulness was mechanical jurisprudence. For Nelson, the will-less judge was a formalist because for Nelson, the opposite of political willfulness was conformity to the moral demands of the Constitution. Cover thought that the abolitionist, if he had a jurisprudence, would reject formalism, whereas Nelson thought that he would embrace formalism.

We are now faced with two rival interpretations of Shaw based on two rival interpretations of formalism: Was Shaw a formalist or an instrumentalist? In a sense, he was both: To address Nelson's argument first, it must be noted that Shaw's appeals to national unity were not rooted in narrow economic or political instrumentalism. Leonard Levy's classic book emphasized the magnitude of the policy choices facing Shaw:

> The fugitive–slavery issue was freighted with perils to the nation. Shaw's thought on the subject was filled with apprehension for the security and harmony of Union. . . . Frenzied provocateurs, vowing obedience not to law and order and the Constitution, but to an unwritten "higher law" of conscience, endangered the political stability

---

21 Nelson, *Impact of the Anti-Slavery Movement*, at 544.
22 Ibid., at 548.

that came from allegiance to the sound nationalist doctrines of Marshall and Webster.[23]

On the other hand, Levy's text also supports Cover's picture of a man blinded by law and who saw himself as hemmed in on all sides by the authority of federal law and the Constitution.[24] Elsewhere, Levy's text supports Nelson's argument that Shaw was as creative and instrumentalist in his approach to the slave cases as he was in his approach to private law.[25] Levy's discussion of *Sims's Case* implied that Shaw went far beyond the confines of "mechanical jurisprudence" in order to reach the result he preferred. One of the main arguments raised by the fugitive Sims was that the Fugitive Slave Act of 1850 was unconstitutional because Congress had no power to command the states on exactly how they were to provide the rendition guaranteed in the Fugitive Slave Clause.[26] In discussing Sims's claim, Shaw made an appeal to instrumentalism on the broadest level:

> It was an appalling picture he sketched of thirteen disunited states embroiled in "constant border wars" that would result from hostile incursions of one sovereignty into another's territory for the purposes of recapturing escaped slaves. Before the thirteen states compacted to relinquish part of their independence and join in a union, their differences on slavery "must first be provided for.". . . Such was Shaw's view of the matter. The important point, of course, is not that his history was wrong but that it was considered essential to a decision of the case for reasons of high policy: the necessity for maintaining peace in the Union.[27]

On one level, the reason Shaw was both a formalist and an instrumentalist is that he was merely human: Unlike a mythical Herculean

---

[23] Leonard Levy, *The Law of the Commonwealth and Chief Justice Shaw* 72 (1957) (hereafter *Law of the Commonwealth*).

[24] In the same passage, Levy stated that, "as a judge, Shaw felt duty-bound to enforce the Constitution as law regardless of whatever moral twinges he may have experienced. When the abolitionists hurled their barbs at him, they aimed at a man who reluctantly regarded the return of runaways as a *legal necessity.*" See Levy, *Law of the Commonwealth*, at 72.

[25] Nelson relied on Levy's discussion of Shaw's decisions concerning railroads, common carriers, and the fellow-servant rule to demonstrate Shaw's use of instrumentalism to bring the common law in line with the needs of Massachusetts's emerging industrial class. Nelson, *Impact of the Anti-Slavery Movement*, at 540. See also Horwitz, *Transformation I*, at 40–1, 52–3, and 209–10.

[26] See Cover, *Justice Accused*, at 176–7; see also Sebok, *Judging the Fugitive Slave Acts*, at 1849–50.

[27] Levy, *Law of the Commonwealth*, at 99, citing 7 Cush. 285, 299 (1836).

judge, he could not achieve perfect jurisprudential consistency (and it is not clear that he would have been a better judge if he had). What is more important and intriguing for our purposes is that not only did Shaw possibly straddle both sides of the formalism/instrumentalism divide but that the divide itself seems in utter dispute. Cover plotted Shaw over a spectrum that contrasted amoral formalism with moral instrumentalism, while Nelson plotted the same spectrum and contrasted moral formalism with amoral instrumentalism. It is easy to see how Shaw could have been both a formalist and an instrumentalist in *either* Cover's or Nelson's world, but not in both.

The exercise we have worked through might suggest that the categories in question are radically indeterminate, and that there really is no core meaning to jurisprudential concepts such as "instrumentalism" and "formalism." This would imply that the ideas to which they refer do not actually matter in the sense that they cannot make a difference ultimately to how a judge decides: To say that Shaw was an instrumentalist is as relevant to explaining why he did what he did as noting that he had brown hair or was right-handed. More important, it is to suggest that were one able to have convinced Shaw to have adopted the opposite of the jurisprudential position he in fact held (whether it was formalism or instrumentalism), it would have made no difference to George Latimer or Thomas Sims.

Thoughtful legal scholars have fought over the definition of words like *instrumentalism* and *formalism* precisely because they thought that the ideas those words represented made a difference to how judges acted and would act.[28] For example, Cover began *Justice Accused* with these words:

> In 1968 I wrote a short polemic against what I characterized as judicial complicity in the crimes of Vietnam. In that piece I compared judicial involvement in the war with judicial acquiescence in the injustices of Negro slavery. Several of my colleagues at the Columbia Law School seemed more upset at the rather facile judgements passed upon the revered and honored dead for their part in slavery than at

---

[28] David Dyzenhaus has made this argument with regard to two other terms in jurisprudence, *natural law* and *legal positivism*. He has tried to prove that whether South African judges tended toward one or the other theory of adjudication made a difference in how they decided a wide range of cases in pre-1994 South Africa, and that these differences developed into doctrinal trends that had significant social and moral consequences. See David Dyzenhaus, *Hard Cases in Wicked Legal Systems* (1991).

the attack upon the sitting bench for its part in Vietnam. From that reaction came the determination to write this book.[29]

Grant Gilmore, in his polemic against formalism, *The Ages of American Law*, left no doubt as to the seriousness with which he took the
formalism/instrumentalism divide, and the degree to which he held
formalism responsible for various painful episodes of American law:

> One of the hidden costs of the national agony which culminated in
> the Civil War may have been the crippling of our legal system. If
> judges like Story and Shaw were driven into formalism, so were
> many lesser judges. And once the tools of formalism have been used,
> even in a good cause, they are there, ready to hand, tempting.[30]

I suspect that it was precisely these sorts of pejorative descriptions
of the awful legal and political consequences which flowed from
the embrace of formalism that led Nelson to reexamine the relationship between formalism and the slave decisions. Nelson must have
been conscious of the political irony implicit in his argument: If natural law formalism had been the legal theory of the abolitionists,
then it turns out that the "liberal" natural rights theory rejected by
Justice Roger B. Taney in *Dred Scott*[31] and Langdell's "conservative"
mechanical jurisprudence were on the same family tree.[32] From
Langdell, it would be only a few short years before the abolitionists'

---

[29] Cover, *Justice Accused*, at xi.

[30] Grant Gilmore, *The Ages of American Law* 38–9 (1977).

[31] *Dred Scott v. Sandford*, 60 U.S. (19 How.) 393 (1857). Nelson saw *Dred Scott* as a
decision crippled by the instrumentalism of its author: "The newly triumphant
forces of antislavery did not deride the Taney Court for its ultimate objectives of economic growth and national unity, for antislavery forces also valued those objectives
highly. Their criticism, rather, was directed at the Taney Court's style of reasoning.
Taney, for instance, was censured because he had 'not hesitate[d] to embody his political principles in judicial decisions.'" Nelson, *Impact of the Anti-Slavery Movement*,
at 549 (quoting *Roger Brooke Taney*, 15 *Atlantic Mo.* 151, 153 [1865]).

[32] Nelson, *Impact of the Anti-Slavery Movement*, at 560–3. Obviously, Nelson was
aware that he was forcing the critic of late-nineteenth-century formalism to take into
account its hallowed origins:

> In most cases, either law as a science or higher law principles provided
> [post–Civil War] judges with a point of reference unalterable by any act of ju-
> dicial will, from which the legal reasoning process could proceed by accepted
> modes of analysis. Men like Thomas Cooley and John Dillon thus drew both
> upon higher law ideas that had been a prominent part of antislavery jurispru-
> dence and upon concepts of scientific legal analysis to synthesize a new ju-
> risprudence of formalism.

Ibid., at 565.

theory of law would ultimately evolve into Justice Rufus Peckham's formalism in *Lochner v. New York*.[33]

3.2. FORMALISM AND ANTIFORMALISM

Given the conflicts between scholarly accounts of formalism, I believe that we might do better if we stop thinking of formalism as a legal theory in and of itself and rather as an artifact of another intellectual movement. Unlike some philosophical movements that either are named or name themselves during their heyday, during the age of formalism (which Grant Gilmore placed between the Civil War and World War I), none of the scholars who were later dubbed formalists seemed to have called himself a formalist or, for that matter, really thought that there was a movement either to defend or to repudiate.[34] In fact, it was not until the antiformalists really came into their own that *formalism,* as a jurisprudential term, was coined. My proposal, therefore, is to examine the basic tenets of antiformalism (especially its most mature form, realism) and reconstruct formalism from the goals of antiformalism. My strategy is borrowed from Morton White, who, in his pathbreaking study on antiformalism, faced the same problem of definition in the larger sphere of social thought. White noted at the beginning of his study that "it is very hard to give an exact definition of the word 'formalism'" and proposed instead that he would define the term through examples drawn from those "who opposed what *they called* formalism in their respective fields."[35] Formalism, so to speak, does not really have an identity of its own: As a theory of law, it exists only as a reflection of scholars like Holmes, Pound, Llewellyn, and Frank.[36]

---

[33]   198 U.S. 45 (1905). Frederick Schauer noted ruefully that "few decisions are charged with formalism as often as *Lochner.*" Frederick Schauer, *Formalism,* 97 *Yale L. J.* 509, 511 (1988) (listing eight articles).

[34]   Gilmore, *Ages of American Law,* at 41. The practice of naming movements seems to have become more popular in the past twenty years. Nonetheless, even in the early years of American jurisprudence certain movements were identifiable, and there were serious disputes over those identities. See, for example, Llewellyn's insistent claim that "there is no school of realism." Karl Llewellyn, *Some Realism About Realism,* 44 *Harv. L. Rev.* 1222, 1233 (1931).

[35]   Morton White, *Social Thought in America: The Revolt Against Formalism* 12 (5th ed., 1976) (emphasis added).

[36]   Neil Duxbury has argued that there was no "revolt against formalism" at the end of the nineteenth century and, more specifically, that Holmes was in important ways a formalist. Neil Duxbury, *The Birth of Legal Realism and the Myth of Justice Holmes,* 20 Anglo-Am. L. Rev. 81, 87 (1991). Duxbury argued that those who self-con-

Antiformalism in law developed during a period when other disciplines were beginning to ask similar questions of their own orthodoxies. As a result, it is hard to know at what point legal scholars began to regard their realist techniques as a form of legal theory, as opposed to treating them as methods borrowed from other disciplines for the benefit of jurisprudence. According to one historian:

> The new legal criticism developed out of the same intellectual environment that generated new attitudes throughout American intellectual life. . . . Large numbers of American thinkers in many diverse fields began to adopt a more empirical, experimental, and relativistic attitude towards the problems and guiding assumptions of their disciplines. The impact of science and pragmatism, together with the desire for the improvement of man's social and political life that many intellectuals shared, brought new vitality, ideas and methods to the expanding social sciences.[37]

As White put it, "Antiformalists like Holmes, Dewey, Veblen, and Beard called upon social scientists in all domains, asked them to unite, and urged that they had nothing to lose but their deductive chains."[38] If we look at White's classic summary of the antiformalist temper, we begin to understand both the soul of antiformalism and its complexity. White argued that antiformalism was built upon two ideas, "historicism" and "cultural organicism."[39] Historicism was antiformalist because it demanded that philosophical concepts be

sciously placed themselves in opposition to formalism used Holmes to project their own picture of formalism: "[V]arious realists, in their desire for an intellectual progenitor, gleaned from Holmes all that corresponded with their particular versions of anti-Formalism, and left behind all that did not." Duxbury, *The Birth of Legal Realism and the Myth of Justice Holmes,* at 100. To the extent that Duxbury tried to prove that Holmes's thought possessed both formalist and antiformalist elements, I think he is basically right. To the extent that Duxbury relied upon the claim that Holmes *himself* did not see himself as an antiformalist, I disagree, although my disagreement is friendly because I do not think that this latter claim is related to the former (and more significant) point. On the other hand, Duxbury's collateral point – that the realists "used" Holmes to help construct their own antiformalist position – is consistent with my claim that formalism was in fact a construction of antiformalists.

[37] Edward J. Purcell Jr., *American Jurisprudence Between the Wars: Legal Realism and the Crisis of Democratic Theory,* 75 Am. Hist. Rev. 424, 424 (1969) (discussing developments in philosophy, economics, history, and political science that affected the growth of realism).

[38] White, *Social Thought in America,* at 12.

[39] Ibid.: "By 'historicism' I shall mean the attempt to explain facts by reference to earlier facts; by 'cultural organicism' I mean the attempt to find explanations and relevant material in social sciences other than the one which is primarily under investigation."

defined not only by reference to abstract categories but also by reference to their particular contingent histories. Cultural organicism was antiformalist because it required scholars to go outside of their own closed and internally consistent systems of thought. I think that White's terms are both obscure and not especially helpful to understanding antiformalism in jurisprudence. White's original terms can be made more comprehensible if we recognize that the consequence of historicism and cultural organicism was that they provided scholars in many fields (especially law) with a contrast to "abstraction, deduction, mathematics, and mechanics."[40] On their own, none of these Enlightenment qualities was especially objectionable: As White noted, Holmes did not criticize syllogistic logic because he was persuaded that the Aristoteleans had been upstaged by modern mathematicians, nor, as we shall see later, did the antiformalists have a low opinion of practical sciences such as mechanics.[41] The antiformalists attacked abstraction and deduction because these ideals produced, in their eyes, a very *un*scientific form of social science. As the antiformalists saw it, they were not against logic or abstraction (what child of Darwin could be?) but the fallacious claim, made by those who championed logic and abstraction, that social inquiry was a process of uncovering an objective and transcendental subject. Formalists insisted that facts generated from one discipline were not relevant to the evaluation of claims in a different discipline because interdisciplinary research raised the prospect that knowledge in any one social science was contingent on what was known in any (or all) other area of scientific inquiry.[42] For example, facts about social well-being were not considered "relevant" in formalist historiography or jurisprudence (or even economics!) because they were not derived from the same premises as the facts with which the formalist historian, legal philosopher, or economist had begun.

---

[40] Ibid., at 11.

[41] Ibid., at 15–16.

[42] Grant Gilmore described formalist legal method in the following terms: "[L]aw was a symmetrical structure of logical propositions, all neatly dovetailed. The truth or error, the rightness or wrongness, of a judicial decision could be determined by merely checking to see whether it fitted into the symmetrical structure: if it fitted, it was right; if it did not fit, it was wrong and could, or at least should, be disregarded." Grant Gilmore, *Legal Realism: Its Causes and Cure,* 70 Yale L. J. 1037, 1038 (1961).

Historicism and cultural organicism were appealing to the antiformalist because they allowed scholars to become heterodox in their work. Historicism and cultural organicism helped dignify claims about social organization that otherwise would have been excluded and trivialized:

> Only those who believe that there is something called the essence of economics, or the essence of sociology, or the essence of history, can draw hard and fast distinctions between the sciences. . . . The great virtue of the American revolt against formalism was its fostering of a flexible and lenient conception of the relation among the social sciences.[43]

The way that historicism and cultural organicism broke the monism of formalism was by asking skeptical questions that were designed to show that formalist history or jurisprudence failed at its own self-appointed tasks. I therefore subscribe to White's characterization of antiformalism, but with the caveat that the ideals of historicism and cultural organicism must be seen as sophisticated placeholders for a certain kind of basic skepticism about the possibility of the objective and transcendental status of facts in social science. By knocking out the formalist's claim that the principles of social science are neither historically nor culturally contingent, the antiformalists made possible the reformation of the social sciences in history, economics, psychology, and, of course, law.

3.3. HOLMES AND ANTIFORMALISM

Oliver Wendell Holmes's famous skepticism is a good illustration of the power of the antiformalist attack on the transcendental status of the social sciences.[44] When Holmes returned to Boston after the Civil War, he encountered a lively group of colleagues who were committed to skeptical inquiry.[45] Within a few years of his demobilization, Holmes joined with William James and a number of Boston's young intellectuals to start a philosophy discussion group.[46] The philosophical scholars of the "Metaphysical Club"

---

[43] White, *Social Thought in America,* at 240.

[44] See, for example, G. Edward White, *The Rise and Fall of Justice Holmes,* 39 U. Chi. L. Rev. 51, 57 (1971) (hereafter *Justice Holmes*) (Holmes, as an antiformalist, "denied the existence of permanent 'laws' that governed intellectual disciplines").

[45] White, *Social Thought in America,* at 59–75.

[46] In 1868 James wrote to Holmes, "When I get home let's establish a philosophical society to have regular meetings and discuss none but the very tallest and broad-

(William James, Charles Saunders Pierce, and Chauncey Wright) symbolized the emerging blend of scientific reasoning and humanism.[47] Few of Holmes's contemporaries intended to become working scientists, yet they were impressed by the clarity and elegance of the scientific method and especially the practical nature of scientific inquiry. For those destined to go into philosophy, or law, or politics, it seemed that perhaps the engineer or the chemist might have something to teach. For example, William James's pragmatism, which evolved out of his interest in science, reflected a clearly practical test for truth:

> The truth of an idea is not a stagnant property inherent in it. Truth *happens* to an idea. It *becomes* true, is *made* true by events. Its verity *is* in fact an event, a process: the process namely of its verifying itself, its *veri-fication*. Its validity is the process of its *valid-ation*.[48]

It must be admitted that the antiformalists were decidedly fickle in their attitudes toward science. On the one hand, they were apt to call a formalist system "mechanistic," thus suggesting that they disapproved of science. But they also idealized science and, like James, viewed the experimental method as a liberating force. As G. Edward White has argued, Holmes, who wrote often about the relationship of science and law, actually had two very different pictures of science in mind. On the one hand he rejected abstract theorizing about formal systems as merely "pure science," while on the other hand he endorsed the "critical evaluation of law," which he called "practical science."[49] "Practical science," which Holmes claimed

---

est questions. . . ." M. H. Fisch, *Justice Holmes and the Predictive Theory of Law, and Pragmatism* 39 J. Phil. 85 (1942) (quoting William James, 1 *Letters* 126 [1920]).

[47] Ibid. The membership of the club was youthful and eclectic, but skepticism seemed to be a theme: "[I]t was a strange sort of metaphysical club, where argument concerned the legitimacy of metaphysics itself. Chauncey Wright, a nominalist, was seen by Pierce and James as an arch positivist, constantly attacking the realism to which they and Abbot ascribed. Wright said no to metaphysics; Abbot, Pierce, and James said yes, but looked to science and scientific method for support." Marcia Speziale, *By Their Fruits You Shall Know Them: Pragmatism and the Prediction Theory of Law*, 9 *Manitoba L. Rev.* 29, 37 (1978) (citing M. Murphey, *The Development of Pierce's Philosophy* 99 [1961]; see also Note, *Holmes, Pierce and Legal Pragmatism*, 84 *Yale L. J.* 1123 (1975).

[48] William James, *Pragmatism: A New Name for Some Old Ways of Thinking* 201 (1910). See also G. Edward White, *The Rise and Fall of Justice Holmes*, 39 *U. Chi. L. Rev.* 51, 57 (1971) ("progressivism denied the existence of permanent 'laws' that governed intellectual disciplines").

[49] White, *Justice Holmes*, at 72.

could be used to criticize formalist legal theory, was in fact "science in a more profound way" than "pure science."[50]

Scientific pragmatism produced in Holmes a deep skepticism of abstract and transcendental claims.[51] The rigorous philosophical skepticism of his Cambridge circle helped Holmes systematize anti-idealist views that he possessed even before the war.[52] Holmes developed a view of human relations that had no room for idealism in either morality or history.[53] Thus, when he said that "the law of fashion is the law of life," he was making a global claim which challenged *any* system that offered a universal explanation of social life.[54] Holmes was unstinting in his skepticism: He deflated universal claims in all fields, from art to law:

[50]   Ibid., at 73.
[51]   As Mark DeWolfe Howe pointed out, even when asked to eulogize those who had given their lives for their country, Holmes began by saying, "I do not know what is true. I do not know the meaning of the universe. . . . [Yet] the faith is true and adorable which leads a soldier to throw away his life in obedience to a blindly accepted duty, in a cause which he little understands." Mark DeWolfe Howe, *The Positivism of Mr. Justice Holmes*, 64 *Harv. L. Rev.* 529, 532 (1951) (quoting Holmes, *Speeches* 59 [1913]).
[52]   Some have suggested that Holmes's moral skepticism was a product of his own traumatic experiences during the war, but his skepticism was so deep and so thoroughgoing that it incorporated but was not produced by his moral philosophy. According to Howe,

> [T]he young man who had joined the army in the conviction that the cause of abolition made the Civil War the moral crusade of the nineteenth century, found that those who saw it as a blundering effort of politicians to achieve through force ends which were beyond the constitutional limits of their power, were capable of heroism equaling if not exceeding his own. What wonder is there, then, that such a young man, *already skeptical* in matters of religious faith, should find himself at the War's end doubtful that "the right" as he conceived it had a better claim to universal validity than "the right" so differently conceived by his neighbor?

Howe, *Positivism of Mr. Justice Holmes*, at 537 (emphasis added). See also Thomas Grey, *Holmes, Pragmatism and Democracy*, 71 *Ore. L. Rev.* 521, 536–7 (1992) (commenting on Holmes's conclusion that personal loyalty was a much more powerful motivation in social life than philosophical beliefs about justice).
[53]   White argued that Holmes adopted skepticism only after growing disillusioned with more conventional scientific social theory: "But as [the twentieth] century dawned, Holmes gave up his effort and came to rest on the belief that the universe was unknowable, that ultimate values were in the end merely personal prejudices, and that change come [sic] through the fluctuating superiority of such prejudices. Ultimately his ideology presumed an open and ever-changing system of intellectual intercourse – an unregulated market of ideas. This was his famous skepticism." White, *Justice Holmes*, at 75.
[54]   Oliver Wendell Holmes, *Law in Science and Science in Law*, 12 *Harv. L. Rev.* 58, 58 (1899).

The crest of the wave of human interest is always moving, and it is enough to know that the depth was greatest in respect of a certain feature or style in literature or music or painting a hundred years ago to be sure that at this point it no longer is so profound. I should draw the conclusion that artists and poets, instead of troubling themselves about the eternal, had better be satisfied if they can stir the feelings of a generation, but that is not my theme. It is more to my point to mention that what I have said about art is true within the possible in matters of the intellect.[55]

Social scientists and lawyers, implied Holmes, ought to be as wary of trying to discover the "eternal" as the poets and artists. The only eternal verity that was itself not subject to the law of fashion was the law of fashion.[56]

There is some reason to believe that Holmes actually could not sustain his thoroughgoing skepticism: His famous refrain, for example, that "the man of the future is the man of statistics and the master of economics" suggests that Holmes privileged economic science and utilitarianism.[57] It would be a mistake to conclude that Holmes was a committed utilitarian because he was such an advocate of economic methodology.[58] The two are quite separate, and it is far more likely that although Holmes was deeply impressed by the emerging importance of economics to law, he probably was not a utilitarian.[59] As Thomas Grey has noted, "while Holmes was a

---

[55] Ibid., at 58.

[56] See, for example, Fisch, *Justice Holmes and the Predictive Theory of Law* at 88 (citing "a Letter to Pollock" (no date): "Sixty years later in a letter to Pollock expounding his own general philosophy, Holmes said: 'Chauncey Wright, a nearly forgotten philosopher of real merit, taught me when young that I must not say *necessary* about the universe, that we don't know whether anything is necessary or not.'"

[57] Oliver Wendell Holmes, *The Path of the Law*, 10 Harv. L. Rev. 457, 469 (1897); Holmes encouraged lawyers to study economics, because in the future lawyers would be "called on to consider and weigh the ends of legislation, the means of attaining them, and the cost. We learn that for everything we have we give up something else, and we are taught to set the advantage we gain against the other advantage we lose, and to know what we are doing when we elect." Oliver Wendell Holmes, *Collected Legal Papers* 195 (1952).

[58] But see H. L. Pohlman, *Justice Oliver Wendell Holmes and Utilitarian Jurisprudence* (1984) and Patrick J. Kelley, *Oliver Wendell Holmes, Utilitarian Jurisprudence, and the Positivism of John Stuart Mill*, 29 Am. J. Juris. 189 (1984) (book review) for an account of Holmes's debt to Mill's utilitarianism.

[59] See Duxbury, *Birth of Legal Realism and the Myth of Justice Holmes* at 97, quoting O. W. Holmes (unsigned), *Summary of Events: The Gas Stokers' Strike*, 7 Am. L. Rev. 582, 583 ("'Why should the greatest number be preferred? Why not the greatest good of the most intelligent and most highly developed?'").

nominal if rather pallid utilitarian, he was much more fervently a moral skeptic."[60] In fact, Holmes's interest in economics supported his skeptical agenda much more than his putative utilitarian world-view, because economics allowed legislators and judges to determine with accuracy which fashions were currently in sway. Had Holmes believed in a scientific utilitarianism, then the precise tools of the social sciences would allow decision makers to determine policy without ultimately resorting to the subjective preferences of "the crowd."[61] But he did not think that social science could identify the objectively "best" choice, only what members of society (given their whims) thought were the best choices. Holmes believed that "the worth of the competing social ends" between which lawmak-ers must choose "cannot be reduced to number and accurately fixed."[62]

Holmes did not deny that there were regularities in any given so-ciety, and that economists or even lawyers could describe those reg-ularities with accuracy in the form of complex correlations. What Holmes rejected was the idea that the regularities observed should somehow take a back seat to the idealistic claims of those who claimed to understand the "true nature" of the system under exam-ination. The social sciences could at best assist in the discovery of the changing preferences of society:

> The true science of law does not consist mainly in a theological working out of dogma or a logical development as in mathematics, or only in a study of it as an anthropological document from the outside; an even more important part consists in the establishment of its postulates from within upon accurately measured social desires instead of tradition.[63]

Social science, on its own, could never produce a set of transcen-dental social rules because its job was "mainly negative and skepti-cal."[64] The measurement of "social desires" helped judges and lawyers "scrutiniz[e] the reasons for the rules which we follow . . . [and] think things not words, [and] translate our words into the facts for which they stand."[65] Because the point of law was to reflect

[60] Grey, *Holmes, Pragmatism and Democracy*, at 531.
[61] Yosal Rogat, *The Judge as Spectator*, 31 *U. Chi. L. Rev.* 213, 249 n182 (1964). As Rogat noted, Holmes thought of "the crowd" more as "the mob" than "the people."
[62] Holmes, *Law in Science and Science in Law*, at 456.
[63] Ibid., at 452.
[64] Ibid.
[65] Ibid., at 460.

social desires and not to promote any single view of the good, Holmes was ultimately skeptical of the idea that there was even a single model of organization to which society should aspire. Holmes bluntly conceded that "the world would be just as well off if it lived under laws that differed from ours in many ways."[66]

It is important for my argument that we pause to note that Holmes's antiformalism included an attack on Austin.[67] Holmes rejected Austin's "sovereign-based" command theory of law as early as 1874.[68] Holmes's rejection of Austin did not (as it did with later twentieth-century critics of Austin) center on Holmes's disagreement with Austin's definition of the sovereign; rather, it focused on what Holmes saw as the formalistic use of logic in Austin and Bentham's sovereign-based command theory.[69] Austin's theory of law contained a specific formalist threat to Holmes because it presupposed that legal commands, whatever their source, had continuing force and authority after their promulgation and upon their receipt by law appliers. The idea that legal commands can have a meaning independent of their application could not be tolerated by Holmes, because law that existed independent of its application presupposed an "essential" content that survived its application. As White

---

[66] Ibid.

[67] White's view was that Holmes was self-consciously positioning himself against the utilitarians. For example, White thought that Holmes's statement at the beginning of *The Common Law* that the legal scholar needed "other tools . . . besides logic" was a thinly veiled attack on the utilitarian tradition. White, *Social Thought in America,* at 14. Further, White claimed, "Holmes selected for his special attack the prime exponent of utilitarian jurisprudence – John Austin" and noted that Mill praised Austin for developing "the logic of law." White, *Social Thought in America,* at 14 n10 (quoting Mill, "Austin on Jurisprudence," in John Stuart Mill 4 *Dissertations and Discussions* 213 [6 vols., 1864–7]).

[68] White, *Social Thought in America,* at 14.

[69] Pohlman argued that Holmes's disagreement with Austin was relatively minor: "Holmes's practical definition of law did not constitute a major departure from the utilitarian tradition. Though Austin defined laws as the commands of the sovereign, he often used judicial enforcement as the criterion of what rules were sovereign commands. . . . So Holmes's practical definition of law as 'the prophesies of what the courts will do' did not diverge much from Austin's views." Pohlman, *Justice Oliver Wendell Holmes and Utilitarian Jurisprudence,* at 60. I agree with Pohlman that Austin's command theory included the delegation of sovereign power to judges, and that this modification shows that his legal positivism is compatible with modern positivist theories that are more focused on the role of judicial discretion. I do not believe that Holmes thought that judges were delegates of the sovereign. Holmes, like the realists (but not necessarily John Chipman Gray), thought that judges exercised sovereign power because legal rules always underdetermine the legal choices available to a judge.

noted, Austin's command theory of law "conflicted with Holmes's main positive view."[70]

White's point would survive even if one were to replace "command of the sovereign" with another source of law. Even though Austin treated common law adjudication differently from statutory interpretation, he recognized that in both cases judges had to identify rules of law.[71] Just because Austin believed that the holdings "established by judicial decision . . . are rather faint traces"[72] from which law may be conjectured does not mean, as some have suggested, that Austin agreed with Holmes that "legal principles were meaningless apart from particular cases" or that the rules of law disclosed by common law "arose after the fact."[73] Holmes rejected, in a way that Austin did not, that in common law reasoning, a holding could act like a major premise:

> It is the merit of the common law that it decides the case first and determines the principle afterwards. Looking at the forms of logic it might be inferred that when you have a minor premise and a conclusion, there must be a major, which you are also prepared then and there to assert. But in fact lawyers, like other men, frequently see well enough how they ought to decide on a given state of facts without being very clear as to the *ratio decidendi*.[74]

Austin believed that *ratio decidendi* could be found in the common law. He had to be sure of the existence of these sorts of major premises, because their existence was crucial to his enthusiastic support for codification:

> Rules of judiciary law are not decided cases, but the *general* grounds or principles (or the *ratio decidendi*) whereon the cases are decided. Now, by the practical admission of those who apply these grounds or principles, they may be codified or turned into statute laws. . . . If it be possible to extract from a case, or from a few cases, the *ratio decidendi*, or general principle of decision, it is possible to extract from all

---

[70] White, *Social Thought in America*, at 14.

[71] As Austin put it, "The truth is . . . that the general grounds or principles of judicial decisions are as completely Law as statute law itself, though they differ considerably from statutes in the manner and form of expression." See John Austin, *Lectures on Jurisprudence in the Philosophy of Positive Law* 375 (5th ed., R. Campbell, ed., 1885) (hereafter *Lectures*).

[72] Austin, *Lectures*, Lect. XXXVII, at 333.

[73] Pohlman, *Justice Oliver Wendell Holmes and Utilitarian Jurisprudence*, at 86.

[74] Oliver Wendell Holmes, *Codes, and Arrangements of the Law*, 44 Harv. L. Rev. 725, 725 (1931) reprinted from *Am. L. Rev.* 5 (1870).

decided cases their respective grounds of decisions, and to turn them into a body of law, abstract in its form, and therefore compact and accessible.[75]

Austin, unlike Bentham, "tolerated" judge-made law because it too could take the form of a rule commanded by a sovereign. For Austin, then, the reason common law was inferior to legislation was not its form but its counterfactual status as a command.[76] If judge-made law could not take on the form of legislation, however imperfectly, then it would not be law at all – an alternative Austin found unimaginable: "Judiciary law consists of *rules*, or . . . it is not law at all."[77] Austin's tolerance of judge-made law simply revealed the central role that rules played within his concept of law. If the command theory plus a grudging acceptance of judicial discretion entailed the sources thesis, then we can see why Holmes would have rejected Austin's positivism regardless of whether it was or was not yoked to legislation. We may therefore conclude that Holmes's antiformalism would have led him to reject not only the command theory, but the sources thesis as well.

Holmes's rejection of classical legal positivism's command theory and sources thesis seems to fly in the face of his enthusiastic embrace of the separability thesis. It is not my aim, in this book, to suppress the fact that Holmes's legal theory overlapped at some places with that of the English positivists. It is well known that Holmes endorsed the separation of law and morals, and this important point of contact between Holmes and classical positivism seems to be what Fuller was thinking about when he launched his famous attack on Holmes's positivism.[78] One of the goals of this chapter is to prove that this point of commonality between formalism and antiformalism obscures the much greater differences that lay between them. Nonetheless, I agree with Grant Gilmore and Neil Duxbury that Holmes was not as much of an antiformalist as the realists who followed. But antiformalism, like all movements, grew over time, and I think that White was absolutely right to place Holmes at the

---

[75] Austin, *Lectures*, Lect. XXXIX, at 377.
[76] P. S. Atiyah and Robert S. Summers, *Form and Substance in Anglo-American Law,* 242 (1987).
[77] Austin, *Lectures*, Lect. XXXIX, at 375.
[78] Fuller, *The Law in Quest of Itself* 5 (1940); but see Mark DeWolfe Howe, *Positivism of Mr. Justice Holmes* at 529; see also Atiyah and Summers, *Form and Substance in Anglo-American Law* at 255–6.

beginning of the antiformalist movement. Holmes's skepticism provided the perfect antiformalist acid test for law. As we saw previously, he could not abide Bentham and Austin *because* they were not skeptics when it came to the existence of legal rules and sovereigns. Holmes's embrace of the separability thesis does not, in the end, tell us very much about his "all things considered" view of positivism. We should avoid the mistake made by Fuller, who confused Holmes's agreement with the separability thesis for agreement with classical positivism.

Holmes's commitment to the separation of law and morals had a very different ground from Bentham's or Austin's. Holmes, as a thoroughgoing skeptic, simply did not believe that moral statements had any meaning other than the behavior that accompanied them. This view was, of course, consistent with his hostility to "essences." For the utilitarian, the ground for the separation of law and morals was not skepticism about the meaningfulness of all moral statements: Bentham's swipe that natural rights were "nonsense on stilts" was the statement not of a moral skeptic, but that of a moralist who happened to believe that rights-based moral philosophy was incoherent.[79]

The different rationales underlying Holmes's and the English positivists' adoption of the separability thesis contributed to the differences between their theories of adjudication. According to Holmes's "prediction theory,"

> the primary rights and duties with which jurisprudence busies itself . . . are nothing but prophesies. One of the many evil effects of the confusion between legal and moral ideas . . . is that theory is apt to get the cart before the horse, and to consider the right or the duty as something existing apart from and independent of the consequences of its breach. . . . [A] legal duty so-called is nothing but a prediction that if a man does or omits certain things he will be made to suffer in this or that way by judgement of the court. . . .[80]

Holmes's prediction theory was a product of the separability thesis plus antiformalism. The prediction theory was a rejection of the Langdellian claim that there was a body of law that preexisted its application in the courtroom.[81] But the prediction theory was not

---

[79] See David Lieberman, *Province of Legislation Determined* 230–1 (1989); and Ross Harrison, *Bentham* 148–62 (1983).

[80] Holmes, *Path of the Law*, at 458.

[81] See Speziale, *By Their Fruits You Shall Know Them*, at 30. Speziale cited Rufus Choate as an example of the kind of formalism Holmes rebelled against: "The judge

just the rejection of the idea that law can exist independent of the courtroom. For if law was, as the antiformalist suggested, application-dependent, *and* morality really made claims on all of us, including judges, then instrumentalist judges would be obliged to use law instrumentally to promote the good. But this is where it is important to remember that antiformalist instrumentalism is not exactly the same as antiformalist prediction theory, despite their common roots. While advocates of the former are moral skeptics, advocates of the latter need not be skeptical about morality.

It is easy to see how there could be moral and amoral versions of instrumentalism. The instrumentalism commonly associated with the antebellum period was portrayed as market driven and pro-industrialization. Horwitz, for example, suggested that the new views of property that fueled the transformation of American common law were produced by capitalist motives.[82] But Horwitz's point (which Gilmore endorsed) was tactical; he was really setting up the argument about the next great period of instrumentalism, the period of strong judicial activism that followed formalism and the demise of the New Deal Court. The judges who oversaw the great changes in criminal procedure, civil rights law, tort law, and many other areas of federal and state law during the 1960s and early 1970s were no less instrumentalist than the courts of the early nineteenth century.[83] Seen from the perspective of a late-twentieth-century liberal, early-nineteenth-century instrumentalism was the pragmatic pursuit of conservative moral ends.[84] Although neither

does not make it [the law]. Like the structure of the State itself, we found it around us at the earliest dawn of reason . . . [and] it executes the will of the departed. . . . [I]t seems more a spirit, an abstraction, – the whispered yet authoritative voice of all the past and all the good, – than like the transient contrivance of altogether such as ourselves." Rufus Choate, 1 *Works of Rufus Choate* 436 (1862). Choate's words are Austinian, despite their apparent appeal to a Blackstonian "dawn of reason." Choate presupposed that the law implements the will of the state, and, although he analogized the law to an abstraction, he never lost sight of the fact that the law is but a collection of authoritative commands from the past.

[82]   Horwitz, *Transformation I*, at 36–40.

[83]   Horwitz and Gilmore must have been acutely aware of the similarity in the judicial styles of Lemuel Shaw and Earl Warren. If all that distinguished instrumentalism in the early nineteenth century from instrumentalism in the mid–twentieth century was the fact that the former promoted commerce and the latter promoted progressive liberalism, then Horwitz and Gilmore had a powerful rebuttal to their conservative colleagues who attacked liberal decisions for being the product of "judicial activism."

[84]   This explains why, for example, both LaPiana and G. Edward White believe that American law in the antebellum period was characterized by natural law. See

Cover nor Nelson realized it, their positions can be reconciled: The early-nineteenth-century legal mind saw a coincidence between an instrumental approach to common law and the morality of commerce.[85]

Amoral instrumentalism, as Holmes argued, is simply about prediction, whereas moral instrumentalism sees law as predictable and *explicable*: Judicial decision should go a certain way because that is what morality requires. An explanation does more than summarize a pattern. An explanation in science attempts to provide principles that characterize physical relationships under a generalization *broader* than the correlation providing primary evidence of the principles. Some skeptics, such as Hume, argued that explanation in science is impossible, and the pragmatists accepted Hume's anti-idealist claim and endeavored to reconstruct science without resorting to idealist assumptions about the nature of explanation.[86] In the same way that Pierce was skeptical about the possibility of "explanation" in science, Holmes was skeptical about the possibility of explanation in law. Holmes's theory of judicial decision eschewed explanation because it was skeptical about all grounds of decision except the empirical fact of the decision itself.[87] The prediction theory was

William P. LaPiana, *Logic and Experience: The Origin of Modern Legal American Education* 32–7 (1994), and G. Edward White, *The Marshall Court and Cultural Change* 1815–1835 135, 153–4 (1991). Stephen Feldman argues that there were both instrumentalist and natural law impulses in antebellum American jurisprudence, and I believe that his attempt to reconcile these apparently irreconcilable approaches matches my account of moral instrumentalism. See Stephen Feldman, *From Premodern to Modern American Jurisprudence: The Onset of Positivism*, 50 Vand. L. Rev. 1387 (1997).

[85] Francis Hilliard wrote that in adjudication, "General expediency, – public policy, – is often the highest measure of right." Francis Hilliard, *The Elements of Law* vi (1835) (1972 reprint). Joseph Story was an excellent representative of moral instrumentalism. Although he believed in natural law, he endorsed instrumentalism, especially in commercial law, as evidenced by his decision in *Swift v. Tyson*, 41 U.S. (16 Pet.) 1 (1842) (overruled by *Erie R. Co. v. Tompkins*, 304 U.S. 64 (1938). Like Hilliard, Story thought that natural law required judges to exercise pragmatic judgment in the pursuit of social advantage: "[The common law] is a system having its foundations in natural reason; but, at the same time, built up and perfected by artificial doctrines, adapted and moulded to the artificial structure of society." Joseph Story, *Miscellaneous Writings* (William W. Story, ed., 1852, reprinted 1972).

[86] "[Pierce] did not look on scientific inquiry as a method of discovering or revealing truth. His hypothesis was that inquiry is a never-ending process whose purpose is to resolve doubts generated when experience does not mesh with preconceived theory. . . . These ideas seem to correspond with the central tenets of Holmes's jurisprudential theory." Grant Gilmore, *The Ages of American Law* 50–1 (1977).

[87] It is unclear whether Holmes would have been sympathetic to the idea that the measurement of "felt social desires" gave lawyers a ground for prediction that

based on what can be at best described as sophisticated correlations: "Holmes told law students to leave axioms and deductions brooding in their omnipresence, and instead to read reports of what past courts had done, to anticipate what future courts in general would do."[88] In contrast, judicial decisions based on a judge's moral convictions could, in theory, be both predictable and explicable (although with independently varying degrees of accuracy), because the predicter could also identify a moral principle under which the decisions could be classified. An antiformalist theory that was skeptical about the existence of legal principles *could* explain legal decisions if it rejected the separability thesis and collapsed legal and moral judgment. Conversely, a formalist theory that was not skeptical about the existence of legal principles but accepted the separability thesis could also explain legal decisions. But an antiformalist theory that was skeptical about legal principles and that accepted the separability thesis would have no basis of explanation and so would be left with a Holmesian, pragmatist, anti-idealist theory of judicial decision based on the correlation of social facts.[89]

was independent of the judges' politics and personality. As we saw previously, Holmes claimed that the ultimate task of the court was to express social desires as measured through the techniques of economics and sociology. If that were the case, then a lawyer who followed Holmes's advice in the first half of *The Path of the Law,* when it came time to predicting the behavior of a sincere judge, should have bet on the choice that was more likely to provide future welfare gains than the choice that appeared consistent with past but suboptimal welfare gains. This was Howe's way of reconciling the first and second halves of *The Path of the Law.* See Howe, *Positivism of Mr. Justice Holmes,* at 542. Grey has argued that the reason the prediction theory limited itself to relatively modest pieces of evidence is that Holmes recognized that litigable issues always arose in the gray area where social forces were in equipoise. See Thomas C. Grey, *Molecular Motion: The Holmesian Judge in Theory and Practice,* 37 *William & Mary L. Rev.* 19 (1995).

[88] Speziale, *By Their Fruits You Shall Know Them,* at 31.

[89] Logically speaking, there are other social scientific principles than just morality. One might think that Holmes and other antiformalists could avail themselves of principles of history, sociology, or economics. This would represent an attractive alternative for an antiformalist theory of adjudication that embraced the separability thesis. I have already argued that Holmes was a global skeptic, which would make his embrace of any social principle equally unlikely. I chose to focus on Holmes's rejection of moral principles not to reintroduce the subject of his use of social science but rather to explain what some see as a point of common contact among Holmes, Austin, and Bentham. I think that it is difficult to support the idea that Holmes was in fact ready to base his prediction theory on the larger explanatory force of history, sociology, or economics. His view of history was especially cynical; his views on sociology were undeveloped; and his views on economics (unlike those of Veblen or Beard) shaded very quickly into a mélange of moral philosophy and political econ-

There is a final point of contact between Holmes and formalism that I must mention. As many commentators have noted, there seems to be a contradiction between the Holmes who wrote *The Common Law* and the Holmes who wrote *The Path of the Law*.[90] In *The Path of the Law,* Holmes stressed his skeptical and antiformalist view of scientific inquiry. *The Common Law,* although informed by Holmes's skepticism, was an impressive attempt to redescribe the law as a "philosophically continuous series."[91] He tried, for example, to show that torts and criminal law rested on the same legal concept of external liability: According to Holmes, primitive societies tried to judge subjective intent, whereas modern societies were gradually recognizing that intent was unknowable and were focusing instead on what could be known – external action.[92] The specific principles Holmes claimed to find deep in the common law were striking and original, but what is more important is that Holmes felt comfortable declaring these principles in very unpragmatic, almost essentialist language. In Holmes's theory of external liability, "logic prevail[ed] over experience. . . . Pierce's philosophy of external knowledge [was] apparently transformed into a tool for demonstrating how *prima facie* distinct legal doctrines are of necessity interconnected by the same philosophical thread."[93] There is no doubt

omy. On Holmes's views of the relationship between economics and morality, see Pohlman, *Justice Oliver Wendell Holmes and Utilitarian Jurisprudence,* at 11–47.

[90] See, for example, Horwitz, *Transformation II,* at 141, and Grant Gilmore, *The Death of Contract* 143 n256 (1974).

[91] Oliver Wendell Holmes, *The Common Law* 104 (Howe, ed., 1963).

[92] As Robert Gordon has noted, Holmes believed that in modern common law, the "standards for imposing liability were general inclusive standards applicable to everyone. . . . [T]he enforcing court need only apply regularities observed in similar factual situations to determine the appropriate legal consequences of the facts in the present case." Robert Gordon, *Holmes's Common Law as Legal and Social Science,* 10 *Hofstra L. Rev.* 719, 728–9 (1982). See also Gilmore, *Ages of American Law,* at 54 ("a legal system approaches maturity to the extent that it succeeds in eliminating any reference to what the defendant actually thought, intended, or willed").

[93] Duxbury, *Birth of Legal Realism and the Myth of Justice Holmes,* at 95. Duxbury has argued that there was a close theoretical relationship between Pierce's theory of scientific knowledge and Holmes's external standard of liability. Duxbury noted that pragmatism, while skeptical, ultimately relied on the community to produce standards of scientific truth: "According to the philosophy of Pierce . . . knowledge is essentially public and communal, acquired through shared, practical experience." Ibid., at 93. According to Holmes's theory, "Legal standards . . . are external, public, communal or objective standards," just like the pragmatist conception of truth. Ibid., at 94. Duxbury, in a separate and very intriguing final step, suggested that Holmes's pragmatism was partially informed by Social Darwinism: "The community, for Holmes, is not the community at large but rather a community of successful social

that, at times, Holmes's doctrinal legal scholarship "talks to us from on high, laying down principles of unrestricted universality."[94] Nonetheless, I am not sure that it would be correct to say that his "theory of external liability is resolutely formalist."[95]

The theory of external standards of liability is one of the cornerstones of Holmes's career. It is as important as his prediction theory or his attack on formalism. It cannot be ignored. To modern eyes, it seems conceptualist if not formalist. Nonetheless, I think that a better way of understanding the theory of external liability is that it is only superficially formalist. It cannot be denied that Holmes's theory of external liability seems wrapped in metaphysical objectivity. Yet I shall argue below that, heedless of the apparent paradox, Holmes endorsed the theory of external liability because he was such an extreme metaphysical skeptic. Thus, the theory of external liability stands, quite appropriately, at a midpoint between the fully formalist theory of classical legal positivism and its advocates, and the legal realists, who rejected formalism more consistently than Holmes.

The theoretical continuity between *The Path of the Law* and the theory of external liability is apparent once one sees that Holmes's arguments in *The Common Law* were motivated by his skepticism. Take, for example, Holmes's observation that the history of tort law was a progression from subjective moralism to objective standards of care:

> The theory of torts may be summed up very simply. At the two extremes of the law are rules determined by policy without reference of any kind to morality. . . . But in the main the law started from those intentional wrongs which are the simplest and most pronounced cases, as well as the nearest to the feeling of revenge which leads to self-redress. . . . But as the law has grown, even when its standards have continued to model themselves upon those of morality, they have necessarily become external, because they have considered, not the actual condition of the particular defendant, but whether his conduct would have been wrong in the fair average member of the community.[96]

But why did Holmes think that tort law moved to external standards? Holmes hypothesized that society recognized in the nine-

competitors, '[t]he more powerful interests' in society." Ibid., at 97 (quoting Oliver W. Holmes [unsigned], *Summary of Events: The Gas Stokers' Strike, 7 Am. L. Rev.* 582).
[94] Gilmore, *Ages of American Law*, at 53.
[95] Duxbury, *Birth of Legal Realism and the Myth of Justice Holmes*, at 94.
[96] Holmes, *The Common Law*, at 128.

teenth century (in a way that it could not in the day of the *deodand*) that no one could know very much about men's moral choices: Courts could not see men as "God sees them," and for that reason the best for which the legal system could hope was to promote a "certain average of conduct."[97] Holmes noted that in the absence of any means by which courts can know anything about men other than their external acts, judgment based on external conduct "is necessary to the general welfare."[98] As Richard Posner noted, Holmes's attraction to objective theories of law resulted not from a substantive theory of law that had an objective or transcendental existence but from his idea that substantive theories of law depended for their content and existence on the nonlegal social base.[99]

But what are we to make of the very complex and subtle system of principles that made up Holmes's external standards of liability? Holmes did not think, as did the realists who followed him, that the midlevel principles of tort law, such as duty, proximate cause, or contributory negligence, were simply arbitrarily selected categories that could be suspended or redefined to fit the immediate needs of society.[100] Holmes seemed to view these principles as part of a coherent whole and argued vigorously that once a legal system had adopted external standards of liability, it was committed to the midlevel principles as well. Ironically, the legal structure generated by Holmes's skeptical inquiry behaved like a set of objective and transcendental norms, and it may be that Holmes embraced external standards of liability because he simply could not resist the temptation to fill the emptiness created by his skepticism.

Assuming that Holmes fell prey to the very human weakness of wanting to offer a theory of tort liability to replace the traditional views that had been washed away by the "cynical acid" of his historical method, why did he opt for an objective theory of liability? Holmes refused the alternatives to the external theory of liability

---

[97] Holmes, *The Common Law,* at 86.

[98] Ibid. Pohlman concluded from quotations like this (of which there are a few) that Holmes's external theory of liability was evidence of his embrace of English utilitarianism. Pohlman, *Justice Oliver Wendell Holmes and Utilitarian Jurisprudence,* at 26–7. Pohlman's error stems from the fact that the external theory of liability is underdetermined: It could be a logical consequence either of skepticism or of utilitarianism. It seems clear to me that Holmes adopted utilitarianism *because* his skepticism had eliminated any other ground for accepting legal rules.

[99] Richard Posner, *The Problems of Jurisprudence* 19 (1990).

[100] See John C.P. Goldberg, *Style and Skepticism in Holmes,* 63 *Brook. L. Rev.* 225, 271 (1997).

partly because, I suspect, he imagined that all the alternatives involved adopting some form of moral instrumentalism. Faced with a
choice between the external theory of liability, which allowed him
to be a moral skeptic at the cost of reproducing formalism at a local
level within tort doctrine, and the alternatives, which allowed him
to escape formalism in tort doctrine at the cost of embracing substantive moral theory, it is easy to see why Holmes chose the former. The main difference between Holmes and the realists is that
the realists tried to escape the dialectic that forced Holmes to embrace formalism in *The Common Law.* Whether the realists succeeded – and what they had to give up in order to succeed – is why
Pound's essay *The Call for a Realist Jurisprudence* is so interesting, despite its crude formulation of realism and its goals.[101]

3.4. ANTIFORMALISM AND
THE GROWTH OF LEGAL REALISM

Obviously, we cannot rely on Holmes alone to develop a picture of
formalism. Nonetheless, our survey of Holmes's antiformalism has
produced certain specific findings: Holmes's skepticism clearly implies that in his own mind, formalism committed the grave error of
idealism. We can summarize this finding as follows. Formalism endorsed what we can call the myth of "transcendentalism":

(1) the view that legal rules exist *a priori*; that is, their existence is a
matter of objective fact unaffected by contingent historical events.

We have, so far, uncovered one element of formalism. This exercise,
however, is only half-complete, because we must look at the second
stage of antiformalism, realism, in law in order to see how the legal
realists described formalism.

Antiformalism in law is at the foundation of legal realism. Probably all realists were antiformalists, but certainly not all antiformalists were realists, if for no other reason than that antiformalism began before realism really cohered as a movement. Despite their
many differences, the early pioneers of antiformalism and the realists who followed them agreed at least upon the same critique of
formalism, if not on the positive program that should follow from

---

[101] Roscoe Pound, *The Call for a Realist Jurisprudence*, 44 *Harv. L. Rev.* 697 (1931).

their common critique.[102] Even where the early antiformalists and the realists differed, such as when Pound attacked Llewellyn and Frank, the grounds for that disagreement will help us understand more deeply to what extent they were constructing a common enemy called formalism. Realism emerged out of antiformalism in three distinct phases.[103] The first phase, which can be described as Holmesian "proto-realism," produced a historical critique of the idea that "the Common Law had a fundamental structure discernible by the architectonic intelligence."[104] This period was marked by the skeptical "critique of conceptualism,"[105] which we explored in the previous section. The second phase, which took place during the Progressive era, can be characterized as "pre-realist." The theorists of this period (Brandeis, Cardozo, Frankfurter, and Pound) were "importantly affected by Progressive politics and Deweyite pragmatism."[106] The third phase belonged to the legal realists, whose work began in the 1920s and reached its maturity in the 1930s. Each of these phases represented different forms of antiformalism. Because we have already examined the proto-realist period, in this section I will focus mainly on the legal realists. I will not examine the pre-realists separately, because in an important sense, the differences between the pre-realists and the legal realists – which were important and deeply felt – were not so much about differences between their particular forms of antiformalism but about other issues.[107] In fact, as we will see, the legal realists adopted, almost wholesale, Pound's antiformalist account of analytical jurisprudence. Because the goal of this section is to define

[102]   The dispute between the antiformalists and the realists achieved its greatest notoriety in the debate between Pound and Llewellyn, illustrating the occasionally sharp distinctions between the realists, who criticized the formalists and the antiformalists, and the antiformalists like Pound, who had initiated antiformalism but could not adopt the entire realist program. See Horwitz, *Transformation II*, at 172–5, for a brief introduction to the Pound–Llewellyn debate.

[103]   Bruce Ackerman, *Law and the Modern Mind*, 103 *Daedalus* 119, 121 (1974).

[104]   Ibid.

[105]   Horwitz, *Transformation II*, at 129.

[106]   Ibid., at 156–7; see Hon. Benjamin Cardozo, *An Address to the New York State Bar Association*, in *Proceedings of the New York State Bar Association* 263, 290 (1932); G. Edward White, *Patterns of American Legal Thought* 113–15 (1978).

[107]   See, for example, Pound, *Call for a Realist Jurisprudence*; and Llewellyn, *Some Realism about Realism* (1931) (the disagreement between pre-realists and realists turned on the role of empiricism in legal theory), and N.E.H. Hull, *Reconstructing the Origins of Realistic Jurisprudence: A Sequel to the Llewellyn–Pound Exchange Over Legal Realism*, 45 *Duke L. J.* 1302 (1989); see also Neil Duxbury, *Patterns of American Jurisprudence*, 74–5 (1995).

formalism by trying to determine how the antiformalists defined it, it will suffice for our purposes to discuss the antiformalism of the pre-realists and legal realists together.

The importance of legal realism and its progenitors is undeniable: Commentators have suggested that "most legal scholars in the United States, from the late twenties on, have been realists in important respects."[108] To take just one example, the use of social science in the law emerged as part of the pre-realist strategy to combat formalism: In 1908 the "Brandeis Brief," designed to educate an appellate court about general social facts relevant to the issues of rule making, first appeared.[109] Yet, from the outset, it is difficult to discuss realism because it is difficult to define who the realists were and when they wrote. On the one hand, it is possible to find legal scholars who were using realist techniques such as Oliver Wendell Holmes and John Chipman Gray as early as the late 1890s.[110] On the other hand, "'legal realism' is an expression that has been used most often to refer to the work of a group of thinkers, the bulk of whose writing appeared in the 1920s and 1930s."[111] Certainly, the pre-realists, whose work appeared between the late 1890s and the early 1920s, were "realistic" in at least their antiformalism.[112]

If we focus on just those in the third phase, we see that the writings of Llewellyn, Frank, Yntema, Arnold, Cohen, and their peers suggest that as a group, the realists were irregularly bound together

[108] Jerome Hall, *Studies in Jurisprudence and Criminal Theory* 136–7 (1958); see also Joseph Singer, *Legal Realism Now*, 76 Cal. L. Rev. 465 (1988). "[Legal realism] constitutes a significant, though not always a dominant, part of the intellectual matrix in which almost all modern lawyers, judges, and scholars of law have been formed." Eugene Rostow, *The Sovereign Prerogative* xvi (1962).

[109] *Muller v. Oregon*, 208 U.S. 412, 419 n1 (1908). See John Henry Schlegel, *American Legal Realism and Empirical Social Science: From the Yale Experience*, 28 Buff. L. Rev. 459 (1979).

[110] See, for example, Holmes, *Path of the Law*, at 457; Holmes, *Law in Science and Science in Law*, at 58; John Chipman Gray, *The Nature and Sources of the Law* (2d ed., 1963) (first published 1909).

[111] Robert Samuel Summers, *Instrumentalism and American Legal Theory* 36 (1982); see also Martin P. Golding, *Jurisprudence and Legal Philosophy in Twentieth Century America – Major Theories and Development*, 36 J. Legal Educ. 441, 453 (1986) ("realism was a movement of the 1920s and 30s"); Edward W. Patterson, *Jurisprudence: Men and Ideas of the Law* 538 (1953) (listing twenty "Realist" authors, citing their scholarship from the 1920s and '30s).

[112] See, for example, Roscoe Pound, *Mechanical Jurisprudence*, 8 Colum. L. Rev., 608 (1908); Roscoe Pound, *The Scope and Purpose of Sociological Jurisprudence*, 24 Harv. L. Rev. 591 (1911), Roscoe Pound, *The Scope and Purpose of Sociological Jurisprudence*, 25 Harv. L. Rev. 489 (1912); T. R. Powell, *The Logic and Rhetoric of Constitutional Law*, 15 J. Phil., Psychol. & Sci. Methods 645 (1918).

by a certain kind of critique. The common thread that held them to-gether was their strong commitment to antiformalism. But their re-jection of the status quo was not an entirely nihilistic view. The real-ists did not attack the established legal academy because they believed that law was a meaningless project. They believed that they were working toward a better view of law. As Dean Anthony Kronman has pointed out, the "negative side of realism" was the means through which they developed their positive views on the answers to the problems of "intelligibility" and "justification."[113] The realists' negative project was complex and consisted of a num-ber of not entirely mutually consistent claims:

> [Realism's] "negation" [of the prevailing orthodoxy] was held on a number of different grounds. On the basis of purely theoretical consid-eration it was argued that rules and principles have no existence; only individual decisions exist. It was also argued that, despite what judges say, rules and principles do not determine judicial outcomes and hence are valueless for a science of law. It was also maintained that since it was impossible to discover what the rules are that were actually being ap-plied, they are valueless. Finally, it was held (by the most moderate Re-alists or by the extreme Realists in their moderate moments) that rules and principles do exist and exercise *some* influence on decisions, but that there are more interesting and important things to study about the law. . . . All of these considerations can be found in the literature of real-ism, and some Realists seem to have entertained all of them at once.[114]

If we are to understand legal realism, and especially its relationship to formalism, we must take seriously its negative project. A close reading of a typical but carefully written realist critique of formal-ism by Felix Cohen will help us grasp the picture of formalism with which the realists operated.

---

[113] Anthony Kronman, *Jurisprudential Responses to Legal Realism*, 73 *Cornell L. Rev.* 335, 336 (1988).

[114] Golding, *Jurisprudence and Legal Philosophy in Twentieth Century America*, at 452. It should be noted that I focus almost exclusively on realism's negative project, which means that its positive project (especially its focus on the role of policy sci-ences in adjudication) will not be explored. For accounts of the positive project, see, for example, Summers, *Instrumentalism and American Legal Theory*, at 60–72 (describ-ing instrumentalist theory of law); Harold D. Lasswell and Myres S. McDougal, *Legal Education and Public Policy: Professional Training in the Public Interest*, 52 *Yale L. J.* 203 (1943) (describing realism as policy science).

In 1935, Cohen summarized the realists' diagnosis of the problems besetting contemporary legal thought.[115] The essay surveyed a variety of doctrinal fields, including corporate and constitutional law, and concluded that all "leaders of modern legal thought in America are in fundamental agreement in their disrespect" for the "traditional legal thought-ways."[116] For example, it seemed absurd to Cohen that empirical evidence about business activity was deemed irrelevant in order to determine "where" a corporation was incorporated, or that the social consequences of a public law would be deemed irrelevant in order to determine whether it was in violation of the Fourteenth Amendment.[117] Cohen referred mockingly to mainstream jurisprudential scholars as "classical jurists"[118] and called the Restatement of the Law by the American Law Institute the "last long-drawn-out gasp of a dying tradition."[119] Cohen attributed the crisis in American law to the hegemonic grip of "mechanical jurisprudence."[120]

Despite its rather scattershot approach, Cohen's critique of formalism was built on two separate claims. Formalism was a bad theory of law because it made two fundamental mistakes: First, it treated law as an autonomous social practice (completely divorced from either morality or social science), and second, it characterized legal reasoning as deductive or mechanical. Although both criticisms are vital elements to the realist critique of formalism, we shall see that Cohen borrowed the latter from Pound, a pre-realist, in order to establish the former. We know this because Cohen, in arguing that the formalist legal reasoning was deductive, selected exactly the same terminology and targets as Pound. Cohen even went so far as to build his argument against formalism around the concept of "mechanical jurisprudence," a term that Pound had made famous. In Pound's essay, mechanical jurisprudence stood for the idea that legal reasoning was deductive.[121] While Cohen did not disagree

---

[115] Felix S. Cohen, *Transcendental Nonsense and the Functional Approach*, 35 Colum. L. Rev. 809, 821 (1935) (hereafter *Transcendental Nonsense*).

[116] Ibid.

[117] Ibid., at 818–20.

[118] Interestingly, Horwitz adopted the term *classical legal thought* to describe late-nineteenth-century legal formalism. Horwitz, *Transformation I*, at 10.

[119] F. Cohen, *Transcendental Nonsense*, at 833. From the perspective of more than a half century later, it appears that reports of the Restatement's death have been greatly exaggerated. But see Anita Bernstein, *Restatement Redux*, 48 Vand. L. Rev. 1663, 1669–75 (1995) (on forces eroding the influence of the Restatement project).

[120] F. Cohen, *Transcendental Nonsense*, at 821.

[121] Pound, *Mechanical Jurisprudence*, at 608.

with this conclusion, he thought it required elaboration. Cohen therefore added a separate and independent argument to Pound's argument that legal reasoning could not be deductive:

> Legal concepts (for example, corporations or property rights) are supernatural entities which do not have a verifiable existence. . . . Rules of law, which refer to these legal concepts, are not descriptions of empirical social facts (such as the customs of men or the customs of judges) nor yet statements of moral ideals, but rather theorems in an independent system. It follows that a [formalist] legal argument can never be refuted by a moral principle nor yet by any empirical fact. Jurisprudence, then, as an autonomous system of legal concepts, rules and arguments, must be independent both of ethics and of such positive sciences as economics or psychology.[122]

This conclusion struck the key theme that ran throughout Cohen's argument, and one that formed the core of the realists' antiformalism: that, at a minimum, any credible theory of law had to reject the idea that law was *autonomous* from either moral theory or the social sciences.

Cohen did not explicitly state what is wrong with treating law as if it were autonomous and independent of other intellectual tasks.[123] Nonetheless, it easy to see how Cohen's rejection of the autonomy of law depended upon Pound's rejection of the idea that legal reasoning could be deductive. According to Pound, the formalist effort to depict law as a science failed because the formalists thought science was a matter of deduction from *a priori* principles:

> I have referred to mechanical jurisprudence as scientific because those who administer it believe it such. But in truth it is not science at all. We no longer hold anything scientific merely because it exhibits a rigid scheme of deductions from *a priori* conception. . . . The idea of science as a system of deductions has become obsolete.[124]

---

[122] F. Cohen, *Transcendental Nonsense,* at 821.

[123] Duncan Kennedy described the formalist commitment to autonomy in law as part of an inescapable liberal dilemma: "The decision process is called rule application only if the actor resolutely limits himself to identifying those aspects of the situation which *per se* trigger his response. . . . The minute he begins to look over his shoulder at the *consequence* of responding to the presence or absence of the *per se* elements [he is no longer acting like a judge]." Duncan Kennedy, *Legal Formality,* 2 J. Legal Stud. 351, 359 (1973); *and see* Paul Shupack, *Rules and Standards in Kennedy's* Form and Substance, 6 *Cardozo L. Rev.* 947, 964 (1985) (on Kennedy's analysis of the dilemma of legal autonomy in a pluralist society).

[124] Pound, *Mechanical Jurisprudence,* at 608.

If legal principles were unverifiable, then they must be true *a priori,* like premises in a syllogism, and if they were like premises in a syllogism, then legal reasoning had to be like elementary logic – that is, matter of proof through deduction. It should be apparent that Pound's claim about the deductive nature of formalist legal reasoning was itself built on an antiformalist claim that legal formalists were committed to transcendentalism. This is because if, as the antiformalists had demonstrated, facts that are provable through verification are not transcendental, then a fact that is believed to be true but cannot be verified must be true by virtue of being an *a priori* truth about the world, like a claim about geometry If transcendentalism entailed the formalist claim that legal concepts are true *a priori,* then transcendentalism entailed a theory of legal reasoning, namely that legal reasoning is deductive. Cohen therefore used Pound as a stepping-stone to the ultimate realist critique of formalism: Pound's argument that the formalism entailed a deductive model of legal reasoning led Cohen to the conclusion that the formalist had to treat law as autonomous and thus made Pound's original antiformalism critique seem even more compelling and prescient.

Cohen used the terms *transcendental nonsense* and *mechanical jurisprudence* to describe legal formalism. Other realists used other terms to denote their antiformalism. For Frank, what was wrong with traditional jurisprudence was that it was governed by "mechanistic law." Like Cohen, Frank faulted the legal formalists for their "obsessive interest in legal rules" and their naïve belief that the science of law could provide "certainty and predictability."[125] Llewellyn, in an ambitious work of historical analysis, determined that from the Civil War until the 1920s, the American legal community had been in the grip of a style of judicial reasoning he designated "the Formal Style." The Formal Style was authoritarian, mechanical, and logical: "[T]he rules of law are to decide cases. . . . Opinions run in deductive form with an air or expression of single line inevitability."[126] "Formalism" may not have been a term of art until after Llewellyn began using the expression (or a shortened version of it). It is currently popular to borrow Llewellyn's analysis of the alternating "styles" of jurisprudence in America and to de-

---

[125] Jerome Frank, *Law and the Modern Mind* 142 (6th ed., 1948).
[126] Karl Llewellyn, *Common Law Tradition,* at 38.

scribe the period between 1860 and 1920 as the Age of Formalism.[127] Nelson has described it this way:

> Formalism – the notion that social controversies could be resolved by deductions drawn from first principles on which all men agreed or by inductions drawn from the "evidence" of past decisions – this became the common denominator of late nineteenth century American jurisprudence.[128]

All of these theorists, regardless of the terms they adopted, subscribed to the same objections to formalism found in Cohen's analysis.

We can now complete the list of antiformalist claims begun with our discussion of Holmes. In addition to transcendentalism, we can add two more elements to the antiformalist picture of formalism:

(2) The "deduction thesis": that formalists thought legal reasoning was deductive.

(3) The "autonomy thesis": that formalists thought that legal reasoning was autonomous from moral or social concerns.

For the sake of brevity, I will refer to this as the "antiformalist list." With this list now complete, we have succeeded in defining formalism by examining the antiformalist argument. From examining the early antiformalism of Holmes and the later antiformalism of the pre-realists and realists, we have constructed a picture of formalism as a theory of law that is transcendental, deductive, and autonomous.

---

[127] The number of modern authors who refer to the "age of formalism" is large. See, for example, Summers, *Instrumentalism and American Legal Theory,* at 138–56; Horwitz, *Transformation I,* at 254; David Lyons, *Legal Formalism and Instrumentalism – A Pathological Study,* 66 *Cornell L. Rev.* 949, 959 (1981); Stephen A. Segal, *John Chipman Gray's Legal Formalism, and the Transformation of Perpetuities Law,* 36 *U. Miami L. Rev.* 439 (1982). In *The Ages of American Law,* Grant Gilmore refers to this era as "the Age of Faith" and characterizes the period as one of expulsion into "the law's black night." Gilmore, *Ages of American Law,* at 41. In contrast to Llewellyn, Neil Duxbury offers an account that emphasizes the continuity between the formalist era and its successors. Duxbury, *Patterns of American Jurisprudence,* at 64 (1995), but see Thomas C. Grey, *Modern American Legal Thought,* 106 *Yale L.J.* 493, 513 (1996) (cautiously endorsing Duxbury's "continuity" argument but noting that Duxbury's argument leaves little room for pre-realism). For recent accounts that offer a revised and more positive perspective on formalism, see Schauer, *Formalism;* Ernest J. Weinrib, *Legal Formalism: On the Immanent Rationality of Law,* 97 *Yale L.J.* 949 (1988); see also William P. LaPiana, *Logic and Experience.*

[128] Nelson, *Impact of the Anti-Slavery Movement,* at 565–6. As we saw earlier, Nelson argued that the antislavery jurisprudence that opposed decisions such as *Dred Scott v. Sandford* (60 U.S. (19 How.) 393 [1857]) helped bolster formalism's rise to preeminence after the Civil War.

As I suggested previously, the antiformalist list is not a view of law that the English positivists would have obviously endorsed. Transcendentalism seems inconsistent with all but the most abstract interpretation of the sources thesis, and the deduction thesis seems flatly inconsistent with the command theory. The only part of the antiformalist list that does not obviously conflict with classical positivism is the autonomy thesis. Something has to give: Either formalism is not really closely related to classical positivism, or (as I tentatively suggested previously) the antiformalist's picture of formalism is inaccurate. Now that we have a clear idea of the antiformalists' version of formalism, we can seriously test the latter option. In the following section I will show that neither of the major American legal scholars who were associated with either analytic jurisprudence or formalism actually endorsed all of the three elements in the antiformalist list.

3.5. THE ANTIFORMALIST CRITIQUE OF LANGDELL AND BEALE

What did the formalists actually say about law? In order to determine what the formalists said, as opposed to what the antiformalists said the formalists said, we have to read the writings of the legal scholars who were the objects of the antiformalists' criticisms. It must be stressed that we will be talking about a group of thinkers and calling them formalists, even though those thinkers and almost none of their critics called them by that name. Dean Christopher Langdell, Joseph Beale, and the Harvard Law School are commonly identified with formalism and bore the brunt of many of the realists' early attacks.[129] Langdell was the first dean of the Harvard Law School, and although his reign did not last into the twentieth cen-

---

[129] See, for example, F. Cohen, *Transcendental Nonsense*, at 821; Karl Llewellyn, *Book Review*, 40 Harv. L. Rev. 145 (1926); William O. Douglas, *A Functional Approach to the Law of Business Associations*, 23 Ill. L. Rev. 35 (1929). See also Summers, *Instrumentalism and American Legal Theory*, at 26 (identifying Langdell and Beale as central figures of formalism); Golding, *Jurisprudence and Legal Philosophy in Twentieth Century America*, at 445 (1986) (the first attack on formalism was led by Holmes against Langdell); Kronman, *Jurisprudential Responses to Legal Realism*, at 335 (equating realism and the attack on "the Langdellian project"); Gordon, *Case for (and Against) Harvard*, at 1231 [1994] (same).

tury, his influence was sustained through his writings and pro-
tégées.[130] As Grant Gilmore put it, "[I]f Langdell had not existed, we
would have had to invent him. . . . However absurd, however mis-
chievous, however deeply rooted in error it may have been,
Langdell's idea shaped our legal thinking for fifty years."[131] In this
section I will determine whether, and to what extent, the antiformalist list's three elements can be found in Langdell and Beale and
then examine the substance of the realist critique of formalism.

Langdell believed that law was a science. He declared in 1886 that:

> [it] is indispensable to establish at least two things; first that law is a
> science; secondly that all the available materials of that science are
> contained in printed books. . . . [T]he library is . . . to us all that the
> laboratories of the university are to chemists and physicists, all that
> the museum of natural history is to the zoologists, all that the botani-
> cal garden is to the botanists. . . .[132]

In his preface to his casebook on contracts, Langdell argued that
study of the law could be reduced to the study of a handful of significant cases, with each case representing a principle of law: "The
number of fundamental legal doctrines is much less than commonly supposed. . . . [Yet] to have such mastery of these as to be
able to apply them with constant facility and certainty to the ever-
tangled skein of human affairs, is what constitutes a true lawyer."[133]
Langdell's "scientific" method resulted in some doctrinal claims
that confounded later scholars.

For example, when Langdell wrote his treatise on contracts, the
"mailbox rule" was on its way to becoming settled law in American
jurisdictions. The rule states that a contract becomes binding when
it is signed and mailed by the offeree, not when the document is received by the offeror.[134] Langdell argued that the very logic of contract law dictated that a written notice stating that a proffered contract had been accepted by the offeree must be received by the

---

[130] Langdell was dean from 1870 until 1895. See Arthur E. Sutherland, *The Law at Harvard,* at 162–205 (1967) ("The Langdell Era"); Thomas C. Grey, *Langdell's Ortho-doxy,* 45 *Univ. Pitt. L. Rev.* 1, 1 (1983).

[131] Gilmore, *Ages of American Law,* at 42.

[132] *Address by C. Langdell to the Harvard Law School Association,* 1886, in Suther-land, *The Law at Harvard,* at 175.

[133] Christopher Columbus Langdell, *A Selection of Cases on the Law of Contracts* vi–vii (1871).

[134] Arthur Linton Corbin, 1 *Corbin on Contracts* 578 (1963).

offeror before the contract could be formed.[135] Langdell argued that the priority of the offeror's receipt of the offeree's acceptance followed from the doctrine that a promise could not be binding unless it was supported by consideration. The consideration for the offer was the offeree's return promise. But a promise by its nature is not complete until communicated; and Langdell reasoned that an unreceived promise was a promise uncommunicated. Therefore, merely the intention to promise, without its receipt, was not consideration.

Langdell thought it was quite telling that, of the many cases that ruled in favor of the party urging a version of the mailbox rule, all but two did so with holdings based on other grounds: either they did not mention the rule, or they referred to it only in dicta. Of the remaining two, he felt that *Thomson* was "neutralized" by the force of the reasoning of its dissenting opinion and *Vassar*'s holding was undermined by the language of the contract it was interpreting.[136] Langdell noted that those who supported the mailbox rule "claimed that the purposes of substantial justice and the interests of the contracting parties as understood by themselves" would be best served by the rule. His response was "the true answer to this argument is that it is irrelevant."[137]

Three aspects of Langdell's treatment of the mailbox rule merit attention. First, Langdell began his analysis of the mailbox rule with a very specific picture of the meaning of a contract. Langdell's general definition of a contract relied upon a specific conception of consideration. While his argument followed logically, it did not allow for a more textured, less general conception of what might count as a contract or of the varying roles that consideration might play in the formation of a contract.

Second, Langdell's rejection of reasons from "substantial justice," or the interests of contracting parties, as "understood by themselves" seems counterintuitive. Assuming that Langdell was right, and the concept of "contract" simply meant bilateral communicated (and heard) consent, why would a complex society ever choose to

---

[135] When Langdell confronted the mailbox problem, the courts of England and New York had adopted the rule, but those of Massachusetts had rejected it. See Christopher Columbus Langdell, *A Summary of the Law of Contracts* 18 (1880) (hereafter *Summary*), citing *Adams v. Lindsell*, 1 B. and Ald. 681 (England, 1818); *MacTier's Admin. v. Frith*, 6 Wend. 101 (N.Y., 1830); *McCulloch v. Eagle Ins. Co.*, 1 Pick. 278 (Mass., 1822).

[136] Langdell, *Summary*, at 18, discussing; *Thomson v. James*, 18 Dunlop 1 (Scot. 1855); *Vasser v. Camp*, 1 Kern. 441 (N.Y. 1854).

[137] Langdell, *Summary*, at 20–1.

retain "contract" law, as opposed to some permutation of contract law that the legal scientist would label under a different name?

Third, and finally, we should note something that was *not* in Langdell's argument. He did not ignore the fact that the courts either did or did not "agree" with the view that the mailbox rule was bad law. He attempted, in at least two ways, to reconcile his conclusion with those jurisdictions that decided "against" what Langdell thought was the "right" view. For the vast majority of courts that upheld the parties who urged the rule but did not build the rule into their holdings, Langdell tried to distinguish: He explained why, in individual cases, the specific facts dictated the outcome without relying on the mailbox rule. For the two cases that flatly contradicted him, Langdell tried to show that they were anomalous. Langdell's efforts at reconciling these cases with his theory illustrates a curious tension between his desire to show how his rejection of the mailbox rule could be found in these cases and his recognition of the actual state of the law.

Langdell's writings do not support the claim that he was a "legal theologian" in the sense that he believed that his "true" rule remained the valid law of every jurisdiction regardless of what the courts actually did.[138] Langdell certainly disagreed with *how* the courts and others determined what was the correct rule of law. Langdell's abrupt dismissal of the concerns of justice reveal a deep commitment to the autonomy thesis. Langdell's insistence on using only reasons from within existing precedent led him to adopt a view of legal reasoning that seems consistent with the deduction thesis (although Langdell's embrace of deductive logic will be explored in greater detail later). But nothing in Langdell's treatment of the mailbox rule proves that he embraced transcendentalism. Nonetheless, Holmes took the mailbox rule to be compelling evidence of Langdell's transcendentalism.[139]

Langdell's discussion of the mailbox rule reflected not a blind obedience to transcendental rules but rather a working out of three closely related claims: (1) that legal conclusions were drawn from legal principles, (2) that legal principles were not determined by

[138] Oliver Wendell Holmes, *Book Review,* 14 *Am. L. Rev.* 233, 234 (1880).
[139] Letter to Sir Frederick Pollock (April 10, 1881), in 1 *Holmes–Pollock Letters* 16–17 (Mark DeWolfe Howe, ed., 1941) (hereafter *Letter to Pollock*). See also Holmes, *Book Review,* at 234.

morality or a survey of individual subjective expectations, and (3) that these legal principles could be discovered only by comparing and interpreting the body of legal decisions found in the law library. And yet, it became commonplace to call Langdell a "legal theologian" who believed that legal principles were eternally inscribed in some "heaven of concepts."[140] This conclusion, in effect, turns Langdell into some sort of "amoral" natural lawyer. By ascribing to Langdell a belief in both pure logic and transcendentalism, the antiformalists conflated contradictory approaches to law and prefigured the later linkage of positivism with elements of realism and authoritarianism.

The claim that Langdell endorsed an "amoral" transcendentalism imputed to him the view that although legal rules had an existence independent of and prior to legal practice, their content was not based in morality. Except for attributing to Langdell a quasi-religious faith in "mere" or pure logic, Langdell's critics never set out in any detail what kind of system of pure reason they imagined he embraced.[141] Nonetheless, the most enduring image of Langdell is precisely that of an amoral natural lawyer. Thus, Richard Posner claimed that Langdell and other nineteenth-century formalists believed that the premises from which judges deduced legal conclusions were "self-evident."[142] Posner argued that the "formalists were Platonists, believing that there existed a handful of permanent, unchanging, indispensable principles of law."[143] Grant Gilmore accused Langdell of believing that "there is one true rule of law which, being discovered, will endure, without change, for-

---

[140] See, for example, H.L.A. Hart, *Jhering's Heaven of Concepts and Modern Analytical Jurisprudence*, in H.L.A. Hart, *Essays in Jurisprudence and Philosophy* 277 (1983); see also Willard Hurst, *Changing Responsibilities of the Law School: 1869–1968*, 1968 Wis. L. Rev. 336, 336 (Langdell thought law is a fixed body of knowledge).

[141] It is difficult to imagine a normative system that is based on pure logic; ostensibly this is supposed to suggest that formalist norms do not privilege one set of ends over another (assuming that one accepts a strict contrast between means and ends). Curiously, to the extent that one could imagine such a system based on pure process, it might be related to certain interpretations of John Rawls made by critics of his argument for the "original position." See, for example, Michael J. Sandel, *Liberalism and the Limits of Justice* 122–30 (1982).

[142] Richard Posner, *Legal Formalism, Legal Realism, and the Interpretation of Statutes and the Constitution*, 37 Case W. Res. L. Rev. 179, 182 (1986).

[143] Posner, *Problems of Jurisprudence*, at 15. To his credit, even though Posner wrongly accused Langdell of transcendentalism, he correctly observed that Langdell was an inductivist.

ever."[144] Lawrence Friedman observed that Langdell's formalism was a form of paradoxical natural law: It was "a geology with only rocks, an astronomy with only stars."[145] William Nelson explicitly equated Langdellian formalism and natural law by attempting to demonstrate that the rise of formalism in the late nineteenth century was a backlash caused by the suppression of "higher law" or natural law jurisprudence before the Civil War. Nelson claimed to find "higher law language" in the treatises of formalists such as Langdell, Thomas Cooley, and John Dillon.[146] Nelson's argument brings us full circle: For him, formalism required that the law applier use adjudication as a tool to promote justice. As Linda Paine has noted, Nelson's "'Formalism' refers to a position which views law as a means for bringing about a society which conforms to natural law."[147] When portrayed in this instrumentalist fashion, formalism becomes indistinguishable from realism, and, bizarrely, formalism is recast as moralized instrumentalism.[148]

The equation of formalism with any form of natural law – which would have shocked Lon Fuller – had its origins in the early antiformalist critique by Holmes of Langdell.[149] It was in reviewing Langdell's *Summary of the Law of Contracts* that Holmes first coined the slogan "the life of the law has not been logic; it has been experi-

---

[144] Gilmore, *Ages of American Law*, at 43. See also James G. Wilson, *The Morality of Formalism*, 33 UCLA L. Rev. 431, 459 (1985) (Gilmore "concluded that Formalism's advocates have always assumed that their work was linked to immutable principles").

[145] Lawrence Friedman, *A History of American Law* 535 (1973).

[146] Nelson, *Impact of the Anti-Slavery Movement*, at 560, 565. See also Comment, *Formalist and Instrumentalist Legal Reasoning and Legal Theory*, 73 Cal. L. Rev. 123, 132–3 (1985) (noting that "[m]any of the cases Nelson uses to describe nineteenth century antislavery 'Formalism' in fact show judges who wholly disregarded existing law in order to bring about justice in accordance with higher law").

[147] Lynda Sharp Paine, *Instrumentalism v. Formalism: Dissolving the Dichotomy*, 1978 Wis. L. Rev. 997, 1013.

[148] Both Paine and Nelson equate realism with instrumentalism. See Paine, *Instrumentalism v. Formalism*, at 1013.

[149] Holmes's critique of formalism predated the appearance of realism. See White, *Social Thought in America, passim* (Holmes, Thorstein Veblen, and John Dewey were the key figures in the "revolt against Formalism"); Golding, *Jurisprudence and Legal Philosophy in Twentieth Century America*, at 452 (realism was based on work of Holmes and John Chipman Gray). Holmes's critique of Langdell, however, was readily adopted by the realists; therefore, for purposes of defining formalism, this section shall treat the aspects that Holmes identified and rejected as virtually the same as those aspects that realism attributed to formalism. See, for example, F. Cohen, *Transcendental Nonsense*, at 827, 835 (noting Holmes's attempts to reduce legal concepts to empirical conditions).

ence."[150] Although Holmes could not help but be impressed by the treatise, he found Langdell's treatment of precedent cramped and unusable: "[Langdell's] explanations and reconciliations of the cases would have astonished the judges who decided them."[151] It seemed to Holmes that in embracing formalism, Langdell sacrificed accuracy and imagination in discussing contract law in order to gain a spurious intellectual tidiness: "Mr. Langdell's idea in the law, the end of all his striving, is the logical integrity of the system . . . [b]ut . . . he is less concerned with his postulates than to show that the conclusions from them hang together."[152] In later essays Holmes expanded his critique of Langdell to cover formalism as a movement. According to Holmes, formalism sought to clothe judicial decisions in the language of formal "logical deduction"[153] and to reason from "general propositions."[154] Formalists sought to make "legal reasoning seem like mathematics" and to convince themselves that, if men differed over a question of law, "it meant simply that one side or the other were [*sic*] not doing their sums right, and, if they would take more trouble, agreement would inevitably come."[155] By emphasizing the role of deduction in formalism, Holmes, like Felix Cohen, linked Langdell to the idea that there were *a priori* legal truths and so connected Langdell (and formalism) to transcendentalism.[156]

The attribution of transcendentalism to Langdell was groundless. It was, in fact, a red herring created to strengthen the nascent theories being developed by Holmes and pre-realist legal scholars like Pound.[157] As Horwitz (who cannot be accused of sympathizing with formalism) has noted, "[T]he Progressive charge that [the for-

---

150 Holmes, *Book Review*, 233.
151 Holmes, *Letter to Pollock*, at 17.
152 Holmes, *Book Review*, at 233.
153 Oliver Wendell Holmes, *Principle, Malice and Interest*, 8 Harv. L. Rev. 1, 7 (1894).
154 Holmes, *Path of the Law*, at 465.
155 Ibid.
156 The transcendentalism Holmes attributed to Langdell has been described by one contemporary scholar as "determinate-formalism." Steven J. Burton, *Judging in Good Faith* 4 (1992). According to Burton, "Langdell's effort to create a determinate-formalist science of law is now a undisputed object lesson [in the failure of a legal theory]." Ibid.
157 Mathias Reimann argued that the attribution of "natural law-like" formalism to Langdell was partly a tactic devised by Holmes to strengthen his argument in *The Common Law*. See Mathias Reimann, *The Common Law and German Legal Science* in Robert Gordon, ed., *The Legacy of Oliver Wendell Holmes, Jr.* 110 (1992).

malists] turned to natural law ... [is] largely a fabrication of Progressive thought."[158] Horwitz understood, better than any other historian of American law, why so many scholars ranging from Pound to Posner could make such a crucial mistake about the nature of formalism. If legal reasoning had to be purely deductive, then one needed legal premises that were not the product of nondeductive processes, such as judicial discretion or legislation. The only premises that could fit this description were *a priori* claims that were either self-evident or true because they reflect some metaphysical reality:

> If general propositions could not decide concrete cases, it was unlikely that one would believe that legal implication from highly abstract conceptions could be non-discretionary. If, by contrast, a concept was thought to have a fixed essence or core of meaning, it was correspondingly easier to derive particular sub-rules or doctrines from more general principles. Much of the Progressive charge that the ... [formalists] turned to higher law was really an expression of Progressive disbelief in the claimed power and scope of traditional legal reasoning.[159]

Thus, according to Horwitz, transcendentalism was not attributed to the formalists as a result of anything they said but rather because it was a necessary step to securing the deduction thesis.

My disagreement with Horwitz is that he did not press his critique of the antiformalist list even further. Just as Horwitz was right to have cast a skeptical eye upon the claim that formalism embraced transcendentalism, he should have taken the next step and cast an equally skeptical eye upon the deduction thesis. Many sophisticated historians, such as Horwitz, were content to leave unquestioned the claim that the formalists embraced the deduction thesis and focused instead their critical attention on the claims that followed from the claim that legal reasoning is deductive.[160] How-

---

[158] Horwitz, *Transformation II*, at 158. Horwitz observed that the story Cover tells in *Justice Accused* about the conflict between natural law and formalism in antebellum America undercut the realists' claim that the formalists embraced "higher law." Ibid.

[159] Ibid., at 157.

[160] See, for example, ibid at 199; Segal, *John Chipman Gray, Legal Formalism, and the Transformation of American Perpetuities Law*, at 447; Comment, *Formalist and Instrumentalist Legal Interpretation Reasoning and Legal Theory*, at 125; Posner, *Legal Formalism, Legal Realism, and the Interpretation of Statutes and the Constitution*, at 182; but see Posner, *The Problems of Jurisprudence*, at 15 (Posner credits Langdell with adopting an *inductive* rather than deductive view of legal science).

ever, it is not clear that Langdell believed that legal reasoning was deductive, at least not in the way that has been attributed to him.

If in fact Langdell was following in the footsteps of Bentham and Austin, one might expect to see in Langdell the influence of the command theory and the sources thesis, because these were two of the three central tenets of classical positivism.[161] An important implication of these two tenets of classical positivism was that law was the product of human will, whether by legislation or judicial discretion. At its very core, classical positivism rejected the idea that legal concepts have an *a priori* existence: Austin and Bentham broke with Blackstone precisely because classical common law theory ignored the contingent and mutable sources of law. If to be committed to the claim that law is deductive entails commitment to natural law, then it is very hard to understand how Langdell could embrace the central principles of classical positivism while at the same time believing that legal reasoning was entirely deductive.

In fact, Langdell's picture of legal reasoning was not completely compatible with classical positivism, but not because he believed that legal reasoning was entirely deductive. Had Langdell believed that, it would be difficult to see how his theory could bear a family resemblance to classical positivism at all. Langdell's theory of legal reasoning was crippled by being "all for logic" (as Holmes would say) – not, as is commonly claimed, *deductive* logic, but rather *inductive* logic.[162] This slight difference will explain how Langdell could have been in important ways both the target that the antiformalists describe and the also the first *American* classical legal positivist.[163]

The difference between the conclusions generated by a deductive and an inductive system may not be dramatic, but the method and assumptions that they require differ significantly. Many of the most influential studies of formalism have assumed that Langdell meant

---

[161] William LaPiana and Stephen Feldman have also noted Langdell's positivism. See LaPiana, *Logic and Experience,* 122–31, and Feldman, *From Premodern to Modern American Jurisprudence* 1426–9.

[162] Holmes, 1 *Holmes–Pollock Letters,* at 16 ("[Langdell] is all for logic and hates any reference to anything outside of it . . ."). A few recent accounts of formalism have noticed that Langdell did endorse induction in legal science, not deduction. See White, *Tort Law in America,* at 30–3 (Langdell displayed "wholesale enthusiasm" for inductive reasoning); Paul Carrington, *Hail! Langdell,* 20 *Law & Social Inquiry* 691, 708–9 (1995).

[163] Paul Carrington makes the same observation but suggests that Ames may have been more aware of Langdell's debt to classical positivism than Langdell himself. Ibid., at 709.

to model legal reasoning after a deductive science like mathematics.[164] Thomas Grey has suggested that the best analogy to Langdell's "conceptually ordered and universally formal legal system" was mathematics: "[Langdell's system] readily suggests a structural analogy with Euclidian geometry."[165] In geometry, "we believe that . . . axioms are not merely human constructs, but rather obvious and indubitable physical truths about the structure of space, from which nonobvious truths (like the Pythagorean theorem) can be proved by sequences of indubitable deductive steps."[166]

Grey looked to Mill's *System of Logic* to explain why Langdell, who spoke so often of the role of observation in law, relied on a nonobservational metaphor like geometry for his model of legal reasoning. In Mill's system, the purpose of observation was to discover principles about the world that "are so well-confirmed by prior experience that no inconsistent observation could rationally overthrow it."[167] As Grey has noted, the systems of reason that rely on these sorts of "objectively true observations" are geometry (in which no one would believe an observation which contradicted the principle that parallel lines intersect) and classical physics (where no one would accept an observation that objects of different masses fall at different rates).[168] According to Grey, it would be reasonable for a proponent of a deductive theory of law to resort to analogizing from other deductive, nonempirical pursuits like mathematics and its cousin, physics.

But Langdell did not think that law was like geometry. Langdell made it clear that he thought that his legal method most closely resembled the *empirical* science of evolutionary biology. Langdell was acutely aware of the fact that legal principle, unsupported by the actual law found in the judgments of courts, was unlikely to be a correct statement of the law. Langdell treated the decisions of courts as results from a "laboratory" from which all reliable conclusions about the principles of law were drawn.[169] The idea that the study

---

[164] But see Reimann, *The Common Law and German Legal Science*, at 106–9 (arguing that Langdell was not the "stubborn logician" portrayed by current scholarship).

[165] Grey, *Langdell's Orthodoxy*, at 16.

[166] Ibid., at 17.

[167] Ibid., at 18–19 (citing John Stuart Mill, *A System of Logic* 151–2 [People's Edition 1889]).

[168] Ibid.

[169] Christopher Columbus Langdell, *Harvard Celebration Speech*, 30 Law Q. Rev. 123, 124 (1887).

of law was an empirical science was a very popular formalist metaphor. Cases were "specimens"; the facts of cases were like "the apple which suggested the law of gravitation."[170] Langdell believed that the law of contracts could be best understood if one were to "select, classify and arrange all the cases which had contributed in any important degree to the growth, development, or establishment of any of its essential doctrines."[171] Although he compared the law library to laboratories of "chemists and physicists," he was at his most eloquent when he argued that the library is "all that the museum of natural history is to the zoologists, all that the botanical garden is to the botanists."[172] Langdell's language evoked biology (especially in the inductive Darwinian mode) much more than mathematics: "Langdell's return to original sources . . . [and] his references to the 'growth' of doctrine, when seen in their late–nineteenth century context, suggest organicism rather than unitary conceptualism."[173] Even Pound, for all his criticisms of Langdell, recognized the biological foundation of Langdell's theory of legal reasoning:

> As teachers of science were slow to put the microscope and the scalpel into the hands of students and permit them to study nature, not books, so we have been fearful of putting reports into their hands and permitting them to study the living law. The merit of revolutionizing legal instruction and putting it on a sound basis in this regard belongs solely to Langdell.[174]

The difference between approaching law as an empirical science and approaching it as a branch of mathematics is most evident in Langdell's view of legal education. Before Langdell, law school education typically took the form of lectures that described the law as

---

[170] William A. Keener, *The Inductive Method in Legal Education,* 28 Am. L. Rev. 709, 713 (1894).

[171] Langdell, *Selections of Cases on the Law of Contracts,* at vii.

[172] *Record of the Commemoration, November Fifth to Eighth* 1886, *on the Two Hundred and Fiftieth Anniversary of the Founding of Harvard College* 86–7 (1887).

[173] Marcia Speziale, *Langdell's Concept of Law as Science: The Beginning of Anti-Formalism in American Legal Theory,* 5 Vt. L. Rev. 1, 35 (1980) and see LaPiana, *Logic and Experience* at 56–7 (Langdell's legal science was not like mathematics).

[174] Roscoe Pound, *The Evolution of Legal Education* 14 (1903). Pound's comments are especially interesting in light of the fact that Pound was trained as a botanist and earned a Ph.D. in that field. He applied the taxonomic approach of botany to law by attempting to categorize legal phenomena according to the social interests they reflected. See Julius Paul, *Foundations of American Legal Realism,* 60 W. Va. L. Rev. 37, 42 (1957).

a fixed body of doctrine in the Blackstonian sense.[175] Wigmore stated that before Langdell, the "didactic method was the same – set lecture and memorized treatise, or both. . . ."[176] Often the students were expected to memorize the text, and there was little or no discussion, because it "was assumed that the author of the textbook had examined the subject and had found out the true rules of law relative thereto. Thus the rules were given . . . [and] it was assumed that the rules were right."[177] The case method, which Langdell introduced in 1870, demanded that students go beyond what Blackstone had said about the law and discover in an "essentially active . . . mode" the law's principles on their own, through an examination of the appellate decisions.[178]

It is ironic that Langdell was considered by his critics to be engaged in a transcendental, nonempirical activity, because the premise of the case method was to inculcate in law students the view that each lawyer had to determine the meaning of a legal principle from the materials before them and not from a treatise or authority:

> Professor Langdell was always willing to reconsider a conclusion in light of new suggestions. . . . A student recently informed me of a course in which Professor Langdell changed his opinion in regard to a case three times in the course of one week, each time advancing with positiveness a new doctrine.[179]

---

[175] See, for example, Samuel Williston, *Life and Law* 198 (1940) ("In the Harvard Law School before 1870, as well as in other law schools, law was taught from treatises and lectures"). See also LaPiana, *Logic and Experience,* at 290 (comparing antebellum and Langdellian legal education).

[176] John H. Wigmore, *Nova Methodus Discendae Docendaeque Jurisprudentiae,* 7 *Harv. L. Rev.* 812, 816 (1896).

[177] Franklin G. Fessenden, *The Rebirth of the Harvard Law School,* 33 *Harv. L. Rev.* 493, 498 (1920).

[178] See Speziale, *Langdell's Concept of Law,* at 15 ("Essentially active, the mode of instruction did not emphasize absorption of information from a book or teacher . . ."); Charles W. Eliot, *Langdell and the Law School,* 33 *Harv. L. Rev.* 518, 518 (1920) ("[Langdell] tried to make his students use their own minds logically on given facts, and then to state their reasoning and conclusions correctly in the classroom"); see also Young B. Smith, *The Study of Law by Cases: A Student's Point of View,* 3 *Am. L. Sch. Rev.* 253, 254 (1913) (the student studies the things to be defined, rather than ready-made definitions); Edwin W. Patterson, *The Case Method in American Legal Education: Its Origins and Objectives,* 4 *J. Legal Educ.* 1, 6 (1951) ("The case method was designed to produce independent and creative thinking"); Carrington, *Hail! Langdell,* at 709 (case method taught students to challenge *stare decisis*).

[179] Charles Warren, 2 *History of the Harvard Law School and of Early Legal Conditions in America* 457 (1908) (quoting W. Schofield 46 *Am. L. Reg.* 273, 276–7 [1907]).

For Langdell, the "truth" of a legal doctrine was like the "truth" about the evolution of an organism: What mattered was not just the final result but also the specific causes and unpredictable forces that got the current doctrine to its current state.[180] Sir Frederick Pollock argued that Langdell's method was primarily about recognizing the dynamic quality of legal doctrine over time:

> [No one] has been more ready than Mr. Langdell to protest against the treatment of conclusions of law as something to be settled by mere enumeration of decided points. . . . Decisions are made; principles live and grow. This conviction is at the root of all Mr. Langdell's work and makes his criticism not only keen but vital. Others can give us rules; he gives us the method and the power that can test the reason of rules.[181]

By treating doctrine as an organic, living thing, Langdell saw himself as making a dramatic break with the Blackstonian treatise tradition that had dominated American law schools throughout the early and mid–nineteenth century.[182] The traditional approach to law that Langdell rejected was itself dependent on deduction to generate legal conclusions from the few legal principles found in the Blackstonian universe.[183] As Hoeflich has noted, "The notion that law must be treated as a deductive science like geometry had several American supporters during the first half of the nineteenth century, including Hugh Swinton Legaré, David Hoffman, and Daniel Mayes."[184] Langdell rejected the treatise tradition that

---

[180] "Langdell's principles grow . . . in fact, their organic nature can be understood only by tracing their development." Reimann, *The Common Law and German Legal Science*, at 108, and see White, *Tort Law in America*, at 30 (characterizing Langdell's "organic" approach to legal science).

[181] *Harvard Law School Association Report of the Ninth Annual Meeting at Cambridge*, June 25, 1895, 17 (Harvard Law School Assn., 1895). The picture of the Langdellian method as extremely rule-oriented is popular among modern critics of legal education. See, for example, John Henry Schlegel, *Langdell's Legacy or, The Case of the Empty Envelope* 36 Stan. L. Rev. 1517, 1533 (1984) (Langdell was successful because he touched a deeply held belief in American society that "law *is* rules").

[182] See Carrington, *Hail! Langdell*, at 711.

[183] See Edward J. Phelps, *Methods of Legal Education*, 1 Yale L. J. 139, 142 (1882) (noting that in contrast to the Langdellian method, pre-1870 law schools had students memorize a few well-established principles because "the habit of reasoning from principles to conclusions gave [the lawyer], if he was capable of attaining it, the large comprehension and strong logical power which are characteristics of the sound lawyer . . .") and see LaPiana, *Logic and Experience*, at 29–54 (describing antebellum legal education as rooted in natural law conceptualism).

[184] H. H. Hoeflich, *Law & Geometry: Legal Science from Leibniz to Langdell*, 30 Am. J. Legal Hist. 95, n112 (1986). Perry Miller thus reported statements such as "'no science

was championed by lawyers like Phelps, Legaré, and Mayes, which is why "old fashioned" teachers like Phelps despised the case method, and why scholars like Wigmore called Langdell's new approach "daring . . . in those days."[185] It was the pre-Langdellian scholars who, under the influence of Blackstone and other Continental theorists, embraced a quasi-natural law model, in which legal conclusions were deduced from *a priori* principles of law.[186] It is ironic that Langdell was associated with a viewpoint that in an important way was the opposite of his own view.

Langdell certainly believed that law was a science, as did the theorists whom he opposed. But instead of believing, as they did, that law was a nonempirical science like geometry or mathematics, Langdell made a radical break that was based on his rejection of the deductive model of legal reasoning and his embrace of an inductive model based on the emerging biological sciences. Langdell was still working with a model that placed logic at the center of legal reasoning, but he had a very different idea of the nature of the principles that formed the system of law. Instead of believing, like Blackstone's American followers in the treatise tradition, that legal principles were transcendental and unchanging, Langdell accepted that legal principles were the product of contingent events and could have been otherwise.[187]

---

among man is more strictly deductive than the science of a true jurisprudence,'" from antebellum legal theorists who only occasionally engaged in inductive legal reasoning. See Perry Miller, *The Life of the Mind in America* 159 (1965) (quoting an 1858 lecture by Professor Theodore Dwight of Columbia University School of Law).

[185] Wigmore, *Nova Methodus Discerdae Docendaegue Jurisprudentiale,* at 817, and Warren, *History of Harvard Law School,* at 372–4 (describing the hostility directed toward Langdell's innovations in pedagogy). I therefore disagree with Hoeflich, who has argued instead that "Langdell's notion of law as a rational science, therefore, was anything but unique or innovative. Indeed, to a very large extent, the Langdellian concept of legal science simply echoed Mayes, Legaré . . . and other earlier jurists." Hoeflich, *Law & Geometry,* at 120. I find Hoeflich's claim implausible given that the contemporaneous descriptions of the reception of Langdell's approach universally describe a great break with the past. The conflict that followed the introduction of the case method clearly reflected a sense within the legal academy that the view of law and law teaching propounded by Langdell was a break with the Blackstonian treatise tradition that dominated American law before 1870.

[186] See Miller, *Life of the Mind in America,* at 165–6 (on the reception of Blackstone's natural law theory in antebellum America). LaPiana, *Logic and Experience,* at 58 (antebellum legal education believed that law consisted of "great universal principles").

[187] For example, Langdell did not believe that a system of contract law *had* to include the element of consideration: "[Langdell] believed that the original adoption of the doctrine of [consideration] had not been logically required by pre-existing law – indeed, going the other way might have been 'the more rational course.'" Grey,

It is precisely Langdell's rejection of the deductive/Blackstonian picture of the origin of legal principles that brings us back finally to formalism's positivist roots. The classical positivists rejected Blackstone because his theory of the common law was inconsistent with the separability thesis, the command theory of law, and the sources thesis. The American treatise tradition of Legaré and Mayes was clearly inconsistent with the command theory and the sources thesis. The treatise tradition, like Blackstone, viewed law as a system of *a priori* principles (a position that followed logically from the embrace of the deductive theory of legal reasoning). Bentham and Austin, on the other hand, believed that legal principles were neither *a priori* nor transcendental. Positivism's rejection of transcendentalism was required by the command theory and the sources thesis: The rules of tort or contract could not be true *a priori* if they were the product of human will and thus were relatively contingent. Furthermore, if legal principles were not transcendental, then they could not, ultimately, be discovered through deduction but instead would have to be located through the quasi-empirical process of induction. We can see, therefore, that Langdell would have rejected transcendentalism and the deduction thesis for the same reasons that Bentham and Austin rejected the transcendentalism and nascent deductivism of Blackstone. We should not be surprised that Langdell followed Bentham and Austin on this point. Langdell's formalism was, after all, a product of classical positivism's appearance in America in the second half of the nineteenth century.

The other theorist who was clearly associated with Langdell whom the realists held up as a paradigm of formalism was Joseph Beale, a colleague of Langdell's at Harvard. Beale gained infamy among antiformalists as the American architect of the "vested rights" theory in the conflict of laws.[188] The problem in the American system of conflict of laws is that a case may be connected to

---

Langdell's Orthodoxy, at 27 (quoting Langdell, *Summary of the Law of Contracts,* at 60–1 [1880]).

[188] In England the vested rights approach was championed by A.V. Dicey. See generally A.V. Dicey and J.H.C. Morris, *Conflict of Laws* (11th ed., 1987). As Amos Shapira noted: "It is not at all surprising that Dicey, usually considered an adherent of Austinian Positivism, was inclined to endorse such territorialist ideas. His version of the vested rights doctrine, however, is said to display both positivist (effectiveness, convenience) and non-positivist (justice in particular cases) notions." Amos Shapira, *The Interest Approach to Choice of Law* 9 (1970) (citing R. H. Graveson, *Philosophical Aspects of the English Conflict of Laws,* 78 L. Q. Rev. 337, 344 [1962]).

more than one jurisdiction. In such a situation, the forum may decide whether to apply its own law or the law of another jurisdiction as the rule of decision in the case.[189] The vested rights approach began with the assumption that in each jurisdiction the legal sovereign has exclusive authority to determine the legal rights of persons within its territory and the legal significance of events occurring there.[190] In a conflicts case, the sovereign can apply its own laws directly or it can create rules about applying other jurisdictions' laws. This decision is an exercise of legislative discretion undertaken by the legislature or the courts in a quasi-lawmaking capacity. Whenever an event occurs to which the territorial law attaches a legal consequence, the consequence vests as a right that "remains" with the relevant legal actor until it is vindicated by that territory's sovereign or some other sovereign. Thus, if an event occurs in a jurisdiction (Territory X) that it invests with legal significance, the right has vested under Territory X's law. If suit is brought in Territory Y to vindicate that right, it is a matter of empirical fact whether the right in question has vested. Under the vested rights approach Y is obliged to recognize the duly created right: "[W]henever a forum encounters a duly created, foreign based right or *obligation* it must accord it respect, by giving it proper effect. Otherwise the territorial-sovereigns' . . . power to create rights entitled to extraterritorial effect' would be unduly denied . . . ."[191] Beale argued that in order for Sovereign X's unfettered discretion to exist, Sovereign Y was necessarily and logically required to recognize the rights created (if at all) by X; and, of course, the same was true in reverse – X was obliged to recognize all and any rights created by Y within Y's territory.

The problem with conflict-of-laws theory before the vested rights approach was that, like other natural law theories, it was impossible to know how to identify the objectively true body of rules, because each interpreter arrived at a different set of "natural" rules. Beale believed that conflict-of-law rules ultimately had to be based on the positive authority of sovereigns and not on an interpreter's

---

[189] Lea Brilmayer, *An Introduction to Jurisdiction in the American Federal System* 215 (1987).

[190] Joseph Henry Beale, 1 *Treatise on the Conflicts of Laws* 219 (1916) (hereafter *Treatise on the Conflict of Laws*, 1916).

[191] Shapira, *Interest Approach to Choice of Laws* at 9 (quoting Michael deB. Katzenbach, *Conflicts on an Unruly Horse: Reciprocal Claims and Tolerances in Interstate and International Law*, 65 Yale L. J. 1087, 1097 [1956]).

insight into the order of things. The vested rights theory had the advantage of solving multistate cases not according to a suprana-tional body of law but according to "the law of the country in whose court [the case] arises."[192] Thus Beale, in a sense, created a transcendental principle of the conflict of laws in order to protect the decidedly nontranscendental foundation of legal rights.[193] Beale's zeal to protect the unfettered capacity of a legal authority to create rights reflected his commitment to classical positivism's com-mand theory of law and the sources thesis. Thus, it is easy to link Beale's vested rights approach to classical positivism, for as Amos Shapira has noted:

> Traditional choice-of-law thinking is deeply rooted in Austinian posi-tivism and the analytical school of jurisprudence. The positivistic fla-vor of the traditional approach is clearly manifested in its celebrated trilogy of principal underlying dogma: the interrelated concepts of territorial sovereignty, legislative jurisdiction and vested rights.[194]

Because a sovereign has, by definition, unlimited legal authority to create rights and obligations,[195] only the sovereign who created the right can destroy a created right. Moreover, a refusal to enforce a right or obligation would have the effect of destroying the expecta-tions established by that sovereign's laws, thus thwarting "a main object of the legal and moral rules whose . . . purpose is the enforce-ment of pacts or agreements."[196] Therefore, the forum sovereign's unlimited power to disturb a vested right must, by logic, be curbed.

Beale did not agree with Austin that every law was nothing more than a command of the sovereign. This was because Beale believed that laws existed only as part of a legal system: Jurisprudence con-cerned "'[n]ot merely laws, expressions of the popular will for the time being, but law, an expression of reason applied to the rela-tions of man with man and of man with the state.' "[197] For Beale, law was ultimately a method of determining the "obligations and

---

192   Beale, 1 *Treatise on the Conflicts of Laws* 1916, at 112.
193   Shapira, *Interest Approach to Choice of Law*, at 9.
194   Ibid.
195   Gerald J. Postema, *Bentham and the Common Law Tradition* 230–7 (1986).
196   John Austin, *The Province of Jurisprudence Determined*, 332 (H.L.A. Hart, ed., 1954).
197   Joseph Beale, 1 *A Treatise on the Conflicts of Laws* §3.4, at 24 (1935) (quoting Pound) (hereafter *Treatise on the Conflict of Laws*, 1935).

rights as are recognized by the State."[198] Nonetheless, the obligations and rights entailed by the legal system were the contingent product of political will: Beale's difference with Austin was not over the sources thesis (because, for Beale, every law had a human source) but over Austin's specific version of the command theory.[199] For Beale, "the sovereign is made such by law" and is not himself above the law.[200] It is important to note that Beale included the following quotation in his casebook on the conflicts of laws: "Whenever, therefore, there is a political society, there must be some complete body of law, which shall cover every event there happening. . . . Law once established continues until changed by some competent authority."[201] This quotation clearly embraces and preserves the command theory but recognizes that in a modern legal system, competent authority may not rest in the hands of an easily identifiable human sovereign.

Furthermore, Beale fully accepted the sources thesis. Beale rejected the idea that law was immutable or had a transcendental existence: It was "wholly fruitless to form *a priori* definitions [about law] and follow them out without getting them from observation of facts."[202] Like Langdell, Beale thought that the scientific method

---

[198] Joseph Beale, "Lectures on Jurisprudence, Harvard Law School, 1909," from Warren Samuels, *Joseph Henry Beale's Lectures on Jurisprudence 1909*, 29 *U. Miami L. Rev* 260, 285 (1975) (hereafter *Lectures on Jurisprudence*). It must be noted that in his lectures on jurisprudence, Beale revealed a tendency toward common law that can be described only as Blackstonian. For example, the basis of law was the "customary morality of the body of the people," ibid., at 291. For Beale, common law was the primary form of law. He accepted the authority of legislation but argued that "common law cannot be effectively changed by legislation, unless the change is in the line of common law," ibid., at 301. On the other hand, as I discuss in the text, Beale had a rather conventional positivist view of both the separability thesis and the sources thesis. The most likely explanation for Beale's unusual views about common law is that he believed that although all law is positive, what is posited are not rules but entire complex sets of rights and relations that are adopted as a whole. These sets are historically contingent, but they are somewhat deeply intertwined: If the state posits any part of the set, the sovereign must accept the whole set. This is not too different from how Langdell understood the relationship between the contract doctrine of consideration and the variety of minor contract rules entailed by the adoption of the doctrine of consideration, such as the mailbox rule.

[199] Ibid., at 284.

[200] Ibid. Beale's argument about the incoherence of Austin's command theory paralleled H.L.A. Hart's argument in *The Concept of Law*, at 51–61. Both Beale and Hart suggested that although Austin was correct to argue that legal authority is posited, Austin was wrong to think that it was posited by the sovereign. Both Beale and Hart argued that legal authority was based on a social rule.

[201] Joseph Beale, 3 *Cases on the Conflict of Laws* 502 (1902).

[202] Beale, *Lectures on Jurisprudence*, at 282.

was more about induction from facts than deduction from fixed principles: "We are living in an age of scientific scholarship. We have abandoned the subjective and deductive philosophy of the middle ages, and we learn from scientific observation and historical discovery. The newly accepted principles of observation and induction, applied to the law, have . . . made possible the intelligent statement of the principles of law."[203]

Nonetheless, the realists subjected Beale to the same antiformalist critique they had used against Langdell. Cook and Yntema mounted a three-pronged attack that borrowed from the antiformalist list almost word for word. First, Beale was criticized for basing conflict of law rules on "metaphysical" concepts such as "right" or "duty." For example, Cook accused Beale of approaching the conflicts of law with an *a priori* definition of legal terms.[204] Cook objected to the vested rights theory because he believed that it did not accurately describe the behavior of courts in the American system: "'right,' 'duty' and other names for legal relations are therefore not names of objects or entities which have an existence apart from the behavior of the officials in question. . . ."[205] By alleging that Beale embraced *a priori* legal principles, Cook was accusing Beale of transcendentalism.

Second, Cook and Yntema attributed to Beale the deduction thesis. Cook claimed that Beale's vested rights approach was a product of mechanical jurisprudence:

> It must be admitted that the "outrageous bit of nonsense" that men think in syllogisms, has apparently ruled in [Beale's theory]. . . . [Realism] points out that [legal reasoning] never can be really mechanical; that the danger in continuing to deceive ourselves into believing that we are merely "applying" the old rule or principle to "a new case" by purely deductive reasoning lies in the fact that as the real thought process is thus obscured, we fail to realize that our choice is really being guided by considerations of social and economic policy or ethics.[206]

Yntema warned that the vested rights theory presupposes a dangerous form of mechanical jurisprudence: "[A]ny system of thought so fragmentary as to base the actual statement or reform of law

---

[203] Joseph H. Beale, *Development of Jurisprudence*, 18 *Harv. L. Rev.* 271, 283 (1905).
[204] See Walter W. Cook, *Logical and Legal Bases of the Conflict of Laws*, 33 *Yale L.J.* 457, 459 (1924) (hereafter *Logical and Legal Bases*).
[205] Ibid., at 476.
[206] Ibid., at 486–7.

upon purely logical deductions from combinations of abstract symbols without careful analysis of the practical purposes of legal traditions and institutions considered with reference to the concrete case is . . . socially dangerous."[207]

Third, Cook and Yntema adopted (or amplified) Felix Cohen's argument about the autonomy thesis. According to the realists, Beale was unscientific because he believed in the autonomy of legal principles. Yntema declared that Beale's theory was "unscientific [in that] . . . [i]t suggests almost no correlation with the studies of a generation in sociological or functional jurisprudence and in inductive logic and scientific method. . . ."[208] Yntema believed that in a conflicts case, other factors should be considered by the court than just the "fact" that the law of another sovereign endowed the parties with certain rights and duties: "One of the primary difficulties with the vested rights theory is the figurative and undifferentiated character of its terminology. . . . The difficulty is rather that the symbols of vested rights theory neither correspond to the social and economic facts with which the courts deal nor even accurately suggest the things which are done in courts."[209]

We may therefore conclude that according to the realists, Beale, like Langdell, viewed law as transcendental, deductive, and autonomous. But, as with their critique of Langdell, we can see that their attribution of much of the antiformalist list to Beale was groundless. Although Beale's casebook reveals a formalist passion with abstraction and completeness in the law, it plainly undercuts the antiformalists' accusation that Beale's formalism embraced transcendentalism. Beale's formalistic claim that every sovereign was the ultimate source of rights in its own jurisdiction was not

---

[207] Hessel E. Yntema, *Hornbook Method and the Conflict of Laws*, 37 *Yale L.J.* 468, 477 (1927) (hereafter *Hornbook Method*).

[208] Ibid., at 474; Cook, *Logical and Legal Bases* at 460; see also Herman Oliphant, *A Return to Stare Decisis*, 6 *Am. L. Sch. Rev.* 215, 221–2 (1928). By "scientific method" Yntema meant something different from the valid operation of logic or the rule-governed operations of mathematics. His meaning is perhaps best illustrated by the following contrast he draws: "The table of logarithms and the formulae of stresses and strains are invaluable to the engineer, but they cannot tell him whether the bridge is to be built or, if so, where, nor how high, and how broad it is to be, and how much it will cost." Yntema, *Hornbook Method*, at 481. Science, in Yntema's mind, has to do with discovering ends *and* fitting means to ends. In this sense, he is adopting a Holmesian perspective: law as a pragmatic science.

[209] Yntema, *The Hornbook Method*, at 476–7.

some strange form of natural law.[210] Thus, although realist critics suggested that Beale, like Langdell, had postulated an "essential nature of law" that would determine eternal principles of conflict rules, regardless of what the courts or legislatures did, this charge simply is false.[211] Beale's purpose in setting up the vested rights theory was to avoid the natural law orientation of traditional conflict-of-law theory. From Beale's perspective, the old theory created an independent body of substantive law that sat above the actual decisions of sovereigns as a separate form of "alleged [private] international law."[212]

It is also not obvious that Beale embraced deductive logic in the way that Cook alleged. Like Langdell, Beale used deductive logic to determine the implications of high-level legal rules or principles. Beale never suggested that the correct answer to a conflicts question could be determined without the introduction of additional facts that themselves could be determined only through a process of induction from empirical facts about the particular legal system. Thus, Beale never claimed that the specific identity of the rights that were the ultimate object of the vested rights approach were themselves deducible. Beale did believe that the question of whether a right had vested was answerable through a process of deductive reasoning.

Of the three formalist "sins" attributed to Beale on the anti-formalist list, the only one that Beale clearly committed was the autonomy thesis. Beale steadfastly rejected the idea that the process of identifying the starting points in a conflicts analysis, and the conclusions one should draw through that analysis, should in any way be affected by sociological or moral principles. It must be noted that the attribution of the autonomy thesis to Beale is consistent with my argument that Beale, as a formalist, was also a positivist. As we will see later, the autonomy thesis captures two of the essential features

---

[210] Even Learned Hand helped promote this myth about Beale. According to Gerald Gunther, in 1959 Hand wrote to A. James Casner that "Beale believed that 'were we only true to ourselves, law would emerge as the will of God,'" and in 1949 he wrote to Samuel Williston that Beale believed that "[a]dequate diligence ... would reveal eternal 'principles of justice' from which specific rules could be readily deduced." Gerald Gunther, *Learned Hand* 48 (1994).

[211] Cook, *The Logical and Legal Bases*, at 459; see also Frank, *Law and the Modern Mind*, at 60 (comparing Beale's approach with Hooker's).

[212] Beale, 1 *Treatise on Conflict of Laws* 1916, at 112.

of positivism, the separation of law and morals and the sources thesis.

3.6. CONCLUSION

I have maintained that American formalism was an heir to English classical positivism. This lineage has been obscured by the antiformalist critique, which manufactured a set of charges that misrepresented formalism's positivist core. In particular, the first element of the antiformalists' three-part indictment – that the formalists believed that legal principles were true *a priori* – was explicitly denied by both Langdell and Beale, as we saw previously. It mistook the highly abstract nature of the contingent principles identified by the formalists to be proof that they believed in some form of transcendentalism.

The second element of the antiformalist indictment was that formalism was committed to a deductive model of legal reasoning. I have argued that Langdell and Beale were committed to an inductive model of legal reasoning. They thought that the sources of law could be found not through pure reason like Platonic forms but through the careful categorization and examination of cases. It is true that *logic* still dominated formalist legal method, but that in itself does not clearly separate the formalists from the antiformalists. The antiformalists respected and employed simple operations of rational method, as their own self-styled attempts to develop a legal science attest. In truth, the antiformalist claim was not really about whether the formalist used logic and the antiformalist did not, but about the number and types of logical operations the formalist found useful or acceptable.

Even if the formalists did not confuse logic with deduction, the antiformalists might still have faulted them for "abusing" logic. According to this more subtle interpretation of the "law as deduction" claim, judges who "abused logic" "reason[ed] from what they claimed to be the *inherent meanings* of words such as 'offer' and 'right.'"[213] The abuse-of-logic argument was more sophisticated than the law-as-deduction argument because it provided a psychological explanation for why inductive legal reasoning could not

[213] Summers, *Instrumentalism and American Legal Theory*, at 155 (emphasis added). According to Summers, if all the antiformalist meant when he criticized the formalist's "obsession" with logic was that the formalist used an inadequate set of initial legal concepts, then he was simply objecting that formalists were conceptualists. See ibid. (on the confusion between the instrumentalist critique of the "abuse of logic" and conceptualism).

supply the formalists with the sort of conclusions they sought. For example, Llewellyn offered a version of the abuse-of-logic argument based on the theory of "rule-skepticism." According to rule-skepticism, even if legal reasoning was capable of being rational, legal argument ultimately was still indeterminate because there were so many precedents and rules of statutory construction that no judge could apply them in a deductive, mechanical fashion. Under Llewellyn's rule-skepticism, indeterminacy had at least two sources: the malleability and variety of sources of law, and the variety of common law principles for interpreting precedent. In the face of such a multiplicity of outcomes, Llewellyn argued that to imagine that rational operations *alone* could ever make up the bulk of legal reasoning was simply wrong. Legal reasoning had to take into account, at least, the problem of selecting sources of law and selecting methods for the treatment of precedent.[214]

Frank offered the other major interpretation of the abuse-of-logic argument. He argued that the formalists were wrong because – to put it simply – judicial reasoning was not really a form of rational activity. Frank took seriously Judge Joseph Hutcheson's argument that judges were ultimately forced to rely on an alogical, nonrational mental leap that Hutcheson called the "judicial hunch."[215] Frank's early writing pursued a twofold project. First, he tried to explain why Hutcheson was correct. Frank suggested that it was because the sources of indeterminacy went deeper than even Llewellyn suspected – the project of trying to expand the range of relevant premises and rules of adjudication was itself of dubious value, because the facts that one would plug into those rules and principles were themselves difficult to identify and often deeply subjective.[216] Second, Frank tried to explain why this deep indeterminacy was so frightening to the formalists. For example, he attributed "Bealism" to subconscious psychological longings interpreted through the theories of Freud or Piaget.[217]

---

[214] William Twining, *Karl Llewellyn and the Realist Movement* 203–10 (1973).

[215] Joseph C. Hutcheson, *The Judgement Intuitive: The Function of the "Hunch" in Judicial Decision*, 14 Cornell L. Q. 274 (1928).

[216] Jerome Frank, *What Courts Do in Fact*, 26 Ill. L. Rev. 645 (1932); Golding, *Jurisprudence and Legal Philosophy in Twentieth Century America,* at 458–9 (on fact skepticism).

[217] Frank, *Law and the Modern Mind*, at 60. Ackerman noted that by "assuming a Freudian point of view, Frank condemned this effort [formalism] as an immature response to the fact that men have only imperfect knowledge and control over reality." Ackerman, *Law and the Modern Mind*, at 122.

The third antiformalist objection was that formalism treated law as an autonomous social institution. To this charge the formalists would eagerly have pled guilty. The realists charged that the top-level concepts employed by Langdell in his analysis of contracts and Beale in his analysis of the conflicts of law did not describe social facts or provide statements of moral ideas. There were at least two senses in which the realist charge made sense.

The first, which we might call the "modest" realist criticism, suggested that the problem with the formalists was not that they were not scientists, but that they were bad scientists. According to this criticism by Holmes and Yntema, the formalists ignored the real and significant differences between various fact situations: that is, in their pursuit of overly abstract top-level categories, Langdell and Beale sacrificed – or purposefully avoided – careful inspections of actual factual differences and similarities among the classifications they created. Although persuasive, this modest critique does not really reject the autonomy thesis.

The second, or "strong," criticism was eventually set out by Llewellyn. According to the strong critique of the autonomy thesis, the formalists erred by refusing to bend rules and precedent to the results that were (or could be determined to be) socially desirable. For Summers, the strong realist objection captured the true difference between formalism and antiformalism: "The [formalist] . . . appeal to notions of consistency, harmony, and coherence is evident. The instrumentalists stressed existing wants and interests, social facts, available legal machinery, community policy, and the predicted effects of alternatives as the primary considerations in lawmaking, not consistency and the like."[218] The lack of social facts or moral ideals in this second sense is not really a lack of analysis or technical knowledge on the part of the formalist but rather a refusal to use legal reasoning in an instrumental fashion. Of course, to the extent that instrumentalism requires a collapse between law and morality, the strong realist criticism is a genuine attack on one positivist aspect of formalism.

Once we have removed from the antiformalist list all the positions that the formalists never really took, we can see just where American formalism overlapped with the core elements of classical positivism. For example, the autonomy thesis was formalism's way of adopting classical positivism's separability thesis and sources

---

[218] Summers, *Instrumentalism and American Legal Theory*, at 143.

thesis. If there is no necessary coincidence between law and morality, and the content of every law can be traced back, at some level, to a legal *source*, then an instrumentalist judge would be violating the sources thesis by adding to the law considerations of morality or politics that were not already there from the beginning, and were that judge to do so *because* the claims of morality could not be ignored, then that judge would have violated the separability thesis.

The idea that law is autonomous from either social science or morality was a virtue in the eyes of classical positivism: It was mandated by the separability thesis. The formalist, like the classical positivist, argued that the acceptability of the content of a legal concept was irrelevant to its existence. However, the formalist did not pretend for a minute that the content of a "top level" legal concept was devoid of either social or moral content. For the formalist, the separability thesis allowed an adjudicator to respect the authority of a valid legal concept regardless of its content. As Beale noted, "law as the lawyer knows it is absolutely distinct from any rule of conduct based on a moral ground no matter how strong."[219] Cook thought that the formalists invoked the separability thesis to escape the moral and social *consequences* of the law.[220] Thus it should not surprise us that the realists (for whom all laws are open to social and moral evaluation) would reject this element of positivism and formalism.

Furthermore, the reasons that led to the attribution of the deduction thesis against formalism would apply equally to classical positivism. Although neither was guilty of the deduction thesis, both formalism and classical positivism were committed to retaining a central role for logic in legal reasoning for the same reasons. The command theory and the sources thesis required that valid legal principles (however identified) generate legal conclusions; otherwise, legal results could not be traced back to the sovereigns that commanded them. But, the realists' real objection to the role of logic in legal reasoning was not that deductive logic was used to produce results from *a priori* principles but rather to the claim that practical reason of any variety (deductive or inductive) limited adjudicators from using reasons based on nonlegal sources such as moral or po-

---

[219] Beale, 1 *Treatise on the Conflict of Laws*, 1935 §4.11, at 44.
[220] Cook found this statement from Beale typical of the formalist's embrace of the separation of law and morals: "A right having been created by the appropriate law, the recognition of its existence should follow everywhere. Thus an act valid when done cannot be called into question anywhere." See Cook, *Logical and Legal Bases* at 460 n10 (quoting Beale, *Summary of the Conflict of Laws* 517 [1902]).

litical theory. Regardless of whether one adopted Llewellyn's rule-skepticism or Frank's more radical fact-skepticism, the real target of the realist attack on formalism's use of logic was the idea that legal reasoning could constrain legal results. The real focus of the realist critique of the deduction thesis was not that it was wrong to think that legal reasoning is deductive but rather that it is wrong to think that legal reasoning can constrain legal reasoners.

The idea that legal reasoning can constrain legal results is in fact central to classical positivism. As I will argue in Chapter 7, *constraint* is the theme that links classical and modern positivism in that in both versions there is a device through which the sovereign constrains adjudication. Antiformalists opposed formalism because it brought to American jurisprudence the "model of rules" that formed the core of classical legal positivism.[221]

What remains of antiformalism, once the antiformalist list is "cleaned up," is that antiformalism was really anti-classical positivism. Formalism was not a theory of transcendental law. It was a form of positivism. But Langdell and Beale's formalism was an imperfect form of positivism for two reasons. First, it failed to cure the problems raised by Austin's command theory of law. All versions of positivism rely, to some extent, on the identification of legal authority, but as Hart and many others since him have argued, Austin's test for sovereignty and his rule of recognition were inadequate.[222] The American formalists rightly perceived that analytical jurisprudence would be better off without Austin's theory of sovereignty, but they failed to provide a satisfactory substitute for the English

---

[221] The term *model of rules* comes from Dworkin. Dworkin characterized (accurately, I believe) the core of legal positivism as a commitment to the idea that "[t]he law of a community is a set of special rules used by the community directly or indirectly for the purpose of determining which behavior will be punished or coerced by public power. These special rules can be identified and distinguished by specific criteria, by tests having to do not with their content but with their *pedigree* or the manner in which they were adopted or developed." Ronald M. Dworkin, *The Model of Rules*, 35 *U. Chi. L. Rev.* 14 (1967). Dworkin's description captures the three elements of classical positivism described at the beginning of this chapter. It is very likely that Dworkin's picture of the model of rules is adequate only for classical positivism, and that Hart has corrected many of Austin's errors. See H.L.A. Hart, *The Concept of Law* 79–98 (2d. ed., 1994), (on the distinction between primary and secondary rules). Furthermore, to the extent that Dworkin is correct in insisting on a theoretical continuity between Austin and Hart, modern positivists have argued persuasively that the model of rules is not the best foundation for legal positivism. See section 7.2.

[222] Hart, *Concept of Law* 18–25; see also Joseph Raz, *The Morality of Freedom* 27–43 (1986).

positivists' command theory. Langdell and Beale thus recognized, as Hart would later, that law is rooted in social rules, not in commands imposed from above, and constructed by the political community. This is why they insisted that legal scholarship's first task was to identify, through a survey of the case law, a legal system's general principles. Unfortunately, Langdell and Beale tended to describe these social rules at such a high level of abstraction that, in practice, they operated like the *a priori* principles they had rejected.

Second, the formalists needlessly limited their picture of legal reasoning by refusing to accept that judges sometimes made law. While Austin's version of positivism required a picture of legal reasoning that provided for the constraint of discretion, neither Langdell nor Beale fully understood the role of discretion. Austin explicitly embraced the idea that judges sometimes made law; unlike Bentham, he felt that a clear-eyed recognition of when judges acted in a sovereign capacity would help law reformers control this inevitable and regrettable feature of law. For example, Austin ridiculed the "childish fiction employed by our judges, that judiciary or common law is not made by them, but a miraculous something, made by nobody, existing from eternity, and merely *declared* from time to time by the judges."[223] Austin was clear, however, in his preference for legislation over judge-made law: "no judicious or candid man will doubt . . . that a well-made statute is incomparably superior to a rule of judiciary law."[224] Langdell and Beale did not see why a judge would need discretion, because the abstract general principles of common law were complete and comprehensive.[225]

The formalists' rejection of discretion was not based on natural law, which, as we saw previously, they explicitly rejected. Instead, their rejection of discretion rested on the idea that the inductive method of legal reasoning could generate an answer to each and every situation that might confront the common law: As Beale said, "the nature of [the common law] is that it is a method of thought

---

[223] Austin, *Lectures*, Lect. xxxvii, at 634.

[224] Ibid., at 661. See also H.L.A. Hart, *Positivism and the Separation of Law and Morals* 71 *Harv. L. Rev.* 593, 610–11 (1958) (on the inevitability of discretion in adjudication because of the penumbral meanings of all legal terms).

[225] Grey, *Langdell's Orthodoxy,* at 6–7; and Beale, 1 *Treatise on the Conflicts of Laws,* 1916, at 133.

rather than a body of fixed rules."[226] For Langdell and Beale, although the content of any legal rule was not fixed and eternal, the
fact that the common law could always generate a legal rule
through the right sort of legal reasoning *was* fixed and eternal. This
embrace of comprehensive inductive reasoning made their approach to adjudication more plausible than the deductive model
that others had attributed to them. Nonetheless, Langdell and
Beale's theory of legal reasoning was a failure because they did not
recognize the limitations of the premises with which they began.
They assumed that through induction the judge or the scholar
would be able to find a legal principle broad enough to fit every legal circumstance. The formalists thus believed in classical positivism's sources thesis to a fault: They believed that if every legal
rule had a source, then there was a legal rule for every case. This is
clearly wrong, but it is not wrong for the reasons proffered by the
antiformalists. The main motivation for their error was to preserve
the core positivist idea that the law constrains judges: "A judge is
always constrained – he is not free to make any rule he sees fit;
therefore he does not make law, but only interprets it as it exists."[227]
Although Austin would have agreed with the first part of Beale's
statement and disagreed with the second, the second part did not
contradict positivism, because it was just an extreme and overzeal-
ous application of the sources thesis.

The antiformalists said they rejected the idea that a legal system
could be based on a small number of abstract principles because
they rejected the idea that legal rules could be true *a priori.* But
when we put that objection to one side, we saw that the antiformalist objection remained even when the number of principles grew
and their metaphysical status became less transcendental. This is
because if a principle posited by society has authority for no other
reason than it was posited under the proper social rule, then it cannot be rejected just because it is unattractive from the point of view
of either social theory or morality, and therefore it constrains the
range of legal results available within the legal system. In order for
authoritative social rules effectively to constrain, they have to apply
beyond their literal meaning and must do so in a way which ensures that the scope and nature of the constraint are ultimately

---

[226] Beale, *Development of Jurisprudence,* at 293.
[227] Ibid., at 289.

within the power of the sovereign.[228] That is why the antiformalists attacked the formalist's model of legal reasoning. What was partly concealed in the realists' antiformalist attack on the use of logic in legal reasoning is an important and profound rejection of Austin's insight that law is an autonomous social practice constrained by the legal sources that happen to compose it.[229]

So antiformalism and legal positivism were, in fact, antagonistic theories. The tensions between them were not well documented because the engagement occurred under other names. To see the state of legal positivism in the United States in the first half of the twentieth century one must look at the substance of the debate, and not the misnomers. Whether we call the object of our search formalism, conceptualism, analytic jurisprudence, Langdellianism, or Bealism is not important. What is important is to identify and understand the relationship between these theories and their contemporary rival (antiformalism) and their jurisprudential source, classical legal positivism.

The relationship between legal positivism and formalism uncovered in this chapter leaves us with two outstanding questions. First, if realism developed, to some extent, in reaction to a specific version of legal positivism, was the same dynamic repeated when realism itself became the object of attack? In the next chapter I will show that a repeat of this dynamic is precisely what happened: The next stage in American legal theory came during the decline of realism, and it was brought about in part by theorists who were positivists. Second, if formalism was, to some extent, an early form of positivism in American jurisprudence, did it evolve into another form

---

[228] Beale, like H.L.A. Hart, believed that the normative content of legal principles could not be reduced to a list of commands because language was too clumsy to express the law's normative content. Beale thought that it was impossible to "express even the simplest ideas in language, much less complex ideas like law." Beale, *Lectures on Jurisprudence,* at 304. Beale believed that a positive legal rule could have meaning even if it could not be reduced to a set of linguistic signs. He disagreed with Hart over discretion: As we saw previously, Beale did not think that the meaning of a law could ever "run out," requiring the judge to engage in law making. Hart, *Positivism and the Separation of Law and Morals,* at 614.

[229] The conflation of formalism's inadequate theory of legal reasoning with its (potentially adequate) theory of law has been noted: "The distinction between styles of reasoning and theories of law has played an important but not entirely clear role in the formalism/instrumentalism controversy. The legal realists, for example, associated formalism with a strictly logical or deductive and quasi-automatic reasoning style, and with theories of law including natural law and judicial conservatism." Comment, *Formalist and Instrumentalist Legal Reasoning and Legal Theory,* at 125.

of positivism that one can identify in modern theory? I will argue in the next chapter that this evolution did occur. The realist attack on formalism did not destroy American legal positivism, but it did change it; in fact, it made it a much better theory. By the middle of the twentieth century American positivism no longer ignored discretion and had deemphasized the role of logic in adjudication. As we will see in the next chapter, the legal process school moved the question of discretion from a position of relative obscurity to the very core of positivism.

Chapter 4

Legal Process
and the Shadow of Positivism

4.1. THE REEVALUATION OF REALISM

It seems commonly assumed by those who study constitutional law or jurisprudence that the legal process school did not possess a legal theory of great sophistication. It is rare, for example, to see the writings of the important scholars of the 1950s and early 1960s in collections that contain realists like Karl Llewellyn and Jerome Frank, or fundamental rights scholars like Ronald Dworkin and Laurence Tribe. Writers working within the legal process tradition did, however, operate with a background theory of law that was a version of legal positivism, although this background theory was not, at the time, called as such.

The point at which I want to begin is, ironically enough, with Henry Hart's 1951 attack on Justice Holmes's alleged legal positivism.[1] Hart attacked Holmes's error of separating law and morality: "The first part [of Holmes's *The Path of the Law*] explains what law really is – something entirely separate from morals."[2] Hart equated Holmes's positivism with the central tenets of Llewellyn-like realism of the 1930s.[3] Hart (not entirely consistently) argued that the logical extension of Holmes's theory of law was the scientific behavioralism of the most extreme realists, in which "[i]t is not what the judges say which is important, but what they do. . . . [W]e seem to arrive, if we take this path, at the monstrous conclusion that reason and argument, the conscious search for justice, are in vain."[4] Hart's response to Holmes was that one cannot wholly sever law

---

[1] Henry M. Hart Jr., *Holmes' Positivism – An Addendum* 64 *Harv. L. Rev.* 929 (1951).
[2] Ibid., at 930.
[3] Ibid.
[4] Ibid., at 933. Hart was referring, in part, to Joseph W. Bingham, *What Is the Law,* 11 *Mich. L. Rev.* 1 (1912); Walter W. Cook, *The Logical and Legal Bases of Conflict*

from morality, and that the latter plays a complex role in shaping the former. Yet Hart was not a natural lawyer – he agreed with Holmes that only a fool would believe "that law was always right, in the sense of embodying eternal truth."[5] But Hart insisted that there is something called "morals-in-the-law" that is "integral in the maintenance of social institutions [because] it tells us that, in some sense at least, what *is* right, providing at least that it is the due result of a fair procedure of institutional settlement, and is subject to change by further and fair procedure."[6]

Hart's comments are worth examining for three reasons. First, it is interesting to discover that Hart – who is best known for his writings on the federal courts – ever ventured so far out into jurisprudence. While Hart's jurisprudential writings are not numerous, they are neither casual nor insubstantial. They are the tip of an iceberg and should give us reason to reevaluate his other writings, which on their surface seem concerned only with the scope of power of the federal courts.[7] Second, I think that Hart is an excellent example of someone who suffered a specific kind of confusion about legal positivism. He equated legal positivism with legal realism, which is peculiar because, as I showed in Chapter 2, legal positivism was the object of realism's attack in the 1920s and 1930s. Bentham and Austin were the intellectual forebears of formalism, and their theories have little in common with legal realism.[8] The great irony, as I hope to show, is that the values that Hart championed in the face of Holmes's separation of law and morality are themselves values central to a coherent and defensible form of legal posi-

---

of Laws, 33 *Yale L. Rev.* 457, 459 (1924); Jerome Frank, *Law and the Modern Mind* 208 (6th ed., 1948).

[5] But see Gary Peller, *Neutral Principles in the 1950s,* 21 *U. Mich. J. L. Ref.* 561 (1988) (an excellent discussion of how Cold War political pressures pushed legal scholars away from realism and toward Legal Process and the antipragmatist political theory that lay behind it).

[6] Hart, *Holmes' Positivism,* at 936–7.

[7] See, for example, Henry M. Hart Jr. and Herbert Wechsler, *The Federal Courts and the Federal System* (1953); Henry M. Hart Jr., *The Relations Between the State and Federal Law,* 54 *Colum. L. Rev.* 489 (1954); and see Herbert Wechsler, *The Political Safeguards of Federalism,* 54 *Colum. L. Rev.* 544 (1954) (a restatement of Hart's views).

[8] As I suggest in Chapter 2, Fuller is responsible for conflating legal positivism and legal realism. See, for example, Lon L. Fuller, *The Law in Quest of Itself* 47 (1940); see also Martin J. Golding, *Jurisprudence and Legal Philosophy in Twentieth Century America – Major Themes and Developments,* 36 *J. Legal Educ.* 475–7 (1986).

tivism.[9] In this way I will demonstrate that Hart and the legal process school embraced, although not very self-consciously, a version of classical legal positivism. Third, and finally, I have begun this chapter on the legal process school with an examination of this short essay by Hart because it portrays in a concise way how the legal process school developed in reaction to (and out of) the success of legal realism. Just because Hart was confused about the equation of legal realism with legal positivism does not mean that he was not right about something. He and others had begun to detect problems with the dominant legal ideology of their time – legal realism – and their early criticisms foreshadow what would eventually become (however briefly) the new dominant ideology of American law – legal process.

Hart's essay was written during a period of transition in American jurisprudence, in which legal realism was coming under serious attack from a new generation of legal scholars. Realism, which had come into prominence in the late 1920s, had come to dominate academic legal discourse by the end of the 1930s. Instead of settling into a period of comfortable orthodoxy, however, the 1940s confronted realism with a wave of reaction that caused the movement to splinter as some realists began to retract some of their more extreme statements.[10] By the end of World War II, professors of jurisprudence could agree that realism included at least the following three tenets: (1) Realism endorsed a temporary divorce of law and morals in adjudication, so that "legal actions, legal decisions, and the law [were] to be judged by their effects."[11] (2) Realists urged a more "institutional" approach to legal processes in America, so that

---

[9] Mark DeWolfe Howe attempted to draw attention to this point in his response to Hart's essay. See Mark DeWolfe Howe, *Holmes' Positivism – A Brief Rejoinder,* 64 *Harv. L. Rev.* 937 (1951).

[10] Robert Summers, *Instrumentalism and American Legal Theory* 277–8 (1982).

[11] Summers, *Instrumentalism and American Legal Theory,* at 53; see Karl Llewellyn, *Some Realism About Realism: A Response to Dean Pound,* 44 *Harv. L. Rev.* 1222, 1236 (1931) ("[By] the temporary divorce of Is and Ought for purposes of study. . . . I mean that whereas value judgments must always be appealed to in order to set objectives for inquiry, yet during the inquiry itself into what Is, the observation, the description, and the establishment of relations between the things described are to remain *as largely as possible* uncontaminated by the desires of the observer or by what he wishes might be or thinks ought (ethically) to be"); see also Walter W. Cook, *Scientific Method and the Law,* 13 *A.B.A.J.* 303 (1927); Underhill Moore, *The Rational Basis of Legal Institutions,* 23 *Colum. L. Rev.* 609 (1927).

legal scholars were encouraged to take note of the role politics and the political branches played in the application of law.[12] Finally, (3) realism repudiated formalism, the theory which purportedly held that deductive logic, applied to legal rules, determined judicial outcomes. In formalism's place the realists argued that "legal rules, principles and precedents had no general applicability"; they were merely artificial constructs designed to conceal the subjective preferences of judges.[13]

There were two waves of reaction to the realist position. The first was directed primarily against realism's first tenet, the temporary divorce of law and morals. For the realist, the practical consequence of this temporary divorce of law and morals was that the scientific understanding of the law would later allow for its reunion with morals so that law became a "means to an end."[14] The realists, however, did not pay much attention to the method by which ends were selected or justified. Most realists seemed content to borrow from early-twentieth-century pragmatism.[15] Most of the realists did not study moral philosophy beyond developing a rough appreciation for the relationship between pragmatism and utilitarianism.[16] Given the diversity among the realists' moral beliefs, and the fact that even the most relativist of realists approved of the policies of the majority during the New Deal, the divorce between law and morality did not become an issue until fascism began to rise in Europe. As Edward Purcell pointed out:

> Although the young [realist] critics were firm believers in democracy, most of them embraced an empirical relativism that raised both prac-

---

[12] Jerome Frank, *Trends in Jurisprudence*, Am. L. Sch. Rev. 1063 (1934); Karl Llewellyn, *A Realistic Jurisprudence – The Next Step*, 30 Colum. L. Rev. 27 (1930); Hessel E. Yntema, *The Hornbook Method and the Conflict of Laws*, 37 Yale L. J. 468, 476–7 (1927).

[13] See Frank, *Law and the Modern Mind*, at 48; Karl Llewellyn, *The Common Law Tradition* 444 (1960); Joseph C. Hutcheson, *The Judgement Intuitive in the Function of the "Hunch" in Judicial Decision*, 14 Cornell L.Q. 274 (1928).

[14] Herman Oliphant, *The New Legal Education*, 131 The Nation 495 (1930) ("Many [liberals] are eager to stop talking and begin studying law as a means to an end").

[15] See, for example, John Dewey, *The Quest for Certainty* 254–86 (1929); John Dewey, *Theory of the Moral Life* 98–101 (1932).

[16] See Summers, *Instrumentalism and American Legal Theory*, at 47–8 ("[M]ost . . . [realists] appeared, at least in their theoretical moments, to adopt conventionalist and utilitarian notions of value. . . ."); see also Walter W. Cook, "My Philosophy of Law," in *My Philosophy of Law: Credos of Sixteen American Scholars* 62–3 (Julius Rosenthal Foundation, ed., 1941) (recommending a scientific theory of the maximization of shared ends); Herman Oliphant, *Current Discussions of Legal Methodology*, 7 A.B.A.J. 241 (1921) (same).

tical and theoretical questions about the nature of democratic government.

. . .

To harm the cause of democratic governments was the last thing the realists hoped to do. . . . [They] were all ardent New Dealers who shared a strong hostility to the method of juristic reasoning that struck down social welfare laws and wrought what they considered great human injustices.[17]

Most of the realists, had they thought about it, would have been wary of any form of moral skepticism that entailed a rejection of the idea that democracy was a pragmatic tool for discovery of the good, or the just.[18] Nonetheless, some realists were far more explicitly relativistic in their metaethical views.[19] Regardless of whether moral relativism could be fairly attributed to realism, by the late 1930s, critics grew concerned that the realists' stinging critique of the operation of law in a democracy would render meaningless the distinction between the competing political theories of the Allies and the Nazis.[20] Thus, Edgar Bodenheimer wrote, "There is a certain danger that the skepticism of realistic jurisprudence may, perhaps very much against the wishes of its representatives, prepare the intellectual ground for a tendency towards totalitarianism."[21] Lon Fuller and Roscoe Pound endorsed and repeated these criticisms of realism.[22]

---

[17]   Edward A. Purcell Jr., *American Jurisprudence Between the Wars: Legal Realism and the Crisis of Democratic Theory*, 75 Am. Hist. Rev. 434, 436 (1969).

[18]   See Neil Duxbury, *Patterns of American Jurisprudence* 95–6 (1995).

[19]   See, for example, Walter W. Cook, *Scientific Method and the Law*, at 305 (1927) (human knowledge has "reached the era of relativity"); Moore, *Rational Basis of Legal Institutions*, at 612 ("ultimates are phantoms drifting upon the stream of day dreams"); Walter Nelles, *Book Review*, 33 Colum. L. Rev. 763, 767 (1933) (reviewing Felix Cohen, *Ethical Systems and Legal Ideals*) ("I deny ethical *right* and *ought* without qualification"); Edward Stevens Robinson, *Law and the Lawyers* 225 (1935) ("there is not now and never has been a deductive science of ethics"); Thurman W. Arnold, *The Symbols of Government* xiv (1935) (morality is "symbolic thinking and conduct which condition[s] the behavior of men in groups").

[20]   See Edgar Bodenheimer, *Jurisprudence* 316 (1940); Francis E. Lucey, *Natural Law and American Legal Reasoning: Their Respective Contributions to a Theory of Law in a Democratic Society* 30 Geo. L. Rev. 494, 533 (1942) ("Democracy versus the Absolute State means Natural Law *versus* realism"); see also Rufus C. Harris, *Idealism Emergent in Jurisprudence*, 10 Tul. L. Rev. 169 (1936).

[21]   Bodenheimer, *Jurisprudence*, at 316.

[22]   See Fuller, *The Law in Quest of Itself*, at 89 (1940); Roscoe Pound, *Contemporary Juristic Theory* 9 (1940). It should be noted that prominent realists attempted to refute the charge that they were moral relativists. See, for example, Karl Llewellyn, *On Reading and Using the Newer Jurisprudence*, 40 Colum. L. Rev. 593, 603 (1940) (offering

The second wave of reaction also used fascism as its foil but focused on the relationship between realism and its attack on the ability of rules to restrain the state. The coalition that propounded this view included critics of the New Deal who had never forgiven the realists for their support of Roosevelt, and Catholic law professors who feared that the realists would aid social reformers who would overturn those legal rules that protected private property and "separate" institutions like the church.[23]

The younger postwar critics for whom Hart spoke were not necessarily sympathetic to either wave of reaction described here. As indicated previously, Hart, like many in his generation, adopted realism's divorce of law and morals.[24] At the beginning of his professional career Hart was sympathetic to the realists who helped build the administrative state. After all, Hart came of age professionally in the midst of the New Deal, and many of his colleagues were enlisted into a war effort that, in the name of fighting fascism, brought large sectors of the economy under central state control.[25]

The postwar attack on realism was directed against the realists' picture of adjudication, not their moral skepticism or progressive politics. Hart and his generation recognized that realism's primary lesson, that judges make the law and do not find it, had a kernel of truth in it; they wanted to refine this truth. They thought that the rule and fact skepticism of Llewellyn or Frank went too far. By teaching that *all* aspects of the legal process are shaped by subjective preferences and acts of power, the realists risked overlooking the critical ways in which rules and principles constrain legal actors. Thus, in his essay on Holmes, Hart argued that we must look

to do "penance" for contributing to the confusion that realism rejected moral truth); see also Jerome Frank, *Fate and Freedom: A Philosophy for Free Americans* 295 (1945); Max Radin, *In Defense of an Unsystematic Science of Law*, 51 Yale L. J. 1275 (1941).

[23] See, for example, Raoul E. Desvernine, *The Creed of Americanism*, 17 Notre Dame L. Rev. 216 (1942); Purcell, *American Jurisprudence Between the Wars*, at 440; Ben W. Palmer, *Holmes, Hobbes & Hitler*, 31 A.B.A.J. 569 (1945); Lucey, *Natural Law and American Legal Reasoning*.

[24] "[Holmes exhibited] a dread of ... any suggestion that law was always right in the sense of embodying eternal truth. In this, almost all of us will follow him." Hart, *Holmes' Positivism*, at 936.

[25] See, for example, Henry M. Hart Jr., *The United States Supreme Court: An Argument on the President's Side*, Harv. Alumni Bull. 767 (1936) and Laura Kalman, *The Strange Career of Legal Liberalism* 18–19 (1996) (noting that Hart wrote a series of unsigned editorials in the *New Republic* attacking the Supreme Court's pre-1937 assaults on the New Deal).

for moral claims in law "because an examination of these claims leads inexorably to examination of the *mechanisms for orderly change*, and thus to the very heart of the *process* by which justice can be achieved through law."[26] (The use of the words *mechanism* and *process* is significant; they will reemerge as important elements in the later writings of Hart and his colleagues.) To put it most simplistically, Hart was saying that Holmes was correct to point to the subjectivity of moral judgment but wrong to conclude from the simple truth that morality is subjective that legal systems cannot organize and constrain the exercise of subjectivity. It is crucial to understand that, when Hart spoke of "morals-in-law," he did not mean that the law's content is based on a single determinate morality. For him, the attack on realism was the defense of reason. Holmes's sin was not, therefore, his separation of law and morals (despite what Hart says elsewhere in the essay) but his widespread cynicism about the role of *reason* in law. That is why Hart attacked the realist slogan that "[i]t is not what the judges say which is important, but what they do" for its complete exclusion of "reason and argument" from law, as opposed to attacking the slogan for excluding morality and justice from law.[27] That Hart then immediately drew a connection between the exclusion of reason from law and the "conscious search for justice" does not mean that he conflated the two sets of values. He may, as I suggest later, have been describing an instrumental relationship between reason in law and the achievement of justice.

The postwar critique of realism scrutinized judicial practices that the realists had identified and to some extent had celebrated. Frank had identified the phenomenon of judicial creativity in fact finding partly to justify judicial creativity in the service of progressive goals; the same could be said of Llewellyn's "demystification" of the binding force of precedent on appellate judges. The realists demonstrated that judges could act disingenuously and argued that in the right circumstances, judicial disingenuity would not be a bad thing. Now, after witnessing the abuse of the rule of law in Germany, the postwar critics of realism began to attack the disingenuous uses of precedent, rule, and doctrine. The postwar critics focused especially on the *reasoning* judges used to justify their decisions.

[26] Hart, *Holmes' Positivism*, at 937 (emphasis added).
[27] Ibid., at 935.

4.2. THE DEVELOPMENT OF REASONED ELABORATION

In the 1950s legal scholars grew increasingly convinced of the importance of practical reasoning in adjudication, and as a result, "judging" judicial performances became a popular activity in the academy.
This new commitment to practical reasoning came to be called "reasoned elaboration."[28] In this regard, the history of the *Harvard Law
Review* foreword to the annual Supreme Court survey (hereafter
"Foreword") is a useful lens through which to chart the development
of reasoned elaboration as a critical institution.[29] The legal process
school's critique of realism should not be seen merely as a reaction to
the excesses of realism but in fact should be seen as a principled attempt to resurrect positivism by reshaping formalism's inadequate
theory of adjudication. The legal process school's work in this area
did not take place only in the shadows of the doctrinal scholarship of
the Foreword. The response to the realist critique of formalism was
set out both in the Foreword as well as in other, more theoretical
texts, such as Henry Hart and Albert Sacks's *The Legal Process*.[30]

The Foreword was first published in 1951 and served as simply
what its title promised: a short introduction written by a member of
the faculty to the student-written summary of important Supreme
Court decisions of the previous year.[31] The Foreword eventually
evolved into an institution in its own right, in which a major scholar
not only reviewed the past year but also took the opportunity to set

---

[28] Legal reasoning, in its various forms, has always been at the center of debates
about law. See, for example, Edward H. Levi, *An Introduction to Legal Reasoning*
(1948) and Steven J. Burton, *An Introduction to Law and Legal Reasoning* (2d ed., 1995).
By saying that "reasoned elaboration" resulted from a "renewed" interest in practical reasoning in law, I am suggesting two things. The first is that *in comparison* to the
preceding period, reasoning regained importance in the eyes of legal scholars; the
second is that a group of scholars were self-consciously attempting to develop a theory of practical reasoning for the legal problems of their day – not that the methods
they ultimately adopted were novel or had never been used by other legal scholars
earlier in American history. See also Neil Duxbury, *Faith in Reason: The Process Tradition in American Jurisprudence*, 15 *Cardozo L. Rev.* 601 (1993), and G. Edward White,
Patterns of American Legal Thought 143 (1978).

[29] See ibid., at 144; Peller, *Neutral Principles in the* 1950s, at 571 (noting connection between Forewords and development of legal process).

[30] Henry Hart and Albert Sacks, *The Legal Process: Basic Problems in the Making
and Application of Law* (William N. Eskridge Jr. and Philip P. Frickey, eds., 1994) (hereafter Hart and Sacks, *TLP*).

[31] For a careful study of the history and influence of the Forewords, see Mark
Tushnet and Timothy Lynch, *The Project of the Harvard Forewords: A Social and Intellectual Inquiry*, 11 *Const. Comment.* 463 (1995).

out a substantive theory of constitutional law.[32] But even the earliest Forewords were, despite appearances, more than a survey. The theme that dominates the first decade of the Foreword was the question of the Supreme Court's competence at legal reasoning. The very first Foreword sets the tone of the debate by raising serious doubts about the abilities of the Vinson Court:

> [Some believe that the Court is] crippled by the presence of three or more lazy, incompetent justices. The Court, lacking manpower, reduces its work load by the refusal of certiorari and the failure to write opinions. So . . . it shirks the elementary business of guidance and direction.[33]

After framing this charge, Louis Jaffe, author of the first Foreword, defended the Court, but his argument was strangely half-hearted. He conceded that the number of written decisions dropped significantly from the heyday of the "activist" New Deal court[34] and conceded as well that through the use of discretionary *certiorari,* the Supreme Court had taken a smaller proportion of appeals than ever before. With regard to this statistic, Jaffe endorsed the criticism that "there is a suspiciously large number of denials in cases of apparent first importance."[35]

Two features of Jaffe's essay are of special importance to us. First, we should note that Jaffe said nothing about the substantive results or general theory he personally would have urged upon the Court. His stated concern was with what he calls the Court's "relative lack of institutional awareness and pride."[36] More than anything else, he wanted to see more open debate and clearer explanations by the Court of its decision-making processes. Jaffe argued that the Court, as an institution, had a duty to produce *legal reasons* that the nation could use in its ongoing debate over the meaning of the Constitution. The Vinson Court's divisions, suggested Jaffe, were based not

[32] Perhaps one of the earliest examples of this use of the Foreword is Alexander Bickel's *The Supreme Court, 1960 Term – Foreword: The Passive Virtues* 75 *Harv. L. Rev.* 40 (1961), which was the foundation for Alexander Bickel, *The Least Dangerous Branch* (1962).

[33] Louis L. Jaffe, *Foreword to The Supreme Court, 1950 Term,* 107 *Harv. L. Rev.* 107, 107 (1951) (quoting Fred Rodell) (hereafter *Foreword 1950 Term*).

[34] Jaffe, *Foreword 1950 Term,* at 108.

[35] Ibid., at 109. See also Fowler V. Harper and Alan S. Rosenthal, *What the Supreme Court Did Not Do in the 1949 Term – An Appraisal of Certiorari,* 99 *U. Pa. L. Rev.* 293 (1950).

[36] Jaffe, *Foreword 1950 Term,* at 113.

on legal analysis but on political allegiances: "One has so often the feeling that the vote of this or that justice is only remotely controlled by his apprehension of the legal issues and represents a judgment based on collateral considerations."[37] Second, Jaffe placed the blame for the decline in the Supreme Court's institutional performance on the shoulders of legal realism: "If reason can be assigned [for this decline] . . . it may be in some measure due to an overstressing by the 'realists' and 'liberals' of the political function of the Supreme Court."[38] In fact, in terms of the controversy over the denial of *certiorari*, Jaffe examines the Court's avoidance of confronting the pressing issues raised in four civil liberties cases and observes sadly that:

> There is irony in the possibility that the "realists" who insisted for so long that the Court's work was not law but politics have made good their claim. . . . The brand of politics [however] will not necessarily satisfy the hopes of the "realist.". . .[39]

As the decade progressed, the Supreme Court's performance, as measured on the scale of its mastery of legal reasoning, became the central axis along which critiques of the Court were mounted. Eventually the rhetoric of blame directed toward realism disappeared; however, one cannot ignore the role this rhetoric played in laying the foundation upon which the legal process school developed reasoned elaboration.

The theory of reasoned elaboration was built in stages, culminating in Hart's famous 1959 Foreword (which was, at the time, one of the most strongly worded critiques of the Court's competency published in a law review since the New Deal). The first stage, as shown previously, concerned the question of "political" judging: The problem with adjudication based on political reasons was that such a decision cannot produce useful legal reasons. The first stage also attempted to criticize the different techniques by which the Supreme Court managed to rationalize the fact that it was not producing useful legal reasoning. In the 1954 Foreword, Albert Sacks praised the Warren Court's desegregation cases but focused most of his attention on the Court's use of "summary opinions" to dispose

[37] Ibid., at 113–14.
[38] Ibid., at 114.
[39] Ibid., at 107.

of some of the year's most difficult legal issues.[40] Thus, the essay not only analyzed the reasoning in the Court's decisions; it also attempted to demonstrate that in a significant number of cases, the Court provided no reasons *at all* where a decision to overturn or affirm demanded an explanation. In these cases, "[j]udgment must be exercised by the Court, and disagreement, if there be any, should be voiced in the same manner."[41] Thus, "[t]he difficulty is not in the result reached, but in the absence of explanation of what was decided."[42] Sacks's concern was about more than the fact that summary decisions produce no precedents and provided no guidance for the public. According to Sacks, summary opinions risked undermining the legitimacy of the Court's power: "At stake is the value which the Court handled so carefully and so well in the Segregation Cases, the acceptability of the Court's decisions to lower courts and to the Bar as a whole."[43]

The second stage of the development of reasoned elaboration began in 1955 and focused on the Court's denial of *certiorari* in clearly ripe but controversial cases. "There will be no praise here for 'judicial statesmanship,'" wrote Robert Braucher in the 1955 Foreword. "Too often 'judicial statesmanship' is used not to describe wise judicial opinions, but to praise unstated and even unjudicial reasons for decisions and failure to decide."[44] The Court evaded a number of difficult cases; as Braucher pointed out, the issues were not just the predictably politically sensitive race and loyalty/security cases but included even an especially difficult conflict-of-laws case.[45] Braucher's criticism was motivated by more than whether his particular political interests had been well served by judicial statesmanship; in fact, he was unhappy with the Court's toleration of unprincipled decision making, regardless of the significance or *in*significance of the case before it:

---

[40] Albert Sacks, *Foreword to The Supreme Court, 1953 Term*, 68 Harv. L. Rev. 96, 99 (1954): The term *summary opinion* as used here is not meant to include all *per curiam* opinions; rather, the term includes those *per curiam* opinions in which the reasons for the decision are either entirely omitted or set forth in a few sentences.

[41] Ibid., at 100.

[42] Ibid.

[43] Ibid., at 103.

[44] Robert Braucher, *Foreword to the Supreme Court, 1954 Term*, 69 Harv. L. Rev. 120, 121 (1955).

[45] *Granville-Smith v. Granville-Smith*, 349 U.S. 1 (1955).

Discretion here should not mean caprice. . . . When the justices can speak with clarity and harmony on a controversial issue which has been fully developed, alternative grounds of decision and even dicta have traditional and legitimate roles in guiding lower courts, government agencies, the bar and the people . . . such pronouncements may perform real public service.[46]

For Braucher, the abuse of discretion meant that future adjudicators would be denied the benefits of a *ratio decidendi,* a loss that sometimes was more important than the original decision makers could ever have predicted.

The third stage of the development of reasoned elaboration was found in Ernest Brown's attack in 1958 on the Supreme Court's practice of reversing lower court opinions through *per curiam* opinions. Brown dedicated his Foreword to the examination of this "increasingly frequent practice."[47] He challenged the suggestion that in many cases, the Court, on the basis of the record, the briefs for and against the petition for *certiorari,* and nothing more, could have had enough information to determine that the lower court's decision was "clearly erroneous."[48] So as not to appear as if he were pursuing this argument for political ends, Brown chose as his example a set of cases "remote from the livelier political and social controversies of the day," the relative status of government and commercial liens.[49] After comparing the appellate court decisions that were overturned with those in the same field left standing, Brown concluded that there was reason for "substantial doubt that the decisions thus reversed are invariably 'clearly erroneous.'. . . It is difficult to resist the conclusion that improper disposition of a case is some indication of less than complete familiarity and understanding."[50] Brown's concern was not only that the lack of reasoned decision making deprives the nation of an important legal resource, or that the Court was avoiding hard cases. His concern was even more basic: To put it bluntly, he was worried that the Court's newfound taste for *per curiam* reversals was evidence of the Court's declining abilities.

---

[46] Braucher, *Foreword to the Supreme Court, 1954 Term,* at 127.

[47] Ernest J. Brown, *Foreword to the Supreme Court, 1957 Term,* 72 Harv. L. Rev. 77, 77 (1958) (hereafter *Foreword 1957 Term*).

[48] Ibid., at 80.

[49] *United States v. R. F. Ball Constr. Co.,* 355 U.S. 587 (1958); *United States v. White Bear Brewing Co.,* 350 U.S. 1010 (1956); *United States v. Colotta,* 350 U.S. 808 (1955).

[50] Brown, *Foreword 1957 Term,* at 94.

The theory of reasoned elaboration received its fullest statement in two articles written by men who would come to symbolize the legal process movement. The first was not a *Harvard Law Review* Foreword. In a commentary on the *Lincoln Mills* case,[51] Alexander Bickel and Harry Wellington, after a searching criticism of the Court's performance in one case, draw the following sweeping conclusion about the Court's performance for the whole term:

> The Court's product has shown an increasing incidence of the sweeping dogmatic statement, of the formulation of results accompanied by little or no effort to support them in reason, in sum, of opinions that do not opine and of per curiam orders that quite frankly fail to build a bridge between the authorities they cite and the results they decree.[52]

Right result without right reason did not further the project of constitutional law, because "such a decision does not attempt to gain reasoned acceptance for the result, and thus does not make law in the sense which the term 'law' must have in a democratic society."[53]

The second article was the 1959 Foreword. Its author was Hart himself, who seemed almost eager to judge the Court's performance for the entire decade. He reviewed all the criticisms described previously, repeated Bickel and Wellington's verdict, and then added the following dark prediction: "It [Bickel and Wellington's conclusion] needs to be said with all possible gravity, because it is a grave thing to say, that the failures are threatening to undermine the professional respect of first-rate lawyers for the incumbent Justices of the Court. . . ."[54] The Court was too busy, argued Hart, and therefore no longer took the time to review and debate the opinions of the various justices. Hart saw a relationship between the rise in summary and vacuous opinions and the rise in individual dissents and fragmented majorities. He argued that, had the Court more time to deliberate and reflect, *and* if all nine justices were to reflect fully on each issue, the Court would have produced more carefully reasoned opinions *and* there would have been greater unanimity among the nine justices. Hart was assuming, of course, that legal reasoning is a bit like shooting at a target: The

---

[51] *Textile Workers Union v. Lincoln Mills*, 353 U.S. 448 (1957).

[52] Alexander M. Bickel and Henry H. Wellington, *Legislative Purpose and Judicial Process: The Lincoln Mills Case*, 71 Harv. L. Rev. 1, 3 (1957).

[53] Bickel and Wellington, *Legislative Purpose and Judicial Process*, at 5.

[54] Henry M. Hart Jr., *The Supreme Court, 1958 Term – Foreword: The Time Chart of the Justices*, 73 Harv. L. Rev. 100, 101 (1959).

more people and more attempts there are, the greater the likelihood of hitting on the "right" answer. Hart based this assumption on the phenomenon he called the "maturing of collective thought":

> Ideas which will stand the test of time as instruments for the solution of hard problems do not come . . . with dependability to any single individual even in much longer periods of study and reflection. Such ideas have ordinarily to be hammered out by a process of collective deliberation of individuals, gifted or otherwise, who recognize that the wisdom of all, if it is successfully pooled, will usually transcend the wisdom of any.[55]

In this case, the right answer would win the assent not only of more of the Court, but of the legal community and the nation as well. Thus, the legitimacy and persuasive power of the Court would be strengthened by better legal reasoning. Furthermore, Hart suspected that eventually the number of petitions going up to the Court would decline if it took fewer cases: "Its dockets would be freed of a large number of cases which now come there only because of the uncertainties which are generated by the failures of reasoning of previous opinions."[56]

We can now summarize the basic tenets of reasoned elaboration as developed by the critics of the Supreme Court in the preceding survey. The fundamental proposition supported by each succeeding set of Forewords was that a judgment accompanied by a reasoned justification – whatever its political outcome – was better than a judgment alone even if it reflected the "right" result. The authors of the Forewords believed this for three reasons. First, as Jaffe suggested, in a "realist" contest of wills within the judiciary, it was difficult to predict whose politics will win; on the other hand, the demand for a reasoned justification cabined the extent to which a single political perspective could capture the Court. Second, as Braucher, Sacks, and Brown suggested, "judicial statesmanship" – through the use of the denial of *certiorari* and *per curiam* affirmances and reversals – denied the nation a crucial resource. The reasoning behind the Court's deci-

---

[55] Hart, *The Supreme Court, 1958 Term*, at 123. Hart revealed a classical liberal assumption in this statement: Like Mill or Madison, he was skeptical of idealism and the utility of abstract reasoning; he placed more faith in the operation of the "marketplace" of ideas, where truth (which exists) is uncovered through the constant friction of conflict and debate. It is interesting that, at the same time Hart made this argument, "pluralism" in political science, which attempted to defend a modernized version of Madison, was becoming dominant within its own field. See, for example, Robert Dahl, *A Preface to Democratic Theory* (1956) and section 4.7.

[56] Hart, *Supreme Court, 1958 Term*, at 125.

sions was critical to the creation of understandable and guiding precedent; and furthermore, only by revealing its reasoning could people grasp the principle underlying a court's decision to let precedent stand. Third, as Bickel and Wellington and Hart suggested, there was likely to be a relationship between the quality of a decision's underlying reasoning and the likelihood of the decision's being "right." The best way to ensure that the Court actually engaged in sufficient reasoning about a case was to demand to see the process in writing; further, the best way to ensure that the Court reasoned well about a case was to demand that it review its reasoning process often and among as many of its members as possible.

Thus, reasoned elaboration was a theory of adjudication in which reason served three functions: It controlled political willfulness, it provided the public with principles around which action could be planned, and it helped increase the likelihood of the right outcome.[57] It is clear that the realists would have denied each of these propositions. The idea that "political" decisions could be cabined by institutional arrangements is, of course, one of the first myths attacked by realism. Similarly, legal realists belittled the value of the public exposition of principles by the courts, arguing that rule making was an act of myth making. Finally, the realists would have been mystified by the idea that there was a "right" legal answer to which the court could be held accountable and toward which judges could be directed through institutional reform.

There was, in fact, a realist reaction to the reasoned elaboration critique of the Court. Judge Thurman Arnold responded to Hart's Foreword with a strongly worded critique in which he attacked Hart's premise that law appliers acted differently from law makers.[58] Arnold questioned whether Hart's ideal could ever be a reality, and he concluded by rejecting the idea of the "maturing of collective thought":

> [T]here is no such process as this, and there has never been; men of positive views are only hardened in those views by such confer-

---

[57]   Hart seemed most concerned with the Court's producing the "right" answers to the substantive legal question presented in the case; he did not raise the question of why the Court, as opposed to another branch of government, should endeavor to produce the right answer. Wechsler was the first legal process scholar to draw an explicit connection between the methodology of reasoned elaboration and the justification of judicial review. See section 5.3.

[58]   Thurman Arnold, *Professor Hart's Theology*, 73 Harv. L. Rev. 1298, 1311 (1960).

ences. . . . The only kind of court that could successfully follow Professor Hart's prescription would be a court composed of men without deep seated convictions about current national problems . . . [s]uch a court might be found in a Trappist monastery.[59]

In the following year's Foreword, Erwin Griswold rejected Judge Arnold's critique: "Arnold's argument wholly fails. . . . To me 'the maturing of collective thought' is a profound reality."[60] Griswold's response was more a rebuke than a rebuttal: He seemed to regard Arnold with the same condescension with which the realists once dismissed Langdell and Beale.

In rejecting the realist model of legal reasoning, the legal process school was resurrecting and reinterpreting the core features of classical positivism. The legal process school's interest in controlling political willfulness reflected an interest in a theory of constraint that took seriously the separation of law and morality. The attempt by adherents of the legal process school to develop strategies for discovering the "right" result in adjudication reflected an attempt to take seriously the sources thesis, and to hold judges accountable to the sources of law in American constitutional law. Finally, the legal process school's interest in the public exposition of principle reflected an attempt to provide a modern application of classical positivism's command theory of law, in that the Harvard Forewords treated the Supreme Court's holdings like the functional equivalents of Austin's sovereign commands. The legal process school differed from classical positivism in its extraordinary interest in adjudication (as opposed to the definition or identification of legal systems). The positivism of legal process was not wholly successful because it was still too wedded to what at best was a modernized version of the command theory: The Forewords were still too focused on the elaboration of legal principle and seemed either to ignore or deny the existence of judicial discretion. Legal process still needed a jurisprudence that would disentangle it from the command theory but would retain the heart of positivism. Legal process found that jurisprudence in the writings of Hart and Sacks.

[59] Arnold, *Professor Hart's Theology*, at 1312–13.
[60] Erwin N. Griswold, *The Supreme Court, 1959 Term – Foreword: Of Time and Attitudes – Professor Hart and Judge Arnold*, 74 *Harv. L. Rev.* 81, 85 (1960).

4.3. THE JURISPRUDENCE FOUNDATIONS
OF LEGAL PROCESS

The generation of Harvard scholars who attacked the realist legacy was supported by an ongoing project led by Hart and Sacks that eventually resulted in a collection of materials entitled *The Legal Process*. The manuscript remained unpublished for thirty-six years, but its typewritten pages had been copied in various formats and used frequently at Harvard as well as other law schools.[61] *The Legal Process* does not have a reputation as one of the major texts of American jurisprudence.[62] Yet a brief examination of the materials reveals that the volume contains – amid the very technical discussions of case law and legislative processes – a substantial (one-hundred-page) discussion of the philosophy of law. This section will briefly sketch the theory of law set out by Hart and Sacks and then argue that their theory of law is rooted in classical legal positivism.

The section in *The Legal Process* on jurisprudence was entitled "Introductory Text Notes on the Nature and Function of Law." It should come as no surprise that Hart and Sacks began the chapter with a rejection of legal realism. They stated that their theory of law "reject[s] the teaching of a vast body of literature which has accumulated during the last half century seeking to equate the method of the various social sciences, and in particular of law, with the methods of the natural sciences."[63] Hart and Sacks put into this latter category Felix Cohen, Walter Wheeler Cook, Jerome Frank, and Oliver Wendell Holmes. They noted that "in the American legal tradition . . . the notion that law can somehow be drawn from the behavior patterns of people has been [linked to] the notion that ethics is a body of thought to be distinguished sharply from law,"[64] a position that Hart and Sacks rejected. On the other hand, Hart and

---

[61] The editors of the 1994 Foundation Press edition are to be credited for facilitating the long-overdue publication of *The Legal Process*. In addition, Professors Eskridge and Frickey have written a very thoughtful critical introduction to the book. See Hart and Sacks, *TLP*, at li–cxxxvi.

[62] I do not mean to suggest that *The Legal Process* was not highly regarded in the academy. It has influenced a wide range of legal scholarship in areas as diverse as procedure, legislation, and statutory interpretation. See Hart and Sacks, *TLP*, at cxxv (noting *The Legal Process*'s influence in legal scholarship). I do think, however, that it has not been given the same regard by legal philosophers. This trend may be changing. See, for example, Duxbury, *Faith in Reason,* at 653 and Anthony J. Sebok, *Reading The Legal Process,* 94 Mich. L. Rev. 2701 (1996).

[63] Hart and Sacks, *TLP*, at 107.

[64] Ibid., at 108 (citations omitted).

Sacks did not reject the temporary divorce of law and morality. Immediately after criticizing Holmes for separating law and morality, they explained that they saw the relationship between law and morality as based on "the principle of institutional settlement," which "requires that a decision which is the due result of duly established procedures be accepted whether it is right or wrong – at least for the time being."[65] Hart and Sacks therefore recognized that there is no necessary connection between law and morality and therefore embraced a central tenet of legal positivism, the separability thesis.

Yet, Hart and Sacks's turn toward legal positivism seems to be contradicted by their own characterization of law:

> [T]he ultimate test of the goodness or badness of every institutional procedure and of every arrangement which grows out of such a procedure is whether or not it helps to further . . . [the task of] "establishing, maintaining and perfecting the conditions necessary for community life to perform its role in the complete development of man."[66]

We should note two aspects of this statement. First, it is about *law* – the concept of law, not Anglo-American law, nor constitutional law, nor law in the twentieth century. Second, it appears to be a definition of law based on the satisfaction of a moral condition: Law is an institutional procedure that helps to establish the conditions necessary for community life to perform its role in the complete development of society. But as natural law theories go, Hart and Sacks offered a very peculiar definition of law. For them, the test was not whether the institutional procedure in question actually promoted the complete development of society; it was whether the institutional procedure promoted *the conditions* necessary for the complete development of society. In fact, for a natural law theory, this definition of law is extraordinarily weak: After all, depending on how loosely Hart and Sacks defined the set of conditions necessary for the complete development of society, the rules of almost any legal system, regardless of their actual evil results, could count as law under Hart and Sacks's definition.

What are the "conditions necessary for the complete development of man"? Hart and Sacks stated that there were three "objec-

---

[65] Ibid., at 109.

[66] Ibid., at 110–11 (quoting Joseph M. Snee, Leviathan at the Bar of Justice, in *Government Under Law* 47, 52 [Sutherland, ed., 1955]).

tives of every society."[67] We can assume that the achievement of these objectives is coextensive with the satisfaction of the conditions necessary for the complete development of man. The three "objectives of group life" were:

i. "to avoid the disintegration of the social order;
ii. "the great *desideratum*: to maximize the total satisfactions of valid human wants, and keep on maximizing them;
iii. "the *pragmatic necessity* of a currently fair division."[68]

I want to reject an easy and tempting interpretation of this test for law: that the use of the word *maximize* in (ii) means that Hart and Sacks were simply Benthamite utilitarians. Hart and Sacks wanted to maximize only *valid* human wants. The question is, what are those? Hart and Sacks explicitly rejected the idea that a valid human want can be found simply by measuring the intensity of human desires.[69] There must be a filter and a ranking mechanism. But then did they mean that the law has to be tested against moral tenets, as some of the Catholic Natural Lawyers from the 1940s argued?[70] The separation of law and morality demanded by the principle of institutional settlement entails that Hart and Sacks wanted to avoid the natural law option. In a deft move that navigated between utilitarianism and natural law, their definition of a valid human want ultimately referred back to the principle of institutional settlement: "To the extent that doubt is possible about the validity or ranking of certain human wants, or of certain wants for certain

---

[67] Hart and Sacks, *TLP,* at 104.
[68] Ibid.
[69] Ibid., at 111.
[70] See text accompanying n23. This is not to suggest that all Natural Lawyers share in the Neo-Scholastics' simple-minded test for law. I bring the Neo-Scholastics up only because they, along with Lon Fuller, were the sort of natural law theorists writing during the 1940s and early 1950s. Although they differed in the type of test they applied, both the Neo-Scholastics and Fuller used morality as a test for the existence of a law or legal system. As I note in Chapter 6, not all natural lawyers are of this epistemic variety. Nonetheless, it is useful to speculate how compatible Hart and Sacks's theory is with other, more sophisticated, nonepistemic natural law theories. For example, up to this point one might have argued that Hart and Sacks's argument is compatible with Finnis's nonepistemic natural law theory. Finnis argued that laws are those rules "[M]ade in accordance with regulative legal rules, by a determinative and effective authority . . . directed to reasonably resolving any of the community's coordination problems . . . for the common good of that community." John Finnis, *Natural Law and Natural Rights* 276 (1980). Nonetheless, as we shall see later, Hart and Sacks's definition of a "valid human want" is far less restrictive than the "basic goods" that constitute the end of community life in Finnis's theory.

people, the procedure of institutional settlement often operates to remove the doubt."[71] Hart and Sacks seem to be saying that in order to know whether a human want is a *valid* human want, we must evaluate it according to a test generated by the "procedure of institutional settlement." Yet we originally wanted to know what was a valid human want in order to determine what sort of social processes were justified under the principle of institutional settlement and thus learn more about the content of the principle of institutional settlement. Their definition of the principle of institutional settlement appears circular. The question then becomes whether this problem can be overcome.

We might try to move our focus onto the third objective of law: the "fairness" condition. Could Hart and Sacks have argued that the *procedure* of institutional settlement which identifies valid human wants was limited to those "ultimate tests of goodness and badness" that are fair? We should be skeptical of any hope of rescue from this direction. Hart and Sacks modified the word *fair* with the phrase "pragmatic necessity." The pragmatic necessity of fairness was a floor – it was based not on a substantive theory of justice or the good but on basic human psychology. The worse-off must see the legal system as "preferable to open revolt."[72] In fact, once the definition of the "objectives of every legal system" is parsed, it turns out that condition (iii) and condition (i) ("avoid the disintegration of the social order") are really the same thing. Neither the "pragmatic necessity of fairness" nor the avoidance of social "disintegration" helps specify the content of either the procedure or principle of institutional settlement; Hart and Sacks in fact admitted this by using a comparative intensifier to describe the condition that really does all the work: Condition (ii) was called the "more important" of the three.[73]

Another way of saving Hart and Sacks's definition from circularity might be to take advantage of the mechanisms of institutional settlement suggested by the text. Hart and Sacks noted that the procedure of institutional settlement "often" tests what is a valid human want, but not always.[74] Institutional procedures further narrowed the range of choices down but still left gaps. Those gaps would be filled by choices channeled but not determined by the in-

71 Hart and Sacks, *TLP*, at 112.
72 Ibid., at 104.
73 Ibid.
74 Ibid., at 112.

stitutional structure. A choice about valid human wants within this narrow range could come through either reasoned elaboration (by a validly empowered individual) or preference (by a validly identified majority). In truth, only the second source is truly an independent source of judgment, because reasoned elaboration is designed to be an application of prior judgments that reflect the preferences on a validly identified majority. Judgment through majority preference is an independent source of normative value but is not necessarily a form of utilitarianism. Voting maximizes first- and second-order preferences, not pleasure (the two values could, but do not necessarily, overlap).[75] A valid human want based on preference reflects a normative judgment, but of what sort? Not utilitarian, but majoritarian (maximizing representation, not welfare). Under this reading of Hart and Sacks's theory of institutional settlement, their theory is saved from empty circularity only by having it revert to a default rule of majoritarianism. Most human wants would be tested against the filter of a current institutional procedure, and an institutional procedure would be deemed "law" if it did a good job of identifying valid human wants. When an institutional procedure suffered failure – where there were "gaps" – it would not necessarily fail to count as law as long as it could take into account a normative judgment rooted in a valid majority preference vote. Left missing from this analysis was how those who were responsible for operating the institutional procedures were supposed to know what was a "valid" method of measuring majority preference. It is likely that Hart and Sacks had not fully considered the possibility that voting procedures may be not only mathematically complex but normatively contestable as well. *Baker v. Carr* had not yet been decided, and when it was, Hart disapproved of the Court's entry into the "political thicket" of reapportionment.[76] Therefore, under my analysis, the principle of institutional settlement was not defended by Hart and Sacks on the basis that it would necessarily produce just results. It was defended on the basis that it would help the majority produce the results that the majority would prefer. It was a test of technical competence.

---

75 See, for example, Ronald Dworkin, *A Matter of Principle* 361 (1985).

76 *Baker v. Carr*, 369 U.S. 186 (1962). Frankfurter warned the Supreme Court away from the "political thicket" of reapportionment in *Colegrove v. Green*, 328 U.S. 549 (1946), a view that Hart endorsed. See Albert Sacks, *Henry Hart*, 82 Harv. L. Rev. 1593, 1594 (1969). According to Laura Kalman, *Baker* so "alienated" Hart that it "sent him over the edge." Kalman, *The Strange Career of Legal Liberalism*, at 31 n32 (1996).

The principle of institutional settlement and Hart and Sacks's definition of law are positivist because they hold that law is an institutional procedure that helps to establish the conditions necessary for a community to achieve the ends of group life as identified by the community's own institutional procedures. Hence, their statement that "law is essentially concerned with the pursuit of purposes"[77] captured the heart of legal process as a theory of law. Law, for Hart and Sacks, was wholly instrumental; it was about achieving society's purposes – whether for good or for evil.[78] To say that, at a minimum, law performs a coordinating function is consistent with recent theories of legal positivism.[79] According to *The Legal Process,* although it was possible to have many different legal systems promoting many different purposes (some moral, some not), it was impossible to construct a legal system that at its most basic level does not issue a purposive command.

An objection one might raise to the foregoing analysis is that Hart and Sacks said that their theory of law-as-purposive-commands was itself based on a claim of morality. One could rightly point to the following passage:

> It is important to see that this distinction . . . is not in a just sense a distinction between law and morals. It is a distinction rather between one aspect of morals in relation to law and another. For the proposition that settled law should be respected, until it is duly changed – that a decision is in some sense "right" simply because it has been duly made – is itself an ethical concept, resting on the recognition that defiance of institutional settlements touches or may touch the very foundations of civil order and that without civil order morality and justice in anybody's view of them are impossible.[80]

It would be a mistake to think that this passage proves that Hart and Sacks believed in a necessary connection between law and

---

[77] Hart and Sacks, *TLP,* at 118.

[78] As I argue in section 4.6, it is for this reason that I believe that Fuller would find Hart and Sacks's definition of law unacceptable. He would have to make the same argument against them that he made against H. L. A. Hart's form of legal positivism. See Lon L. Fuller, *Positivism and Fidelity to Law – A Reply to Professor Hart,* 71 *Harv. L. Rev.* (1958); but see Lon L. Fuller, *The Morality of Law* 223 n32 (2d ed., 1969) (suggesting that Henry Hart and he might agree on the ends of law).

[79] See, for example, Joseph Raz, *The Morality of Freedom* 101–4 (1986); Joseph Raz, *The Authority of Law* 116–21 (1979).

[80] Hart and Sacks, *TLP,* at 119–20.

morality and therefore rejected legal positivism.[81] In the same way that they carefully resisted the temptation to invest the phrase "valid human wants" with natural law, Hart and Sacks resisted the temptation to invest the phrase "ethical concept" with natural law. In the foregoing quotation, Hart and Sacks distinguished a second sense of morality that is not like what we usually mean by that term. They argued that the *duty* to obey the law is itself a reason based in morality. This argument is not at all uncontroversial, but even if it were true it is not clear to what extent it serves the natural lawyer.[82] All the positivist needs to argue is that the *existence condition* for a legal system (or the definition of a rule of recognition) need not rely on claims about morality. That position is compatible with the claim that someone has a moral reason (even a duty), once the legal system or the law has been identified, to obey the law.

The only claim that the positivist cannot concede, and that Hart and Sacks's statement did not imply, is that the identification of the law which one has a moral duty to obey necessarily relies upon the truth status of the moral content of the law. Hart and Sacks's position is compatible, however, with a large set of morally suspect legal systems, and that is because it says nothing more than that one has a duty to promote those conditions which allow a community to flourish. Unless one operates with an unnaturally narrow definition of what it means to flourish or is a skeptic of the possibility of a variety of social systems' being able to promote flourishing, their definition of law is consistent with a variety of legal systems, not all of them rooted in what is usually called moral truth.

The claim that all humans thrive in communities organized through law is not an exclusive basis for a natural law (or any other) argument. This point could be argued by a positivist with utilitarian tendencies like Bentham or a positivist with natural rights tendencies like H.L.A. Hart. Ultimately, the natural law interpretation of Hart and Sacks's quotation cannot be based on the argument that the norm "obey the law" is a moral principle, because without any independent moral content as to what counts as a valid rule of recognition, any norm valid according to its own legal system will

[81] See Vincent A. Wellman, *Dworkin and the Legal Process Tradition: The Legacy of Hart and Sacks*, 29 *Ariz. L. Rev.* 413, 470–1 (1987) (despite affinities with Dworkin, "Hart and Sacks did not advocate anything like a natural law theory. . . . What can be gleaned from their views about the nature of laws suggests a positivistic orientation instead").

[82] See M.B.E. Smith, *Is There a Prima Facie Obligation to Obey the Law?*, 82 *Yale L. Rev.* 950 (1973).

carry with it a *prima facie* moral duty for obedience, because no reason not generated by the system's own rule of recognition can validly change what will count as a valid norm under that rule of recognition.[83] But the foregoing reasoning simply restates the proposition that, if one has a duty to obey law because it is law, then the test of legal validity cannot be identical with the test for moral truthfulness. The claim that all humans thrive in communities is consistent with the separability thesis.

Hart and Sacks's idea that law was a system of general directive arrangements that creates a set of *human* obligations demonstrates their debt to the sources thesis. If one of the purposes of the principle of institutional settlement was to determine who can decide certain questions, and to ground a decision maker's authority in practical reasoning distinct from moral reasoning, then, like Bentham, Hart and Sacks were committed to the idea that every legal result has a "pedigree" and ultimately a human source.

Furthermore, Hart and Sacks were clearly concerned with focusing on law as an *authoritative* system. Building on the basic definition of law examined previously, they argued that legal systems are "general directive arrangements":

> The establishment of a system of institutionalized procedures of settlement necessarily implies general understandings about the kinds of questions which each of the procedures in the system, whether official or private, is going to settle and something about how it is going to settle them. The system has necessarily to include one or more institutions authorized to reach additional general understandings for handling new problems or dealing more effectively with old ones.[84]

This description corresponds with the position developed by H.L.A. Hart about the relationship between primary and secondary rules, which in turn grounded Hart's argument for the existence of a rule of recognition that would provide members of the community with a social rule for legal validity.[85] Although Hart insisted

---

[83] This assumes that when Hart and Sacks referred to "duly established procedures" they referred to nothing more than conformity with the procedures that the system requires of itself. It should be noted that by using the locution "due result of duly established," Hart and Sacks invoke an important (albeit inscrutable) phrase from the U.S. Constitution. See, for example, Edward S. Corwin, *The Doctrine of the Due Process of Law Before the Civil War*, 24 *Harv. L. Rev.* 366, 368–73 (1911).

[84] Hart and Sacks, *TLP*, at 113.

[85] H.L.A. Hart argued that a legal system relies upon secondary rules to distinguish which normative problems it will concern itself with; these secondary rules, in

that his "social rule thesis" represented a complete rejection of Austin's command theory, Hart's alternative shared with Austin the basic premise that the ultimate rule of a legal system was, in some sense, obligatory.[86] The great difference between Austin and Hart was that the former believed the obligation arose from the threat of sanction, whereas the latter thought it arose from a more complex psychological phenomenon called the "internal point of view."[87]

By rejecting the command theory (in at least its Austinian form), Hart and Sacks succeeded in breaking free from the weakest aspect of classical legal positivism. The command theory posed problems for legal process not only because it could not explain the origin of rules in a modern democracy but also because, as we saw previously, it was silent as to the nature of discretion. To the extent that the Austinian idea of a command relied on a hypothetical threat of sanction, it gravely mischaracterized the interpretive posture of the law's subjects. As Hart noted in his discussion of "power-conferring" rules, laws that allow subjects to create new legal relationships require the law applier to take a more active role in the interpretation of the law than does a legal system built entirely of criminal laws:

> What is distinctive [about power-conferring rules], as compared with individuated face-to-face orders which an official, like a policeman on traffic duty, might give to a motorist, is that the members of soci-

---

turn, generate primary rules that make up the system of legal obligations we face every day. See H.L.A. Hart, *The Concept of Law* 91–9 (2d ed., 1994).

[86] For Austin, any law was obligatory in the crude sense that one is "obliged" to obey the instructions of a person holding a gun. See H.L.A. Hart, *Positivism and the Separation of Law and Morals*, 71 *Harv. L. Rev.* 593, 603 (1958). In contrast, rules of recognition were obligatory in that, to the extent that they were accepted by the bulk of "officials of the system," these officials "regard [them] as common standards of official behaviour and appraise *critically* their own and each other's deviations as lapses." Hart, *Concept of Law*, at 117 (emphasis added).

[87] See Hart, *Concept of Law*, at 89–91. Raz noted that Hart's account of "duty" in *The Concept of Law* was obscured only by the concept of the internal point of view and suggested that Hart's idea could be best expressed through the notion of a norm. See Joseph Raz, *The Concept of a Legal System* 148–50 (2d ed., 1983). Raz's observation leads me to suspect that Hart erroneously focused on the *motivation* for members of a legal system to regard a rule as a norm, as opposed to the more important question of the definition of a norm. I think this is illustrated by Schauer's suggestion that Austin's phrase *general prescription* better captures what we mean by a rule than the word *command*. Frederick Schauer, *Playing by the Rules: A Philosophical Examination of Rule-Based Decision-Making in Law and in Life* 24 n11 (1991). To the extent that the command theory relies upon the rather unreal notion that every law is necessarily backed by a sanction, it is easy to see why Hart and any other positivist would reject it.

ety are left to discover the rules and conform their behavior to them; in this sense they "apply" the rules to themselves.[88]

Subjects of the laws who measure their successful conformity to the law against the presence or absence of a sanction do not engage in the "reasoned elaboration" of the law; they are merely looking for uniformities and patterns in their immediate environment. According to Hart, a system of rules defined entirely on their sanctions (if such a scheme were even possible) would deprive its subjects of the opportunity to be "private legislators."[89] I think that Hart and Sacks viewed the law in a very similar way. As we will see later, Hart and Sacks emphasized the inevitability *and* virtue of discretion in adjudication. By rejecting the command theory, Hart and Sacks both abandoned one of positivism's greatest embarrassments and moved the question of discretion to the center of their theory of positivism.

4.4. REASONED ELABORATION
AS NONCONTINUOUS DISCRETION

Hart and Sacks made a connection between their definition of law as institutional settlement and the theory of reasoned elaboration as developed in the Forewords. They set out a typology of different types of law possible under their theory and suggested that the An-glo-American system has opted for one particular theory, the theory of reasoned elaboration. What made reasoned elaboration attractive, according to Hart and Sacks, was that it imposed two important duties on decision makers. The first was consistency or uniformity: "the idea that like cases should be treated alike."[90] The second obliged decision makers to understand the *purpose* behind a legal argument before they attempted to apply it: "[E]very statute and every doctrine of unwritten law developed by the decisional process has some kind of purpose or objective, however difficult it may be on occasion to ascertain it or agree exactly how it should be phrased."[91] These two values of reasoned elaboration – consistency and purpose – were essential features of a legal system.

---

[88] Hart, *The Concept of Law*, at 39.
[89] Ibid., at 41. Hart called the power to help make law within the constraints of power-conferring rules a "huge and distinctive amenity." Id.
[90] Hart and Sacks, *TLP*, at 147.
[91] Ibid., at 148.

Hart and Sacks's defense of reasoned elaboration was built on a typology of distinctions. Hart and Sacks distinguished among types of laws, types of purposes laws could serve, and finally the types of discretion allowed under the law. To define the types of laws, Hart and Sacks distinguished between laws that were rules and laws that were standards. A rule was "a legal direction which requires for its application nothing more than a determination of the happening or non-happening of physical or mental events – that is, determinations of *fact*."[92] A standard did not require the happening or nonhappening of an event to be put into operation: It was triggered by a "qualitative" change in circumstances.[93] An example of a rule would be the prohibition against driving faster than fifty-five miles per hour, and a familiar standard in law would be the due care requirement in torts.

To define the different purposes of the law, Hart and Sacks next drew a distinction between principles and policies. A policy "is simply a statement of an objective (*e.g.*, full employment)."[94] A principle differs from a policy "in that it asserts that the result *ought* to be achieved and includes, either expressly or by reference to well understood bodies of thought, a statement of *the reasons why* it should be achieved."[95] Thus, in its every application a principle evidences its normative coherence with the legal system as a whole. A policy, on the other hand, need not provide its addressees any principled reasons for action at all.[96]

Finally, Hart and Sacks distinguished between "continuing discretion" and "noncontinuing discretion." Continuing discretion occurred when "the power-holder is without obligation to relate in any formally reasoned manner the grounds upon which he acts in one instance with those upon which he acts in another."[97] Noncontinuing discretion was the opposite: The power holder cannot "think of himself as in the same position as a legislator taking part in the enactment of the [norm] in the first place."[98] He must relate the decision to the norm in a reasoned fashion. Hart and Sacks

[92] Ibid., at 139.
[93] Ibid., at 140.
[94] Ibid., at 141.
[95] Ibid., at 142.
[96] "Arguments of policy justify a political decision by showing that the decision advances or protects some collective goal of the community as a whole." Ronald Dworkin, *Taking Rights Seriously* 82 (1977).
[97] Hart and Sacks, *TLP,* at 144.
[98] Ibid., at 143.

thought that any legal system (and every law) authorized varying degrees of discretion. A legal system that tried to give judges complete discretion would inevitably fail.[99] Such a legal system would still have law, just not very much of it. The rule or standard that authorized continuing judicial discretion in the first place would be law because it would be directive, authoritative, and general. But the reasoning in which judges would then engage after they determined the scope of their discretion would not be legal reasoning (although it could nonetheless be a valid form of reasoning). This is because the law can only constrain discretion, and so someone exercising continuing discretion cannot, within the scope of that discretion, claim to be employing legal reasoning because legal principles and policies are used to *control* discretion.[100]

If a decision maker is free to choose to obey or not the guidance of either a principle or a policy, then the fact that the principle (or policy) is authoritative, general, and directive is not the decision maker's reason for action. Rather, it is simply the content of the principle (or policy) that is doing the work; the relation of the principle (or policy) to the decision maker is the same as if the words had been delivered by a well-intentioned friend as advice: The listener is absolutely free to adopt or ignore them.[101] It is the use of principles and policies to *constrain* discretion authorized by law that is called "reasoned elaboration."[102]

The fact that a legal system reflects the complex structure of reasoned elaboration does not mean that the legal system is necessarily just. The desirability of using legal norms to control judgment instead of granting continuing discretion depends on the extent to which a given society wanted to organize its social life around the values of consistency and obedience to purpose. Hart and Sacks never imagined that a legal system could be a pure instance of dis-

---

[99] Ibid., at 162. Martin Golding, a legal philosopher at Columbia who was sympathetic to legal process, made much the same point in a discussion of American constitutional law: "Our legal system has no privileged status. Not only are systems possible that differ from ours in content, but so also can principled decisions occur within the framework of such systems. . . . Principled judicial decision-making is possible in a tyranny." Martin P. Golding, *Principled Decision-Making and the Supreme Court*, 63 Colum. L. Rev. 35, 42–3 (1963).

[100] Hart and Sacks, *TLP*, at 147.

[101] This analysis adopts an understanding of discretion that is relatively uncontroversial. It conforms, for example, with Dworkin's use of the term in *The Model of Rules I*. See Dworkin, *Taking Rights Seriously*, at 23.

[102] Hart and Sacks, *TLP*, at 143.

cretion – the question was about matters of degree. Even where judges are given a vast amount of discretion, it must be true that those judges have that authority because of a legal process whose application did not itself allow for continuing discretion. Thus, Hart and Sacks pointed out that the key to understanding the process of adjudication was not, as the realists would have it, of deciding whether or not all law allows discretion, for "reasoned elaboration and uniformity of application are *always* called for up to the point where discretion begins – in defining, in other words, the permitted scope of discretion. . . . The problem is [therefore] one of the appropriate degree of elaboration."[103] When judges elaborate on a legal norm, they are essentially trying to provide an answer to the same question that must have confronted whoever wrote the law: Given that the point of law making is to achieve some future result, "how far should the present go in trying to plan the future?"[104] For Hart and Sacks, the realists' interest in discretion was basically right but misplaced: Discretion mattered to the legal theorist because wherever discretion is found, so also will be found attempts to control it, and that is where reasoned elaboration enters the picture.

The subject of *The Legal Process*, therefore, was the control of discretion – the reasoned elaboration of law – at "all levels": "private, judicial, legislative, administrative, and constitutional."[105] Hart and Sacks offered a visual metaphor ("The Great Pyramid of Legal Order") to describe orderly, almost scientific ratios among these different degrees of discretion. At the base of the pyramid are the "billions and billions of events and nonevents" in which members of society make laws through private orderings; apply those laws by complying with contracts, leases, and the like; and apply the public laws made by the state by complying with the public laws. Here the decision maker (the private citizen) exercises the greatest degree of discretion. At the next level are those "situations in which established general arrangements are claimed to have been violated," but no action is taken by the unhappy party.[106] The next level represents those cases in which the parties to a dispute settle their legal

---

[103] Ibid., at 146 (emphasis added).
[104] Ibid.
[105] Ibid., at 107. See also ibid., at 112 ("The further examination of the nature of the process of institutional decisions, and of the problems involved in making and appraising the decisions, in each of the major types of institutional processes is the concern of these materials from this beginning to the end").
[106] Ibid., at 286.

disagreement privately, through "agreement and formal release, arbitration, and decision by private associations."[107] The fourth level captures those cases that are "instituted in courts or other tribunals endowed with powers of formal adjudication" but that are settled.[108] The fifth level concerns those cases that are ultimately never contested in court but are disposed of through a final judgment, such as a "default or consent judgment," or a dismissal or plea of guilty.[109] The sixth level consists of litigated cases in courts, and the seventh level "include[s] all the cases which go to some reviewing tribunal."[110] The pyramid illustrated that the technique which appropriately regulates the legal relationship between private citizens (such as a contract) must be different from the technique appropriate to the regulation of the legal relationship at issue in an arbitration, or an administrative procedure, or an appellate court argument. A recurrent theme in *The Legal Process* was the idea that a good lawyer should be able to pick the degree of discretion appropriate for the type of problem at hand, which is why the book frequently asked the student to weigh the comparative advantages of legal decision making through private agreement, majority voting, administrative dictate, arbitration, or adjudication.[111] Although the vast majority of the examples scattered throughout the book involve *judicial* decision making, it would be a mistake to conclude that *The Legal Process* was about only adjudication by courts. If it were, then Hart and Sacks would have called it *The Judicial Process*.[112] It is one of their great achievements that they were able to take Cardozo's insights about adjudication and apply them to law outside the courtroom. Thus, although all of the examples in *The Legal Process* concerned institutional decisions that involve the reasoned elaboration of law, not all involved reasoned elaboration of law by courts.

---

[107]   Ibid.

[108]   Ibid., at 287.

[109]   Ibid.

[110]   Ibid. "How many sub-layers there are at this level depends, of course, on how many reviewing tribunals are available."

[111]   This list is meant to be illustrative, not exhaustive, of what Hart and Sacks meant when they referred to the "choice among several [institutional] procedures" that society must make in order to take advantage of the principle of institutional settlement. Ibid., at 112.

[112]   See, for example, Benjamin N. Cardozo, *Elements of the Judicial Process* 13 (1921).

4.5. THE VALORIZATION OF ADJUDICATION

It is important to stop for a moment to consider the degree to which Hart and Sacks equated adjudication and reasoned elaboration. They noted that most, but not all, acts of reasoned elaboration occur in courts, and that for this reason judges are often viewed as the typical adjudicator.[113] Accordingly, Hart and Sacks initially developed their view of adjudication by looking at reasoned elaboration in the common law.[114] In Problem No. 10 Hart and Sacks illustrated why they clearly rejected the view, which they attributed to Jerome Frank, that it is impossible to distinguish between issues of fact and law.[115] Furthermore, they believed that judges, who find and apply the law, should minimize the discretion of juries, who find the facts.[116] One might imagine that the reason why Hart and Sacks thought the jury's role should be minimized was that laypeople simply are not as good at judgment as the educated, elite judiciary. But subsequent comments by Hart and Sacks suggest that they would have also disapproved of a judge's acting like a jury. For example, in a case where a judge sits without a jury, they thought it would be an abdication of the judicial role for the judge "to state only his naked conclusions: [for example] that 'the defendant is guilty of driving an automobile so as to unreasonably en-

---

[113]   Hart and Sacks, *TLP*, at 178.

[114]   See, for example, ibid., at 345 (Problem No. 10: Law, Fact, and Discretion in the Application of Law) (reviewing Holmes's decisions in *Commonwealth v. Wright*, 137 Mass. 250 [1884] and *Commonwealth v. Sullivan*, 146 Mass. 142 [1888]).

[115]   Ibid., at 344 (citing Jerome Frank, *A Plea for Lawyer-Schools*, 56 *Yale L.J.* 1303 [1947]; Jerome Frank, *Courts on Trial* [1949] and Hart and Sacks, *TLP*, at 349).

[116]   Problem No. 10 concerns jury instructions in which the defendant was accused of promoting a lottery. The defendant admitted that he had promoted the game described by the prosecution but denied that what he had done was a lottery. Hart and Sacks asked the student to pick between the following jury instructions:

(a) A request by defendant's counsel for an instruction that if the jury believed beyond a reasonable doubt that the defendant had set up and promoted a lottery for money, they should find him guilty;

(b) A request by the prosecuting attorney for an instruction that if the jury believed beyond a reasonable doubt that the defendant had conducted a game having the following described characteristics (specifically enumerating all of the characteristics of the game which the defendant had admittedly conducted) then they should find him guilty; otherwise not guilty.

Hart and Sacks, *TLP*, at 345 ([b] and [c] have been combined for reasons of exposition). Hart and Sacks's dislike of (a) is expressed pretty clearly at Hart and Sacks, *TLP*, at 353.

danger life.'"[117] Hart and Sacks thought that it would be wrong for a judge to deliver a verdict by stating his or her conclusions and nothing more:

> [I]t will make a great deal of difference if he chooses [this] way out. The parties will have no idea of the basis of his decision; and the losing party, being left in the dark, may be harder to convince that the decision is just. And an appellate court will have trouble in reviewing the decision to decide whether or not it involves error, unless it retraces the whole process of decision *de novo*. Compare the difficulty of reviewing an arbitrator's award or an administrative order which is unexplained by an articulate findings or reasons. Perhaps more important, other private persons will have no aid in planning future conduct.[118]

This statement led into a section entitled "The Reason-for-Being of Judicially Declared Law," which used Lon Fuller's *The Forms and Limits of Adjudication* to set out the essential features of adjudication.[119]

Although the Fuller article was presented as just another selection for the student to read, Fuller was not merely just another author whose views Hart and Sacks thought should be represented in the text.[120] They cited to Fuller so frequently, and used his terminol-

---

[117] Ibid., at 356. Note that this option resembles jury instruction (a) quoted in Problem No. 10, ibid., at 345.

[118] Ibid., at 357.

[119] This section actually begins with two problems that illustrate successful and unsuccessful approaches to adjudication. The first problem is based on *Norway Plains Co. v. Boston & Maine R.R.*, 1 Gray 263 (1854). Chief Judge Shaw's decision, in which he limited the extent of a railroad's duty as a common carrier, might be seen as an example of "instrumentalism." See Morton J. Horwitz, *The Transformation of American Law, 1780–1860* 90–7 (1977). Although used primarily to demonstrate the desirability of common law courts to make law, *Norway Plains Co.* also serves as an example of adjudication that was successful (more or less) because the decision maker gave the reasons for his decision. (It should be noted, however, that notwithstanding their general satisfaction with Shaw, Hart and Sacks still thought that he had not done as well with his own method as possible, and they point out that Shaw's conclusion that the railroad's obligations as a common carrier ended at the platform did not follow from his argument.) The next problem, "The Need for the Reasoned Elaboration of Precedent: The Case of the Faithless Fiduciary," was chosen, I suspect, because it is based on a decision that lacks the imagination and creativity of *Norway Plains*. See Hart and Sacks, *TLP*, at 397 (reviewing *Berenson v. Nirenstein*, 326 Mass. 285 [1950]). In addition to teaching the student about how common law courts make law by choosing between competing lines of precedent, this problem is also an example of a court that failed to give adequate reasons for its adjudicative act.

[120] As Eskridge and Frickey noted, Hart and Sacks reproduced an excerpt "from '[a]n unpublished paper presented by Professor Lon L. Fuller to a group of Harvard University faculty members on November 19, 1957.'" *TLP*, at 397, n.* (citing the 1958 version of *The Legal Process*) (hereafter Fuller, Manuscript). This paper – much like *The*

ogy so naturally, that there is good reason to believe that Hart and Sacks self-consciously adopted his view of adjudication.[121] Fuller began his argument, like Hart and Sacks, by noting that laws must be based "upon some rule, principle, or standard,"[122] and, like Hart and Sacks, connected the rationality of law to its being "purposive."[123] Fuller, however, was far more systematic in organizing a conceptual picture of adjudication, and it is difficult to imagine that Hart and Sacks were not familiar with at least the general outlines of Fuller's theory.[124] Fuller tried to identify the conditions under which adjudication might occur in its ideal form, so that he could then determine at what point legal process ceased to be adjudicative and deteriorated into either "a Mixed, Parasitic, or Perverted Form of Adjudication."[125] Fuller thought that for a decision-making process to be adjudicative, it had to possess the following features: (1) The process must be adversarial – "the arguments of counsel hold the case, as it were, in suspension between two opposing interpretations of it."[126] (2) "The adjudicative process should not normally be initiated by the tribunal itself."[127] (3) The tribunal should aspire to base its decision (as much as possible) on the proofs and arguments presented by the parties.[128] Fuller was

---

Legal Process itself – was famous and often cited during Fuller's lifetime and yet it remained unpublished. See Summers, *Instrumentalism and American Legal Theory*, at 10. A later, substantially revised version of the essay was published posthumously. See Lon L. Fuller, *The Forms and Limits of Adjudication*, 92 Harv. L. Rev. 353 (1978) (hereafter *Forms*).

[121] See Duxbury, *Faith in Reason*, at 633. The picture of adjudication attributed to Fuller in the following pages of this work bears a strong resemblance to the five features of adjudication that Abram Chayes attributed to the "received tradition" civil litigation in the 1950s and '60s. Abram Chayes, *The Role of the Judge in Public Law Litigation*, 89 Harv. L. Rev. 1281, 1282–3 (1976). For a more complete analysis of Fuller's picture of adjudication that places it within his theory of law, see Robert S. Summers, *Lon Fuller* 90–100 (1981).

[122] Hart and Sacks, *TLP*, at 398 (quoting Fuller, Manuscript). In their introductory section on "general directive arrangements," Hart and Sacks had organized laws according to the degree they possessed either the features of a rule or standard, and promoted either a principle or a policy. See Hart and Sacks, *TLP*, at 138–43.

[123] Ibid., at 400 (quoting Fuller, Manuscript).

[124] See Duxbury, *Faith in Reason*, at 633.

[125] Fuller, *Forms*, at 381.

[126] Ibid., at 381, citing Lon Fuller and John D. Randall, *Professional Responsibility: Report of the Joint Conference*, 44 A.B.A.J. 1159, 1160–1 (1958), and see Summers, *Lon Fuller*, at 91. Hart and Sacks say something similar in Hart and Sacks, *TLP*, at 633 and 643 ("Adjudication implies . . . [a] tribunal imposing a solution upon the parties to a dispute in the respects in which they have failed to agree. . . . [T]he process is *not* one of mediation").

[127] Fuller, *Forms*, at 385.

[128] Ibid., at 388–91.

well aware that this condition is more often honored in its breach, but he was emphatic about pointing it out as one of the early warning signs of a procedure crossing the invisible line between a mixed form of adjudication and a perverted form.[129] (4) The tribunal must be impartial.[130] Hart and Sacks said something similar but added a criterion: "[A]djudication implies that the deciding officers are not politically accountable to anyone for any particular decision . . . [they are] subject only to their own consciences."[131] (5) The tribunal's decision must be retroactive – that is, it may have prospective effects, but it must also have a retroactive effect.[132] (6) The tribunal "must . . . at some appropriate point . . . give reasons for the result reached."[133] This is one of Fuller's most difficult claims to interpret, and while I tend to agree with Summers's attribution of this position to Fuller, in *The Forms and Limits of Adjudication* Fuller made a slightly weaker claim.[134] On the other hand, in the same essay Fuller also said that "it seems clear that the fairness and effectiveness of adjudication are promoted by reasoned opinions [in which the tribunal states its reasons]."[135] It is very likely that if

---

[129] Ibid., at 388 ("We need to remind ourselves that if . . . the grounds for the decision fall completely outside the framework of the argument, making all that was discussed or proved at the hearing irrelevant – then the adjudicative process has become a sham"). Summers pointed to another reason as well: "As [Fuller] saw it, 'the essence' of [adjudication] is to give each side a chance to know what the other is saying and to afford an opportunity to refute the other." Summers, *Lon Fuller*, at 92. Robert Bone argued that this feature of Fuller's theory of adjudication reveals its progressive potential, which has been ignored by later critics. Robert Bone, *Lon Fuller's Theory of Adjudication and the False Dichotomy Between Dispute Resolution and Public Law Models of Litigation*, 75 B.U.L. Rev. 1273, 1306–7 (1995).

[130] Fuller, *Forms*, at 391.

[131] Hart and Sacks, *TLP*, at 642.

[132] "It is not the function of courts to create new aims for society or to impose new basic directives." Fuller, *Forms*, at 392; see also Summers, *Lon Fuller*, at 92. Hart and Sacks seem to have been less hostile to prospective decision making than Fuller. See Hart and Sacks, *TLP*, at 600–15; but see Hart and Sacks, *TLP*, at 630–40 (Problem No. 23, Advisory Opinions: The Case of Mr. Jefferson's Incompleted Forward Pass).

[133] Summers, *Lon Fuller*, at 92.

[134] See Fuller, *Forms*, at 387.

[135] Ibid., at 388. What Fuller ultimately believed is not so important, because Hart and Sacks appear to agree with the position Summers attributed to Fuller. They said that "it is an integral part of the concept of adjudication as exemplified in the conventional forms of the judicial process that decision is to be arrived at *by reference* to impersonal criteria of decision applicable in the same fashion in any similar case." Hart and Sacks, *TLP*, at 643 (emphasis added). If "by reference" means that the tribunal must publicly state its reasons, then Hart and Sacks were taking an even stronger position than Fuller on the connection between the giving of reasons and the having of reasons in adjudication. It is interesting that in the version of *The Forms*

Fuller believed, like Hart, that adjudication depended, in some way, on the presence of reasoned opinions, he also believed that the adjudicator should articulate those reasons. Obviously, the idea that an adjudicator should be required to make a public statement of his or her reasons is an idea that we have already encountered in the earlier discussion of Hart's Foreword and the development of reasoned elaboration.

Hart and Sacks recognized that given the complexity of the definition of adjudication they adopted, adjudication was appropriate for only a fraction of institutional decisions. They followed Fuller by declaring that adjudication was much more effective at resolving conflicts that result from human organization through "common ends" or "shared purpose," as opposed to organization "by reciprocity."[136] In a system defined by reciprocity, people could rely on market mechanisms to mediate their interests and regulate their transactions peacefully. Fuller defined "order by reciprocity" by contrasting it with "organization through common ends":

> *Order (or organization through common ends)* can be illustrated by the following situation: A common road gives access to two neighboring farms. A boulder rolls across this road, blocking it. . . . Joining together [the two farmers] are able to remove the obstacle. Here an association of two men makes both of them richer. . . . *Organization by reciprocity*, on the other hand, requires that the participants differ in their "values," that is, that they evaluate differently the same objects. . . . By a trade of [the objects], both farmers can become richer.[137]

According to Fuller, problems of reciprocity, unlike problems of shared ends, have no rational solution and therefore should not be solved by adjudication but through other forms of institutional decision making, such as negotiation (private law making) or voting (legislation).[138] There is something almost perverse about Hart and Sacks's simultaneous embrace of the form of common law adjudication while they rejected as a subject for adjudication conflicts resulting from the private sphere – after all, the common law is mostly

and *Limits of Adjudication* that Hart and Sacks quoted in *The Legal Process*, Fuller seems to assume that the tribunal will state to the losing party the reason for its decision. See Hart and Sacks, *TLP,* at 644.

[136]   Hart and Sacks, *TLP,* at 647; see also ibid., at 402 (quoting Fuller, Manuscript).

[137]   Ibid., at 647. It is important to note that Fuller accepted that problems stemming from incommensurable values ("organization by reciprocity") are technically susceptible to regulation by *either* the market or politics.

[138]   Ibid., at 645, and see Fuller, *Forms,* at 363.

concerned with disputes in contract, property, and torts. Fuller anticipated and answered this problem: He argued that although *creating* and *policing* the rules of the market is a shared purpose and therefore an appropriate subject of adjudication, the *outcome* of the market is not a shared purpose and therefore an inappropriate subject of adjudication.[139] It is for this reason that Hart and Sacks concluded that "questions arising within the regime of reciprocity with respect to what constitutes a satisfactory exchange are not ordinarily appropriate for adjudication."[140] For similar reasons, Hart and Sacks followed Fuller in concluding that, if a problem involves the application of many rules and principles – even if any one of them could be solved rationally – then it is "polycentric" and "require[s] handling by the method of either *ad hoc* discretion [managerial dictate] or of negotiation or of legislation."[141]

Fuller did not argue in *The Forms and Limits of Adjudication* that adjudication is superior to other institutional procedures from the perspective of either morality or philosophy, although he did make this argument in *The Morality of Law*.[142] In fact, as Hart and Sacks suggested, Fuller was well aware that adjudication can sometimes

---

[139] "A market is a regime of reciprocity; it presupposes *and requires* a divergence of individual objectives. Establishing the rules necessary for the functioning of such a mechanism is a meaningful task for adjudication; performing the tasks of the mechanism itself is not." Hart and Sacks, *TLP*, at 402 (quoting Fuller, Manuscript). This distinction between the rationality of social rules and their outcomes is based, in part, on Hart and Sacks's adoption of the Fullerian idea of the "fallacy of the static pie." Ibid., at 102–3 (attributing the phrase to Hart and Fuller). Hart and Sacks seem to have assumed, contrary to Rawls, that although institutional arrangements concerning the market have a rational structure, the distribution of goods in a society governed by a rational institutional structure is not, in itself, subject to rational analysis. See John Rawls, *A Theory of Justice* 83–90 (1971), and Duxbury, *Faith in Reason*, at 653. See also Fuller, *Forms*, at 404 ("The court gets into difficulty, not when it lays down rules about contracting, but when it attempts to write contracts").

[140] Hart and Sacks, *TLP*, at 646.

[141] Ibid., at 674 and see ibid., at 647 ("[a]djudication of disputes about management decisions involving the selection of a course of action for the future among many possible courses is not ordinarily satisfactory, if it is feasible, at all, because of the numerous variables to be taken into account"). See also Fuller, *Forms*, at 394–404; Chayes, *Role of the Judge*, at 1289–92 (on "the demise of the bipolar structure" in modern litigation) and Melvin Aron Eisenberg, *Participation, Responsiveness, and the Consultative Process: An Essay for Lon Fuller*, 91 *Harv. L. Rev.* 410, 424–5 (1978) (Fuller's polycentric model is partially a result of the parties to the dispute not being evaluated by the same criteria). For a criticism of Fuller's distinction between bipolar and polycentric problem solving, see Owen Fiss, *Foreword: The Forms of Justice*, 93 *Harv. L. Rev.* 1, 39–44 (1979).

[142] Fuller, *The Morality of Law*, at 157–62.

be less effective than other techniques at settling disputes.[143] He suggested, however, that because adjudication concerned itself solely with disputes that can be rationally resolved, it was "a tendency of the adjudicative process to induce voluntary acceptance of its results."[144] Hart and Sacks rejected the idea that "there are no disputes of any kind which cannot be effectually settled by establishing an impartial and sufficiently prestigeful tribunal to hear them, giving both sides or all sides of the dispute an opportunity to present their evidence and argument, and then having the tribunal make its decision."[145] Hart and Sacks's chapter on the common law, like Fuller's essay, is explicitly about defining adjudication and then determining when it should be chosen in favor of some other method. Hart and Sacks agreed with Fuller that knowing the *limits* of adjudication was as important as knowing its form.[146] This is true for two reasons. First, "[w]here adjudication is used to settle disputes not subject to rational decision, the *moral force* of the institution suffers." Second, "if the dispute is not susceptible to a reasoned solution, then the attempt to force it into the mold of adjudication will render unavailable the very means which are rationally best calculated in most situations to a produce a satisfactory settlement."[147] In *The Legal Process* Hart and Sacks attempted to identify the "kinds of disputes which lend themselves to reasoned decision."[148] The resulting list shows a extraordinary bias toward disputes that arise in common law.[149] Hart and Sacks clearly believed that there was a relationship between the *form* of adjudication and the inherent rationality of common law: Because a common law decision maker restricts itself to choosing between "limits fixed by es-

---

[143] "To the extent that the resolution of the dispute depends essentially upon what Professor Fuller calls the principle of order by reciprocity, as distinguished from the principle of order through common ends (including the maintenance of a regime of reciprocity), the method of adjudication operates to eliminate the *best judges* of a satisfactory exchange – namely, the parties to the exchange themselves." Hart and Sacks, *TLP,* at 645 (emphasis added).

[144] Hart and Sacks, *TLP,* at 400 (quoting Fuller, Manuscript).

[145] Ibid., at 644.

[146] Ibid., at 401 (quoting Fuller, Manuscript; emphasis added).

[147] Ibid., *TLP,* at 645.

[148] Ibid., at 646.

[149] Because the "remedies available in the armory of the common law courts [are] few and relatively well defined," Hart and Sacks argued that they are especially well suited to the conditions imposed by adjudication, in contrast to remedies available in equity (for example) that "strained" the "integrity of the adjudicatory function." Ibid.

tablished remedies ... it provides a comprehensive, underlying body of law adequate for the resolution of all disputes that may arise within the social order."[150] But the valorization of common law was not designed to shrink the range of application of *The Legal Process*; rather, it was designed to suggest that, to the extent that other legal techniques are susceptible to rational analysis, they ought to adopt the form of adjudication.

The concept of adjudication was, for Fuller, an ideal type, and he recognized that it could manifest itself in the world in greater and lesser degrees. Thus, he was very interested in the problem of "mixed" forms of adjudication such as arbitration or administrative law. Fuller noted that "tripartite" arbitration, which during the 1940s and '50s was becoming a popular element in the emerging field of labor law, "tends to deteriorate ... into a kind of continuation of bargaining behind closed doors, or ... into an empty form."[151] Fuller was equally skeptical about new forms of administrative law that failed to adopt the central features of common law

---

[150] Ibid., at 647. See also Duxbury, *Faith and Reason,* at 661 ("Hart & Sacks purport to favor neither common law nor legislation, yet they seem to display a peculiar preference for the judicial decision") (footnote omitted). Hart and Sacks's celebration of the range of the common law has a distinctly nineteenth-century sound. See, for example, Address by David D. Field on September 21, 1859, "Magnitude and Importance of Legal Science," in *Speeches, Arguments, and Miscellaneous Papers of David Dudley Field* (I. Sprague, ed., 1884) ("the more perfect is the civilization, the more complete is the law"). It is a peculiar coincidence worth noting that the example Fuller used to demonstrate his theory of the inherent rationality of the common law is the problem of what rule to apply "when the acceptance and revocation of an offer cross in the mail." Hart and Sacks, *TLP,* at 401 (quoting Fuller, Manuscript). Fuller noted that although honest minds might disagree over the proper solution, the choice between the modern rule (acceptance is effective upon dispatch) and its alternative is not "purely arbitrary" but "may be derived rationally from the purposes shared by a commercial community." Ibid. It is unclear whether Fuller was, like Langdell, invoking "higher level" legal principles or solving this legal problem by invoking policy. See Christopher Columbus Langdell, *A Summary of the Law of Contracts* 20–1 (2d ed., 1880); Thomas C. Grey, *Langdell's Orthodoxy,* 45 *U. Pitt. L. Rev.* 1, 25 (1983), and James Boyle, *Legal Realism and the Social Contract: Fuller's Public Jurisprudence of Form, Private Jurisprudence of Substance,* 78 *Corn. L. Rev.* 371, 372–3 (1993) (on the tension between Fuller's instrumentalist tendencies in his contracts scholarship and the formalism that pervades his jurisprudential writings).

[151] See Hart and Sacks, *TLP,* at 330 (citing Edgar L. Warren and Irving Bernstein, *A Profile of Labor Arbitration,* 4 *Ind. & Lab. Rel.* 200, 217 [1951]), and Fuller, *Forms,* at 397. Hart and Sacks were equally critical of arbitration in nonlabor cases. At the end of Problem No. 8 ("Private Arbitration: The Case of the Litigious Investor") they skeptically examined the arguments made in favor of voluntary arbitration. See, for example, Hart and Sacks, *TLP,* at 314–21 (questioning the alleged advantage of private arbitration's speed, lack of rancor, technical expertise, privacy, freedom from precedent, and finality).

adjudication. According to Fuller, the War Manpower Commission, the Office of Price Administration, and the War Production Board, despite their effectiveness, did not "act adjudicatively"; conversely, the FCC was doomed to failure despite its adoption of an adjudicative procedure because the task of awarding television and radio licenses was not susceptible to reasoned solution.[152] He argued that decision makers were tempted to solve polycentric problems (like the awarding of licenses) through adjudication because "[t]he instinct for giving the affected citizen 'his day in court' pulls powerfully toward casting exercises of government power in the mold of adjudication, however inappropriate that mold may turn out to be."[153]

At a certain point, problems that are "not susceptible of a reasoned solution" will no longer fit into the mold of adjudication without the law applier's cutting corners and cheating.[154] When that point is reached, according to Fuller, the legal process in question becomes a perversion of adjudication that survives by drawing its "moral strength" from institutions of true or real adjudication.[155] Hart and Sacks took up Fuller's arguments and cautioned that American lawyers should stay away from the "many well-intentioned bandits [who] engage in attempted raids upon [adjudication's] prestige. . . . [T]hey want the benefits of judge-made law without having to accept the conditions of decision which are necessary to secure the benefits."[156] As this language suggests, Hart and Sacks were quite anxious about the threat posed by "parasitic" adjudication: They argued that not only do parasitic forms of adjudication deny disputants a process better suited to solve their problem,[157] but notwithstanding the success of any individual episode of parasitic adjudication, the practice has a corrosive effect on the legal system overall.[158] Fuller took only a slightly less hostile view of parasitic forms of adjudication: "In labeling [a form of decision making] 'parasitic,' I intend no more condemnation than when a botanist calls a certain fungus 'parasitic.' Just as, from the stand-

---

[152]   Fuller, *Forms,* at 400–3.
[153]   Ibid., at 400.
[154]   The phrase is Hart and Sacks's. See Hart and Sacks, *TLP,* at 645.
[155]   Fuller, *Forms,* at 406.
[156]   Hart and Sacks, *TLP,* at 642 (discussing whether an institutional procedure for obtaining advisory opinions would qualify as adjudication).
[157]   Ibid., at 645.
[158]   Ibid., at 644 (quoting Fuller, Manuscript).

point of human interest, there are good and bad fungi, so parasitic forms of order may be good or bad."[159]

Reasoned elaboration was supposed to ensure that adjudication was used only where it was needed and in circumstances in which it was appropriate. Hart and Sacks's fear of perverted adjudication led them to oppose activist approaches to law and put them in conflict with the Warren Court. The specter of *Brown v. Board of Education* hung over *The Legal Process* when Hart and Sacks wrote that "[t]he present question is whether the enthusiasts for adjudication as a method of settling every kind of social problem may not be open to the charge of trying to make a similarly parasitic use of the prestige of the method."[160] Nonetheless, it is important to realize that nowhere in their arguments do Fuller or Hart and Sacks explicitly reject judicial activism because of the substantive political results it might bring. As Eskridge and Frickey point out, both Hart and Sacks were politically liberal.[161] Of course, it is very possible, as Gary Peller has argued, that Hart and Sacks's commitment to legal process and the demanding form of adjudication it entailed was itself inextricably tied to a politically conservative agenda.[162] I think that Peller's conclusion is too sweeping. As the foregoing discussion shows, Hart and Sacks, like Fuller, were less concerned about the specific political consequences of applying their theory of the legal process than they were about ensuring that the law did not mis-

---

[159] Fuller, *Forms,* at 406. Hart and Sacks even offered an exercise designed to help the student identify parasitic adjudication in which they asked the student to decide whether adjudication would be a good way to solve any one of the fictional disputes they set out in a list. The list describes a set of problems along a spectrum that ranges from the award of a license to an international crisis. The examples are: the allocation of a broadcast license among a set of applicants, the solution of a labor dispute, the final formulation of a zoning plan, the resolution of a dispute between the United States Treasury Department and the Federal Reserve Board about a set of regulations, the resolution of a deadlock between the two houses of Congress over the amending of the Labor Management Relations Act of 1947, and a dispute between two countries over the alleged attempts by one country to change the form of government in the other country. Hart and Sacks, *TLP,* at 641. Hart and Sacks stressed that the question was not whether these disputes should be solved in court but rather whether they should be solved by any of the "tribunals which clothe their proceedings in some or all of the conventional trappings of adjudication." Ibid., at 641.

[160] Ibid., at 642.

[161] Ibid., Introduction at cxiii.

[162] See Peller, *Neutral Principles in the 1950s,* at 608 (arguing that the connection was inevitable) and Elizabeth Mensch, "The History of Mainstream Legal Thought" in *The Politics of Law* 30 (David Kairys, ed., 2nd ed., 1990) (same). But see Duxbury, *Faith in Reason,* at 667 (questioning whether the connection is "exaggerated").

treat complex social problems *either* by forcing them into an adjudicative process when they were not susceptible to rational analysis *or* (if one of the problems was susceptible to rational analysis) through the application of a legal process that was insufficiently adjudicative.[163]

Hart and Sacks were committed first and foremost to the *idea* of adjudication as reasoned elaboration, and although they were worried that too many complex social problems were being brought under its mantle, they were equally upset when a judge "abdicated" his or her judicial responsibility by refusing to decide. Thus, Hart and Sacks were very critical of Justice Hugo L. Black, probably one of the Court's most committed realists, for his "perversion" of adjudication in the name of judicial humility. For example, in *Halcyon Lines v. Haenn Ship Ceiling and Refitting Corp.* the Court was asked to decide whether admiralty allows contribution as between joint tortfeasors on account of claims by third persons, and if it does, whether a federal maritime statute limited an employer-defendant's contribution to the compensation that a plaintiff-worker was owed.[164] Justice Black, writing for the Court, held that "it would be unwise to fashion new judicial rules of contribution and that the solution of this problem should await congressional action."[165] Hart and Sacks mercilessly criticized the Court's argument that admiralty law had not already provided both precedent and principle upon which to extend the doctrine of contribution from collision cases to noncollision cases.[166] They argued that *Halcyon* was driven

---

[163]   See Norman Dorsen, *In Memoriam: Albert M. Sacks*, 105 *Harv. L. Rev.* 1, 12 (1991) (contesting the criticism made by progressive lawyers that legal process was steeped in "conservative and procedural fetishism").

[164]   U.S. 282 (1952). In this case, a worker who was covered by the Longshoremen's and Harbor Workers' Compensation Act (LHWA) sued and received judgment against Halcyon, the owner of the ship upon which the worker was injured. In the same action, the jury returned a special verdict finding Halcyon 25 percent responsible and the worker's employer, Haenn, 75 percent responsible for the injury. Halcyon then sued Haenn for contribution.

[165]   Hart and Sacks, *TLP*, at 498 (quoting Black, J.). Justices Reed and Burton dissented. The Court reserved the question of whether, if Congress chose to extend the right to contribution among joint tortfeasors to admiralty cases, the contribution should be limited by the LHWA. Ibid., at 499 n12 (quoting Black, J.).

[166]   They concluded that "at one stroke the Court (1) reached an unsound conclusion in the case before it, (2) destroyed the harmony of the underlying maritime law in this general area, and (3) established a precedent which puts into question *the continued vitality in the federal courts of the whole Anglo-American tradition of growth of decisional law.*" Ibid., at 515 (emphasis added). Furthermore, Hart and Sacks argued that by denying the common law right to contribution, the Court turned tortfeasors like

not by its doctrinal reasoning (which Hart and Sacks called "so much eyewash"[167]) but by Justice Black's willful misunderstanding of the Court's job. Black's opinion tried to determine whether Halcyon had a right to contribution by asking whether in this matter "the method of legislative growth is to be preferred to the method of judicial growth," and, in concluding the former, pretended that by deferring to Congress, the Court was in fact not making law.[168] Hart and Sacks suggested that Black's "profoundly anti-constitutional and indeed unconstitutional" reasoning was motivated by a lack of respect for adjudicative values.[169] Black supported his decision to defer to Congress because Congress had entered the sphere of maritime personal injury, which demonstrated that "many groups of persons with varying interests are vitally concerned with the proper functioning and administration of [maritime torts] . . . [Therefore] legislative consideration and action can best bring about a fair accommodation of the diverse but related interests of these groups."[170] Black noted that the only party apparently "in favor" of allowing contribution was the appellant.[171] Hart and Sacks accused Black of trivializing the interests of the parties to the suit and of taking into account "the wishes" of economic interest groups not even before the Court.[172] Hart and Sacks basically accused Black

---

Halcyon into absolute indemnitors of joint tortfeasor employers, because the LHWA (being a form of workman's compensation) naturally allowed the employer to recover its payments from the employee if the employee successfully sued a third party like Halcyon. Ibid., at 508–9. It is worth noting that Hart and Sacks unfavorably compared Black's refusal to use the Court's earlier collision cases to solve this noncollision case with Shaw's application of case law on common carriers to the railroads in *Norway Plains*. Ibid., at 501.

167   Ibid., at 516.
168   Ibid., at 517. See also ibid., at 515 ("There can be no doubt, can there, that the Court actually 'fashioned new judicial rules' while asserting that it was 'unwise' and 'inappropriate' to do so . . . ?").
169   Ibid., at 517.
170   Ibid., at 498 (quoting *Halcyon*).
171   Ibid., at 498 (quoting *Halcyon*).
172   Ibid., at 517 ("could unconcern for the interests of the parties before the Court be made more explicit?"). One might think that *Halcyon* anticipated the modern trend toward expanding the set of parties of interest in public law litigation. See Chayes, *Role of the Judge in Public Law Litigation*, at 1291; Richard Stewart, *The Reformation of American Administrative Law*, 88 Harv. L. Rev. 1667, 1723–47 (1975). However, Hart and Sacks's poor opinion of Black's decision went beyond accusing him of careless legal reasoning. They suggested, ultimately, that Black's decision was designed to ensure that the worker's employer in *Halcyon* would have an incentive to advance the worker money while he sued the employer's co-tortfeasor. Thus, *Halcyon* – its language about deference to Congress notwithstanding – was really about "securing

of stripping away from the case many of the elements that they deemed central to adjudication; according to them, by ignoring the parties in interest the Court did not stand "suspended" between two advocates; the Court made and interpreted law but gave no reasons. Finally, instead of limiting itself to the remedies available to it, it enthusiastically embraced a polycentric task.[173] This was not a case of a nonjudicial body's adopting a perverted form of adjudication but of a court's adopting a perverted form of law making.

Because they were deeply committed to the idea of adjudication, and not just to adjudication by judges, Hart and Sacks were just as supportive of nonjudicial actors who, where appropriate, faithfully adopted the forms of adjudication as they were critical of judges who, like Black, evaded or perverted adjudication. For this reason Hart and Sacks were most approving of agencies when they incorporated adjudicative values. For example, in Problem No. 43, which was aptly named "Drafting an Administrative Opinion: The Oil Pump Fiasco," an actual Federal Trade Commission decision was compared with a hypothetical decision written by Hart and Sacks.[174] Whereas the FTC issued a decision that consisted of nothing but findings of fact, a conclusion, and an order, Hart and Sacks's decision looked like a judicial opinion, with sections entitled, "analysis of issues," "findings of adjudicative fact," and "conclusions of law."[175] Hart and Sacks made no attempt to hide their pref-

a tactical advantage . . . which will predispose a negligent employer to finance the employee in the employee's own lawsuit so as to pass the whole buck of the loss in a polite way to the employer's co-tortfeasor." Hart and Sacks, *TLP,* at 521. Hart and Sacks opined that this result would appeal to Black because it would make it easier for workers to sue negligent third parties like Halcyon, proving, in their minds, the truly unprincipled (and realist) roots of the decision. Ibid.

[173] Despite the fact that the result of the Court's process was to defer to a legislative body, the question that Black asked – who should decide whether there is a right to contribution in this case – was "not susceptible of reasoned elaboration and . . . ought to be made by the political arm of the government" and had been already answered by Congress. Ibid., at 516. Hart and Sacks therefore understood Black's act of judicial passivism with regard to statutes as an act of judicial activism with regard to the Constitution.

[174] Ibid., at 1083. The decision upon which this example is based, *Matter of Standard Oil Co. of New Jersey,* Docket No. 337, 2 F.T.C. 357 (1920), involved Standard Oil's practice of leasing gasoline pumps at below cost to retail gasoline dealers with the restraint that the pumps can be used to pump only Standard Oil's gasoline. The Commission found that the leasing arrangement violated Section 5 of the Federal Trade Commission Act of 1914 and Section 3 of the Clayton Act of 1914. The Commission's findings were invalidated in *Federal Trade Commission v. Standard Oil Company* (New Jersey), 261 U.S. 463 (1923).

[175] Ibid., at 1084–92.

erence for their hypothetical opinion.[176] Hart and Sacks believed
(contrary to Justice McReynolds) that the only reasonable interpretation of Section 5 of the Federal Trade Commission Act was that it
required the FTC to "build up a body of administrative law through
the articulation of grounds of decision intelligible enough and well
enough reasoned to have an impact at the stage of primary private
activity."[177] In other words, the Commission, like a court, was responsible "in the determinations of matters of law,"[178] and, as with
a court, the more its procedures reflected adjudicative values, the
better it would do its job.[179] Hart and Sacks's assumption about the
centrality of adjudication in the legal process of agencies is evident
in their theoretical discussion of the interpretation of statutes by
agencies. Hart and Sacks approved of Justice Jackson's view that
when Congress writes a law like the Federal Trade Commission Act
of 1914 (which forbade "unfair methods of competition"), the relevant agency is required, in interpreting the "inchoate" law, to make
law.[180] But in doing so, the agency is in the same position as a court
interpreting an "avowedly indeterminate direction."[181] Because
Hart and Sacks minimized the difference between the judicial interpretation of a statute and legislation,[182] it should not be surprising

---

[176] The only secondary source they included, Gerard Henderson, *The Federal
Trade Commission* (1924), is clearly the inspiration for their hypothetical decision: "'It
seems to me that the most important single step which the Commission could take
. . . would be to abandon the formal and legalistic "findings" to which it is now ad-
dicted, and to adopt instead the . . . signed opinions of the kind employed in the
courts of England and of the United States.'" Hart and Sacks, *TLP*, at 1105 (quoting
Henderson, *Federal Trade Commission*).

[177] Ibid., at 1103.

[178] Ibid., at 1107.

[179] Hart and Sacks said that the FTC's standard practice failed to satisfy a number of the conditions for adjudication listed *supra*. (1) The process was not truly adversarial, because the decision maker was not technically choosing between two
competing legal arguments; (2) the tribunal did not, in its decision at least, base its
decision on the proofs and arguments presented by the parties; (3) the decision written by the tribunal did not deal impartially with the arguments presented by both
sides and set out the reasoning for its decision. See ibid., at 1109 (citing Henderson,
Federal Trade Commission). Neither Henderson nor Hart and Sacks discussed how an
administrative agency could satisfy the adjudicative ideal that the decision maker be
impartial.

[180] Ibid., at 1309–10 (quoting *Federal Trade Commission v. Ruberoid Co.*, 343 U.S.
470 [1952] [Jackson, J., dissenting]).

[181] Ibid., at 150 (a "broad standard . . . backed up and informed by principles
and policies implicit in the history and general scheme of the statute").

[182] See, for example, ibid., at 126 ("Enacted law may displace decisional law as
a means of initial formulation of legal arrangements, but not as a means of elaboration . . . for enactments need to be interpreted . . .").

that they saw little difference between adjudication in a court and that in an agency: "an agency can formulate law in the same form and manner as a court."[183]

So far, we have seen that Hart and Sacks privileged adjudication when it was associated with the courts and hypothesized that greater allegiance to adjudication could improve the work of administrative agencies. A final piece of evidence of *The Legal Process*'s commitment to the primacy of adjudication was its treatment of legislation. When Hart and Sacks found legislation wanting (and they often did) it was because it lacked one or more of the essential qualities found in adjudication. They argued that the real mistake made by those who distinguish between common law and legislation was not that they focus on the fact that the former is announced by judges and the latter created by politicians, but that they thought that the former resides in principles and that the latter in a set of rules.[184] Hart and Sacks challenged this idea, as evidenced by the following rhetorical question: "[C]annot there also be postulates of reasoning, which limit and control, behind the words of statutory provision. . . . [C]annot a legislature effectively state its postulates and tell the courts that they are to treat them as lifting and controlling in their reasoning?"[185] The rest of the chapter was designed to

---

[183]   Ibid., at 1311–12. In this section, Hart and Sacks argued for the distinctiveness between agencies and juries and ended up proving that judges and agencies share many adjudicative features: (1) both are able to "formulate legal standards and rules" to guide future conduct (e.g., explain their reasoning); (2) both must be as "even-handed as possible"; and (3) both must formulate the governing rules and standards in the case before them (e.g., restrict themselves to the arguments of the parties before them).

[184]   Hart and Sacks clearly disagreed with the sentiment that "a code must be dogmatic . . . a statute must never be either a reasoning or a dissertation." Ibid., at 781 (quoting Ernst Freund, *Legislative Regulation* [1932]).

[185]   Ibid., at 783. Hart and Sacks illustrated their point with an example based on *Roberson v. Rochester Folding Box Co.*, 171 N.Y. 538 (1902), in which they proposed three alternative hypothetical acts of legislation that would have enforced the common law right to privacy that the New York Court of Appeals had (in Hart and Sacks's opinion, as well as those of other courts and the New York legislature) erroneously denied. The alternative they preferred "avoids the difficulties . . . [of] fragmentary codification by a level of generality that leaves all of [the difficulties in elaborating the principle] to be resolved by future judicial action." Hart and Sacks, *TLP*, at 783. See also Duncan Kennedy, *Legal Formality*, 2 J.Leg. Stud. 351, 396 (1973) (doubting that Hart and Sacks's "third way" is sustainable) and Kathleen M. Sullivan, *Foreword: The Justices of Rules and Standards*, 106 Harv. L. Rev. 24, 79 n395 (1992) (noting that the Court adopted reasoned elaboration in *Planned Parenthood of Southeastern Pennsylvania v. Casey*, 505 U.S. 833 [1992]).

show that statutes should reflect, as much as possible, the sort of principles found in common law.

For example, in Problem No. 29 ("Revision of Judicial Interpretation of an Existing Statute") Hart and Sacks used a lengthy excerpt from a congressional hearing to illustrate the dangers of encouraging the idea that a statute is all rule and no principle. The purpose of the hearing was to pass a relatively simple piece of legislation to reverse a Supreme Court decision that had held that the Federal Food, Drug, and Cosmetic Act did not require a manufacturer to permit entry by a federal inspector.[186] Hart and Sacks disapproved of the Court's handing the "mess" created by Congress back to it for the reason that as long as Congress treated its laws like rules, interested parties would be able to exploit the unfortunate logic of this approach.[187] In the relatively insignificant episode they documented, an industry lobbyist tried to get a congressional committee to state in the legislative history that the clarification of the Food and Drug Administration's right to entry (which confirmed a previous FDA construction) should not be seen by the courts as a confirmation of *other* previous administration constructions of the same act.[188] The only cure to this problem, Hart and

---

[186] Hart and Sacks, *TLP*, at 810–33 (discussing *United States v. Cardiff*, 344 U.S. 174 [1952]).

[187] Ibid., at 817. There is every reason to believe that the Court knew that Congress would have wanted to have written a statute that required entry to federal inspectors and that the Court found against the government in order to punish Congress for writing an incoherent statute. See *Cardiff*, 344 U.S. 174, quoted in ibid., at 816.

[188] Ibid., at 814. As Hart and Sacks observed, the congressmen had backed themselves into a corner: By allowing their statute to be treated like a limited rule, they had no alternative but to tell the courts that their approval of a subsequent reasonable interpretation of their act by the FDA should not be used to evaluate the reasonableness of other FDA interpretations of the same statute based on the same reasoning. From the questions Hart and Sacks asked, it is clear that, *given the premises upon which the statute had been drafted*, the committee had failed to meet the objections raised by the lobbyist at the hearings. See ibid., at 833.

This case, like others in their chapter on statutory interpretation, illustrates Hart and Sacks's rejection of the view that legislation should be seen as directed toward addressing a specific state of affairs. The first rule of statutory interpretation Hart and Sacks offered at the end of *The Legal Process*'s seventh chapter was that "a court . . . is to decide what meaning ought to be given to the directions of the statute in the respects relevant to the case before it. . . . [This] does not say that the court's function is to ascertain the intention of the legislature with respects to the matter at issue." Ibid., at 1374. Hart and Sacks filled *The Legal Process*'s fifth chapter with examples of statutes that had failed to serve the public interest because they were designed to ad-

Sacks seem to have said, is to treat legislation like principles of common law.[189]

We may therefore conclude that Hart and Sacks's theory of law relied upon many, but not all, of the same elements found in the definition of classical positivism. First, Hart and Sacks's claim that law was instrumental is essentially the same as the separability thesis. Second, Hart and Sacks's claim that law required the application of practical reasoning in order to identify norms and to determine the scope of authority granted by the law maker was essentially the same as the sources thesis. Third, Hart and Sacks's claim that law was a set of purposive commands was a modern revision of the command theory of law in the style of H.L.A. Hart. Not only was Hart and Sacks's theory fundamentally continuous with classical positivism, but their theory improved upon Langdellian formalism. Hart and Sacks took seriously, in a way that the formalists did not, the role of discretion in the application of rules.

dress specific (often private) needs instead of to create "general directive arrangements." For example, Problem No. 35 ("Provision of Government Services and Pecuniary Inducements: The Uses of Insurance, Especially Against Floods") and Problem No. 36 ("A Special Law Dealing with a Municipal Disaster") are textbook examples of what would later be understood as rent-seeking legislation. See William N. Eskridge, *Politics Without Romance: Implications of Public Choice Theory for Statutory Interpretation,* 74 *Va. L. Rev.* 275, 288 (1988); see also James Buchanan and Gordon Tullock, *The Calculus of Consent* 233–48 (1962) (on rent seeking in public choice). Eskridge and Frickey suggested that Hart and Sacks may not have been aware of the pessimistic implications of their picture of legislative failure. See Hart and Sacks, *TLP* Introduction, at cxxi–cxxii, and see William N. Eskridge and Philip P. Frickey, *Legislation Scholarship and Pedagogy in the Post–Legal Process Era,* 48 *U. Pitt. L. Rev.* 691, 705–7 (1987) (Richard Posner's "legisprudence" corrected Hart and Sacks's naïve views of legislation).

[189] Hart and Sacks implied that they did not want to overstate the difference between the adjudication of common law and statutes when they discussed their general principle of law – the reasoned elaboration of general directive arrangements – without distinguishing between statutes and common law. Hart and Sacks, *TLP,* at 147–8. Their sense that statutory interpretation should mainly be about the search for principle explained, for example, their rejection of the "literal approach" (ibid., at 1116–48) and their skepticism of the utility of legislative history (ibid., at 1212–54). Hart and Sacks clearly reflected the influence of Edward Levi in this view. Levi was as skeptical about overstating the differences between statutory interpretation and common law interpretation as Hart and Sacks. See, for example, Edward H. Levi, *An Introduction to Legal Reasoning,* at 29–30 (1949). Levi, however, urged a theory of statutory interpretation that was more deferential to early judicial interpretations of legislative intent than the view indicated by *The Legal Process.* See ibid., 31–2 (in trying to construct legislative intent, a court has "more discretion than it has with case law" and for that reason must be more deferential to precedent), and Hart and Sacks, *TLP,* at 1343 (commenting on Levi's theory).

4.6. HOW COULD HART AND SACKS
HAVE AGREED WITH FULLER?

Thus far, I have argued that Hart and Sacks shared with Fuller a common view of adjudication. I have also argued that Hart and Sacks adopted and improved upon classical legal positivism and that legal process, as a movement, was in fact a modern form of positivism. Yet if these arguments are correct, we are confronted with yet another jurisprudential mystery, for the simple reason that Fuller is well known as the single most important critic of legal positivism in postwar America.[190] Fuller (who equated positivism with legal realism) rejected positivism because he rejected its "fundamental postulate": "that law must be strictly severed from morality."[191] Fuller believed that law could not be separated from morality because law, even "considered merely as order, contain[s] its own implicit morality."[192] Fuller thought he was making a conceptual argument that, in other contexts, was quite unremarkable. We would agree, argued Fuller, that there are "natural laws" governing "particular kind[s] of human undertaking[s]" such as carpentry.[193] In the same way that there are natural laws governing good carpentry, there must also be natural laws that govern the "enterprise of subjecting human conduct to the governance of rules."[194]

Fuller called the natural laws of governance of rules the "internal morality of law."[195] The modifier *internal* was supposed to distinguish his theory from the more demanding forms of natural law that used moral philosophy to test the content of individual laws.[196] The internal morality of law therefore placed a limit on *how* laws were made and applied, not on *what* values they promoted:

> What I have called the internal morality of law is in this sense a procedural version of natural law.... The term "procedural" is, however, broadly appropriate as indicating that we are concerned, not

[190] See, for example, Summers, *Lon L. Fuller,* at 10 (1984) and Ernest Nagel, *Fact, Value and Human Purpose*, 4 Nat. L. Forum 26, 26 (1959).
[191] Fuller, *Positivism and Fidelity to Law,* at 656.
[192] Ibid., at 645.
[193] Fuller, *Morality of Law,* at 96.
[194] Ibid.
[195] Ibid.
[196] Ibid., at 104; Fuller, *Positivism and Fidelity to Law,* at 660 and see Roger Cotterrell, *The Politics of Jurisprudence* 130 (1989) (on Fuller's "distancing" himself from classical natural law).

with the substantive aims of legal rules, but with the ways in which a system of rules for governing human conduct must be constructed and administered if it is to be efficacious and at the same time remain what it purports to be.[197]

The internal morality of law blended the perspective of both a legislator and a judge: It demanded that the law maker focus not only on the substantive ends he or she wishes to achieve, but also on how those to whom the law is directed will come to know what those ends are. For Fuller, more traditional natural law theory had put the cart before the horse by asking what the law should achieve before fully understanding how the law was to achieve anything.

Fuller determined that the morality of law consisted of eight jointly necessary conditions: (1) A legal system must have rules, because a legal system cannot decide everything on an "ad hoc" basis; (2) the rules must be publicized; (3) the rules may not be retroactive; (4) the rules must be comprehensible; (5) the rules may not contradict other rules in the same legal system; (6) the rules may not demand the impossible; (7) the rules may not be changed constantly; and (8) the rules' administrators may not ignore the rules.[198] These conditions represented the minimum floor below which a legal system could not fall, as well as the heights to which a legal system could aspire.[199] A legal system that consistently failed most of the eight conditions simply had no law, while a legal system that satisfied most of the conditions most of the time had law, albeit in varying degrees.[200]

Fuller thought that positivism was wrong because it had the wrong definition of the "floor" described by the morality of law. Classical legal positivism's conception of the line separating law from not-law was the command theory set out by Austin and Bentham. According to Fuller, the positivist's test was incoherent because "law cannot be built on law" – for example, the test by which we recognize the sovereign who issues valid commands cannot it-

---

[197] Fuller, *Morality of Law,* at 97.

[198] Ibid., at 39.

[199] According to Fuller, all normative conduct took place on a spectrum that fell between "morality of duty" (the minimum required of a normative system) and the "morality of aspiration" (the end to which any normative system aspires). Ibid., at 5–10.

[200] Ibid., at 39. The morality of law "confronts us with the problem of knowing where to draw the boundary below which men will be condemned for failure, but can expect no praise for success, and above which they will be admired for success and at worse pitied for the lack of it." Ibid., at 42.

self be a command issued by the sovereign.[201] According to Fuller, if law must be built on something other than law, it must be built on morality.[202]

The modern positivist response to Fuller's argument was to note that there was a third option that Fuller was ignoring – that law could be based on neither "more law" nor morality, but on social fact.[203] One reason why Fuller did not think that law could be based on "fact" – social or material – was that facts could not guide human conduct. If the purpose of law is to "[subject] human conduct to the guidance and control of general rules," then law cannot be just a "datum of nature" because the very idea of "guidance" presupposes a teleology or morality.[204] It is important to recognize that for Fuller, the opposite of the internal morality of law is not a regime of substantive evil but a regime of "uncontrolled administrative discretion."[205] Fuller phrased this contrast differently at different points in his career, but the dichotomy always indicated the same stark choices: between reason and fiat,[206] adjudication and arbitration,[207] law and "managerial direction."[208] In each of the second terms, the regime described is one in which no one's conduct – neither the commander's nor the subject's – is governed by a norm. Just as the commander cannot look to past decisions as reasons for how to decide in the future, the subject cannot conform his or her behavior to meet the commander's norm (nor could the subject have any grounds upon which to defend his or her choices were the commander to criticize them).[209]

The main response by H.L.A. Hart to Fuller's argument about the necessary relationship between purpose or *telos* and the internal

[201] Fuller, *Positivism and Fidelity to Law,* at 645. It is doubtful that any positivist, with the possible exception of Hans Kelsen, believed that legal validity was a self-referential concept. See Raz, *Concept of a Legal System,* at 136.

[202] Fuller, *Positivism and Fidelity to Law,* at 645.

[203] Hart, *Concept of Law,* at 112.

[204] Fuller, *Morality of Law,* at 146 and see Lon L. Fuller, *Human Purpose and Natural Law,* 53 J. Phil. 697 (1956).

[205] Fuller, *Positivism and Fidelity to Law,* at 654.

[206] See Lon L. Fuller, *Reason and Fiat in Case Law,* 59 Harv. L. Rev. 376 (1946).

[207] See Fuller, *Forms,* at 397.

[208] Fuller, *Morality of Law,* at 207.

[209] Ibid., at 218–19. Of course, Fuller recognized that, as a matter of "expediency," certain patterns may evolve in managerial relations or in the course of repeated arbitrations, but the fact of those patterns is not a reason for future decision in one direction or another; at best, they contribute to an efficiency calculation. Ibid., at 208.

morality of law was to note that even if Fuller was correct about the internal structure of law, it simply was not clear what the morality of law, as defined by Fuller, had to do with *morality*, and hence, why the truthfulness of morality of law proved that the separability thesis was wrong. Hart argued that purposive behavior, including behavior in conformity with a norm, was compatible with evil ends. For example, he noted that "poisoning is no doubt a purposive activity, and reflection on its purposes may show that it has its internal principles."[210] We would certainly understand the use of the word *ought* by a baffled poisoner who said after witnessing the failure of his attempt, "I ought to have given her a second dose."[211] But if it is true that someone pursuing substantively immoral purposes can satisfy the morality of law, then what do we really gain by connecting the analysis of purposive behavior to morality or justice? A rigorous application of the minimum demands of the "floor" of the morality of law might allow us to declare a number of inefficacious legal system not-law, but it would not tell us anything about efficacious evil legal systems, such as (Hart seemed to suggest) Nazi Germany.[212]

Fuller felt quite strongly that there was a connection between the morality of law and substantive justice.[213] Much of his 1958 response to Hart's Holmes Lecture was devoted to showing that the Nazis in fact did not have a legal system. He argued, for example, that a German woman who was prosecuted in 1949 for turning her husband in to the Nazi police in 1944 in accord with anti-sedition laws passed in 1934 and 1938 (resulting in the husband's prosecution for the capital offense of slandering the Führer) was not acting under the valid law of the land when she turned her husband in, because the 1938 law was never law.[214] Fuller subjected the Nazi anti-sedition laws to the test of the morality of law and found them

---

210 H.L.A. Hart, *The Morality of Law*, 78 Harv. L. Rev. 1281, 1286 (1965) (book review). For example, one might command a poisoner in one's service to "avoid poisons however lethal if their shape, color or size is likely to attract notice." Hart, *Morality of Law*, at 1286.

211 H.L.A. Hart, *Positivism and the Separation of Law and Morals*, at 613.

212 Ibid. ("Under the Nazi regime men were sentenced by courts for criticisms of the regime. Here the choice of sentence might be guided exclusively by consideration of what was needed to maintain the state's tyranny effectively").

213 Fuller, *Morality of Law*, at 153–5.

214 Fuller, *Positivism and Fidelity to Law*, at 653–5 (discussing Judgment of July 27, 1949, Oberlandesgericht Bamberg, 5 *Süddeutsche Juristen-Zeitung* 207 [Germany 1950], 64 *Harv. L. Rev.* 1005 [1951] [case comment]).

wanting. The 1938 law, which forbade "publicly seek[ing] to injure or destroy the will of the German people [in wartime]," failed, at a minimum, condition eight (which requires the administrator of the law to follow the rules he or she sets down) because the husband had spoken against Hitler in private with his wife, not in public.[215] The 1934 law, which forbade public or private statements that "disclose a base disposition toward the leading personalities of the nation or of the [Nazi] Party . . . and of such a nature as to undermine the people's confidence in their political leadership, shall be punished by imprisonment," failed the morality of law because it was so "overlarded and undermined . . . by uncontrolled administrative discretion" that a judge would have no choice but "to declare this thing not a law."[216] Fuller offered other examples of Nazi "laws" that failed to satisfy the morality of law, such as the "Roehm purge" in which the Nazis tried, convicted, and then sentenced to death more than seventy party members *after* they had been killed,[217] and the "laws" that forced Jewish store owners to display signs saying "Jüdisches Geschäft" ("Jewish business") except in Berlin during international events (when the Nazis wanted to appear more humane to foreign visitors).[218] According to Fuller, the Roehm purge law failed to be "law" not because it was substantively horrific, but because it was retroactive (condition three); similarly, the "Jüdisches Geschäft" law failed because it was never publicly enacted (condition two).[219]

Elsewhere, Fuller suggested that other evil legal systems (or at least the substantively evil laws produced by those systems) would have failed to reach the floor set out by the morality of law.[220] How-

---

[215] Ibid., at 653–4 (citing section 5 of Kreigssonderstrafrecht Law of Aug. 17, 1938, [1939] 2 *Reichsgesetzblatt* pt. I, at 1456).

[216] Ibid., at 654–5 (citing Article II of *A Law Against Malicious Attacks on the State and the Party and for the Protection of the Party Uniform,* Law of Dec. 20, 1934 [1934], I *Reichsgesetzblatt* 1269). Fuller highlighted the facts that, unlike the 1938 law, this law set out *only* imprisonment as punishment for its violation, and that the definition of a "leading personality" was left open to interpretation by the National Minister of Justice.

[217] Ibid., 650 (citing *N.Y. Times,* July 4, 1934, p. 3, col. 3, and July 14, 1934, p. 5, col. 2).

[218] Fuller, *Morality of Law,* at 158.

[219] Fuller, *Positivism and Fidelity to Law,* at 650 and Fuller, *Morality of Law,* at 158.

[220] Fuller suggested that the Soviet Union's retroactive imposition of the death penalty for violations of currency regulations violated the morality of law, as did South Africa's racial classification laws, which relied on the unbridled discretion of the courts.

ever, classical legal positivism did not deny that evil regimes often cut corners and abandoned the rule of law, or that evil regimes abandoned the rule of law more often than good regimes. The separability thesis claimed only that there was no *necessary* relationship between substantively evil regimes and the presence or absence of the rule of law. For example, one might argue that postwar South Africa posed exactly this dilemma: Throughout the 1950s and '60s South Africa erected an evil, racist regime that (arguably) did satisfy the eight conditions of the morality of law. Fuller responded by noting that even South African law was infected by procedural immorality, in that in its zeal to regulate the races according to the rule of law, the South African government created a set of rules that degenerated through their own complexity into a set of managerial dictates no less arbitrary than the Nazi anti-sedition laws.[221]

For Fuller, the fact that every modern regime which attempted to achieve substantively evil aims failed to conform to the morality of law evidenced a necessary relationship between substantive justice and procedural justice.[222] Fuller argued that the reason why evil regimes like those of Nazi Germany, Stalinist Russia, and South Africa could never, in principle, have law is that "coherence and goodness have more affinity than coherence and evil":

> [The positivist] seems to assume that evil aims may have as much coherence and inner logic as good ones. I, for one, refuse to accept that assumption. . . . [Therefore] I believe that when men are compelled to explain and justify their decisions, the effect will generally be to pull those decisions toward goodness, by whatever standards of ultimate goodness there are.[223]

The connection, therefore, between the retroactivity condition of the morality of law and justice is that if the Nazi or Soviet law makers had been forced to frame in advance the general norm that governed the Roehm purge or the imposition of the death penalty for currency offenses, they would have, like Fuller's failed imaginary sovereign Rex, failed to make law and would have been forced to

---

[221] Ibid., at 160. Fuller thought that the view that South Africa was a combination of "strict observance of legality" with "a body of law that is brutal and inhuman" arose from a confusion "between deference for constituted authority and fidelity to law." Ibid., at 160.

[222] Fuller, ibid., at 153 and Fuller, *Positivism and Fidelity to Law*, at 645.

[223] Fuller, *Positivism and Fidelity to Law*, at 636.

fall back on issuing managerial directives, not norms.[224] Further-more, the demand of prospectivity, like the demand of publicity, forces the law makers to confront the substantive evilness of the ends served by the state's power. It is a natural reaction on the part of law makers, when confronted by the ugliness of their own hand-iwork, to try to hide their evil from others through secret laws, and from themselves through retroactive laws (which legitimate, after the fact, acts that are often the result of inchoate, hidden passions such as cruelty, racism, or greed).[225]

Fuller's assumption that justice is more "coherent" than evil is extraordinarily important to his attack on positivism. If the coher-ence thesis (as we may call it) is not true, then Fuller's theory about the morality of law could be absolutely true and yet entail nothing about the separability thesis. Fuller admitted that he had not proven the coherence thesis, and it is obvious that it is a controver-sial claim that touches on some of the most difficult problems of moral philosophy.[226] Although the coherence thesis might have been supportable if one stayed at the level of crude historical gener-alization, it seems to miss the point about what made certain uses of state power immoral. For example, Fuller argued that what made the laws ordering the extermination of Jews in concentration camps a violation of natural law was that they were passed in secret, thus violating condition two of the morality of law.[227] But of course, Ger-many's actions would have been no less immoral had it chosen to exterminate the Jews after a long, public debate. The coherence the-sis notwithstanding, it is not obvious that Germany would have re-treated from the Holocaust had it been forced to engage in open and prospective law making. Would the evil goals of the anti-sedition laws discussed here have been less achievable had they been writ-ten in conformity with the morality of law? The 1938 law failed to

[224] Fuller, *Morality of Law*, at 40–1.
[225] "But, as with retroactivity, what in most societies is kept under control by the tacit restraints of legal decency broke out in monstrous form under Hitler. In-deed, so loose was the whole Nazi morality of law that it is not easy to know just what should be regarded as an unpublished or secret law." Fuller, *Positivism and Fi-delity to Law*, at 652.
[226] Ibid., at 636; Cotterrell, *Politics of Jurisprudence*, at 132; and see, for example, Anthony D'Amato, *Lon Fuller and Substantive Natural Law*, 26 Am. J. Juris. 202 (1981).
[227] Fuller, *Positivism and Fidelity to Law*, at 651 (citing Gustav Radbruch, *Die Erneuerung des Rechts*, 2 Die Wandlung 8, 9 [Germany 1947]). Of the secret laws order-ing the Holocaust, Fuller said, "[n]ow surely there can be no greater legal monstros-ity than a secret statute." Ibid.

be law because it did not explicitly forbid private slanders against the state. Would the law have become more palatable had it been amended to take into account private statements? The 1934 law failed because it delegated too much discretion to the Ministry of Justice in the definition of its scope of application. If the problem therefore was that it was void for vagueness, it is not clear that the law really was infirm: The 1934 law did not look that different from certain American loyalty statutes such as the Alien and Sedition Acts in the late 1790s and the Espionage Act during World War I.[228] As David Luban has pointed out, in the case of the Nazi anti-sedition laws, what made these laws "bad" laws was that they violated substantive moral principles, either because they were designed to defend an evil state or, more controversially, because any law designed to limit dissent regardless of the moral status of the state is evil; but they were "law" just as much as America's (arguably evil) anti-sedition laws were law.[229]

H.L.A. Hart's view of Fuller's argument was that immoral laws could satisfy the internal morality of law, and that Fuller's theory of law was therefore compatible with legal positivism. Fuller vigorously denied both of Hart's claims and insisted that the morality of law was incompatible with legal positivism. Hart and Sacks left little evidence as to where they would have come out on this debate.

---

[228] The Alien and Sedition Laws, June and July 1798, cited in Norman Dorsen et al., 1 *Political and Civil Rights in the United States* 26–7 (1976); for a discussion of the Espionage Act, see David Luban, *A Report on the Banality of Evil: The Case of the Nazi Judges*, 61 Brook. L. Rev. 1139, 1145 (1995) (citing Zechariah Chafee, Jr., *Freedom of Speech* 57–8 [1920]).

[229] Luban, *A Report on the Banality of Evil*, at 1146. Ingo Müller has turned Fuller's position on its head and argued that the Nazi legal system would have been *less* evil had it been *more* positivist. According to Müller, German jurisprudence in the 1930s had adopted a view very similar to the theory of teleological reasoning demanded by Fuller's procedural natural law theory that, when directed toward substantively evil ends, allowed Nazi judges to achieve far more evil than had they been acting like positivists. Ingo Müller, *Hitler's Justice: The Courts of The Third Reich* 220–2 (Deborah L. Schneider, trans., 1991). One problem with Müller's argument is that he confuses classical legal positivism, which must include the separability thesis, the sources thesis, and the command theory, with a kind of judicial passivism, in which the judge is constrained by both formalistic reasoning and a crabbed form of textualism. See Markus D. Dubber, *Judicial Positivism and Hitler's Injustice*, 93 Colum. L. Rev. 1807, 1820–1 (1993) (reviewing Müller, *Hitler's Justice*). Sometimes legal positivism will result in judicial passivity, but not necessarily. Furthermore, although it may be true, for contingent reasons, that less evil would have been done by Nazi judges had they adopted a passive role in the interpretation of statutes, it would be a mistake to believe that judicial passivity is an effective tool with which to achieve substantive justice (compare the U.S. Supreme Court in the 1940s with that of the 1960s).

It is unlikely that they were not aware of the differences between H.L.A. Hart and Fuller. Henry Hart, Sacks, and Fuller were colleagues at Harvard, and in 1956–7 H.L.A. Hart visited the law school and began his extended debate with Fuller that ultimately culminated in H.L.A. Hart's defense of legal positivism in the 1958 Holmes Lecture.[230] Despite the almost wholesale insertion of Fuller's theory of adjudication into the theory of reasoned elaboration, the theory of law in *The Legal Process* is closer to H.L.A. Hart than Fuller. It is very likely that Hart and Sacks were not even aware of the degree to which they were disagreeing with their friend and would have been embarrassed by the fact had it been pointed out to them. Nonetheless, when it comes to the point where Fuller and H.L.A. Hart clashed, Hart and Sacks seemed to lean toward positivism.

Although *The Legal Process* made almost no mention of H.L.A. Hart, there are points where Hart and Sacks used language that seemed to challenge the coherence thesis. As we saw previously, the principle of institutional settlement, which based legal authority on the idea that one ought to obey "a decision which is the due result of duly established procedures," used the concept of "due" as a proxy for a social fact such as a majority preference. It is unlikely that Fuller would have thought that every human want identified as valid by the principle of institutional settlement was substantively moral (or, to put the same point differently, was not substantively *im*moral). Hart and Sacks, in their effort to make the principle of institutional settlement a universal principle, stressed that the usefulness of their theory of law did not depend on the substantive morality of the legal system to which it was applied:

> Are the positions which have been taken thus far in these materials conventional and generally acceptable? Might a representative chairman of the Republican National Committee, for example, be expected to agree with them? A chairman of the Democratic National Committee? A representative union leader? A representative president of the United States Chamber of Commerce? Of the American Bar Association? A representative member of the Soviet Russian Politburo? A younger professor of anthropology in an American university representative of the most recent trend of thought in this field? Of economics? History? Philosophy? Political Science? Psychology? Sociology?[231]

[230]   See H.L.A. Hart, *Positivism and the Separation of Law and Morals*.
[231]   Hart and Sacks, *TLP*, at 113.

It is true that this passage did not explicitly reject the coherence thesis, but it seems clear that, unlike Fuller, Hart and Sacks were not confident that one could assume that any substantive set of aims could not conform to the theory of law set out in *The Legal Process*. In the one place where Hart and Sacks discussed H.L.A. Hart – a lengthy footnote – they took Hart's definition of duty and made it even more positivistic by arguing that one does not need to identify the purpose of a duty in order to define what a duty is.[232]

4.7. INSTITUTIONAL SETTLEMENT AND PLURALISM

The key to the mystery concerning Hart and Sacks, Fuller, and legal positivism is the principle of institutional settlement. It was not defended by Hart and Sacks on the ground that it would necessarily produce just results. It was defended on the basis that it would help society produce the results that the society wanted: first by guaranteeing stability and second by producing a mechanism through which society's ends could be achieved. Without the coherence thesis, the principle of institutional settlement was just an instrument of technical competence. It is likely that Hart and Sacks believed, like Fuller, that duly organized social institutions would produce

---

[232] Hart and Sacks argued that the following is a perfectly adequate definition of the concept of a "duty": "A duty is a position of a person in relation to an authoritative directive arrangement in which the person is obliged to do something, or not to do it, or do it if at all only in a particular way, subject to some officially imposed disadvantage for failure to comply." Hart and Sacks, *TLP*, at 128–9 n5. There is other evidence of nascent sympathies between H.L.A. Hart and Henry Hart. During his visit to Harvard, H.L.A. Hart participated in the Legal Philosophy Discussion Group at the law school (which seemed to be administered that year by Julius Stone). H.L.A. Hart presented a paper entitled "Discretion" in which he distinguished between "Avowed Discretion" and "Tacit Discretion" in a way that paralleled the distinction between continuing and noncontinuing discretion in *The Legal Process*. See H.L.A. Hart, "Discretion" 11 (November 19, 1956) (unpublished manuscript, on file with the Harvard University Law School Library). Hart also argued that one reason why discretion was a necessary part of law is that the law cannot precisely capture the purposes of the law makers (what Hart called the problem of "Indeterminacy of Aim"). Id., at 12. The indeterminacy of aim argument anticipated Hart's later dispute with Fuller over whether the legal norms had to be teleological in the way suggested by the morality of law. (Hart even used the example of a rule "excluding vehicles from the park," which would reappear as his chief example in *Positivism and the Separation of Law and Morals*.) Henry Hart thereafter gave a talk in which, in his notes, he explicitly refers approvingly to H.L.A. Hart's paper and especially to the concept of the indeterminacy of aim. See Henry Hart, "The Place of Discretion in the Legal System" 2 (November 20, 1956) (unpublished manuscript, on file with the Harvard University Law School Library).

just results. But as we have seen, it is equally likely that Hart and Sacks did not agree with Fuller that one could guarantee just results through legal arrangements alone. What must be explained is what it was that could have led Hart and Sacks to ignore the problems raised by their rejection of the coherence thesis. Why, for example, were they not more concerned that the principles of *The Legal Process* might be used for substantively evil ends?

The answer to this question can be found by looking outside of law and at the dominant theory of political science and political sociology during the 1950s. The reason why Hart and Sacks were not worried by the fact that they agreed with H.L.A. Hart and not Fuller with regard to the coherence thesis is that they thought that the protective role that Fuller attributed to law was actually being played by the political theory of pluralism.[233] As Neil Duxbury has noted, there is more than a passing similarity between the structure and concerns of political science during the 1950s and legal process.[234] Pluralism provided a theory of intergroup competition that could explain how a political system could maintain a permanent set of procedures for identifying and maximizing valid human wants in a world that had accepted relativism. Pluralism was the result of the confluence of two trends in social thought that had developed during the early twentieth century: pragmatism and interest-group political science.

Pragmatists (especially John Dewey) had argued against philosophical absolutism on a variety of fronts including aesthetics, ethics, metaphysics, and political theory.[235] In *Reconstruction in Philosophy*, Dewey analogized between absolutism in thinking and authoritarianism in politics and argued that the same reasons for adopting democracy compelled us to adopt relativism, which was

---

[233] See Gary Minda, *Postmodern Legal Movements* 34 (1995) and Kalman, *The Strange Career of Legal Liberalism*, at 25–6.

[234] Duxbury, *Patterns of American Jurisprudence*, at 242–8; and see Edward A. Purcell Jr., *The Crisis of Democratic Theory: Scientific Naturalism and the Problem of Value* 203–9 (1973). For a comprehensive account of the interrelationships among political sociology, pluralist political science, and legal process in postwar America, see David M. Weber, *Reasoned Elaborations: Consensus Liberalism, Legal Process, and the Discourse of Democracy, 1950–1962* (1996) (Ph.D. dissertation, University of California, Los Angeles).

[235] John Dewey, *Ethics* (1908, revised 1932); John Dewey, *Democracy and Education* (1916); John Dewey, *The Quest for Certainty* (1919); John Dewey, *Human Nature and Conduct* (1922); John Dewey, *Experience and Nature* (1925); John Dewey, *Reconstruction in Philosophy* (1930); John Dewey, *Art as Experience* (1934).

simply the "democracy of individual facts equal in rank."[236] The advent of fascism gave pragmatists proof of the connection between absolutism and authoritarianism, and conversely, of the connection between relativism and democracy. As Purcell noted, for the pragmatists "democracy was therefore justified, not because anyone could prove or demonstrate certain ethical propositions, but because the idea of an absolute moral demonstration was itself a rational impossibility."[237]

Even before philosophers like Dewey were developing the theoretical connections between relativism and democracy, political scientists were developing a theory of American democracy based on the struggle of interest groups. Beginning in the Progressive era, political scientists shattered the static nineteenth-century formalist model of society by observing that political power behaved dynamically, flowing away or toward groups depending on various conditions, including the activities of the state and the laws it imposed.[238] Arthur Bentley, in his influential book *The Process of Government*, stressed the fundamental role that groups played in American democracy.[239] According to the interest-group theory of democracy, whichever groups controlled the political system defined the terms in which group competition would occur: "It is these group pressures, indeed, that not only make but also *maintain* in values the very standards of justice, truth, or what not that reason may claim to use as its guides."[240] One consequence of this new approach to politics was the complete abandonment of the idea that democracy was necessarily about the identification and influence of the "ma-

---

[236] Dewey, *Reconstruction in Philosophy*, at 65–6; see also Alan Ryan, *John Dewey and the High Tide of American Liberalism* 230–1 (1995), and see Hilary Putnam, *A Reconsideration of Deweyan Democracy*, 63 S. Cal. L. Rev. 1671, 1696 (1990) (on Dewey's "radical democracy").

[237] Purcell, *Crisis of Democratic Theory*, at 205 and see Robert Booth Fowler, *Believing Skeptics: American Political Intellectuals, 1945–1964*, 121 (1978) (pragmatism's value-relativism was most attractive when it was placed in opposition to totalitarianism).

[238] See Herbert Croly, *The Promise of American Life* 281 (1909); and see Charles Beard, *An Economic Interpretation of the Constitution of the United States* (1913); Walter Lippmann, *The Phantom Public* (1925). On the relationship between the rise of value-relativism and the assault on formalism in the social sciences, see Purcell, *Crisis of Democratic Theory*, at 15–46 and Stephen M. Feldman, *Republican Revival/Interpretive Turn*, 1992 Wis. L. Rev. 679, 683 (1992).

[239] Arthur Bentley, *The Process of Government*, 225 (1949, originally published in 1908) ("[w]hen the groups are adequately stated, everything is stated").

[240] Bentley, *Process of Government*, at 447.

jority," as opposed to government by numerically small but politically influential groups.[241]

The pragmatists and political scientists who wrote before World War II were skeptics whose work challenged the status quo in America. Like the legal realists, they came under fierce attack from scholars based in Catholic universities, as well as from secular idealists like Robert Maynard Hutchins, the president of the University of Chicago.[242] Although the war may have strengthened the resolve of philosophical relativists like Dewey, the spread of fascism forced his followers to defend themselves against the charge that they were weakening, not defending, democracy. Just as the war had given new life to the critics of legal realism, pragmatists in the social sciences confronted a challenge similar to that posed to the legal realists: Could a theory based on relativism provide a bulwark against totalitarianism?[243]

The theory of pluralism arose from the need of social scientists to reinterpret the elements of pragmatism and interest-group politics into a theory that could explain, justify, and even celebrate American democracy. The twin pillars of pluralism were value relativism and group conflict. Political scientists like Robert Dahl and David Truman saw the relativity of value as a positive source of stability in a democracy. The fact that people differed in their fundamental views of the good meant that it would be more difficult for any one view to tyrannize the others: "a relatively high degree of group autonomy combined with a relatively high degree of disagreement over goals will act as an important limitation on the capacity of any putative majority to control government policy."[244] The fact that individuals were molded by broad economic and social forces into groups was also a positive source of stability, because in a modern

---

[241]   See, for example, Charles Merriam, *Political Power* 31 (1934); Harold D. Lasswell, *Politics: Who Gets What, When, How* 13 (1958, originally published in 1936).

[242]   Purcell, *Crisis of Democratic Theory*, at 180–1 (on Thomistic social science) and 147–9 (on Hutchins).

[243]   See John G. Gunnell, *The Descent of Political Theory: The Genealogy of an American Vocation* 129 (1993) and Purcell, *Crisis of Democratic Theory*, at 235. As Purcell noted, during the postwar period political theory witnessed a fierce war of words between two camps: the liberal relativists (represented by the pluralists) and the conservative absolutists (represented, most famously, by Leo Strauss); yet by the midsixties it was clear that the latter group had lost. Ibid., at 327.

[244]   Dahl, *Preface to Democratic Theory*, at 79 (1956) and see David B. Truman, *The Governmental Process: Political Interests and Public Opinion* (2d ed., 1971, originally published 1951).

society (with mass media and mass democracy), only through groups could individuals express their interests.[245] Dahl crafted a theory of group competition, which he called polyarchy, that explained how the pursuit of political power by groups actually produced moderation in democratic systems in a way that externally imposed norms or principles of justice never could.[246]

Pluralism was clearly well suited to the mood of American scholars in the 1950s: It defended American democracy by arguing that group conflict and value relativism were the best defense against totalitarianism.[247] The question still remained, however, why, in a democratic system that rejected *a priori* principles of justice, majority rule would never generate unjust (even antidemocratic) results. The pluralists' answer to this question was not that a democracy could be protected from failure by laws and constitutions: They clearly rejected Fuller's procedural natural law approach.[248] If democracies were to resist collapse into majority tyranny, it would be because of the health of the democracy's nonlegal institutions.

Democratic pluralism was a product not of laws but of culture: "without these social checks and balances, it is doubtful that the intragovernmental checks on officials would in fact operate to prevent tyranny. . . ."[249] Truman referred to the norms that permitted pluralism to flourish as the "political culture" and argued that what made these norms effective was that they were "pervasive and generally accepted."[250] A shared culture enabled Americans to "combat the weaknesses of human nature and to correct the natural defects of democracy."[251] William Kornhauser argued that in America, "intermediate organizations" made it difficult for elites to control any large portion of the nonelite population, thus preventing the sort of antidemocratic politics of mass culture that occurred in both Ger-

---

[245] Truman, *Governmental Process*, at 46. Dewey made a similar argument just before the start of World War II began. See John Dewey, *Freedom and Culture*, 56 (1963, originally published in 1939).

[246] See Dahl, *Preface to Democratic Theory*, at 78 and Purcell, *Crisis of Democratic Theory*, at 260–1.

[247] See Feldman, *Republican Revival*, at 685.

[248] Dahl, *Preface to Democratic Theory*, at 18.

[249] Ibid., at 22; see also Gabriel A. Almond and Sidney Verba, *The Civic Culture: An Analytic Study of Political Attitudes in Five Nations* 366 (1965) ("unless the political culture is able to support a democratic system, the chances for the success of that system are slim").

[250] Truman, *Governmental Process*, at 513.

[251] Ibid., at 311.

many and Russia.[252] The political culture upon which the pluralists relied was not like the natural law of either Fuller or the Neo-Scholastics, because it was not a transcendental norm that could be used to criticize society without some shared empirical judgments.[253]

The pluralists found support for their sociological assumptions in the work of Talcott Parsons. Parsons "treated societies as wholes, emphasizing their self-maintenance as systems and their efforts at collective goal-attainment. . . . [His] wholly descriptive focus deprived it [sociology] of any basis for social criticism."[254] Parsons believed that American society, which was highly relativist, could resist totalitarianism because America's individualist and capitalist social order had been rationalized.[255] Parsons applied Max Weber's theory of bureaucracy to twentieth-century America and concluded that modern capitalism's values of instrumentalism and expertise provided a set of ultimate ends. Parsons did not deny the deep roots of individualism in American society: He turned it on its head, making it the source of consensus. Individual action in American society was not "amoral undisciplined greed for gain" but rather "systematic, continuous rational honest work in the service of economic acquisition."[256] Like Dahl, Parsons found a set of important antitotalitarian values in certain "scientific" principles that were not ideological and hence were not tainted with the stain of sectarian debate.[257] That is why, as one critic argued a decade later, the pluralists were able to convince themselves that the preservation and promotion of liberal democracy was not itself a normative value judgment: Their idea of political culture was based on "the tacit assumption that reasonable men agree on what constituted the fundamental procedures of democracy."[258]

---

[252] William Kornhauser, *The Politics of Mass Society*, 99–100 (1959).

[253] According to Putnam, contemporary critics have failed to appreciate the extent to which Dewey rejected transcendental arguments for democracy. Dewey thought that the only arguments that could be made to an antidemocratic despot were empirical and that if the method of pragmatism were properly applied, empirical arguments should be sufficient. Putnam, *A Reconsideration of Deweyan Democracy*, at 1687–8.

[254] Purcell, *Crisis of Democratic Theory*, at 262, and see Talcott Parsons, *The Structure of Social Action* (1937).

[255] See William Buxton, *Talcott Parsons and the Capitalist Nation-State: Political Sociology as a Strategic Vocation* 33–5 (1985).

[256] Ibid., at 62 (citing Parsons, *The Structure of Social Action*, at 515–16).

[257] See Dahl, *A Preface to Democratic Theory*, at 75–7.

[258] Peter Bacharach, *The Theory of Democratic Elitism: A Critique* 52 (1967).

Pluralism had its own version of the coherence thesis, but it was not Fuller's version.[259] Whereas Fuller believed that the imposition of procedural natural law would prevent the law from being used for evil ends, the pluralists believed (perhaps naïvely) that the right sort of political culture would prevent the law from being used for antidemocratic ends.[260] Paul Freund argued that in a pluralist system, "intermediate principles of democracy" would substitute for dogmatic faiths.[261] American pluralism "fortunately avoid[ed] any commitment to theories of truth or any alliance with schools of skepticism or belief" and therefore fostered antitotalitarian values.[262]

Whether or not the pluralists' belief in the power of political culture to protect democracy was any more plausible than Fuller's belief in the power of openness and prospectivity is a profound question that is tangential to the question we are trying to answer. On the other hand, it is important to recognize that Hart and Sacks could have adopted the pluralist belief about political culture without in any way compromising their commitment to legal positivism. The political culture to which the pluralists referred was a contingent social fact that they believed existed in the United States and could be developed elsewhere. Fuller, on the other hand, believed "that human beings are equally devoted to and united in their conception of aims (the pursuit of knowledge, justice to their fellow men) . . . and that these dictate a further necessary content to a legal system."[263] Assuming that Hart and Sacks were influenced

[259] "Thus Fuller objected to those political theories popular in his day, such as interest group pluralism, that viewed politics in terms of power." Bone, *Lon Fuller's Theory of Adjudication and the False Dichotomy Between Dispute Resolution and Public Law Models of Litigation*, at 1288 n50 (citing Lon L. Fuller, "On Legal Education," in *The Principles of Social Order* 277–81 [Kenneth I. Winston, ed., 1981]).
[260] "Truman is unable to explain how elites themselves might be kept within constitutional bounds." Duxbury, *Patterns of American Jurisprudence*, at 246.
[261] Paul Freund, *The Supreme Court of the United States: Its Business, Purposes, and Performance* 82 (3rd. ed., 1972, first published in 1949). Freund's argument is very similar to Cass Sunstein's concept of the "incompletely theorized agreement." See Cass Sunstein, *Incompletely Theorized Agreements*, 108 Harv. L. Rev. 1733 (1995).
[262] Freund, *The Supreme Court of the United States*, at 82. According to another influential pluralist, "the tendency to abstract the principles of political life . . . becomes idolatry when it provides statesmen or a people with a blueprint for their society . . . [and] one of the many good fortunes of American civilization has been the happy coincidence of circumstances which has led us away from such idolatry." Daniel Boorstin, *The Genius of American Politics* 3 (1954).
[263] Hart, *Positivism and the Separation of Law and Morals*, at 623. Hart was summarizing the difference between his views and Fuller's. Furthermore, the value-rela-

by pluralism, then one reason why they were not concerned over the fact that they did not accept the coherence thesis is that pluralism offered the same result as the coherence thesis, but through a different set of premises.[264] If pluralism was correct, then the rejection of the coherence thesis would not necessarily mean that legal process would have to explain how American law could resist capture by groups intent on promoting injustice. The question did not seem very pressing in the 1950s because, according to pluralism, the capture of the legal system by injustice could occur only if the political culture as a whole dramatically changed, which was a matter for the sociologist, not the legal theorist. From Hart and Sacks's perspective, pluralism moved the problem that the coherence thesis was designed to solve out of law, thus leaving to jurisprudence the smaller but more tractable problems addressed by the theory of reasoned elaboration.

4.8. CONCLUSION

The overall view endorsed by the various arguments contained in the Harvard Forewords and the theory of law developed in *The Legal Process* is that reasoned elaboration demands that the law applier engage in a self-conscious search for the limits of discretion set out in the law. This view explains how a law applier should view his or her task *if* the architects of a given society have chosen to employ a legal system that contains a complex ordering of discretion, as opposed to a relatively simple, almost invisible, legal system in which there is no attempt to control discretion through reasoned elaboration. It is not yet clear, however, given that a legal system could privilege one or the other form of social organization, why we would want to emphasize the practice of reasoned elaboration. As discussed previously, reasoned elaboration imposes two duties on the decision maker. The first is consistency or uniformity: "the

---

tivism that formed part of the foundation of pluralism was utterly incompatible with Fuller's antirelativism.

[264] There is little extant evidence of Hart and Sacks's reading or general views on political science in the 1950s, but it is likely that Hart and Sacks, who were part of the academic status quo, would have embraced the status quo's reigning ideology. Gary Minda has argued that there is a theoretical relationship between the pluralist theory of democracy and the role that reasoned elaboration plays in Hart and Sacks's private law theory. See Minda, *Postmodern Legal Movements,* at 35 (1995).

idea that like cases should be treated alike."[265] The second is that the decision maker try to understand the *purpose* behind a legal argument before attempting to apply it: "[E]very statute and every doctrine of unwritten law developed by the decisional process has some kind of purpose or objective, however difficult it may be on occasion to ascertain it or agree exactly how it should be phrased."[266]

These two values of reasoned elaboration – consistency and purpose – are necessary assumptions to understanding a norm as a law, because they are the essential features of a legal system. The desirability of treating norms as laws instead of one of the other forms described by Fuller (such as managerial dictate or arbitration) depends on the extent to which a society wants to organize its social life around the essential features of reasoned elaboration. Given what was said earlier about the necessity for some general directive arrangements in social systems, the question is about matters of degree. If a society is to enjoy the benefits of law, then every decision, including those that seem to allow the decision maker continuing discretion, is regulated by a legal process whose application did not itself allow for continuing discretion. Even a president exercising executive privilege when choosing an appointee is acting under a thin layer of noncontinuing discretion.[267] Hart and Sacks's argument, however, was based on more than just the observation that discretion is an inevitable feature of law. They argued that law is a good thing precisely because of (not in spite of) the fact that it is a mechanism for harnessing discretion: "Discretion is a vehicle of good far more than evil; [i]t is the only means by which the intelligence and good will of a society can be brought to bear directly upon the solution of hitherto unsolved problems."[268]

The relationship between the tenets of reasoned elaboration derived from the Harvard Forewords and the underlying theory of law developed by Hart and Sacks reviewed in the foregoing sections should now be somewhat more clear. Hart and Sacks grounded their rejection of "political" decision making on the distinction between continuing and noncontinuing discretion. Judicial decision making should be constrained by law; judges should not rely on the sort of reasons used by legislators. The rejection of "judi-

---

[265] Hart and Sacks, *TLP,* at 116.
[266] Ibid., at 166.
[267] Ibid., at 144.
[268] Ibid., at 158.

cial statesmanship" was based on the two values of reasoned elaboration. To deny *certiorari* in one case and not in another when the
two were alike from the perspective of legal principle violated the
requirement of treating like cases alike. To generate summary reversals without any explanation betrayed the underlying principle that
each law has a purpose (in the form of either a principle or a policy)
to which a judge can relate his or her decision. Finally, the recommendation that the Court take advantage of the "maturing of collective thought" was based on Hart and Sacks's claim that law is a
set of general directive arrangements that can "speak from one
point in time to another" – that is, that there is some meaning which
laws convey, and that the interpreters of that meaning can get it
right or wrong.[269]

It seems, therefore, that Hart was taking his jurisprudence seriously in the 1959 Foreword. He really believed that judges can identify and act upon the principles and policies embedded in the law;
further, he believed that those principles and policies can really
constrain those judges. Thus Hart's hope that more careful deliberation would help produce "better" decisions was rooted in what he
wrote in *The Legal Process.* Judges could do better or worse, *qua* legal
reasoning, depending on how faithfully they interpreted and
obeyed the principles and policies embedded in the law.

[269] Ibid., at 124.

Chapter 5

The False Choice Between
the Warren Court and Legal Process

Thus far, the theory of reasoned elaboration seems both workable and attractive. Yet it is apparent that despite the presence of *The Legal Process* in the Harvard curriculum, its reputation as a theoretical text and even a teaching material has declined.[1] Not only has Hart and Sacks's theory lost its audience, but it has developed a distinct and unsavory reputation as a theory steeped in "conservatism and procedural fetishism."[2] One might wonder how *The Legal Process* came to merit this reputation; the answer is found in the fact that in the eyes of many observers, Hart and Sacks's theory met "a formidable opponent" – and not an ally – "in the Warren Court."[3] Thus, we must turn toward an episode in the history of legal process that, although central to the argument of this book, has not yet been mentioned: Herbert Wechsler and the theory of neutral principles.

Wechsler's 1959 Holmes Lecture, entitled *Towards Neutral Principles of Constitutional Law,* was published at the same time as Hart's Foreword.[4] It is probably the most important of the legal process writings, not because it is the best (clearly *The Legal Process* itself

---

[1] The legal process movement had been "sapped, if not altogether drained . . . [of its]vitality" since the 1960s. Vincent A. Wellman, *Dworkin and the Legal Process Tradition: The Legacy of Hart and Sacks* 29 *Ariz. L. Rev.* 413, 473 (1987). By the 1980s the movement had "collapsed." William N. Eskridge Jr. and Gary Peller, *The New Public Law Movement: Moderation as a Postmodern Cultural Form,* 89 *Mich. L. Rev.* 707, 710, 743 (1991).

[2] Norman Dorsen, In Memoriam: Albert M. Sacks, 105 *Harv. L. Rev.* 1, 12 (1991).

[3] Jan Vetter, *Postwar Legal Scholarship on Judicial Decision Making,* 30 *J. Legal. Educ.* 412, 414 (1983). See also G. Edward White, *Patterns of American Legal Thought* 150 (1978) ("Reasoned education was incompatible with the brand of activism that emerged in the Warren Court").

[4] Herbert Wechsler, *Towards Neutral Principles of Constitutional Law,* 73 *Harv. L. Rev.* 1 (1959) (hereafter Wechsler, *Neutral Principles*).

best expresses its own theory) but because it applied reasoned elaboration to the most pressing problem in constitutional law at the time – racial equality under the federal constitution – and, by assuming that challenge, drew the attention of a wide audience of lawyers and nonlawyers.[5] Because Wechsler used a version of reasoned elaboration to criticize the Supreme Court's performance in cases involving the white primary,[6] the enforcement of racially restrictive covenants,[7] and the segregation of public education,[8] his essay became an infamous symbol of the legal process school's hostility to civil rights. In my opinion, the essay prejudiced an entire generation of liberal scholars to the point where few chose to look past Wechsler's presentation of reasoned elaboration before rejecting the project out of hand.

In *Neutral Principles,* Wechsler employed reasoned elaboration to answer Judge Learned Hand's charge, made a year earlier, that judicial review by the Supreme Court should be exercised only within very narrow limits.[9] Wechsler rejected Hand's extreme theory of judicial restraint. The Court, argued Wechsler, "cannot escape the duty of deciding whether actions of the other branches of the government are consistent with the Constitution."[10] He questioned the criteria that could justify the Court's exercise of judicial review. The question that Wechsler asked is not necessarily unique to constitutional cases. It is a question of adjudication applicable to any occasion where a court applies a law. Wechlser's argument in response to Hand began with Wechsler's denouncing the idea that a judge should choose a result based merely on its outcome, because that would turn the courts into "naked power organs," not courts of law.[11] The essential element to legal reasoning was that "it must be

---

[5] Some years later, Wechsler commented he doubted that he would have "provoked substantial disagreement" had he not tested his theory against the Fourteenth Amendment. Herbert Wechsler, "The Nature of Judicial Reasoning," in *Law and Philosophy* 290, 294 (S. Hook, ed., 1964).

[6] *Smith v. Allwright,* 321 U.S. 649 (1944).

[7] *Shelley v. Kraemer,* 334 U.S. 1 (1948); *Barrows v. Jackson,* 346 U.S. 249 (1953).

[8] *Brown v. Board of Education,* 347 U.S. 483 (1954).

[9] Learned Hand, *The Bill of Rights* (1958). For an excellent discussion of Hand's theory of judicial review, see Gerald Gunther, *Learned Hand* 226–72 (1994).

[10] Wechsler, *Neutral Principles* at 10.

[11] Ibid., at 12. Wechsler did not specify who endorses the view that judges should decide cases according to their political preferences, but because he cited to Fuller in developing it, I assume that Wechsler attributed this view to the various instrumentally oriented realists, such as Cook and Oliphant, whom Fuller attacked. See Lon L. Fuller, *Reason and Fiat in Case Law, 59 Harv. L. Rev.* 376 (1946).

genuinely principled, resting with respect to every step that is involved in reaching judgment on analysis and reasons quite transcending the immediate result that is achieved."[12]

There were four elements to Wechsler's idea of neutral principles. First, judges should not decide a certain way because they approve of the results of the verdict. Second, judges must test their neutrality by ensuring that cases like the one at hand have been decided in a similar fashion, as would be "others that the principles imply."[13] Third, although a principle (or policy) *in* a law may be the result of a political process and may reflect political interests, judges must not decide whether to apply[14] that political principle (or policy) on the basis of reasons unrelated to the political ends of that principle (or policy). Fourth and finally, the reasons judges may use to apply the principles (or policies) found in the law must be presented in a form of reasoned explanation unlike the sort of justifications required of politicians.[15]

Wechsler's theory of neutral principles was rooted in the theory of reasoned elaboration. The demand that judges not decide because they approve of the *effects* of their decisions was a practical application of Jaffe's caution against political judging and Hart and Sacks's distinction between continuous and noncontinuous discretion. The demand that judges test themselves to see if they have decided a case the same way they have decided other cases, like criticisms of the Court's seemingly political use of *certiorari* and *per curiam*, was another practical application of Hart and Sacks's distinction between continuing and noncontinuing discretion. The recognition that the principles or policies judges have to apply neutrally are themselves not neutral but the result of politics simply repeated Hart and Sacks's point that the purpose of adjudication was to discover where law ends and the realm of continuing discretion begins. Finally, the demand that judges publicly explain their reasoning was, as has been pointed out in section 4.2, one of Hart's main points: There are norms embedded in the law for judges to discover, and the dual pressures of public explanation and thorough review helps push judges toward better (more accurate) discoveries.

---

[12] Wechsler, *Neutral Principles*, at 15.
[13] Ibid.
[14] Wechsler in fact used the word *application*. Ibid., at 15.
[15] Ibid., at 16.

According to these criteria, the Supreme Court had not succeeded in deciding according to neutral principles in civil rights cases. As if borrowing from the Forewords, Wechsler noted that the Court had disposed of important cases through opaque *per curiam* opinions.[16] The most important test of the Court's performance according to neutral principles, however, came when Wechsler discussed the reasoning contained in the written opinions in a number of major race cases. With regard to the white primary cases, Wechsler asked whether the principle upon which the Court based its decision could be extended to parties that excluded on the basis of religion. If not, he asked rhetorically, could anyone then be "able to discover in the opinions thus far written in support of this result [the prohibition of all-white parties] . . . neutral principles that satisfy the mind[?]"[17] In the case of restrictive covenants, Wechsler could not see how the decision in *Shelley v. Kraemer* could not be logically extended to cases that Wechsler was sure the Court would not affirm. Thus, he declared that in the absence of "a principle susceptible of broad extensions . . . I do not hesitate to say that I prefer to see the issue faced through legislation, where there is room for drawing lines that courts are not equipped to draw."[18]

Finally, with regard to the school segregation cases, Wechsler – with a heavy heart, he claimed – criticized the reasoning of *Brown v. Board of Education.* The Court, he said, was disingenuous: It really meant to say that racial segregation was, in principle, a denial of equality, whereas the Court made it sound as if its decision was based on the force of empirical fact. Wechsler was concerned that the argument that racial segregation was in principle unconstitutional could not be upheld without infringing the bigot's constitutional right not to associate. He thought that someone should be able to identify a principle in the Constitution whose neutral application would result in placing a black citizen's right to integration

---

[16] Wechsler reviewed the *per curiam* disposal of five censorship cases and noted that if the Court could not come to an agreement in these cases of obvious importance, "[i]s it not preferable . . . indeed, essential, that if this is so the variations of position be disclosed?" Ibid., at 21. He then made the same critique of the Court's extension of the antisegregation principle in *Brown* to public facilities such as parks and pools by *per curiam* decision. Ibid., at 22.

[17] Ibid., at 29.

[18] Ibid., at 31.

over the bigot's right to associate only with white citizens, "but," he said, "I confess that I have not yet written the opinion."[19]

5.2. CRITICAL REACTION TO NEUTRAL PRINCIPLES

Because of his criticisms of the race cases, Wechsler's essay became notorious; furthermore, because he was seen as applying Hart and Sacks's principles, Wechsler was seen as speaking for the legal process school. This perception is unfortunate because his discussion of reasoned elaboration was incomplete, and his application of it to the race cases was simply wrong.

There were four types of response to Wechsler's article. The first group, the realist critics, rejected the concept of neutral principles in its entirety, and not just its application to the race cases. The second group, the internal critics, took issue with Wechsler's criticism of the race cases; they thought he had misunderstood the principles upon which they were being decided. The third group, the conservative critics, took Wechsler's argument and turned it into an argument for "judicial restraint." The fourth group, the liberal critics (or fundamental rights school), attacked Wechsler's theory from the perspective of the larger project of the Warren Court.

The realist critics recapitulated the debate we have already seen in the Forewords. They had four main criticisms. The first was that Wechsler was wrong that judges should not be concerned for the consequences of their decisions. Thus, Eugene Rostow declared that, "Wechsler's lecture . . . represents a repudiation of all we have learned about law since Holmes . . . and Pound [with their] . . . pathbreaking pleas for a result-oriented, sociological jurisprudence, rather than a mechanical one."[20] Second, the realists rejected the demand of generality. Addison Mueller and Murray Schwartz argued that the term

> "[G]enerality" leads nowhere. A decision holding a statute which forbids all Negroes to drive automobiles is unconstitutional because it discriminates against Negroes enunciates a reason which is general. The question is: Is it adequately general? The next question must be:

---

[19]   Ibid., at 34.
[20]   Eugene W. Rostow, *The Sovereign Prerogative* 28 (1962).

Adequate for what purpose? The answer would seem to be: general enough to be neutral.[21]

Third, the realists challenged Wechsler's claim that, as happened in the school segregation cases, where two constitutional principles were in conflict, a unifying neutral principle must be found to mediate between them. Thus, Mueller and Schwartz produced the following explanation for why the Supreme Court would never be able to satisfy Wechsler's test for legitimacy: "The difficulty we have found is that there will *always* be a point at which an extension of the logic of any constitutional principle of decision will run into the similarly extended logic of competing principles."[22] A court trying to apply Wechsler's theory would therefore always be faced with either choosing one constitutional principle over another for nonlegal reasons, or doing nothing, which in effect would be a backhanded endorsement of the constitutional choices of others. Fourth, the realists argued that Wechsler's demand for generality was a sham because what counts as "sufficient" generality in Wechsler's model is determined not by legal reasoning but by reference to current public sentiment. Jan Deutsch therefore argued that "since one man's 'relatively fundamental rules of right'" may well be another person's "particular set of ethical or economic options . . . historical context may well determine the proper classification of a given principle as either a 'fundamental right' or a 'particular opinion.'"[23] Thus, neutral principles that were supposed to constrain the judge or the majority were inevitably defined by a judge or the majority.[24]

---

[21] Addison Mueller and Murray L. Schwartz, *The Principle of Neutral Principles,* 7 *UCLA L. Rev.* 571, 577 (1960) ("[Wechsler] must not insist, therefore, on decision based on principles that push value choices beyond the realm of choice"). For similar reasons, Arthur S. Miller of Emory Law School and Ronald Howell, a political scientist at Emory, who saw themselves as building on the realists' work, rejected Wechsler's use of the word *neutrality* in relation to constitutional adjudication. They cited scholarship from various disciplines outside law to demonstrate that "neutrality or objectivity was essentially impossible of attainment." Arthur S. Miller and Ronald F. Howell, *The Myth of Neutrality in Constitutional Adjudication,* 27 *U. Chi. L. Rev.* 661, 676 (1960).

[22] Mueller and Schwartz, *Principle of Neutral Principles* at 586; also see Jan G. Deutsch, *Neutrality, Legitimacy and the Supreme Court: Some Intersections Between Law and Political Science,* 20 *Stan. L. Rev.* 169, 192–3 (1968).

[23] Deutsch, *Neutrality, Legitimacy and the Supreme Court,* at 195.

[24] In labeling these reactions to Wechsler's essay "realist," I do not mean to diminish the importance of the behavioralist study of public law that was beginning to reach maturity in the late 1950s. To take but one example, it is clear that the work of

184

The internal critics were those who were either sympathetic or indifferent to Wechsler's theory of law and objected only to his specific application of it to the race cases. Louis Pollak, in his first article on Wechsler, endorsed the theory of neutral principles.[25] He even conceded that in the white primary and restrictive covenant cases, the Court could have been more forthcoming with principles that covered cases that were not before them; he thought he could provide them.[26] In the restrictive covenant case, Pollak argued that the principle should have been that the state cannot "assist a private person in seeing to it that others behave in a fashion which the state could not itself have ordained."[27] With regard to the all white primary, Pollak argued that the Court had the right principle but had picked the wrong amendment on which to base its decision: "[T]he [Fifteenth] Amendment must impose on the states a heavier

Glendon Schubert applied a realist point of view in that it emphasized that value preferences and policy attitudes determined judicial decisions. Schubert's understanding of the Constitution was similar to that of the older realists: From a behavioral standpoint, the Constitution is what a majority of justices agree it ought to be said to mean, or what the president or Congress may declare by speech or action. In an even broader sense, Schubert held that the Constitution is embedded in "the consensually dominant patterns of values that constitute American political ideology." Glendon Schubert, *Quantitative Analysis of Judicial Behavior* 2 (1959); see also Glendon Schubert, *The Rhetoric of Constitutional Change*, 16 J. Pub. L. 38 (1967); Glendon Schubert, *The Future of Public Law*, 34 Geo. Wash. L. Rev. 593 (1966). The new realism, wrote Martin Shapiro, "was basically an attempt to treat the Supreme Court as one government agency among many – as part of the American political process, rather than as a unique body of impervious legal technicians above and beyond the political struggle." Martin Shapiro, *Law and Politics in the Supreme Court: New Approaches to Political Jurisprudence* 21 (1964).

On the other hand, Peller argued that the techniques of behavioralism and other forms of "value-free" social science were inextricably interrelated with the legal process school's project of legitimizing the sort of pluralism portrayed in Daniel Bell's theory of the "end of ideology." See Gary Peller, *Neutral Principles in the 1950s*, 21 U. Mich. J. L. Ref. 561, 585 (1988) (citing Daniel Bell, *The End of Ideology: On the Exhaustion of Political Ideas in the Fifties* [1960]). At the end of Chapter 4 I argued that there was a close connection between legal process and pluralism, and so I am inclined to agree with Peller that Schubert's behavioralism was at least as much a product of legal process as it was a vestige of realism.

[25] "No attempt is here made to dissent with Professor Wechsler's concept of neutrality of constitutional adjudication." Louis H. Pollak, *Racial Discrimination and Judicial Integrity: A Reply to Professor Wechsler*, 108 U. Pa. L. Rev. 1, 5 (1959).

[26] It is interesting to note that some of Wechsler's more realist critics attacked Pollak for stating that "if the Court decisions in recent race cases 'are not supportable on the basis of neutral constitutional principles, they deserve to be jettisoned.'" Miller and Howell, *Myth of Neutrality* at 682 (citing Pollak, *Racial Discrimination and Judicial Integrity*, at 31).

[27] Pollak, *Racial Discrimination and Judicial Integrity*, at 23.

affirmative duty than does the Fourteenth," and therefore all-white parties may be unconstitutional whereas all-Catholic parties are not.[28]

Further, Pollak conceded that the Warren Court's attempt to decide *Brown* on the basis of the claim that separate education entailed unequal education was doomed to failure. Pollak rewrote the opinion (literally), basing the wrong of segregation on the stigma it currently produced in America, and on the fact that the equal protection clause of the Fourteenth Amendment was designed to forbid the use of state power to stigmatize blacks, who were (when the amendment was written) newly freed from slavery.[29] While this is not the proper place to engage in a lengthy review of Pollak's arguments, it seems that, in retrospect, he (as well as the other internal critics) had a better grasp of the implications of Wechsler's argument (as a matter of constitutional law) than Wechsler himself.

For example, Martin Golding, who called himself a "friendly critic" of Wechsler, argued that he could use neutral principles to support *Brown* "without overstretching Professor Wechsler's language."[30] Golding, like Pollak, thought that the Constitution contained a neutral principle that would prohibit segregated schools. Using an approach quite different from Pollak's, Golding attempted to use the equal protection language in *Cooper v. Aaron* to support the conclusion that "principled decision requires sameness of treatment in public education – unless some justification can be offered for the different treatment."[31]

Golding's methodological criticism of Wechsler suggests that he would have had Wechsler rethink the theory of neutral principles in a manner consistent with Hart and Sacks. Golding noted that in general, "principled legal judgment is not so much a matter of content as it is of form. . . . Principled judicial decision-making is possi-

---

[28] Ibid., at 13.

[29] Ibid., at 28; see also Louis Henkin, *Some Reflections on Current Constitutional Controversy*, 109 U. Pa. L. Rev. 637, 653 ("I, like Professor Pollak, believe that the particular cases which bother Professor Wechsler can be justified in 'neutral principles' although the Court perhaps did not do so effectively. But Professor Wechsler's basic thesis seems to me unchallengeable").

[30] Martin P. Golding, *Principled Decision-Making and the Supreme Court*, 63 Colum. L. Rev. 35, 36 (1963).

[31] Ibid., at 56, citing *Cooper v. Aaron*, 358 U.S. 1, 19 (1958) ("the right of a student not to be segregated on racial grounds in school so maintained is indeed so fundamental and pervasive that it is embraced in the concept of due process of law").

ble in a tyranny."[32] The question was not whether principled decision making was inconsistent with segregation but whether the
framers had delegated to the Court the task of balancing the principle of equality against the principle of freedom of association. Golding thought that Wechsler was right to note that the Supreme Court
was required to base its decision on values found only in the Constitution: "A legal system, then, may broadly fix the starting-points
of deliberation. . . . [Our legal system] has no higher guide than the
Constitution itself."[33] But Golding was baffled by Wechsler's claim
that a constitutional value must be so general that it never conflicts
with another constitutional value:

> I fail to grasp Professor Wechsler's position if it consists in the state-
> ment that one ought to, or even can, supply "neutral principles" for
> "choosing" between competing values. I can, of course, choose be-
> tween competing values by reference to a third value which is more
> comprehensive or supreme, that is, when there is an ordering of values.
>
>   . . .
>
> [But even where] a tribunal is faced with two competing values and
> there is no good reason to be advanced for preferring one value over
> another, so that the preference to one value is entirely arbitrary, if you
> please, we may still require that the tribunal formulate a standard or
> criterion that shall function as a principle of decision in this and other
> cases of its type. This principle is general in the sense that it covers but
> also transcends the instant case. It is not, of course, inherently "neutral"
> in any sense, except that there may be neutrality in its application.[34]

Golding's suggestions improved Wechsler in a way that brought
the constitutional analysis in *Neutral Principles* to the point where it
began to look like something that might have been endorsed by
Hart and Sacks.

The third group, the conservative critics of Wechsler, saw themselves as the true heirs of the theory of reasoned elaboration.[35] Their
interpretations of Wechsler and legal process were so different from

---

[32] Ibid., at 42–3. Golding made a Fullerian caveat, however: "there is . . . a point
at which the form and content of the tyranny become inseparable, making it impossible to speak of principled judicial judgment." Ibid., at 43.

[33] Ibid., at 43.

[34] Ibid., 48–9. It is interesting to note that Golding's first insight (that the law can
set out a series of "ordered" values) was echoed by some members of the fundamental rights school. See Walter F. Murphy, *An Ordering of Constitutional Values*, 53 S. Cal.
L. Rev. 703 (1980).

[35] See Isidore Silver, *The Warren Court Critics: Where Are They Now That We Need
Them?*, 3 Hastings Const. L.Q. 373, 374 (1976).

Hart and Sacks's original theory, however, that they should be seen as usurpers of the legal process tradition, and not its heirs. The conservative critics were skeptical about the objective existence of moral concepts and thought that the moral language of the Constitution could have no referent other than the original intent of its authors. Through their intervention, the conservative critics succeeded in making original intent – or interpretivism – the ultimate form of legal process.

The most prominent of this group was Alexander Bickel. Bickel's primary idea – perhaps forged during his time as clerk to Justice Felix Frankfurter in 1954 – was that while it is true that judges must obey the demands of reasoned elaboration, it is also true that the Supreme Court is a political institution and that sometimes the demands of principle must be ignored for the moment if the Court is to survive to promote principle in the future. Thus, Bickel implicitly approved of the very same tendency toward "judicial statesmanship" that was criticized by other legal process scholars in the early Forewords.[36] In his 1961 Foreword, Bickel celebrated various techniques for the denial of *certiorari* – dismissal for lack of ripeness, jurisdiction, and so on – as "passive virtues" that allowed the Court to avoid giving the "right" answer when, in a sense, the truth would have been too costly.[37]

Bickel's concern was shared by Philip Kurland, another of Frankfurter's former clerks. In 1964, Kurland accused the Court of insisting "that its rulings be carried to their dryly logical extremes."[38] His warning was intended to produce the opposite result from that hoped for by Pollak or Henkin, who wanted to see Wechsler's the-

---

[36] Alexander Bickel, *The Least Dangerous Branch* 173 (1962). ("[I]t will not do to exalt an individual claim to particular justice over all the other problems that adjudication may have to solve and over all other problems that it perhaps entails.")

[37] Alexander Bickel, *The Supreme Court, 1960 Term – Foreword: "The Passive Virtues,"* 75 Harv. L. Rev. 40, 43 (1961).

[38] Philip Kurland, *The Supreme Court, 1963 Term – Foreword: "Equal in Origin and Equal in Title to the Legislative and Executive Branches of the Government,"* 78 Harv. L. Rev. 143, 165 (1964). Ironically, Bickel and Kurland criticized the Court for taking reasoning too seriously – just the opposite argument made by Hart and others in the *Forewords* a decade earlier. As Purcell noted: "In *The Least Dangerous Branch*, Bickel had seen the courts as the special voice of reason, uniquely suited to elaborate proper principles; the political process had appeared erratic and given to excess. When principles became 'ideological' in the late sixties and Bickel's primary goal shifted from achieving moral reform to ensuring social tranquility, the judgment had to be reversed. The judiciary became erratic, the political system rational." Edward A. Purcell Jr., *Alexander M. Bickel and the Post-Realist Constitution,* 11 Harv. C.R.-C.L. L. Rev. 521, 554 (1976).

ory vindicated through its extension to every available incidence of the appropriate principle.

Robert Bork carried Wechsler's project further toward the conservative camp than anyone else. He argued in 1971 that "[w]e have not carried the idea of neutrality far enough."[39] Bork argued that for too long the theory of reasoned elaboration concerned only the *application* of principles and had ignored the *derivation* of these principles. Bork agreed with Wechsler that the principles in question were of course nonneutral in their content, because they were the product of political choices. Bork challenged, however, what he saw as the realist notion that judges should be able to replace the law maker's nonneutral preferences with their own nonneutral preferences: "If [a judge] may not choose lawlessly between cases in applying principle X, he may certainly not choose lawlessly in defining or in choosing X. . . ."[40] We should nonetheless note that Bork's argument was a non sequitur. The original theory of reasoned elaboration *assumed* that judges can in fact be directed by law to apply standards that require the "working out" of a system of belief in their application, or even to assume varying degrees of continuing discretion. (Recall that according to Hart and Sacks a judge could be authorized to act like a legislator.)

Bickel and Bork nonetheless raised difficult questions for their legal process colleagues. Their writings suggested that the internal critics were wrong to attack Wechsler's conservative interpretation of Hart and Sacks. If anything, Bickel and Bork would have argued that Wechsler did not go far enough with his own argument. Bickel and Bork assumed that Wechsler, had he adopted the terminology of *The Legal Process*, would have endorsed the view that the Constitution provided for noncontinuing discretion. Furthermore, they would have agreed with the internal critics that Wechsler must have believed that the Constitution commanded judges to determine the limits of their own discretion. What Bickel and Bork rejected was the internal critics' claim that Wechsler should have recognized that the Constitution commanded judges to exercise discretion when interpreting the moral language of the Fourteenth Amendment. The reason the conservative critics could agree with the internal critics that law concerns the delegation of noncontinu-

---

[39] Robert H. Bork, *Neutral Principles and Some First Amendment Problems*, 47 Ind. L.J. 1, 7 (1971).

[40] Ibid., at 8.

ing discretion yet deny that the Fourteenth Amendment delegated to adjudicators the power to use noncontinuing discretion to determine the meaning of the moral terms in the Constitution is that the conservative critics were convinced that noncontinuing discretion was impossible where the law incorporated moral commands.

Because Hart and Sacks rejected the idea that the Constitution commands judges to exercise *continuing* discretion in order to achieve the Constitution's purposes,[41] the issue upon which Bickel and Bork and the internal critics differed was how a Wechslerian judge should interpret the rules and standards that limit judicial discretion. (In fact, the real question related to the interpretation of constitutional standards because very few norms in the Constitution are rules; with the exception of the age requirements and a few other provisions, very few constitutional determinations rely upon the occurrence or nonoccurrence of an event.) The application of a standard cannot be an act of continuing discretion, or what H.L.A. Hart would call "rule-making."[42] It must be an act of elaboration or interpretation of existing law, not the creation of new law.

As we saw in section 4.4, Hart and Sacks argued that all standards are based in either principle or policy. Bickel and Bork thought it was clear that Wechsler understood – as the internal critics did not – that discretion cannot be cabined by a standard derived from a principle. If that were true, then all standards could be cabined only by treating them as if they were policies. A policy, according to Hart and Sacks, is "simply a statement of an objective."[43] Given that the application of a standard already required judges to interpret the instant case in the context of "the quality or tendency of happenings in like situations,"[44] it would seem that Wechslerian judges ought to be able to identify an objective if they were to base their decisions on policy. In common law, the identification of policy objectives is a constant concern of tort and contract scholars – for example, one group of commentators thinks that the objective of

---

[41] Hart and Sacks thought that, although common law judges may have once had such discretion, the Constitution does not give complete continuing discretion even to Congress and the President. See Hart and Sacks, *The Legal Process: Basic Problems in the Making and Application of Law* (William N. Eskridge Jr. and Philip P. Frickey, eds., 1994) (hereafter *TLP*).

[42] See H.L.A. Hart, *The Concept of Law* 141 (2d ed., 1994).

[43] *TLP*, at 141.

[44] Ibid., at 140.

private law is economic efficiency.[45] But no answer based on policy-driven goals is helpful at the level of constitutional interpretation. It is doubtful that Hart and Sacks thought that constitutional standards like due process could be based on policy. They probably believed that policy could be a foundation for standards in other parts of the law, like common law or statutory law, whereas constitutional law is rooted only in principles.[46]

If reasoned elaboration in constitutional law relies upon the derivation of standards from principles, then it follows that Hart and Sacks must have had some idea of what kind of principles could do the job. It was precisely Bickel and Bork's contention that the genius of Wechsler's argument was that it exposed the sad fact that there are no principles that can do the work of generating a constitutional standard. According to Hart and Sacks, a principle describes a rationale for the achievement of a goal: It limits the sort of reasons judges can have for action to reasons that are part of a "clearly thought-out and justified system."[47] The conservative critics' challenge to those internal critics who thought they could put a liberal spin on legal process was to ask, whose system of reason? The judge's? The original founders'?

The conservative critics doubted the existence of "systems of reason" that could supply principles to the Constitution. For example, Bork argued that in morality as in economics, people's preferences are, at a certain level, impossible to justify or explain through reason.[48] Because *systems* of moral reasoning are in principle impossi-

---

[45]   The literature on this question is enormous. See generally Guido Calabresi, *The Cost of Accidents: A Legal and Economic Analysis* (1970); Jules L. Coleman, *Markets, Morals and the Law* (1988); Richard A. Posner, *Economic Analysis of Law* (3rd ed., 1986). But see, for example, Ronald M. Dworkin, *Is Wealth a Value?*, 9 J. Legal Stud. 191 (1980) (maximization of social wealth cannot by itself motivate a principled reason for action).

[46]   Hart and Sacks disagreed with Harry Wellington on this point. Wellington based his analysis of constitutional language on the *similarity* between constitutional principles and common law principles. See Harry H. Wellington, *Common Law Rules and Constitutional Double Standards: Some Notes on Adjudication*, 83 Yale L.J. 221 (1973); see also Harry H. Wellington, *The Nature of Judicial Review*, 91 Yale L.J. 486 (1982). Wellington's most recent views on this subject have been outlined in Harry H. Wellington, *Interpreting the Constitution: The Supreme Court and the Process of Adjudication* (1990), and his views have changed somewhat since the 1973 article. For the purposes of this chapter, which is primarily on the legal process school and its evolution from the 1950s to the 1970s, I have chosen to focus primarily on Wellington's views as set out in the earlier essays.

[47]   Hart and Sacks, *TLP*, at 159.

[48]   Bork, *Neutral Principles and Some First Amendment Problems*, at 10. "There is no principled way to decide that one man's gratifications are more deserving of re-

ble, all the law can do is embed the majority's choices – representing the *result* of practical moral reasoning by the majority at that moment – about what the Constitution should command judges to do on specific, well-defined occasions. When an occasion comes to pass for which the majority has not provided, and there is nothing in the Constitution to command judges one way or the other, judges without continuing discretion should defer to the next level of instructions in the Constitution, which happen to refer to the democratic process by which the majority generates specific responses to concrete problems.[49]

Bickel was also skeptical of the existence in constitutional law of what Hart and Sacks called principles. In *The Least Dangerous Branch*, an early study of this problem, he merely alluded to this skepticism,[50] while in his last writings Bickel revealed a full-scale value-skepticism quite similar to that of his colleague and friend Bork – and quite similar to that of some of the more extreme realists whom both he and Bork scorned. Bickel, like Bork, did not argue that the founders could have embedded principles into the Constitution but chose not to; both Bickel and Bork argued that the founders could not have successfully embedded principles *even if they had tried.* Bickel wrote that he came to realize that, although concepts of justice and injustice were once thought to have some stable content, "[t]he words are used in a different sense now [the late twentieth century] because they are no longer rooted in a single, well-recognized ethical precept."[51] In making this argument, Bickel in fact denied the existence of the distinction between principle and policy set out by Hart and Sacks. The inescapable implication of his writing is that, in the end, all government under law, whether by legislatures or by courts, was rooted in policy.[52]

---

spect than another's or that one form of gratification is more worthy than another." Ibid., at 10.

[49] Ibid., at 11.

[50] "Which values, among adequately neutral and general ones, qualify as sufficiently important or fundamental or what-have-you to be vindicated by the Court against other values affirmed by legislative acts?" Bickel, *Least Dangerous Branch*, at 55.

[51] Alexander Bickel, *The Supreme Court and the Idea of Progress* 84 (1970). See also William Haltom and Mark Silverstein, *The Scholarly Tradition Revisited: Alexander Bickel, Herbert Wechsler, and the Legitimacy of Judicial Review*, 4 Const. Commentary 25, 29–30 (1987) (according to Bickel, value choices in adjudication ought to reflect consensus).

[52] Bickel, *Supreme Court and the Idea of Progress*, at 177.

There was one conservative critic who did not share Bickel and Bork's extreme skepticism of moral principles: Harry Wellington. He attempted to distance himself from Bickel and Bork by interpreting legal process through the lens of the common law. Wellington noted that the problem of interpreting rules and standards in terms of principles and policies was not new – Anglo-American courts had dealt with this problem since the early history of the common law.[53] Wellington admitted that it is rare that constitutional interpretation was rooted in policy and therefore focused his discussion about constitutional adjudication on the problem of interpreting legal rules by reference to principle.[54]

In either common law or constitutional law, Wellington argued, the problem Bickel and Bork raised is the same. The fact that in common law the legislature could correct a judge who decided "wrongly" doesn't change the problem for a common law judge who wants to get it right. Wellington argued that judges who want to apply a principle in a tort case must perform the same interpretive act as judges applying a principle in a constitutional case. He must "take a moral point of view."[55] But Wellington stressed that recognizing that an adjudicator must identify the moral principle embedded in the law does not mean that the moral principle found by the adjudicator is the same principle that the adjudicator would have embedded into the law had he or she been the law's mythical author: "I doubt that one would want to say that a court is entitled or required to assert *its* moral point of view. . . . Unlike the moral philosopher, the court is required to assert *ours*."[56]

Note that Wellington did not argue that all judges can do is refer to the specific "choices" made by society at a certain time with regard to a specific set of events (which, in this case, would mean the

---

[53] Wellington accepted some of Hart and Sacks's terminology. He adopted their distinction between principle and policy but not rules and standards; the latter distinction he simply collapsed and called any legal norms enforceable by a judge a "rule." Wellington, *Common Law Rules and Constitutional Double Standards*, at 222–3.

[54] When the Supreme Court bases a decision on considerations of policy, it is almost always when interpreting a congressional statute, such as the National Labor Relations Act or Federal Communications Act (in which case the federal courts treat these statutes as if they were common law sources). On those occasions when the Constitution is being interpreted and there is nothing for the Court to refer to except policy, Wellington counseled the Court to defer to the more *competent* judges of policy – elected officials. See ibid., at 269–70.

[55] Ibid., at 244.

[56] Ibid.

LEGAL POSITIVISM IN AMERICAN JURISPRUDENCE

complete collapse of tort law into the realist view that all aspects of tort law should be treated as questions of policy). But, if judges can locate coherent, closely reasoned moral systems with which to interpret tort law, why could they not find such systems when faced with problems in constitutional law? The possibility of moral-type reasoning doesn't change because judges put down a Restatement of Torts and pick up the Constitution.

Wellington seemed to concede to Bickel and Bork that a principle embedded in a law cannot remain a useful source of "close reasoning" over time. Because he doubted that the law can express moral principles adequately or fully, Wellington recommended that judges refer not to a system of moral reasoning as it ideally would have been set out in the law, even if it could have been, but rather to the "conventional morality" of one's time."[57] When Wellington cryptically refers to "our morality" in the foregoing quotation, he really was referring to the community's conventional morality. According to Wellington, "conventional morality is not necessarily the best morality," but it is the only sure moral concept at the judge's disposal.[58] The alternative would be judicial deference whenever the Constitution's instructions were not clear.[59] Wellington's theory, therefore, was a well-intentioned attempt to save the intelligibility of principle in Hart and Sacks's theory of constitutional interpretation, but it did so only at the cost of making the content of constitutional principles rely upon current conventional preferences, which ultimately turns out to be the preferences of the majority.[60] One might observe that, in his attempt to defend neutral principles, Wellington had all but conceded Deutsch's "realist" criticism explored previously.

Calling Bickel, Bork, and Wellington "conservative" critics of Wechsler suggests a bit of a double entendre. In the beginning of his

[57] Ibid., at 280.
[58] Ibid.
[59] It seems that for Bork, Bickel, and Wellington, a moral principle embedded in a law could be interpretable and acted upon only if it were framed as a rule – that is, a clear norm whose action could be clearly determined by the occurrence or nonoccurrence of some act. A paradigmatic example of this would be Justice Hugo Black's reading of the First Amendment's free speech clause (see Hugo Black, *A Constitutional Faith* 17–18 [1969]), or the almost universally accepted reading of the Thirteenth Amendment.
[60] Wellington claimed that current conventional morality might be countermajoritarian, but his argument is unpersuasive. See John Hart Ely, *Democracy and Distrust* 63–9 (1980) (collapsing conventional morality into majoritarianism).

194

career, Bickel saw himself as a political liberal, and Wellington, to some extent, still sees himself that way.[61] Bork has been more cryptic as to his political preferences, although he dedicated a significant portion of the first of his post–confirmation battle books to rebutting the charge that he was a "conservative extremist."[62] The conservative critics claimed to be conservative in their method of interpretation of the Constitution; they disclaimed any relationship between their personal politics and either the norms they claim the Constitution commands or the particular liberal or conservative color of those norms. The double entendre has force in that it is obvious that, given the political climate of the 1950s and '6os, the civil rights decisions that were the target of Bickel and Bork (but not Wellington) were supported by political liberals and opposed by political conservatives. Furthermore, these gains were not likely to have been produced by the political system left to its own democratic devices.[63]

The fourth group of Wechsler's critics faulted Wechsler on grounds similar to those raised by Bickel and Bork; furthermore, they agreed with Bickel, Bork, and Wellington that it was impossible to embed principles in constitutional standards. Their reaction was not, however, to declare the project of constitutional adjudication of the Fourteenth Amendment hopeless or to revert to the majority. They took this tragic fact about the limitations of the law as proof of the necessity for judges to treat the Fourteenth Amendment as an invitation to reflect seriously on the moral foundations of American democracy and to adjudicate constitutional questions according to the correct applications of those moral norms. The members of this last group were "liberal" in that they found the political consequences of Wechsler's approach to the race cases unacceptable, and their interest in defending and promoting civil rights through the courts provided a practical motivation for them to formulate a theory to rebut Wechslerian neutral principles. This fourth

---

[61] Ely noted that Bickel, who was a "Robert Kennedy liberal . . . as late as 1968," may have moved toward political conservatism by the end of his life. Ibid., at 70–1. Wellington has consistently supported the pro-choice position from the perspective of "political morality." See, for example, Wellington, *Common Law Rules and Constitutional Double Standards*, at 156.

[62] See Robert Bork, *The Tempting of America* 323–36 (2d ed., 1990).

[63] This point was profoundly illustrated by Richard Kluger in *Simple Justice* (1975) and well understood by the Supreme Court in the 1950s. See, for example, Bickel, *Least Dangerous Branch*, at 245–7.

group also embraced a methodology that appeared "liberal" in that it called for a more expansive set of civil rights than Wechsler's would have supported. This was not, as the realists might have it, because of any felt political necessity on the part of the interpreter of the Constitution, but because the Constitution demanded it: The Fourteenth Amendment guaranteed the moral rights fundamental to all persons. For this reason, this last approach – albeit politically liberal – is more accurately called the "fundamental rights" critique of Wechsler.[64]

A good example of the early fundamental rights critique can be found in the arguments made by Arthur Miller and Ronald Howell in 1960. They criticized Wechsler's theory of neutral principles for many of the reasons raised by the realists. They broke with the realists, however, in the end and criticized the realist conclusion that adjudication is essentially politics. "[Our] formulations," they wrote, "are attempts to build on the shambles of classical jurisprudence left after the attack of the legal realists had crumbled the edifice of the phonograph theory of law."[65] Thus, Miller and Howell rejected the emphasis on indeterminacy that rule skeptics such as Felix Cohen or the early Jerome Frank built into their analyses of the Constitution. Miller and Howell believed that the Constitution imposes a duty on judges to promote justice, but they did not believe that the Constitution, as law, could constrain either the ends or the means by which judges pursued justice. They offered, for example, two versions of the conception of justice that were supposed

---

[64] The term *fundamental rights* did not come into vogue until the 1970s, at which point the term described a fully developed method of constitutional adjudication. See, for example, Walter F. Murphy et al., *American Constitutional Interpretation* 929–30 (1986) (discussing fundamental rights as a "mode" of constitutional interpretation). Attribution of the term to this last group of Wechsler's critics is appropriate for two reasons. First, the reasoning applied by this group to their critique of Wechsler's theory of neutral principles is substantially identical to the reasoning underlying the fundamental rights scholarship that appears later. Second, the language of "fundamentality" began to appear even in these earlier texts: In one essay discussed below, the authors recommended a "teleological" approach to interpreting the Constitution, in which the justices craft constitutional decisions that exemplify the "goals of American society" or "the democratic ideal." Miller and Howell, *Myth of Neutrality in Constitutional Adjudication*, at 690–3.

[65] Ibid., at 692. The "phonograph theory" – which it seems Miller and Howell equated with Wechsler – was originally a realist expression for legal positivism. See, for example, Morris R. Cohen, *Positivism and the Limits of Idealism in the Law*, 27 Colum. L. Rev. 237, 238 (1927).

to guide constitutional interpretation: The Supreme Court should interpret the Constitution to promote either "human dignity" or "welfare."[66]

Judging according to human dignity or welfare was a form of "teleological jurisprudence."[67] According to this approach, "judicial decisions should be gauged by their results and not by either their coincidence with a set of allegedly consistent doctrinal principles or by an impossible reference to neutrality of principle."[68] Therefore, legal reasoning was not really distinguishable from prudential or moral reasoning. Hart and Sacks were wrong when they concluded that judges' first task in adjudication was to determine the degree of continuing discretion that they have been given. There was nothing for the judge to determine, because all judicial action was the result of continuing discretion. What distinguished these acts of discretion from the typical legislative act of continuing discretion was that judges were not supposed to act on the basis of the politics of self or (enlightened) class interest but rather on the basis of moral beliefs that the judges had examined carefully and (one hoped) had subjected to rigorous scrutiny.

Few other writers applying the fundamental rights critique in the 1960s were as forthright about their reasons for rejecting Wechsler as Miller and Howell, but close examination of Pollak's further reflections on Wechsler illustrates how Pollak moved from being a friendly "internal" critic of legal process to ultimately adopting the fundamental rights perspective. For example, at the end of an article in which he defended his criticism of Wechsler's misapplication of neutral principles to *Brown*, Pollak revealed that he had earlier been under the impression that he and Wechsler had not really disagreed about the general principles of constitutional interpretation, and that their disagreement involved only the narrow question of

---

[66] Miller and Howell, *Myth of Neutrality in Constitutional Adjudication,* at 693. See, for example, Myres MacDougal, *Perspectives for an International Law of Human Dignity,* 1959 *Am. Soc'y Int'l. Proc.* 107, 130 (1959) (human dignity); Alexander H. Pekelis, *The Case for a Jurisprudence of Welfare,* in *Law and Social Action* 1 (Milton R. Kovitz, ed., 1950) (welfare).

[67] Miller and Howell, *Myth of Neutrality in Constitutional Adjudication,* at 690. Fuller, it should be remembered, also used the phrase *teleological jurisprudence* to describe his form of natural law. See Lon Fuller, *The Morality of Law,* 146 (2d ed., 1969).

[68] Miller and Howell, *Myth of Neutrality in Constitutional Adjudication,* at 690.

[69] Louis H. Pollak, *Constitutional Adjudication: Relative or Absolute Neutrality,* 11 J. *Pub. L.* 48, 61 (1962).

how to apply neutral principles in the race cases.[69] As a result of further discussions with Wechsler, Pollak admitted that he had misunderstood the scope of his differences with Wechsler. Pollak had suggested to Wechsler that the Constitution *requires* judges to evaluate a putative constitutional principle in light of whether it would "contribute to the quality of our society."[70] Wechsler answered that "[A decision to treat the] "quality of our society" as a constitutional threshold must "rest . . . on neutral principles, i.e., was not merely an ad hoc disposition of [the court's] immediate problem unrationalized by a generalization susceptible to application across the board."[71] Pollak concluded this article by reflecting on the fact that he vigorously disagreed with Wechsler's caveat. But in doing so, Pollak took issue not with Wechsler's application of Hart and Sacks to the race cases but with Hart and Sacks's more general claim that all law (including the Constitution) granted law appliers no more than limited or "noncontinuing" discretion.

What was the cause of Pollak's new-found disagreement with Hart and Sacks? They had said, in effect, that a consideration of social justice may be a contingent but never a necessary or sufficient condition of reasoned elaboration in law. Pollak seemed to be saying that considerations of social justice were *always* a sufficient condition (at least in American law): That the norm "x is law if x makes an enduring contribution to the quality of our society" was itself a constitutive principle of American law.

An inevitable consequence of Pollak's argument was that, in describing the condition of reasoned elaboration so broadly, he simply abandoned the idea of interpreting law on the basis of the kind of principle envisioned by Hart and Sacks. The norm of social justice cannot *constrain* a law applier, and hence it collapses noncontinuing discretion into continuing discretion. The norm is on such a global scale that it would amount to a grant of continuing discretion to its bearer to promote justice in the guise of a grant of noncontinuing discretion to secure a specific, contingent, and (possibly) unjust state of affairs.

True to his new theory, Pollak objected to the suggestion that there may be other necessary conditions (such as consistency and

[70] Ibid., at 61. It must be noted that this test for constitutionality was first suggested by Pollak to Wechsler in 1962; it played no role in Pollak's 1959 *University of Pennsylvania Law Review* article.

[71] Ibid. (quoting response from Wechsler).

generality) that must be conjoined to the purposeful pursuit of justice in order for there to be a principle cognizable by the law that can inform adjudication. He argued that when one's principle is "improve the 'quality of society'" *simpliciter,* any other norm that improves the "quality of society" is, by definition, necessarily authorized by the principle "improve the 'quality of society,'" and conversely, no other norm that does not ultimately improve the "quality of society" has an independent ground for authority.[72]

The ultimate conclusion of Pollak's argument was a version of the fundamental rights argument: that the rights the Constitution guarantees are substantially related to the achievement of justice in American society. Once the Constitution was reduced to being a single standard that is to be interpreted in light of a principle as broad as "promote justice" or "promote the good life," then Hart and Sacks's careful typology collapsed and the American legal system ceases to be a "general directive arrangement." If the distinction between "law-as-morals" and "law-as-purposive-commands" was collapsed, then the idea that law controls the limits of continuing discretion was effectively replaced by the idea that all law was necessarily an exercise of continuing discretion.[73]

5.3. SAVING LEGAL PROCESS FROM ITS FRIENDS

As a result of the critical reception of Wechsler's article, the legal process school was soon seen only through the lens of the conservative version of neutral principles. A combination of forces guaranteed that Wechsler, Bickel, and Bork's interpretation of legal process soon became what people believed to be legal process. The scholarly community was far more aware of the fact that Wechsler had criticized *Brown* in 1958 than the fact that Sacks had endorsed it in 1954.[74] The conservatives obscured Hart and Sacks's actual understanding of the role that principles played in constitutional adjudication and as a result created a very specific version of legal positivism that was, in its own way, as unattractive as legal formalism.

---

[72] Ibid., at 61–3.
[73] For a realist critique of Wechsler that also anticipates the fundamental rights approach, see Mueller and Schwartz, *Principle of Neutral Principles,* at 588 (indicating that judges must select the fundamental rights the Constitution is designed to protect).
[74] See Albert M. Sacks, *The Supreme Court,* 1953 Term – Foreword, 68 *Harv. L. Rev.* 96, 103 (1954).

As with formalism, which foundered on an overly narrow view of the autonomy thesis, the conservative interpretation of legal process took Hart and Sacks's positivist theory of adjudication and attributed to it an autonomy thesis that was unnecessarily skeptical of moral principles.

It is clear that Hart and Sacks believed that laws can contain moral principles. The claim that moral principles can be part of the law is perfectly consistent with the separability thesis, the command theory, and the sources thesis. Furthermore, Hart and Sacks suggested that laws can incorporate moral principles not only through the exercise of noncontinuing discretion but by the reasoned elaboration of moral terms as well.[75] This latter point is one of the most important contributions the legal process school could make to improving upon formalism's simplistic application of the sources thesis.

According to the conservative critics, Hart and Sacks were misled: Only *rules* could put into effect a law maker's preferences. Because all one had to do to apply a rule was to determine a matter of fact, it made no difference what the source of the rule had been – it could have been the result of the operation of reason or merely the expression of an ill-considered preference. In either case, it manifested itself as a "fact" that could be determined without interpretation. That is why Wechsler and his conservative critics assumed that although a law could contain a command that expressed the law maker's preference about some state of affairs at some certain time, a law could not contain a command that expressed the law maker's preference that the judge apply the law maker's "system of reason."

As we saw previously, the conservative critics believed that a *standard* could not implement a law maker's preferences if those preferences were based on principles. Under the Hart and Sacks model, in order to apply a standard, one had to do more than observe a fact; one had to make a "qualitative appraisal" [of facts] "in terms of their probable consequences, moral justification, or other aspects of general human experience."[76] But according to Bickel and Bork, a judge could not make a qualitative appraisal of others' systems of reasoning and still faithfully obey their will. On the other hand, they argued, a judge *could* make a qualitative appraisal of

---

[75] Hart and Sacks, *TLP*, at 168.
[76] Ibid., at 157.

others' preferences based on policy and still faithfully obey their will.[77] Why did the conservative critics think this? What could make a standard based on principle different from a standard based on policy? The answer must be that a standard based on policy is a statement of an objective that is knowable without one's necessarily knowing anything about the reasons for its being preferred. Such an objective would be knowable without the interpreter's needing to understand, agree, or disagree with the thought process that generated the stated preference. There are "naked" preferences like this in politics all the time. One example is when something is declared the "preference" of the group because more people voted for it than the other choices.[78]

When Hart and Sacks spoke of policy, they meant "naked" preferences.[79] This feature of policies – that policies can be acted upon without the law applier's understanding why the preference was preferred – holds the key to Bickel and Bork's claim that a standard could be based only upon a policy. Because, for the conservative critics, judges would not need to understand the reason why a law maker preferred the policy identified in the law in order to identify it as the thing that must be done, adjudication based on policy must be a matter of empirical observation.[80]

Bickel and Bork basically believed that legal commands could communicate only matters of empirical fact to their listeners. They certainly would not have denied that legal commands could, through the establishment of factual conditions, communicate when someone was entitled to act with continuing discretion (e.g., that the Constitution could have given the president the power to propose a budget without regard to any restriction). Because, however, they denied that there could be any conceptual space between

[77] Bickel and Bork do not explicitly limit their discussion to standards. It is a conclusion I force upon them because of the obvious yet sometimes overlooked point that the Constitution does not contain many rules. Constitutional litigation focuses, for the most part, on the interpretation of standards such as due process, cruel and unusual punishment, and the like.

[78] This term is borrowed from Sunstein, *Naked Preferences and the Constitution*, 84 Colum. L. Rev. 1689 (1984).

[79] A policy may be a matter "of unreasoned preference." Hart and Sacks, *TLP*, at 159.

[80] The policy of "bringing inflation down to 6.0 percent" is a good example, as would be the policy of "minimize traffic accidents." Ibid., at 159. It therefore turns out that a standard designed to promote a policy is essentially the same as a rule designed to promote a policy (the former may simply be a more complex version of the latter).

the application of matters of fact (which was the province of adjudication) and the application of continuing discretion (which was the province of politics), they denied that law appliers could perform reasoned elaboration on principles in the same way they could on simple, empirically verifiable terms. Therefore, these conservative critics did not accept Hart and Sacks's idea that laws could be based on principles; for them law was necessarily a system of rules. The view that legal meaning relied upon empirical, not moral, judgment came to be known as interpretivism.[81] Laws, however, often contained moral terms. What did Bickel and Bork think judges should have done with these terms? Of the two, Bork put the more energy into developing an answer. Because laws must ultimately refer to empirically verifiable terms, the moral terms found in the law (such as "cruel," or "unfair competition") must refer to empirically verifiable events, which in the case of normative terms could mean only the intentions of the authors of those terms.[82] Following Bork, most conservative legal process scholars turned to original intent as a necessary tool for interpreting the normative language of the Constitution.[83]

---

[81] Labels are not very important, but it is valuable at least to be able to understand with whom someone is allying him- or herself when he or she writes approvingly of one or another group. As I shall discuss shortly, the interpretivists contained (uneasily) various subgroups, most notably a set of conservative opponents of the fundamental rights school who were generally committed to the idea that legal texts should be interpreted according to the meanings that the texts' authors would have given. See, for example, Raoul Berger, *Government by Judiciary: The Transformation of the Fourteenth Amendment* (1977); Bork, *Tempting of America;* Robert Bork, *Styles of Constitutional Interpretation, So. Tex. L.J.* 383 (1985); William H. Rehnquist, *The Notion of a Living Constitution,* 54 *Tex. L. Rev.* 693 (1976).

[82] "Legislation requires value choices and cannot be principled in the sense under discussion. . . . The bare concept of equality provides no guide for the courts." Bork, *Neutral Principles and Some First Amendment Problems,* at 11. See also Bork, *Tempting of America,* at 144: "All that counts is how the words used in the Constitution would have been understood at the time. The original understanding is thus manifested in the words used and in secondary materials, such as debates at the conventions, public discussion, newspaper articles, dictionaries in use at the time, and the like."

[83] Those who joined with Bork eventually came to be known as originalists. See, for example, Berger, *Government by Judiciary;* Henry Monaghan, *The Constitution Goes to Harvard,* 13 *Harv. C.R.-C.L.L. Rev.* 118 (1978); Rehnquist, *The Notion of a Living Constitution,* at 693. Originalism is but one variety of interpretivism. See Ely, *Democracy and Distrust,* at 1–9 (discussing Interpretivism); Paul Brest, *The Fundamental Rights Controversy: The Essential Contradictions of Normative Constitutional Scholarship,* 90 *Yale L.J.* 90–2 (1981), discussing Berger and Bork; Aviam Soifer, *Protecting Civil Rights: A Critique of Raoul Berger's History,* 54 *N.Y.U. L. Rev.* 651 (1979) (book review); Ronald Dworkin, *A Matter of Principle* 34–57 (1985) (on intention in legal theory).

As a result of the conservative critics' rejection of Hart and Sacks's idea that legal principles could express moral principles, interpretivism has become the modern face of legal positivism. Bickel and Bork's position is what many think positivism must say.[84] If we are to understand how positivism and legal process could have taken a different path, we must see why Bickel and Bork were wrong about the relationship between legal principles and moral principles.

One reason why it is easy to dismiss Bickel and Bork is that their desire to base law on empirically verifiable rules seems grounded in their moral skepticism. It is unlikely, however, that the defenders of the conservative interpretation of legal process would give up just because their metaethical positions were proven wrong.[85] Bickel and Bork's main argument must have looked something like the following: They might have asked, "Why assume that a legal system can contain more than one 'system of reason'?" Hart and Sacks spoke as if a system of reason were like a complex rule, under which only some legal problems were subsumed. If by "system of reason" they meant to include a set of moral principles whose norms were not applicable to every putative legal problem faced by the system, how was this set of principles cabined? If we reject moral skepticism, then does not the decision to determine the institutional rights in the legal system relevant to one set of problems necessarily commit the law applier to use the *same* system of moral reasoning the next time he or she wants to determine institutional rights in the legal system according to "a" system of moral reasoning, but for a *different* set of problems?

There are two responses to this argument. First, not all "systems of reason" are systems of *moral* reasoning. For example, not all forms of practical reasoning are forms of moral reasoning.[86] Second, not all systems of practical reasoning that incorporate moral principles must be insatiable in the way Bickel and Bork have implied.

---

[84] The degree to which this final version of Bickel and Bork's position on law as a set of rules resembles Dworkin's description of positivism as a "semantic theory of law" is uncanny: "[The positivist believes that] we will understand the legal process better if we use 'law' only to describe what lies in the core of that concept, if we use it, that is, to cover only propositions of law true according to the central or main rule for using 'law' that everyone accepts, *like the propositions of the highway code.*" Ronald Dworkin, *Law's Empire* 40 (1986) (emphasis added).

[85] In fact, there is no reason to believe that all interpretivists are moral skeptics. Neither Berger nor Monaghan has displayed skeptical tendencies.

[86] See, for example, Joseph Raz, *Practical Reasons and Norms* 107–23 (2d ed., 1990) (on varieties of normative systems).

They made the same assumption that the fundamental rights theorists made: They assumed that the principles invoked by a law are global (e.g., "promote autonomy" or "promote dignity") and thus if applied in one part of the law, they must be extended to all. Bickel and Bork's argument, once one gets beyond the moral skepticism, shared a common foundation with the fundamental rights school; they just choose one extreme on the spectrum as opposed to its alternative.

Both schools, in assuming that legal norms must be either matters of empirical fact or "global" systems of moral reasoning, made an unwarranted leap. Both groups assumed that if the legal system authorized a law to interpret some of its institutional rights according to a norm, then the *truthfulness* of the norm becomes a reason to apply the norm to questions of institutional rights for which no authorization had been given by the legal system. But that assumption ignores, of course, the argument made previously that the reason the norm has any force at all with regard to the interpretation of the institutional rights of the legal system is that it was authorized by that system. Its authorization, being provisional, can never validly assume more authority than was granted initially. The conditional status of legal norms was the lesson of Hart and Sacks's distinction between grants of continuing and noncontinuing authority.[87]

Both the fundamental rights school and the conservative critics assumed that if a legal system incorporated a moral principle, it must have incorporated a global system of moral reasoning, but empirically this is not so in our legal system. As Wellington pointed out, in the common law, different departments of the law rely simultaneously upon different types of principles (some of which may represent mutually exclusive systems of reasoning).[88] Yet

[87] Martin Golding made exactly the same point when he pointed out that "principled decision-making" (reasoned elaboration) was very similar to moral decision making except for two provisos. First, "a legal system is able to stipulate in a large measure the principles that must be employed in deliberation," and second, "a legal system may stipulate what grounds are and are not legitimate grounds" for adopting new principles. Golding, *Principled Decision-Making and the Supreme Court*, at 42. This is identical to the point just made in the text, in that because legal systems can cabin the scope of moral principles, unlike in a system of moral decision making, the legal system can stipulate where and up until what point moral reasoning will be employed. Ibid., at 43: "A legal system, then, may broadly fix the starting points of deliberation and the criteria of relevant distinctions."

[88] See Wellington, *Common Law Rules and Constitutional Double Standards*, at 233 (strong duty in tort law not to harm versus other weaker duties of efficiency). Some scholars have argued that contract law is more sensitive to the demands of allocative

Wellington, as we saw previously, lacked the courage of his convictions. While he seemed comfortable with raising the possibility that the common law is filled with different moral principles of which judges can and do take note, he seemed unwilling to extend the same possibility to constitutional law. Wellington correctly directed judges to apply the principles *in* the law but then leapt to the conclusion that moral principles cannot be embedded into a "system of reason" in the law unless it is through a *global* system of moral reasoning (which cannot be adequately or fully expressed by the law); that is why he argued that the "systems of reason" judges should employ, when ordered by the Constitution to apply a moral term, must be obtained from the judge's view of contemporary society's conventional morality.

There was no reason for Wellington to make this leap in the case of constitutional law. After all, the moral principles expressed by the common law are not obviously developed by judges with an eye toward how "conventional morality" might deal with the same question. Common law shows us that it is possible that moral principles can be used in a system of practical reasoning that is not itself a global system of moral reasoning.[89] Hart and Sacks's legal process, if properly applied, would lead one to conclude that the moral terms in the Constitution reflect a commitment by the founders that those terms be treated as moral principles and interpreted with the sort of serious reflection that moral concepts require.[90] Although it may not be easy to apply the moral principle of prohibiting cruel punishment to a question of institutional rights, it is not obvious why the reasoned elaboration of the word *cruel* is qualitatively different from the reasoned elaboration of the word

efficiency than tort law. See Jules Coleman, *Risks and Wrongs* 185–6 (1992). One could observe at this point that law and economics are least convincing when they attempt to fit different departments of law into their own global legal principle, efficiency.

[89]   One could argue that Hart and Sacks's treatment of normative terms in administrative law makes the same point. See Hart and Sacks, *TLP,* at 169–70.

[90]   There is no reason to believe that an interpreter of a moral principle that was identified through a system of nonmoral practical reason cannot treat the problem of determining the meaning of that moral concept as a problem about the objective meaning of that moral concept. A law applier engaging in the reasoned elaboration of a normative term must assume that the term has objective content. See ibid., at 168: "In these circumstances [interpreting normative terms] there may be thought to be a justification for describing the act of interpretation as one of discretion. . . . But this would be to obscure what seems to be the vital point – namely, the effort, and the importance of the effort, of each individual deciding officer to reach what he thinks is the right answer."

unfair by a court interpreting the Federal Trade Commission Act of 1914.[91] The key point to note is that regardless of how difficult the act of interpretation might seem, it would never be necessary for interpreters to reconcile the moral content of the moral principle they applied in one part of the Constitution with the principle applied by them or by others in another.[92] This is not to say that conflict among the moral implications of different parts of the law might never occur. Just as in common law or administrative law, there would probably be a great deal of convergence – certainly no less than what we have today in constitutional doctrine – and perhaps no less than we would have under a regime developed by any one fundamental rights theorist.

5.4. THE RISE OF FUNDAMENTAL RIGHTS

The critical reaction to Wechsler's interpretation of the principles of legal process framed the debate in American constitutional law and jurisprudence for the next generation of academic lawyers and judges. Of the four sets of reactions described in this chapter, two would form the poles between which most debate would take place. The fundamental rights argument against Wechsler soon widened into a methodological program designed not only to protect the Warren Court's decisions in the area of race but also to guide the Supreme Court to identify constitutional rights in cases that touched upon other socially controversial issues, such as sexual autonomy, poverty, and education.[93] Running parallel to the funda-

---

[91] Act of September 26, 1914, 38 Stat. 717. See Hart and Sacks, *TLP,* at 169: "The framers of a general directive arrangement may not think it wise, or they may not be able, to give it even the degree of definiteness of [a] speed statute.... In these circumstances, a possible technique is to provide for the development of subsidiary guides to meaning by the exercise of discretion, and for the reasoned elaboration of these subsidiary guides thereafter. The field of administrative law is replete with examples."

[92] See Louis Henkin, *The Supreme Court* 1967 Term, Foreword: On Drawing Lines, 82 *Harv. L. Rev.* 63, 63–5 (1968) (recognizing lack of consistency within Constitution); see also Louis Henkin, *Privacy and Autonomy,* 74 *Colum. L. Rev.* 1410 (1974).

[93] As the editors of *American Constitutional Interpretation* have pointed out, John Ely's *Democracy and Distrust* is responsible to a great extent for placing the term *fundamental rights* in the center of the debate over constitutional interpretation in the 1970s and '80s, as well as potentially confusing the term with the idea of "fundamental values." See Murphy et al., *American Constitutional Interpretation,* at 929 n1. Brest's discussion of the debate over constitutional interpretation in the 1970s also established fundamental rights as a term of art. See Brest, *Fundamental Rights Controversy.* Others have tried to describe the same concept through other terms. See, for exam-

mental rights school, the "conservative critics," who saw Wechsler as insufficiently skeptical of the possibility of reasoned interpretation of constitutional language, formed themselves into a counter-school known as Interpretivism.

The remaining two sets of reaction described in this chapter diminished in importance as the 1960s progressed. Those supporting the realist critique generally belonged to an older generation, and their students, to the extent that they shared their mentors' perspective, usually joined (and thus were absorbed into) the fundamental rights school.[94] The "internal critics" of Wechsler faded from importance as well. Some, like Pollak, seemed to join the fundamental rights school; others, like Henkin, simply did not enter the debate. Of course, both Hart and Sacks continued to teach the legal process materials at Harvard; neither, however, made a significant effort either to rebut or endorse Wechsler's treatment of their ideas or the criticisms of those who attacked Wechsler's version of legal process.[95]

In Chapter 4 I argued that Hart and Sacks's theory of law was essentially identical to a thin theory of positivism and that their interpretation of the U.S. Constitution (using their theory of law) generated a theory of adjudication associated with the legal process school. If I am correct in arguing that legal process relies upon the

ple, Henry Monaghan, *Our Perfect Constitution,* 56 N.Y.U. L. Rev. 353, 356 (1981) ("due substance"); Laurence Tribe, *The Puzzling Persistence of Process-Based Constitutional Theories,* 89 *Yale L. J.* 1063, 1064 (1980) ("substantive rights and values"). In my judgment, *fundamental rights* is the best phrase if for no other reason than that it represents the largest plurality among all the possible terms.

94   In time, even explicitly realist writings were used by younger scholars to support the fundamental rights approach directly. For example, Myres McDougal's explicitly (and famously) realist arguments were mined as a source of fundamental rights by Miller and Howell. See Miller and Howell, *Myth of Neutrality in Constitutional Adjudication,* at 691. Laura Kalman has suggested that the debate framed by Wechsler's Holmes Lecture and the retirement of the chief justice was a "family quarrel between . . . two wings of the realist tradition" – Warren Court activists (who disagreed with Wechsler) and process theorists (who agreed with Wechsler). Laura Kalman, *The Strange Career of Legal Liberalism* 49 (1960) (hereafter *Strange Career*).

95   Hart and Sacks's curious refusal to resume work on their unfinished yet widely accepted theory was noted and commented upon. See, for example, J. D. Hyman, *Constitutional Jurisprudence and the Teaching of Constitutional Law,* 28 Stan. L. Rev. 1271, 1286 n70 (1976) (book review) (noting Dean Sacks's unwillingness to put further work into *The Legal Process*). The purpose of this book is, in one sense, an attempt to make an argument that Hart and Sacks could have made but did not make. The fact that Hart and Wechsler were close collaborators in the field of federal courts does not in itself prove that Hart agreed with Wechsler's interpretation of legal process (it may explain, however, why Hart never explicitly repudiated Wechsler on this issue).

central tenets of legal positivism, then the fact that the fundamental rights/interpretivism debate originated in the rejection of legal process by members of the fundamental rights school suggests that the modern debate between fundamental rights and interpretivism was, to some extent, over the validity of some or all of the central tenets of legal positivism.[96] Some have been quick to embrace this conclusion.[97]

Of course, there is another possibility: that one of the other two positions that did not survive the immediate debate surrounding Wechsler better represented both legal process and positivism. According to this possibility, perhaps the perspective I attributed to the "internal critics" captured better the fundamental elements of Hart and Sacks's theory and thus truly captured the positivist content of legal process. This is the position I prefer. Nonetheless, the historical fact that only the fundamental rights and interpretivist schools emerged from the debate surrounding Wechsler lends *prima facie* support to the idea that a rejection of the fundamental rights analysis entails embracing the interpretivist position. I reject that claim, partially because I reject the interpretivist analysis as vigorously as I reject the fundamental rights analysis.

In the late 1960s and '70s scholarship about the Supreme Court was dominated by theorists who used the concept of fundamental rights to justify the Court's decisions and to lay out new directions for the Court to pursue.[98] The fundamental rights theorists on the

[96] Obviously, not all versions of legal positivism are compatible with Hart and Sacks's legal process. In Chapter 4 I argued that legal process contains the essential elements of any positivist theory. I will argue in the next chapter that in addition to correctly rejecting the flawed "positivism" of Wechsler and Bickel, the fundamental rights school incorrectly rejected the claims that are essential to a defensible "thin" theory of legal positivism.

[97] See, for example, Ronald Dworkin, *Taking Rights Seriously* vii (1977); Laurence Tribe, *American Constitutional Law* (2d ed., 1988) at 872; Mark Tushnet, *The Dilemmas of Liberal Constitutionalism*, 42 *Ohio St. L.J.* 411, 423 (1981).

[98] Mark Tushnet noted that "[a]ttempts to reinfuse constitutional law with principles of justice persisted into and throughout the 1970's." Mark Tushnet, *Truth, Justice, and the American Way: An Interpretation of Public Law Scholarship in the Seventies,* 57 *Tex. L. Rev.* 1307, 1316 (1979). According to Tushnet, the "typical constitutional law article" of 1979 was based on the assumption that "Supreme Court decisions are, and in any event can easily become, embodiments of principles of justice, defined as the standard political principles of the moderate-left of the Democratic Party." Ibid., at 1322. See also Brest, *Fundamental Rights Controversy*, at 1067 (describing a "profusion of articles supporting fundamental rights adjudication" and "relatively few unsympathetic analyses" of the fundamental rights school in the late 1970s); Monaghan, *Our Perfect Constitution*, at 358–9 (recent constitutional theory assumes that "prop-

whole endorsed a form of "legal liberalism" that consisted of "political liberalism and judicial activism in equal parts."[99] From a doctrinal perspective, the fundamental rights school's influence grew as
the fundamental rights methodology that had been used so effectively to criticize Wechsler was applied to constitutional cases concerning "privacy, procreational choice, sexual autonomy, lifestyle
choices, and intimate associations."[100]

It is not surprising that the fundamental rights school blossomed
as soon as its methods were transferred from the task of interpreting the equal protection clause of the Fourteenth Amendment to the
task of interpreting the due process clause of the Fourteenth
Amendment, given that arguments concerning fundamental rights
are far more easily bottomed upon the due process clause. This is
because, since the 1960s, "strict scrutiny" had been applied under
the equal protection clause in cases where *either* a "suspect" class *or*
a fundamental interest was implicated. The language and structure
of the suspect class prong of the equal protection clause, while the
obvious candidate by which to pursue the interests of racial minorities, did not offer much promise to liberals who wanted to expand
the constitutional protections of sexual autonomy and privacy.
The fundamental interest prong, which will be discussed in greater
detail later, was essentially identical to the conception of fundamental right used in due process analysis.[101] Because the case for non-

---

erly construed, the constitution" guarantees "most equality and autonomy values
which the commentators think a twentieth century Western liberal democratic government ought to guarantee" [emphasis omitted]).

99   Kalman, *The Strange Career,* at 43.
100   Brest, *Fundamental Rights Controversy,* at 1064. See, for example, *Griswold v.
Connecticut,* 381 U.S. 479 (1965) (state may not prohibit use of contraceptives by married couples); *Eisenstadt v. Baird,* 405 U.S. 438 (1972) (state may not prohibit distribution of contraceptives to unmarried couples); *Roe v. Wade,* 410 U.S. 113 (1973) (state
may not prohibit abortion before viability); *Roe v. Commonwealth's Attorney,* 403 F.
Supp. 1199 (E.D. Va. 1975), aff'd mem., 425 U.S. 901 (1976) (state may prohibit homosexual sodomy).
101   See *Harper v. Virginia State Board of Elections,* 383 U.S. 663, 669 (1966) ("We
have long been mindful that where fundamental rights and liberties are asserted under the Equal Protection Clause, classifications which might invade or restrain them
must be closely scrutinized and carefully confined"); see also *United States v. Carolene
Products Co.,* 304 U.S. 144 n4 (1934) (setting out a two-pronged test for strict scrutiny
of state legislation: whether the legislation implicates a fundamental right [either an
explicit right guaranteed by the Bill of Rights and incorporated through the due process clause of the Fourteenth Amendment] or a right to political participation [im-
plied in the Bill of Rights] or the interests of a "discrete and insular minority").

racial civil rights would be virtually the same regardless if approached through the equal protection clause or the due process clause, many liberals preferred to move directly through the due process clause.[102]

The content of the rights contained in the due process clause had been the site of great debate ever since the *Slaughterhouse Cases* foreclosed the possibility of using the privileges and immunities clause as an original source of rights against the states.[103] One important source of the rights found in the Fourteenth Amendment is the Bill of Rights itself: Through incorporation, almost all of the first eight amendments have been found in the due process clause.[104] The Court had also experienced varying success in finding various economic and noneconomic rights in the due process clause itself that were not necessarily explicitly named in the Bill of Rights.[105] Certainly the early writings of various scholars of the Constitution made it clear that the unspecified noneconomic rights suggested by Justice Harlan F. Stone in *Carolene Products* could be a rewarding point of departure for many liberals.[106] Thus, notwithstanding

[102] Compare *Brown v. Board of Educ.*, 347 U.S. 483, 493 (1954) ("Does segregation in public schools . . . deprive the children of the minority group of equal educational opportunities?") with *Griswold v. Connecticut*, 381 U.S. 479 (1965) (Goldberg, J., concurring) (right to marital privacy a "fundamental right" guaranteed by the due process clause of Fourteenth Amendment).

[103] U.S. 36 (1873); see Edward Corwin, *The Constitution of the United States of America* 965 (1953) (privileges and immunities clause "rendered a practical nullity" by *Slaughterhouse Cases*).

[104] See *Palko v. Connecticut*, 302 U.S. 319, 323 (1937) (describing process of incorporation); see also J. Israel, *Selected Incorporation: Revisited*, 71 Geo. L. Rev. 253, 336–8 (1982).

[105] See, for example, *Meyer v. Nebraska*, 262 U.S. 390 (1923) (state prohibition on the teaching of German a violation of the liberty necessary for the "orderly pursuit of happiness by free men"); *Palko v. Connecticut*, 302 U.S. 319 (1937) (due process clause of Fourteenth Amendment incorporates "scheme of ordered liberty" against the states); *Rochin v. California*, 342 U.S. 165 (1952) (invasion of bodily integrity is violation of due process clause of Fourteenth Amendment because act "shocks the conscience").

The baleful history of the rise and fall of "economic" rights substantive due process during the "laissez faire" period of American history is beyond the scope of this chapter. The period began approximately with *Allgeyer v. Louisiana*, 165 U.S. 578 (1897) (liberty of contract a fundamental right protected by the Fourteenth Amendment), reached its zenith with *Lochner v. New York*, 198 U.S. 45 (1905) (state may not regulate contracts between bakery and employees), and was finally repudiated by the Supreme Court in *West Coast Hotel Co. v. Parrish*, 300 U.S. 1 (1937) (state may force employers to pay minimum wage for women).

[106] It must be admitted that political scientists and historians were probably more perceptive about this prospect than lawyers and law professors, who, as I sug-

some noteworthy pre–Warren Court cases identifying noneconomic fundamental rights, academic and judicial efforts to define the range of fundamental rights contained in the due process clause of the Fourteenth Amendment did not gain momentum until after the civil rights cases.[107]

Of course, there was no logical necessity to the order in which the fundamental rights school analyzed the different clauses of the Fourteenth Amendment. From the point of view of fundamental rights theorists, the fact that their critique of Wechsler's attack on *Brown*'s interpretation of the equal protection clause may have helped the Warren Court develop a fundamental rights theory of the due process clause simply supported their argument that the task of constitutional interpretation – regardless of which part of the Constitution one faced – was a matter of developing a unified theory of fundamental rights.[108]

Further proof of the fundamental rights school's argument that the Constitution is best understood through the lens of a unitary theory of rights was provided by the construction of a new category of equal protection doctrine in the 1960s which required enhanced scrutiny of state actions that implicated a "fundamental interest."[109]

gest, needed the object lesson of the NAACP's successful equal protection litigation before recognizing the potential of working through the due process clause. See, for example, Edward Corwin, *The Basic Doctrine of American Constitutional Law*, 12 *Mich. L. Rev.* 247 (1914) (example of early pioneer in modern fundamental rights/due process analysis by a political scientist).

[107] As the editors of *American Constitutional Interpretation* noted, paragraph two of *Carolene Products* footnote four (which suggests strict scrutiny of legislation affecting the unenumerated fundamental interest to participate in the political process) did not come to "full flower" until the Warren Court. See Murphy et al., *American Constitutional Law*, at 491. One can, I suggest, draw the same conclusion about paragraph one, which suggests strict scrutiny for legislation affecting enumerated fundamental rights, and about paragraph three, which suggests similar protections for "discrete and insular minorities." Murphy and his co-editors draw their conclusion about the Warren Court's role in the development of the due process clause notwithstanding their acknowledgment of earlier courts' attempts to develop the meaning of due process. See ibid. (noting C. Herman Prichett's analysis of pre–Warren Court civil liberties in C. Herman Pritchett, *The Roosevelt Court* [1948]; C. Pritchett, *Civil Liberties and the Vinson Court* [1954]).

[108] See, for example, Tribe, *Puzzling Persistence of Process-Based Constitutional Theories,* at 1067: "Even the Constitution's most procedural prescriptions cannot be adequately understood, much less applied, in the absence of a developed theory of fundamental rights. . . ."

[109] See Gerald Gunther, *Foreword: In Search of Evolving Doctrine on a Changing Court: A Model for a Newer Equal Protection,* 86 *Harv. L. Rev.* 1, 12–18 (1972). Until the category of fundamental interests was developed and applied to equal protection doctrine, it was generally accepted that there were two models of equal protection

The idea that the equal protection clause was triggered if state action affected a fundamental right was first explored in *Skinner v. Oklahoma*.[110] Building on *Skinner*, the Warren Court developed the category of fundamental interest analysis in equal protection by borrowing heavily from its methods of discovering fundamental rights in due process analysis. The Court identified fundamental interests in voting,[111] access to the judicial process,[112] and travel[113] and came close to adding welfare[114] and education[115] to the list. The distinction the Supreme Court drew between fundamental rights and fundamental interests and the different parts of doctrine they addressed was irrelevant to the fundamental rights theorists; what was far more important to most of them was that the Court was be-

---

analysis. The first test focused on classifications based on race or other "suspect" criteria and entailed strict scrutiny; the second model focused on classifications in the economic or social realm (the police powers) and entailed a "rational basis" review. See Geoffrey Stone et al., *Constitutional Law* 751 (1986).

[110] 316 U.S. 535 (1942) (state may not sterilize a thrice-convicted larcenist because "marriage and procreation" are "basic civil rights of man," and because the state could not justify its decision to sterilize larcenists and not other criminals, the state's action violated the equal protection clause). It is worth noting that Chief Justice Stone, in a concurrence, argued that he would have found the state's action unconstitutional because of a concern not for equal protection but for due process. *Skinner*, 316 U.S. at 543–5. As Justice Harlan noted in his dissent in *Shapiro v. Thompson*, 394 U.S. 618, 628 (1969), the equal protection doctrine requiring strict scrutiny if a fundamental interest is affected is "of relatively recent vintage;" and although it was "foreshadowed" by Skinner, it "reemerged" "after a long hiatus" under the Warren Court.

[111] *Harper v. Virginia State Board of Elections*, 363 U.S. 663 (1966) (state may not impose poll tax).

[112] *Griffin v. Illinois*, 351 U.S. 12 (1956) (state must provide indigent criminal defendant with a free trial transcript); *Douglas v. California*, 372 U.S. 353 (1963) (state may not require state appellate courts to make independent investigation of utility of appointment of counsel on appeal for indigent criminal defendant).

[113] *Shapiro v. Thompson*, 394 U.S. 618 (1969) (state may not impose waiting period on residents who have recently returned from out of state in welfare applications), and see *Crandall v. Nevada*, 73 U.S. 35 (1868) (state may not charge a tax upon persons leaving the state through commercial transport). Some have criticized Shapiro's conjoining of equal protection and the fundamental right to travel. See, for example, Thomas R. McCoy, *Recent Equal Protection Decisions – Fundamental Right to Travel or "Newcomers" as a Suspect Class?*, 28 Vand. L. Rev. 987, 996–9 (1975) (*Shapiro* did not have to be decided through reference to right to travel).

[114] *Dandridge v. Williams*, 397 U.S. 471 (1970) (state may limit welfare payments despite calculable "standard of need").

[115] *San Antonio Ind. School District v. Rodriguez*, 411 U.S. 1 (1973) (education not a fundamental interest), but see *Plyer v. Doe*, 457 U.S. 202 (1982) (state may not deny public education to children who had not been "legally admitted" into the United States).

ginning to recognize how similar its mode of analysis was in both sets of cases.[116]

There was probably a causal connection between the fundamental rights criticism of the Wechsler/Bickel version of legal process and the development of the fundamental rights school.[117] In 1981 Richard Parker suggested that the "burgeoning" of fundamental rights scholarship was a consequence of a generational split between the "'generation of the 1960s' who are now doing constitutional law" and the "process"-oriented theories of an earlier generation.[118] This "generational" split between the fundamental rights school and the conservative legal process scholars does not completely explain the direction that fundamental rights took as it developed. Thus, although it may have been inevitable that members of the "generation of the 1960s" were going to break from their elders on questions of legal theory because legal process was compromised by its doctrinal errors, it was not inevitable that the alternative theory that the younger generation would develop would be something like fundamental rights.

---

[116] Thus, from the fundamental rights perspective, it made sense for Walter Murphy to criticize Justice Jackson for "[m]ixing and confusing a doctrine of fundamental, substantive rights with Justice Stone's prescription in *Carolene Products* [304 U.S. 144, 152 n4 (1938)] limiting the judicial role to keeping the political processes free of impediments to exchanges of ideas and discriminations against 'insular' minorities." Murphy, *Ordering of Constitutional Values*, at 731. For Murphy, the constitutional protections of the freedom of press, speech, religion, to marry, citizenship, privacy, reproduction, travel, to possess property, to choose a profession, and (possibly) to have an education are "constitutional rights" validated by the same test: Is the proposed right implied by the fundamental values of the Constitution? Ibid., at 731, 745.

[117] See Brest, *Fundamental Rights Controversy*, at 1067 (discussing the connection between the rejection of Bickel's criticisms of the Warren Court's equal protection jurisprudence and the development of the fundamental rights school's due process jurisprudence).

[118] Richard Parker, *The Past of Constitutional Theory – and Its Future*, 42 *Ohio St. L.J.* 223, 223–24 (1981). See also Kalman, *The Strange Career*, at 50 (describing the "new generation who went to law school during the Warren years and entered teaching" during the 1960s) and Martin Shapiro, *Fathers and Sons: The Court, The Commentators, and the Search for Values*, in *The Burger Court: The Counter-Revolution That Wasn't* 219 (Vincent Blasi, ed., 1984) (on the new generation of scholars whose "consciousness-shaping crisis was not 1937 but 1954"). At the same symposium where Parker made his comments, Mark Tushnet suggested that American constitutional law experiences periods of "Grand Theory," and that fundamental rights and interpretivism were two modern attempts at Grand Theory; the last attempt at Grand Theory immediately prior to the most recent period "can be dated from Herbert Wechsler's Holmes Lectures and Alexander Bickel's early work . . . [on] neutral principles." Tushnet, *Dilemmas of Liberal Constitutionalism*, at 411–12.

As we saw previously, there were other choices: Parker and his generation could have accepted Pollak and Golding's original invitation and rejected Wechsler and Bickel as incompetent interpreters of legal process. For whatever reasons, the younger generation did not choose another alternative. Instead, they rejected every variety of legal process theory and turned their energies toward developing the fundamental rights criticism. Critical to a complete explanation of how constitutional theory developed in the recent past is the conflation by fundamental rights scholars of legal process with the conservative politics and particular methodological beliefs of Wechsler and Bickel. This conflation explains why the fundamental rights approach gained dominance, which in turn explains why interpretivism – the reaction to fundamental rights – became the leading alternative school.

Furthermore, the theoretical commitments that the "younger generation" attributed to legal process explain, at least proximately, the theoretical commitments the younger generation built into its own alternative theory. Thus, for example, when Judge Skelly Wright reviewed the impact of legal process upon Supreme Court scholarship on the Warren Court (as of 1971), he picked Bickel as the primary exemplar of what he called the "Wechslerians of the 1950s and 1960s."[119] Obviously Judge Wright (J.D. 1934) was not a member of the younger generation to which Parker referred. His article, however, was quite self-consciously designed as an articulation of the ideals and methods of "an identifiable new generation of lawyers ... educated in a new 'tradition.'"[120] A brief review of Wright's argument will illustrate upon which elements of legal process the "younger scholars" chose to focus, and in turn, the theoretical needs they felt their own theory of fundamental rights would have to satisfy.

First, Wright turned briefly to Wechsler's arguments for neutral principles and pointed out (as did so many before him) that, while Wechsler explicitly recognized that the Constitution selects certain

---

[119] J. Skelly Wright, *Professor Bickel, the Scholarly Tradition, and the Supreme Court,* 84 *Harv. L. Rev.* 769, 783 (1971) (hereafter *Professor Bickel*). I do not fault Judge Wright for focusing on Bickel and Wechsler: By 1971, they had seized the mantle of the heirs of Hart and Sacks. The argument made here is not about "blaming" the younger scholars for responding to the conservative wing of legal process, or even for conflating all the other varieties of legal process with its conservative form. The argument is designed to explain how the fundamental rights school developed, and why it apparently contains an irreducible commitment to some version of natural law.

[120] Ibid., at 804.

values, he demanded a test for the identification of those values that could never be met.[121] Wright then noted that Bickel himself recognized the paradox Wechsler set for himself[122] and argued that Bickel drew the wrong lesson from Wechsler's failure. Bickel had "'come to doubt in many instances the Court's capacity to develop "durable principles," and to doubt, therefore, that judicial supremacy can work and is tolerable in broad areas of social policy.'"[123] As Wright correctly observed: "[O]ut of [Bickel's] profound value relativism emerges the view that the Court simply must stay out of most important policy questions."[124] Wright then made explicit the force of the generational split:

> [Bickel's] rather audacious commentary on the Warren Court invites an examination of the relevance and vitality of his own mode of judicial criticism. To put it another way: How is the general approach of Professor Bickel and his colleagues in [legal process] likely to relate to the concerns of a new generation of lawyers?[125]

According to Wright, Bickel and his colleagues could not relate to the concerns of the new generation: Legal process could not accommodate the Warren Court's decisions and therefore had to be replaced. But by what? Wright again returned to Bickel as the source – in reverse – for the content of the new generation's theory. Wright certainly agreed with Wechsler's insight (borrowed from Hart and Sacks) that legal principles can intelligibly identify certain values for enforcement. But from Bickel's sly observation that Wechsler failed to actually name any single value correctly identified and applied by the Warren Court, Wright concluded that Wechsler failed for the reason suggested by Bickel. As Bickel (and Bork) had suggested, adjudication could not intelligibly identify *moral* principles, just the majority's policies.[126]

---

[121]   Ibid., at 777–8.
[122]   Ibid., at 778 ("[Bickel] admits his doubt that the Court has ever fully met the Wechslerian standards and recognizes that he does not know whether the Warren Court fell any further short than its predecessors").
[123]   Ibid., at 781 (quoting Bickel, *Least Dangerous Branch*, at 298). Note that the expression *durable principles* is a classic legal process phrase. Here, Bickel was quoting Wechsler, who was quoting Henry Hart's 1959 *Harvard Law Review* Foreword. See Henry M. Hart, *The Supreme Court*, 1958 Term – Foreword: The Time Chart of the Justices, 73 Harv. L. Rev. 84, 99 (1959).
[124]   Wright, *Professor Bickel*, at 781.
[125]   Ibid., at 781.
[126]   Wright adopted the position that regardless of how a moral value is referred to in a law, further moral choices will have to be made by the interpreter of the law in

Wright therefore presented the problem as a choice between two stark alternatives. On the one hand there was Bickel's moral relativism, in which legal principles could not be based in morality because there were no "real" moral values for the law to enforce anyway. This alternative comported neatly with Bickel's conservative politics, because Bickel regarded the majoritarian imposition of conservative values as a matter of policy, not morality. On the other hand, the rejection of moral relativism seemed (according to the Bickel/Wright analysis) to entail that moral values enforced by judges had to come from outside the law itself. In the 1960s this option would have been very attractive to anyone with progressive politics, because it would leave open the possibility that judges could import moral values that would be more liberal than the values evidenced by the language of the Constitution.[127] Given these two choices, it is not surprising that Wright picked the second and predicted that the "new generation" of lawyers would pick that choice too.[128] Therefore, for Parker's generation, under fundamental rights there was "no theoretical gulf between the law and morality."[129]

order to apply the value the law contains: "Wechsler and his followers seem to assume [incorrectly] that the simple application of reason will answer the hard question" of how to interpret the moral terms found in the Constitution. Ibid., at 780. Here Wright was explicitly endorsing Deutsch's rule-skeptical argument reviewed previously. See Deutsch, *Neutrality, Legitimacy and the Supreme Court.*

[127] This is not to suggest that this alternative cannot be attractive to activist judges with conservative politics, as the 1991 nomination and testimony of Judge Clarence Thomas illustrated.

[128] Wright then turned around and suggested that Bickel's loyalty to neutral principles was a façade: Unmasked, Bickel turned out to be a fundamental rights theorist, albeit one who embraced conservativism: "It is useful, then, to pierce the veil of the scholarly tradition [of neutral principles] and to see its quarrel with the Warren Court for what it really is. It is, I believe, a fundamental dispute over the good society as well as over judicial method. And Professor Bickel – his protestations of rational skepticism notwithstanding – is quite prepared to assert certain values as paramount." Wright, *Professor Bickel,* at 803.

[129] Ibid., at 804.

Chapter 6

Fundamental Rights and the Problem of Insatiability

Judge Skelly Wright's critique of legal process revealed two basic theoretical commitments of the fundamental rights approach: (1) that legal principles cannot fully or adequately identify moral values; and (2) that judges must choose (at some level and only sometimes) upon which moral values to rely when adjudicating a legal claim. We should be clear about what we are attributing to Wright. When Wright suggested that a judge must make a moral choice when interpreting a legal principle that expressly refers to a moral concept, he was saying that the judge must do something different from interpreting the moral concept to which the law refers. When a law refers to a nonlegal concept (such as "subsequent" or "adjacent"), we accept the inevitable difficulties of interpretation, but we do not readily assume that the interpretation of a temporal concept (for example) requires the judge to supplement the temporal concept with another concept instantiating another value of equal weight (such as morality or aesthetics).[1] Nowhere did Wright (or

---

[1] Some theorists have said this, of course. The realists argued that any and every step in legal reasoning potentially involved questions of policy (as well as other, more idiosyncratic factors). See, for example, Felix S. Cohen, *Transcendental Nonsense and the Functional Approach*, 35 Colum. L. Rev. 809, 839 (1935) (discussing how to analyze the existence of a contract); see also Justice Cardozo's opinion in *Hynes v. N.Y.C.R.R.*, 231 N.Y. 229, 235–6 (1921) (whether landowner owed duty to boy standing on plank extending over public right of way): "Here structures and ways are so united and commingled, superimposed upon each other, that the fields are brought together. . . . The law must say whether it will subject him to the rule of the one field or of the other, of this sphere or of that. . . [according to]considerations of analogy, of convenience, of policy, and of justice." Critical legal studies would suggest that each and every step of legal reasoning is simply the reproduction of roughly the same hegemonic system of liberal rationality. See, for example, Gary Peller, *The Metaphysics of American Law*, 73 Cal. L. Rev. 1151, 1194–1219 (1985) (discussing the nonneu-

any other fundamental rights theorist) suggest that the problem of interpreting moral concepts in law is a subset of the more general problem of interpreting concepts in law. Nor did it seem that it is a problem that could be solved by better draftsmanship: The Eighth Amendment unambiguously states that prohibited punishments are to be measured against the standard of "cruel and unusual," yet it is clear that Wright thought that the application of the Constitution's prohibition against cruel and unusual punishment required some prior moral choice by a judge.[2] Thus, Wright was saying that something about the moral content of moral concepts necessarily caused them to be underdefined when they were used to provide the normative content of a legal principle.[3]

It might be argued that this summary forces too skeptical a view of legal reasoning on Wright (and by extension the fundamental rights school) in that Wright wrote only about the Constitution, not law in general, and that he could be read as meaning only that the Constitution does not fully or adequately identify moral principles.[4] Two possibilities present themselves. Either Wright accepted that (1) other types of laws could fully or adequately identify moral

---

tral implications of the temporal and spatial metaphors used in early-twentieth-century contract and tort law).

[2] I attribute this position to Wright as a logical extension of his basic argument. Tribe, a reliable representative of the fundamental rights school, did take this position. Laurence Tribe, *American Constitutional Law* 919 (2d ed., 1988); see also *Gregg v. Georgia*, 428 U.S. 153, 232 (1976) (Marshall, J., dissenting); Margaret Radin, *The Jurisprudence of Death: Evolving Standards for the Cruel and Unusual Punishments Clause*, 126 *U. Pa. L. Rev.* 989, 1039–42 (1978) (discussing Justice Marshall's application of the Eighth Amendment). For a view which suggests that the Eighth Amendment can be interpreted without the introduction of new moral premises, see Michael Moore, *A Natural Law Theory of Interpretation*, 58 *S. Cal. L. Rev.* 277, 394 (1985).

[3] I note that in section 5.4 I wrote that Wright agreed with Bickel's claim that "legal principles cannot intelligibly identify moral values for enforcement," and in this paragraph I characterize Wright's position as "legal principles cannot *fully* or *adequately* identify moral values." The shift from *intelligibly* to *fully or adequately* is necessitated by the fact that although Wright and Bickel agreed that legal principles cannot constrain action through the incorporation of moral norms, they disagreed on the reason why this is so. Bickel thought it is so because he doubts the very existence of moral principles, anywhere and at any time, Wright because he doubted the capacity of legal principles to capture or express moral principles with any specificity.

[4] See J. Skelly Wright, *Professor Bickel, the Scholarly Tradition, and the Supreme Court* 84 *Harv. L. Rev.* 769 at 784 (1971): "Of course the Constitution is written in broad, majestic language. How else should it have been written? The framers were not so dim-witted as to believe that times would not change, that unforeseen problems would not arise." See also Walter F. Murphy, *An Ordering of Constitutional Values* 53 *S. Cal. L. Rev.* 703, at 704 (1980) (noting sources of vagueness).

principles, just not constitutions, or (2) although constitutions can fully or adequately identify moral principles, the U.S. Constitution does not. With regard to the first option, it is unclear why a *constitutional provision*, as opposed to a statute, would *necessarily* be any less capable of adequately describing a moral principle.[5] As Wellington pointed out, the fact that a judge's interpretation of the Constitution is not reviewable by a legislature does not make the Constitution more inscrutable than a statute; nor does the fact that a constitutional provision will be interpreted for more years than a statute make the statute's meaning more tractable.[6] I think Wright would have agreed, because when he argued that moral principles cannot be fully or adequately described by a legal principle, he did not distinguish between constitutions and other forms of law.[7] With regard to the second option, it is unclear why we should assume that the framers would not place adequately described moral principles into the Constitution if such an option were available.[8]

We can now hazard a working definition of the theory of fundamental rights. It makes a claim about the concept of law. According to the fundamental rights theorists, legal principles cannot adequately or fully communicate moral principles to the law's intended audience. Because a constitution is a form of law, albeit a special form, the theory of fundamental rights is committed to a

---

[5] Many fundamental rights theorists think that constitutions do the best job of all forms of law in capturing the meaning of moral claims. See, for example, Sotirios Barber, *On What the Constitution Means* 42 (1984) (a constitution is a form of law that conveys "aspirational meanings"). On the other hand, it may be that given the very high stakes, the logic of bargaining in a constitutional convention would generate incentives among all factions to accept vaguely worded language that contained as little normative content as possible (on the assumption that case-by-case interpretation of empty phrases may provide opportunities for the control of judicially created constitutional meaning).

[6] Harry H. Wellington, *Interpreting the Constitution* 30 (1990) (constitutional adjudication is like other forms of adjudication).

[7] Wright, *Professor Bickel*, at 778; see also Thomas Grey, *Do We Have an Unwritten Constitution?*, 27 *Stan. L. Rev.* 703, 715–16 (1975) (suggesting that positive law – of any form – could not completely codify the moral principles the framers wanted to put into the Constitution).

[8] It is far more likely that whatever limitations are faced by the 1787 Constitution are faced by all constitutions. After all, Chief Justice Marshall did not distinguish the 1787 Constitution when he said, "we must never forget, that it is *a constitution* we are expounding." *McCulloch v. Maryland*, 17 U.S. (4 Wheat.) 316, 321 (1819). See also Murphy, *Ordering of Constitutional Values*, at 705 (noting the fundamental similarities among the problems of interpreting the U.S. Constitution and other written constitutions).

certain view about constitutional interpretation: If legal principles cannot adequately or fully communicate moral principles to the Constitution's intended audience, then at least some decisions under the Constitution will be decided according to moral principles that have been identified as constitutionally authoritative *because of* the fact that they are objectively true.[9] The adoption of the fundamental rights approach to law and constitutional interpretation necessarily entails a certain view about the correct theory of adjudication for the U.S. Constitution. If an interpreter wishes to avail him- or herself of moral principles in the course of determining what the Constitution requires and must do so regardless of the language contained in the law, then the interpreter's choice of moral principles will be independent of (even if parallel to) any command found in the Constitution. This entails that the interpreter's choice of moral principle will be based upon a moral or political theory that the interpreter believes to be objectively true.[10]

For purposes of illustration, here is a partial list of theorists who have been members of the fundamental rights school, as well as the "theory of moral value" each used to determine the meaning of the moral terms they find in the Constitution: the early Laurence Tribe

[9] I think it is obvious that one's constitutional theory must be the same for every legal institution plausibly described as a constitution. This is not to say that the content of every constitution is identical: The contents of specific constitutions may differ, as may the theory of adjudication demanded by the content of various constitutions. That is to say, *how* we interpret a constitution cannot change as we move from document to document (or regime to regime), but the answers to the questions of *what* a constitution means and *who* determines what it means may vary tremendously from constitution to constitution. (I am indebted to Walter Murphy for educating me on these three questions.)

That the answer to the question "How should we interpret this constitution?" should be the same regardless of the constitution one is interpreting is, I believe, a point of fundamental agreement between positivists and the fundamental rights scholars discussed in this chapter. Thus, even if I may disagree with Murphy about whether a "set of traditions" is a constitution, I believe he and I would agree that once the question of inclusion and exclusion has been settled, each member that has been included in the "set of constitutions" should be interpreted the same way – that is, according to the theory of interpretation one believes is correct. See Walter F. Murphy, *Slaughter-House, Civil Rights, and the Limits of Constitutional Change*, 32 Am. J. Juris. 1, 11 (1987).

[10] It is beyond the scope of this chapter to discuss the details of the kind of theories of adjudication that are compatible with the fundamental rights theory of constitutional interpretation. It should be noted that fundamental rights authors in law schools focus on the question of adjudication so much that they often fail to distinguish it from the question of interpretation.

(equality and autonomy),[11] Frank Michelman ("just wants of citizens"),[12] Kenneth Karst ("the dignity of full membership in society"),[13] Ronald Dworkin ("equal concern and respect"),[14] Michael Perry (a theory of human rights determined by "orthopraxis"),[15] David Richards (Rawls's theory of justice),[16] Thomas Grey (natural rights),[17] Walter Murphy (human dignity),[18] Sotirios Barber (justice),[19] Jim Fleming (deliberative autonomy),[20] and Larry Sager (justice).[21] This list could be criticized for flattening the differences between these scholars, of which there are many. Nonetheless, this

---

[11]   Tribe, *American Constitutional Law*, at chs. 15–17 (2d ed., 1988).

[12]   Frank Michelman, *The Supreme Court, 1968 Term – Foreword: On Protecting the Poor Through the Fourteenth Amendment*, 83 Harv. L. Rev. 7, 11–13 (1969); Frank Michelman, *In Pursuit of Constitutional Welfare Rights: One View of Rawls' Theory of Justice*, 121 U. Pa. L. Rev. 962, 966, 997 (1973); but see Frank Michelman, *Welfare Rights in a Constitutional Democracy*, 1979 Wash. U.L.Q. 659, 674–80 (moving away from fundamental rights to ground theory on Ely's representation-reinforcing model).

[13]   Kenneth Karst, *The Supreme Court, 1976 Term – Foreword: Equal Citizenship Under the Fourteenth Amendment*, 91 Harv. L. Rev. 1, 5 (1977).

[14]   Dworkin, *Taking Rights Seriously* 277 (1977) (hereafter *TRS*). Dworkin's later writings reveal an acute discomfort with the idea that his legal theory endorses any particular set of moral values in adjudication. See Ronald Dworkin, *Law's Empire* 358–9 (1986) (hereafter Dworkin, *Empire*). But see Ronald Dworkin, *Freedom's Law: The Moral Reading of the American Constitution* 75 (1996) ("the Constitution guarantees the rights required by the best conceptions of the political ideals of equal concern and basic liberty . . .").

[15]   Michael J. Perry, *The Constitution, the Courts, and Human Rights* 110 (1982); see also Michael J. Perry, *Morality, Politics & Law* (1988). It must be stressed that Perry is included here for the sake of completeness and illustration: As I argue later, he took a peculiar path to his ultimate fundamental rights stance, a path that took him (in the opinion of others listed here with him) far too close to embracing strong epistemic natural law. His current positions – especially on the relationship between law and religion – are not easily categorized in those terms in which the debate over constitutional interpretation are usually conducted.

[16]   David Richards, *Commercial Sex and the Rights of the Person: A Moral Argument for the Decriminalization of Prostitution*, 127 U. Pa. L. Rev. 1195, 1228–31 (1979); David Richards, *Sexual Autonomy and the Constitutional Right of Privacy: A Case Study in Human Rights and the Unwritten Constitution*, 30 Hastings L.J. 957, 970–2 (1979) (hereafter *Sexual Autonomy*).

[17]   Grey, *Do We Have an Unwritten Constitution?*, at 717.

[18]   Murphy, *Ordering of Constitutional Values*, at 746; see also Murphy, *The Art of Constitutional Interpretation*, in *Essays on the Constitution of the United States* 130 (M. Harmon, ed., 1978).

[19]   Sotirios Barber, *The Constitution of Judicial Power* (1993); Barber, *On What the Constitution Means*.

[20]   James Fleming, *Securing Deliberative Autonomy*, 48 Stan. L. Rev. 1 (1995).

[21]   Lawrence Sager, *Justice in Plain Clothes*, 88 Nw. L. Rev. 410 (1993); Lawrence Sager, *The Incorrigible Constitution*, 65 N.Y.U. L. Rev. 893 (1990).

group captures, I believe, the relevant range of theories that share the basic premises of the fundamental rights position: that law cannot adequately or fully communicate moral principles, and that judges must interpret moral language in law by referring to the moral theory they believe to be true.

Some of the books and articles that I take to be examples of the fundamental rights approach are seen by many today to be exemplars of a style of interpretation known as "justice-seeking" constitutional theory.[22] There is an overlap between the fundamental rights approach and justice-seeking constitutional theory, because the former simply sets out a distinctly liberal, substantive theory of justice that is often seen as the best interpretation of the latter.[23] Because the fundamental rights approach sets out a potentially more narrow area upon which to deploy any given interpreter's conception of justice, it shall be the preferred term in this chapter.

6.2. THE FUNDAMENTAL RIGHTS APPROACH AND NATURAL LAW

One of the most common criticisms leveled against the fundamental rights approach is that it is a form of natural law theory revived to serve certain political ends.[24] Given the summary of the

---

[22] Sotirios Barber defined "the family of justice-seeking constitutionalists" as anyone "who can accept (1) a description of the Constitution as an instrument of justice, conceived as a substantive state of affairs; (2) some conception of the Constitution's affirmative ends; and (3) the view that the Constitution obligates elected officials to pursue such ends." Sotirios Barber, *Justice-Seeking Constitutionalism and Its Critics* (presented at New York University School of Law, April 20, 1995), at 2–3.

[23] Mark Tushnet claimed that fundamental rights scholars acted as if it were mere coincidence that most mainstream constitutional law scholarship agreed with the editorial page of the *New York Times*. Mark Tushnet, *Truth, Justice, and the American Way: An Interpretation of Public Law Scholarship in the Seventies*, 57 Tex. L. Rev. 1307, 1322 (1979). The conception of justice identified by justice-seeking constitutional theorists has followed recent liberal political philosophy by shifting its focus away from rights in order to incorporate a broader set of liberal concerns, including equality and community. Compare Michelman, *In Pursuit of Constitutional Welfare Rights* (using Rawls's *Theory of Justice* to construct the Constitution's theory of justice) with Fleming, *Securing Deliberative Autonomy* (using Rawls's *Political Liberalism* to do the same).

[24] See, for example, Henry Monaghan, *Our Perfect Constitution*, 56 N.Y.U. L. Rev. 353, 358–9 (1981) (recent constitutional theory assumes that "properly construed, the constitution" guarantees "most equality and autonomy values which the commentators think a twentieth century Western liberal democratic government ought to guarantee" [emphasis omitted]); Tushnet, *Truth, Justice and the American Way*, at

fundamental rights approach just presented, this objection seems peculiar. It would be strange to imagine the authors of a law (much less a constitution) who did not think that they were crafting an instrument that they hoped would lead to results that were just. Why would the claim that the U.S. Constitution is an "instrument" of justice commit its speaker to natural law theory? The answer, of course, depends on which definition of natural law one chooses to adopt.

One traditional criticism of natural law focuses on its failure to provide an answer to the question of legal validity:

> Kelsen correctly points out that according to natural law theories there is no specific notion of legal validity. The only concept of validity is validity according to natural law, i.e., moral validity. Natural lawyers can only judge a law as morally valid, that is, just or morally invalid, i.e., wrong. They cannot say of a law that it is legally valid but morally wrong. If it is wrong and unjust, it is invalid in the only sense of validity they recognize.[25]

Natural law's critics have typically held the view that natural law must endorse some version of the infamous maxim *"lex injusta non est lex"* (an unjust law is not law), often attributed to Aquinas.[26] This model of natural law focuses on the connection between the moral truthfulness of the values contained in a law and the existence of the law. It seems to suggest, in this stark form, that any putative law

---

1316 (justice-seeking constitutional theory "attempt[s] to recast constitutional law as natural law"); and see Laura Kalman, *The Strange Career of Legal Liberalism* 62–8 (1996) (noting confluence between the political liberalism and "legal liberalism" of fundamental rights scholars) and Ronald Dworkin, *"Natural" Law Revisited,* 34 U. Fla. L. Rev. 165, 165 (1982) (noting criticism of "natural law" elements in his theory).

[25] Joseph Raz, *Kelsen's Theory of the Basic Norm,* 19 Am. J. Juris. 94, 100 (1972).

[26] According to John Finnis, there is no record of Aquinas's actually stating the maxim attributed to him. See John M. Finnis, *Natural Law and Natural Rights* 364 (1980) (noting that the closest Aquinas ever came to this statement was "injustum judicium non est" ["unjust judgment of a court is not a judgment"]); see also Norman Kretzman, *Lex Iniusta Non Est Lex: Laws on Trial in Aquinas' Court of Conscience,* 33 Am. J. Juris. 99, 101 n5 (1988) (traces H.L.A. Hart's misquotation of Aquinas). For a powerful (but flawed) refutation of the claim that any natural lawyer could have adopted the position attributed to Aquinas, see Deryck Beyleveld and Roger Brownsword, *The Practical Difference Between Natural Law Theory and Legal Positivism,* 5 Oxford J. Legal Stud. 1, 2–6 (1985). Michael Moore attributed the statement to Augustine. See Michael S. Moore, *Law as a Functional Kind,* in *Natural Law Theory: Contemporary Essays* 198 (Robert George, ed., 1992).

can be declared a nullity if the norm it contains is not consistent with the objectively true theory of morality.[27]

A theory that provides a test for the "standard that one can use to identify, validate, or discover a community's law" is an "epistemic" theory of law.[28] A theory that sets out moral truth as the test for legal validity is an epistemic natural law theory.[29] This approach to natural law makes sense if one thinks that the purpose of all theories of law is to identify the sources of law. If morality is the source of law, then no putative law that is not derivable (directly or indirectly) from morality along these lines is a true law.[30] Anglo-American jurisprudence has been dominated by theorists asking varying versions of the "sources of law" question.[31]

The impression one might have that natural law theory offers a test to evaluate an individual law's relation to its source is reinforced to some extent by Fuller. In his famous exchange with H.L.A. Hart, Fuller (perhaps because he felt he had to respond to Hart point by point) began his argument by pointing out how different positivists have failed to set out an adequate theory of the positivist sources of law.[32] He then couched his entire discussion of his version of natural law – the "morality of law" – in terms of its superiority as a test of the validity of laws. Of course, Fuller's theory really is no such thing: It is a theory about how to evaluate *legal systems*.[33] There clearly is a relationship between the existence of a legal system and the test for valid laws, but the relationship is difficult and often not very profitable to express, at least from the

---

[27] See, for example, H.L.A. Hart, *Positivism and the Separation of Law and Morals*, 71 *Harv. L. Rev.* 593, 620 (1958) (natural law holds that "what is utterly immoral cannot be law").

[28] Jules Coleman, *Negative and Positive Positivism*, 11 *J. Legal Stud.* 139 (1982), reprinted in Jules Coleman, *Markets, Morals and the Law* (1988).

[29] As Coleman noted, the epistemic function in legal positivism can serve to validate or identify putative laws. Jules Coleman, *Authority and Reason*, in *The Autonomy of Law* 288, 291 (Robert George, ed., 1996). In the case of natural law, however, these two epistemic functions collapse.

[30] See Roger Cotterrell, *The Politics of Jurisprudence* 121 (1989).

[31] See, for example, Joseph Raz, *The Authority of Law* 45–52 (1979). Bentham and Austin grounded the authority of law in the existence of habitual obedience to a sovereign, a purportedly objective "test" to distinguish law from nonlaw and identify legal authority. Hart and Kelsen focused on the social acceptance of a rule of recognition or a basic norm as the fundamental prerequisite for a determination of legal authority.

[32] Lon Fuller, *Positivism and Fidelity to Law – A Reply to Professor Hart*, 71 *Harv. L. Rev.* 630, 633–5 (1958).

[33] Lon Fuller, *The Morality of Law* 39 (2d ed., 1969).

224

perspective of one who wants a test for valid and invalid laws.[34] Nonetheless, Fuller said that his natural law theory provides a test for the validity of law. Under his test, the elements of the "morality of law" are necessary conditions for any law.[35]

Many self-described natural lawyers reject epistemic natural law. Thus, while Raz may have defined "natural law theorists" as "those philosophers who think it a criterion of adequacy for theories of law that they show . . . that it is a necessary truth that every law has moral worth,"[36] Finnis's response was:

> For my part, I know of no philosopher who fits, or fitted, such a description, or who would be committed to trying to defend that sort of theoretical or metatheoretical proposal. . . . Suffice it to say that the root of the misunderstanding seems to be the failure of the modern critics to interpret the texts of natural law theorists in accordance with the principles of definition which those theorists have, for the most part, consistently and self-consciously used.[37]

The modern critics to whom Finnis referred made the mistake of assuming that legal theory has only one task: constructing a test for putative laws. Natural law theorists like Finnis (or his American counterparts, Lloyd Weinreb and Robert George) "reject[ed] any claim to judge the legal validity of rules and so avoid any confronta-

---

[34] While Fuller made a persuasive case that the Nazi legal system did not satisfy the morality of law, his discussion of the "grudge informer" law simply does not prove his point. The law he cited probably does satisfy the eight criteria of the morality of law, to the extent that the morality of law can be used to evaluate a single law in isolation. Compare Fuller, *Positivism and Fidelity to Law* at 652 (discussing Judgment of July 27, 1949, Oberlandesgericht Bamberg, 5 Suddeutsche Juristen-Zeitung 207 [Germany 1950] [German citizen may be prosecuted for harms caused in the course of obeying valid Nazi law in 1944]) with Walter Murphy et al., *American Constitutional Interpretation* 260 (1986) (discussing Judiciary Act of 1789, Section 25 [Alien and Sedition Act]); see also Cotterrell, *Politics of Jurisprudence*, at 132 (Fuller fails to connect his criticism of the Nazi legal system with his discussion of individual laws).

[35] See Fuller, *Positivism and Fidelity to Law*, at 661: "In other words, where one would have been most tempted to say, 'This is so evil it cannot be law,' one could usually have said instead, 'This thing is the product of a system so oblivious to the morality of law that it is not entitled to be called a law.'"

[36] Joseph Raz, *Practical Reasons and Norms* 162 (2d ed., 1990).

[37] Finnis, *Natural Law and Natural Rights* at 26–7. According to R. George Wright, natural lawyers have rejected the epistemic project because epistemic natural law (if it were possible) would end up being more indeterminate than epistemic legal positivism. See R. George Wright, *Is Natural Law of Any Use in Constitutional Interpretation?*, 4 S. Cal. Interdisc. L.J. 463, 469–75 (1995).

tion with Legal Positivism."[38] Weinreb, George, and Finnis are therefore "traditional natural law theorists" in constrast to Dworkin and other fundamental rights theorists, who are "modern natural law theorists."[39]

Instead, Finnis's natural law theory provides an evaluative function; it acts as a standard against which a legal system may be tested. Finnis was concerned with what he understood, following Aristotle, as a "focal" conception or "central case" of law.[40] This focal conception is an ideal or pure form, of which actual existing forms are mere derivatives or imperfect examples.[41] In fact, it turns out that Finnis's theory of natural law is more like an exercise in moral philosophy than in epistemic jurisprudence: Instead of using the term *natural law,* one "could, without loss of meaning, have spoken instead of 'natural right,' 'intrinsic morality,' 'natural reason or, right reason, in action,' etc."[42] The result is a complex metaethical analysis that generates a focal conception of a legal system that is measured against the degree to which it allows for human flourishing through "complete" communities.[43] Finnis, like Fuller, saw the rule of law as the central legal value recognized by natural law: Rules bring clarity and predictability to human interactions and allow individuals to adjust their circumstances rationally within a

[38] Cotterrell, *Politics of Jurisprudence,* at 145–6; see also Finnis, *Natural Law and Natural Rights* at 278: "I have by now sufficiently stressed that one would be simply misunderstanding my conception of the nature and purpose of explanatory definitions of theoretical concepts if one supposed that my definition 'rules out as non-laws' laws which failed to meet, or meet fully, one or other of the elements of the definition." It should be noted that there are many significant differences between Weinreb and Finnis; however, they share the same general approach to the relationship between natural law theory and jurisprudence. See Lloyd C. Weinreb, *Natural Law and Justice* (1987); see also Robert George, *Recent Criticism of Natural Law Theory,* 55 *U. Chi. L. Rev.* 1371 (1988) (book review) (comparing Finnis and Weinreb).

[39] See Brian Bix, *Natural Law Theory,* in *A Companion to Philosophy of Law and Legal Theory* 223–40 (Dennis Patterson, ed., 1996).

[40] Finnis, *Natural Law and Natural Rights,* at 9–13.

[41] Ibid., at 280: "'Natural law' – the set of principles of practical reasonableness in ordering human life and human community – is only analogically law, in relation to my present focal use of the term."

[42] Ibid., at 280–1. In light of this comment by Finnis, it is interesting to recall that he very clearly distinguished between legal reasoning and the sort of practical reasoning that he thought is properly the subject of natural law theory. According to Finnis, "[i]t is a philosophical mistake to declare, in discourse [about natural law], that a social order or set of concepts must either be law or not be law, be legal or not legal." Ibid., at 280. The latter question, which concerns the existence of a law or a legal system, is of no interest to Finnis's natural lawyer.

[43] Ibid., at 147.

rule-governed environment. Because Finnis's developed conception of the good life according to natural law depends heavily on the community's creating the conditions for individual flourishing, he was less committed – even in the central case – than the fundamental rights theorists to specifying the fundamental individual rights that the law must respect.[44] Ultimately, Finnis's distinction between the legal systems in the world and the standard against which they are measured, *and* his strong interest, even in his central case, in allowing the community to develop its own idea of the good through the rule of law, generates a theory that is more about the moral life the law should promote than about the morality of law.[45] Thus, even H.L.A. Hart, who opposed the first version of natural law examined previously, found this second version relatively congenial: It is "in many respects complementary to rather than a rival of positivist legal theory."[46] Under this second view, natural law theory is not epistemic but semantic, in that it describes the relations between moral and legal concepts without providing a test for the validity of the latter.[47]

Notwithstanding Finnis's efforts, when critics such as Monaghan or Ely faulted the fundamental rights approach for the sin of nat-

---

[44] See, for example, Robert George, *Individual Rights, Collective Interests, Public Law, and American Politics,* 8 *Law and Philosophy* 245, 254–5 (1989) (contrasting Finnis's natural law theory with the "campaign" by American liberals "to obtain legal immunities for controversial activities they believe to be matters of individual right").

[45] Cotterrell noted that Finnis's natural law theory is ultimately weaker than Fuller's. See Cotterrell, *Politics of Jurisprudence,* at 149: "At the point at which Finnis's natural law theory meets legal positivism's direct concern with working systems of legal rules, it restricts itself, like Fuller's theory, to elaborating and lauding the virtues of the Rule of Law." But whereas Fuller attacked positivism for its inadequate treatment of the rule of law, he offered no challenge to positivism on its own ground. Natural law has, it seems, become an ally of and supplement to legal positivism.

[46] H.L.A. Hart, *Essays in Jurisprudence and Philosophy* 10 (1983). Hart may have felt that there was no remaining conflict between him and Finnis because they both agreed that all legal systems share the same "minimum content of natural law," that is, certain rules that are essential if individuals are to live together at all. H.L.A. Hart, *The Concept of Law* 195 (2d ed., 1994). Hart would be wrong to base his reconciliation on this idea. If the minimum content theory is to act as a test of the existence of legal systems, then it is an "epistemic" natural law theory of the first type, albeit a very "thin" theory (similar) to Fuller's and not like Finnis's evaluative theory. If the minimum content theory is supposed to be a description of the "focal" conception of law, then it is simply very different from Finnis's conception. See M. Martin, *The Legal Philosophy of H.L.A. Hart: A Critical Approach* 181–90 (1987).

[47] It is likely that this "second view" is the natural law equivalent of what Coleman called the "semantic" theory of legal positivism. See Coleman, *Negative and Positive Positivism,* at 141.

ural law, they meant the first form of natural law attacked by Raz and Hart. The reason for this is simple: Because this debate takes place among politically motivated constitutional scholars, it is to the advantage of each side to produce a test that would condemn the other's interpretation of the Constitution as not-law. Thus, the conservative opponents of the fundamental rights school have developed an originalist theory of constitutional adjudication that is consistent with (although by no means a natural consequence of) an epistemic version of positivism and have attributed to the fundamental rights school the epistemic natural law theory described previously. Under the most extreme vers ons of epistemic natural law, moral truthfulness operates not only as a test for not-law but also as the only positive source of law.[48] The advocates of semantic natural law theory seek to distance themselves from fundamental rights on the grounds that because it uses justice as the source of law, the fundamental rights approach must be an epistemic theory of natural law.[49] Legal positivists and semantic natural lawyers have a *prima facie* case for their view. Fundamental rights theorists not only criticize their conservative opponents' proposed interpretations of the Constitution but energetically propose alternative interpretations based on the application of justice, *qua* justice, to the Constitution.

It is for reasons such as those sketched here that many fundamental rights theorists preemptively strike and affirmatively argue that they do not share a connection with any form of natural law.[50] They assume that "natural law" necessarily must mean epistemic natural law, and epistemic natural law is unpalatable to them for three reasons. First, it seems indistinguishable in form from the theory of substantive due process that supported the economic rights

---

[48] Semantic natural law theorists oppose attributing to natural law theory a sources thesis that claims that all moral obligations are part of the law: "[D]oes logic compel us to hold that (MO) [moral obligation to comply with a rule] entails (LV) [legal validity]? . . . This [conclusion] . . . is flawed for it commits the fallacy of Affirming the Consequent." Beyleveld and Brownsword, *The Practical Difference Between Natural Law Theory and Legal Positivism*, at 6.

[49] See, for example, George, *Individual Rights, Collective Interests, Public Law, and American Politics*, at 254 and John Finnis, *Natural Law and Legal Reasoning*, 38 Clev. St. L. Rev. 1, 7 (1990).

[50] See, for example, Dworkin, *"Natural" Law Revisited*, at 165 ("I have of course made the pious and familiar objection to this charge [of natural law]"); Tribe, *American Constitutional Law* at 1309 ("natural law" inadequate to establish right to personhood); David Richards, *The Moral Criticism of Law* 31–2 (1977) (denying that his method is natural law theory).

argument of the *Lochner* era.[51] Second, it leaves unclear whether a constitution could authorize laws that were clearly in violation of the moral values each theorist held to be true.[52] Third, it implies that justice is prior to politics, and thus that the most basic political acts of constitution making, such as ratification and amendment, are unnecessary or purely symbolic.[53] While the first of these concerns might be dismissed as an *ad hominem* attack, the second and third concerns would, if true, cause most American constitutional lawyers to stop and reconsider their commitment to the fundamental rights approach.

Epistemic natural law, as I have described it so far, seems outrageously inconsistent with our traditional understanding that the rights and powers possessed by American citizens, whatever their moral status, did not exist as *legal* rights and powers until the Constitution was brought into existence through the act of ratification described in its own Article VII.[54] Even Lysander Spooner based his argument that slavery was illegal in the United States on the fact that the Constitution of 1787 was *ratified*; had it not been, then he would not have had a standard against which to find the Fugitive Slave Clause inconsistent.[55] A view even tougher than Spooner's – which would hold slavery illegal, any other political or legal act re-

---

[51]   See Grey, *Do We Have an Unwritten Constitution?*, at 711 n35 (citing *Lochner v. New York.*, 198 U.S. 45 [1905]).

[52]   See Dworkin, *"Natural" Law Revisited*, at 186 (discussing the adjudication of the Fugitive Slave Acts).

[53]   It is this fear that I believe ultimately motivated Bruce Ackerman's rejection of the fundamental rights approach. Ackerman replaced justice with certain political acts (constitutional moments) that are, for very precise historical reasons, *prior* to "normal" politics. See Bruce Ackerman, *We the People: Foundations* (1991); Bruce Ackerman, *A Generation of Betrayal?* 65 Fordham L. Rev. 1519 (1997).

[54]   See Frederick Schauer, *Constitutional Positivism*, 25 Conn. L. Rev. 797 (1993). The idea that ratification is a necessary existence condition for a constitution is a modern innovation – classical political theory did not distinguish between ratified, written constitutions and unratified, unratifiable constitutional texts. Arguably, neither does the United Kingdom. It can be argued that there must be normative preconditions in place in order for the ratification of a constitution to be valid under its own terms. See Frank Michelman, *Always Under Law?*, 12 Const. Commentary 227 (1995) and William F. Harris II, *Bonding Word and Polity*, 76 Am. Pol. Sci. Rev. 76 (1982), but both Michelman and Harris insist that the necessity of normative conditions prior to the valid ratification of a constitution by political acts does not entail the conclusion that those normative conditions are themselves positive sources of constitutional law.

[55]   Lysander Spooner, *The Unconstitutionality of Slavery* 94 (1860) and see Robert Cover, *Justice Accused* 150–5 (1975) (discussing the debate between the Garrisonians and "Constitutional Utopians" like Spooner).

garding slavery notwithstanding – is clearly an example of what we can call strong epistemic natural law. If epistemic natural law were available only in this strong form, then it would be understandable if fundamental rights theorists chose to abandon epistemic natural law for epistemic positivism and then adopted Finnis's semantic natural law. Justice would then be the metric against which to measure the laws we have. According to Finnis, however, adopting his version of natural law would mean losing the one reason liberal constitutional scholars love epistemic natural law: If justice is a source of law, judges can use moral philosophy to give content to the moral principles that have been referred to by the law.

The obvious response to this argument by fundamental rights theorists is to challenge the all-or-nothing description of strong epistemic natural law given previously. Assuming that no one endorses strong epistemic natural law, which identifies justice as the source of *all* supreme law, it is still possible that many might want to articulate and defend weaker versions of epistemic natural law in which some political act authorizes the members of the political community to act like epistemic natural lawyers from that moment on. There is a range of weaker epistemic natural law arguments of this sort, some more plausible than others. They fall roughly into three categories, ranging from the least weakened (and least plausible) to the most weakened (and most plausible).

1. Almost Strong Epistemic Natural Law: *The existence of a constitution entails the identification of justice as the source of supreme law.* This is a version of the "morality of law" view attributed by Hart to Fuller. Fuller clearly believed that the very fact of a legal system automatically committed the state to certain moral norms. Of course, Fuller emphatically denied that the substance of that commitment was very great; nonetheless, he believed that the morality of law is incompatible with an identifiable set of unjust behaviors by both the state and its citizens. David Dyzenhaus made a similar argument. He argued that the concept of "common law," at least as it is understood in the Commonwealth system, entails certain background norms that no legislation can violate.[56]

---

[56] Thus, South African judges had a legal duty to ignore or overturn a racist law designed to achieve a clearly articulated, morally repugnant end. The judge "does not exclude the plain fact intention solely because it is morally repugnant.... But... [because it violates] a principle of South African common law" of equality that "is

2. Not Very Strong Epistemic Natural Law: *The ratification of a consti-tution that refers to unenumerated rights entails the identification of justice as the source of supreme law.* This is also known as the "unwritten consti-tution" view. According to the unwritten constitution view, the au-thors of the Constitution "generally recognized that written constitu-tions could not completely codify higher law [moral principles]," so the text refers the law applier to another source of law in those cases where the law applier is attempting to apply a legal principle that con-tains a moral term.[57] Unlike the morality of law view, under the un-written constitution view, justice is a source of law only if a constitu-tion exists *and* that constitution refers to rights outside of the constitution.[58] The rights identified by justice preexist the constitution and are possessed by persons *qua* persons, yet it is only because the framers assert that these rights exist that justice has any epistemic value for constitutional law. The argument for the unwritten constitu-tion view is that *if* the framers had wanted a source of law that could do something their original source, the constitutional text, could not do, they would not have turned to more text, and so their statement that we are to take note of rights that are not in the text entails that something else (justice) is supposed to serve as the source of the rights.

Both the morality of law view and the unwritten constitution view reflect what Ely has called "noninterpretivism."[59] Neither view is interpretivist because in neither view does the content of the

presumed to be in place prior to interpretation and [so] the repugnant intention is ex-cluded because it cannot compete as an intention in such a context." David Dyzen-haus, *Hard Cases in Wicked Legal Systems* 60 (1991).

[57] Grey, *Do We Have an Unwritten Constitution?*, at 716. In the first half of this century there was a great deal of discussion over the nature of the values that were implicit in the Constitution. See, for example, Edward Corwin, *The "Higher Law" Background of American Constitutional Law, Parts I & II,* 42 Harv. L. Rev. 149 & 365 (1928); see also Howard Lee McBain, *The Living Constitution: A Consideration of the Re-alities and Legends of Our Fundamental Law* (1927); William Bennett Munro, *The Makers of the Unwritten Constitution* (1930); Charles Edward Merriam, *The Unwritten Consti-tution and the Unwritten Attitude* (1931).

[58] Under the morality of law view, a constitution merely had to exist and could therefore exist as a social fact in the way that Hart and Kelsen viewed the constitu-tions of common law countries. Because the unwritten constitution view trades on a reference to rights "outside" of the constitution, it applies only to constitutions that have defined content – hence the reliance on the metaphor of writtenness.

[59] As Ely noted, for many fundamental rights theorists the Ninth Amendment has been the specific positive law mechanism by which the unwritten constitution is incorporated into the text of the written constitution. John Hart Ely, *Democracy and Distrust* 38 (1980). For example, the Ninth Amendment was the foundation of Justice Goldberg's concurrence in *Griswold v. Connecticut,* 381 U.S. 479 (1965).

source of law depend on the propositional content of the constitution. Under the morality of law view, justice is the source of law if there is a constitution (the content of the constitution is irrelevant to the requirements of justice, which, after all, is a matter of moral philosophy). Similarly, under the unwritten constitution view, justice is the source of law if there is a constitution and it refers to unenumerated rights (again, the content of the constitution is irrelevant to the requirements of justice, which, after all, is a matter of moral philosophy). As Dworkin pointed out recently, there was a period when fundamental rights theorists accepted the allegation (made by their critics) that they were not interpreting the Constitution and attempted to defend their methods by defending, in part, noninterpretivism.[60] Grey was one of the first to recognize that the fundamental rights approach was interpretive in that the conception of justice that formed the source of law for unenumerated rights itself depended, to some extent, on the propositional content of the constitution itself.[61] The bulk of fundamental rights theorists therefore endeavored to weaken their commitment to epistemic natural law enough so that they could base their inquiry into justice on the *interpretation* of some constitutional text, no matter how thin. This leads us to the last and weakest of the weakened epistemic natural law theories.

[60] Ronald Dworkin, *The Moral Reading of the Constitution, The New York Review of Books* 46 (March 21, 1996) ("The theoretical debate was never about whether judges should interpret the Constitution or change it – almost no one really thought the latter"). See also Barber, *The Constitution of Judicial Power,* at 157 (on the rise and fall of the interpretivist/noninterpretivist distinction). But see Thomas B. McAffee, *Substance Above All: The Utopian Vision of Modern Natural Law Constitutionalists* 4 *S. Cal. Interdisc. L.J.* 501, 502–3 (1995) (suggesting that natural modern law constitutionalists "transcend" the interpretivist/noninterpretivist distinction by offering a theory that "[embodies] both a preferred constitutional jurisprudence and a more accurate interpretation of the original constitutional design").

[61] See Thomas Grey, *The Constitution as Scripture,* 37 *Stan. L. Rev.* 1 (1984). Perry underwent a similar conversion. In his earliest work, Perry adopted a form of noninterpretivism that looked a lot like the morality of law view: Although neither the intentions of the framers nor the constitutional text supported using justice as the source of rights, such a practice was a necessary consequence of democracy under a constitution. See Michael J. Perry, *Noninterpretive Review in Human Rights Cases: A Functional Justification,* 56 *N.Y.U. L. Rev.* 280, 281–2 (1981). When Perry abandoned the interpretivist/noninterpretivist distinction he began to abandon the fundamental rights approach. See Michael J. Perry, *The Authority of Text, Tradition, and Reason: A Theory of Constitutional "Interpretation,"* 58 *S. Cal. L. Rev.* 551 (1985) (accepting interpretivism) and Perry, *Morality, Politics, & Law,* at 74–5 (adopting a skeptical view of the concept of justice).

3. Weak Epistemic Natural Law (or Justice-Seeking Interpretivism): *The ratification of a constitution that specifies a conception of justice the constitution is supposed to instantiate entails the identification of that conception of justice as the source of supreme law.* I call this the *"summum bonum"* view of interpretation because it defines the scope and content of a legal system's supreme law as coextensive with the "unitary vision of an ideal political society" identified by the text of the constitution.[62] The *summum bonum* view asks us to take notice of the fact that from the perspective of practical reasoning, every constitution is designed to achieve some principal good. Sometimes this principal good is (inadequately) described through a term or phrase in the constitutional text,[63] although it also can be described by some more general phrase that construes the constitution's principal good from its language and structure.[64] The fundamental rights theorists who urge a constitutional *summum bonum* would admit that the good they identify becomes a source of moral principle in constitutional interpretation only because the framers

---

[62] Augustine, *The City of God* 309 (David Knowles, ed., 1972); and see Laurence Tribe and Michael Dorf, *On What the Constitution Means* 24 (1991). Tribe and Dorf rejected the *summum bonum* view, which they called "hyper-integration," and associated this approach with Walter Murphy, John Hart Ely, Richard Epstein, and David Richards. Tribe's emphatic repudiation of hyper-integration must be read in light of his endorsement of an approach which accepts that there may be great variance between what the Constitution's text and "architecture" require and what justice or popular sovereignty might demand. See, for example, Laurence Tribe, *Taking Text and Structure Seriously: Reflections on Free-Form Method*, 108 Harv. L. Rev. 1221, 1236 (1995). It is arguable that Tribe was not always such a pessimist about the possibility of a coincidence between interpretation and justice. See Tribe, *American Constitutional Law*, at chaps. 15–17 (on equality and autonomy as the *summum bonum* of the Constitution).

[63] The Preamble is often used for this purpose; according to one fundamental rights theorist, it lists "national integrity, 'obtaining domestic tranquility,' securing 'the Blessings of Liberty,' and, not least, advancing justice" as its ends. Murphy, *An Ordering of Constitutional Values*, at 747.

[64] Notwithstanding Monaghan's suggestion (unsubstantiated in his article), terms like *the common good* or *the general welfare* are rarely used in this sense probably because fundamental rights theorists are generally anti-utilitarian. See Monaghan, *Our Perfect Constitution*, at 369–70. The principal good cited by fundamental rights theorists almost always implies the liberal principle of incommensurability – that is, that inequalities cannot be compensated through a single welfare metric. See Joseph Raz, *The Morality of Freedom* 198–9 (1986) (on "public goods" and liberalism). Frank Michelman, for example, set out the norm of "just wants," in Michelman, *The Supreme Court*, 1968 Term – Foreword at 11; Kenneth Karst set out the norm of "equal citizenship," in Karst, *The Supreme Court*, 1976 Term – Foreword, at 5. Barber set out the norm of "justice" in Barber, *The Constitution of Judicial Power*, at 215 (quoting the Federalist Papers); and Fleming set out the norm of "deliberative autonomy," in Fleming, *Securing Deliberative Autonomy*, at 10–12.

chose that good.[65] Had the nation not chosen that good, it is implied, the particular *summum bonum* endorsed by each theorist would have no more than a hortatory function. If a fundamental rights theorist were to argue that the particular *summum bonum* was a source of supreme law regardless of what a constitution actually said, then their view would collapse back into either the unwritten constitution or morality of law view. Therefore, unlike a noninterpretivist epistemic natural lawyer, the proponent of the *summum bonum* view may say that, "once it [the *summum bonum*] was adopted, the courts could . . . honestly defend an unpopular decision to a protesting public with the transfer of responsibility: 'We didn't do it – you did.'"[66]

We have seen that there are four types of epistemic natural law: the strong version, which sets out a source of moral principles independent of any authorization from a positive source of law, and three weak versions, which rely on a prior epistemic positivist theory to allow a citizen to know if a legal system exists and (with increasing degrees of specificity) the identity of the source of moral norms that form the substantive content of the legal system's norms. A version of Weak Epistemic Natural Law would seem compatible with Hart's original formulation of legal positivism (because the existence condition for the legal system is ultimately a social fact) and Wright's critique of Wechsler and Bickel (because it rejects moral skepticism). It may be that some version of Weak Epistemic Natural Law is compatible with legal positivism. But the three versions of weak epistemic natural law adopted by the fundamental rights approach, the morality of law, the unwritten constitution view, and the *summum bonum* view do not work. As I shall show in the next section, all of them collapse into strong natural law.

6.3. THE STRANGE FATE OF WEAK EPISTEMIC NATURAL LAW

We can see how the collapse occurs by tracing the fate of David Richards's Weak Epistemic Natural Law theory. From a juris-

---

[65] The *summum bonum* view is similar to the posture of a "constitutional democrat" who embraces a form of liberal republicanism. See Frank Michelman, *Can Constitutional Democrats Be Legal Positivists? Or Why Constitutionalism?* 2 *Constellations* 293, 295 (1996).

[66] Grey, *Do We Have an Unwritten Constitution?*, at 710.

prudential perspective, he accepted legal positivism.[67] But he saw no reason why legal institutions cannot incorporate moral principles.[68] He therefore introduced a form of the *summum bonum* view of weak epistemic natural law, which he called "methodological natural law":

> [The theory has] two central characteristics: (1) the analytic focus is the moral dimension of laws, unlike forms of Legal Positivism which have tried to characterize the purely legal element of law in general; and (2) the moral principles, on which this theoretical account rests, *are objective principles of moral reasonableness,* very similar to the kinds of moral principles in terms of which natural law theory traditionally assessed legal systems.[69]

Richards thought that methodological natural law is appropriate to interpret the Constitution, because the framers "believed some such theory" of "contractarian moral rights."[70] Our job as methodological natural lawyers is to determine the "objective principles" of contractarian moral theory: "The choice to adopt or reject such a theory is not an open question in the United States; it is part of the warp and woof of constitutional design."[71] In fact, recognizing the unwritten constitution the framers selected limits our range of theories about the Constitution:

> In general, contractarian theory does not start from premises of the ultimate good of majority rule or of neutral principles, nor does the theory rest on skepticism about the possibility of giving reasonable expression to the moral notions implicit in the constitutional order.
>
> . . .
>
> [O]ne form of constitution that is clearly justified by [contractarian theory] would be one in which certain requirements of justice, for

---

[67]   Richards, *Moral Criticism of Law,* at 26: "[T]he main thesis of legal positivism remains intact: legal systems may exist which are substantially evil. Nothing in the language or thought of law ensures its morality."

[68]   Ibid., at 33: "Legal positivism . . . can be compatible with the general view that moral ideas importantly influence and shape legal development, that concrete legal institutions often rest on moral ideas."

[69]   Ibid.

[70]   Ibid., at 44.

[71]   Ibid., at 44–5. Elsewhere, Richards described contractarian moral theory as the "unwritten constitution." Richards, *Sexual Autonomy and the Constitutional Right to Privacy,* at 960. Like other fundamental rights theorists, Richards agreed that the Constitution incorporates moral principles that could not have been fully or adequately instantiated by legal principles: "[A]ttempts to define the specific content of constitutionally protected moral rights are frustrated by the fact that articulation of such rights typically rests on constitutional provisions strikingly general in form." Ibid., at 962.

example, those established by [Rawls's] principle of greatest equal liberty, are embodied in the constitution itself as conditions of legal validity.[72]

Under methodological natural law, the positive acts of the framers make Rawls's principle of greatest equal liberty the source of moral principles used to interpret the legal principles found in the Constitution.

It is not important at this moment to evaluate Richards's claim that the framers endorsed a contractarian rights theory, or that the best expression of contractarian rights theory is Rawls's principle of greatest equal liberty. Richards could have claimed that Dworkin's theory of equal concern and respect is the best expression of contractarian rights theory.[73] On the other hand, Richards strenuously denied that Dworkin's theory of law is compatible with methodological natural law, notwithstanding the fact that Richards and Dworkin seemed to have endorsed very similar theories of the *content* of the Constitution. Therefore, it is critical that we evaluate Richards's claim that Dworkin's conclusions, which were almost identical to Richards's, are based on "strong natural law," and that Richards's theory avoids that fatal mistake.[74] Where, according to Richards, did Dworkin go wrong?[75]

Dworkin's theory of law begins with the assumption that all laws involve determining, at some level, the rights people have as citizens of their state.[76] But Dworkin denied that the rights people have as citizens are coextensive with the rights people have as persons *qua* persons:

> [We must] distinguish between background rights, which are rights that provide a justification for political decisions by society in the ab-

[72] Richards, *Moral Criticism of Law*, at 49–50.

[73] It could be argued that Dworkin made this claim. See Ronald Dworkin, *Justice and Rights*, 40 U. Chi. L. Rev. 500 (1973).

[74] David Richards, *Taking* Taking Rights Seriously *Seriously: Reflections on Dworkin and the American Revival of Natural Law*, 52 N.Y.U. L. Rev. 1265, 1300 (1977) (hereafter *Taking* TRS *Seriously*).

[75] Richards's critique was based on the fundamental rights argument set out by Dworkin in the 1960s and '70s. One might argue that the "law as interpretation" argument developed in the mid-1980s, or the "majoritarian premise" argument developed in the early 1990s, cured Richards's objections. While *Law's Empire* and *Freedom's Law* certainly advance Dworkin's basic argument, they did not break with the original position set out in *Taking Rights Seriously*.

[76] "The rights thesis . . . [is] that judicial decisions enforce existing political rights." Dworkin, *TRS*, at 87.

stract, and institutional rights, that provide a justification for a decision by some particular and specified political institution. Suppose
that my political theory provides that every man has a right to the
property of another if he needs it more. I might yet concede . . . that
he has no institutional right that the present legislature enact [or a
judge impose] legislation that would violate the Constitution. . . .[77]

Legal rights, therefore are a specific form of institutional right.[78]

Some institutional rights can be identified without the introduction of any moral principles: The process might involve only principles of aesthetics or intellect.[79] But why should a participant in an
institution accept the *authority* of the relevant system of institutional
rights (why can't one insist that a rule based upon an aesthetic principle trump an institutional right in chess based upon an intellectual principle)? The answer, according to Dworkin, is:

> [that] the general ground of institutional rights must be the tacit con-
> sent or understanding of the parties. They consent, in entering a
> chess tournament, to the enforcement of certain and only those rules,
> and it is hard to imagine any other general ground for supposing that
> they have any institutional rights.[80]

Dworkin left open the possibility that for different practices, there
may be different sorts of "general grounds." What Dworkin insisted upon, however, is that in "hard cases" (where the proper in-

---

[77] Ibid., at 93.

[78] Ibid., at 101 ("the concrete rights upon which judges rely must have two other
characteristics. They must be institutional rather than background rights, and they
must be legal rather than some other form of institutional rights").

[79] See, for example, Dworkin's discussion of the institutional rights of chess: "[A
referee] might hold, as a matter of political theory, that individuals have a right to
equal welfare without regard to intellectual abilities. It would nevertheless be wrong
for him to rely upon that conviction in [determining institutional rights in chess]. . . .
Since chess is an intellectual game, he must apply [a] rule in such a way as to protect,
rather than jeopardize, the role of intellect in the contest." Ibid., at 102. Dworkin
made the same argument about the role of aesthetic principles in literary interpretation. See Dworkin, *"Natural" Law Revisited*, at 169–73, and Ronald Dworkin, *A Matter
of Principle*, 158–66 (1985). Consistent with his rejection of value-skepticism, Dworkin
assumed that there are such things as principles of intellect, aesthetics, morality, and,
presumably, legality upon which to interpret one's institutional rights in chess, literary theory, and law. See Dworkin, *"Natural" Law Revisited*, at 175 (rejecting the
"threat of skepticism") and Dworkin, *Empire* at 78–85 (on internal and external skepticism).

[80] Dworkin, *TRS*, at 104.

terpretation of an institutional right is not clear) the interpreter must refer to the "general grounds" upon which the institution rests: "If the decision in a hard case is a decision about which rights [participants in the practice] actually have, then the argument for the decision must apply that general ground to the hard case."[81]

The general strategy for determining institutional rights in controversial cases is the same regardless of the practice. The judge (or referee, or critic) must strive to make the practice "the best it can be": "We must distinguish between two dimensions of a successful interpretation. An interpretation must 'fit' the data it interprets . . . and it must also show that data in its best light, as serving as well as can be some proper ambition of [the practice]."[82] In the case of law, Dworkin argued that a legal interpretation's "fit" can be measured against legal history[83] and its "best light" can be measured against "the substantive ideals of political morality."[84] As Dworkin pointed out, however, a theory of the interpretation of law (and ostensibly all other practices) must have a theory of mistakes, for the threshold of fit relies on being able to measure consistency. Any mechanical test of consistency "will prove too strong, unless [the judge] develops it further to include the idea that he may, in applying this requirement, disregard some part of institutional history as a mistake."[85] The theory of mistakes helps the judge determine whether a novel doctrine that is supported by principles of political morality must nonetheless be rejected because it fails the threshold of fit. If the decision(s) the novel doctrine contradicts are mistakes, then the new doctrine can be included without any loss of fit. Dworkin's theory of mistakes tests a past decision on two axes. First, the judge must determine whether the putatively mistaken decision "is now widely regretted within the pertinent branch of the profession"; and, second, whether "he believes, quite apart from any argument of consistency, that [the] particular statute or decision was wrong because unfair, within the community's own concept of fairness."[86]

---

[81] "In chess [for example] the general ground of institutional rights must be the tacit consent or understanding of the parties." Ibid., at 104.

[82] Dworkin, *"Natural" Law Revisited*, at 170.

[83] See, for example, Ibid., at 171: "How many decisions (roughly) can an interpretation set aside as mistakes, and still count as an interpretation of the string of decisions that includes those 'mistakes'?"

[84] Ibid.

[85] Dworkin, *TRS*, at 119.

[86] Ibid., at 122.

If a decision fails either of these tests, it is vulnerable to being declared a mistake.

Richards thought that Dworkin's theory is not compatible with methodological natural law because it is a form of "sporadic" strong natural law. In hard cases, "a judge *must* have recourse to a set of principles. . . . [And the] determination of which set of principles to apply will in part be a decision about which set 'best' expresses a particular morality."[87] If, in hard cases, the particular morality the judges use were one "determined by some empirical method separable from moral concerns," then Dworkin's theory would collapse into methodological natural law, because, counterfactually, the judges could have adopted some other "particular morality."[88] Dworkin clearly rejected this option. For him, the political morality upon which an interpreter bases the "best light" part of his or her interpretation is not authorized by some empirical method; it is determined according to the interpreter's own convictions about what is objectively the best political morality.[89] If this is the case, said Richards, then the institutional rights judges interpret in hard cases will ultimately be based only on objective morality. Dworkin's distinction between institutional rights and justice collapses, and in hard cases (at least) the theory of mistakes reveals the strong natural law foundation of Dworkin's theory.[90]

Dworkin's response to this criticism was to say that a critic like Richards simply misunderstood what is "natural" in his theory: In hard cases all people must "naturally" make the law the best it can be (that is the "nature" of interpretation). No one must "naturally" adopt the institutional right that he or she believes is the most morally adequate (that would be a matter of the "nature" of moral

---

[87] Richards, *Taking* TRS *Seriously,* at 1299. "There will, in short, be a group of cases in which legality will be dictated by morality, and, for those cases, the separability thesis will be controverted." Ibid.

[88] Ibid., at 1299–1300.

[89] Ibid., at 1300. Dworkin would deny the possibility of the law's identifying a particular morality through empirical method for the same reason he denies that the law can identify institutional legal rights through empirical method: the error of the "semantic sting." See Dworkin, *Empire,* at 31–46.

[90] Here is an example of Dworkin's theory of law in practice, according to Richards: "[We must] use Dworkin's overriding moral imperative – equal concern and respect for all citizens – as the single moral theory to which Hercules [Dworkin's judge] must look. . . . [But then] Dworkin's assertion of an overlap between law and morality in the process whereby Hercules identifies his set of principles . . . puts [Hercules] in something of a dilemma." Richards, *Taking* TRS *Seriously,* at 1300–1.

philosophy, not interpretation).[91] According to Dworkin, then, Richards (or his equivalent) ignored the role of the theory of fit in constructing a theory of mistakes. Political morality, the principles that show law in its best light, must constantly interact with the criteria of fit. If strong natural law means that an interpretation of the law must always instantiate moral truth in hard cases, then Dworkin denied that he is a strong natural lawyer, for the criteria of fit often act to produce interpretations of the law that are not moral from the point of view of the interpreter.[92]

But Richards did not have to end his argument here. He might have asked about how fit constrains interpretation. We know that when judges are "checking" the fit of a novel proposition of law, they are actually deciding whether to select a new legal principle (supported by justice) over a settled legal principle (supported by institutional history) or vice versa. Adjudication is not always about this choice, but adjudication is always about this choice when the theory of fit is involved. The procedure for deriving a novel proposition based on justice is relatively straightforward moral reasoning. The procedure for evaluating the force of institutional history is a bit more complex. The critical point to understand is that the theory of mistakes is simply the inverse of the theory of fit: *Either* the novel proposition fits because the settled proposition was a mistake, *or* the novel proposition does not fit because the settled proposition was not a mistake. Put this way, it almost seems that the theory of mistakes is prior to the theory of fit, but this orderly picture is an illusion: In fact, as I will soon show, the evaluation of the force of the institutional history of the settled proposition uses exactly the same moral judgment that identified the new proposition as the more just legal principle.

As we saw previously, the putative "mistake" is known to be a mistake for one of two reasons: Either the institutional history behind the principle is "widely regretted" by the relevant legal elites, or the interpreter believes that the principle simply violates "the community's own concept of fairness."[93] Because the first test is ba-

[91] See Dworkin, *"Natural" Law Revisited*, at 165 (on the difference between natural law theory and "naturalism").

[92] Ibid., at 186 (discussing the Fugitive Slave Acts); Dworkin, *Empire*, at 103–8 (discussing Nazi legal systems).

[93] "If [Hercules] believes, *apart from any argument of consistency,* that a particular statute or decision was wrong because unfair, within the community's own concept of fairness . . . ." Dworkin, *TRS*, at 122 (emphasis added).

sically a tautology,[94] the only test with any critical bite is the second. How does it operate in practice? First, note that Dworkin required the interpreter to determine the community's concept of *fairness*. Why fairness and not political morality or justice, or any one of a broad range of moral and nonmoral concepts? Dworkin required fairness because in a rights theory, it would be *unfair* to disturb settled expectations without good reason.[95] Second, note that Dworkin required the interpreter to determine the *community's* concept of fairness. Why the community's and not the interpreter's? Given that the theory of mistakes plays a role in the question of fit, and fit is a constraint on the individual interpreter's own idea of true political morality, and fairness is (arguably) a subset of political morality, it would be *circular* to allow the theory of mistakes to rest on the interpreter's idea of fairness.[96] Finally, note that Dworkin required the interpreter to determine the community's *concept* of fairness. Why its concept and not its conception? Regardless of what he said, Dworkin must have meant either that a decision is a mistake if the interpreter believes that it was unfair, according to *the* concept of fairness, or that it was unfair according to the community's *conception* of fairness.[97] But, of course, Dworkin could not have said that

---

[94] This is easy to see: If an old precedent was "widely" regretted by the relevant legal elites (judges, lawyers, legislators, scholars, etc.) how could it be supported by nontrivial institutional history? Remember the sort of example Dworkin used: *MacPherson v. Buick Motor Co.*, 217 N.Y. 382, 111 N.E. 1050 (1916) was a hard case because tort doctrine concerning duties for consumer products, while criticized and ripe for review, was not "widely regretted." Dworkin, *TRS*, at 122. In fact, it is precisely because the institutional history of a case (the precedents and commentary) is supported by a wide portion of the relevant legal community that a change in doctrine confronts a judge as a hard case.

[95] Ibid.

[96] There is no point to dwelling on whether Dworkin could defend this last argument: It is mooted by the next one.

[97] The distinction between concept and conception, if it is to mean anything at all, turns on the fact that the former refers to a "preinterpretive" stage where everyone "agree[s] about the most general and abstract propositions" that make up the idea to which the concept refers. A concept is a logically necessary "plateau on which further thought and argument are built. . . . [Someone who stands outside that plateau] is mark[ed] as outside the community of useful or at least ordinary discourse about the institution." Dworkin, *Empire*, at 70–1. A conception, on the other hand, is one of many competing models of how the concept should look at a less abstract level, especially when applied to controversial cases. See ibid., at 71 and Dworkin, *TRS*, at 134. By definition, then, concepts are not perspectival, because all possible "possessors" of the concept would share the same concept. Conceptions, however, are certainly perspectival; furthermore, moral conceptions are reported from the perspective of what the possessor believes is objectively true. Thus, Dworkin states that while groups have a concept of fairness, each mem-

the community has a conception of fairness. In *The Model of Rules II* Dworkin argued, *contra* Hart, that social rules are necessarily interpretive, with the result that when we ask someone about a social rule, we will necessarily discover no more than that person's conception of the social rule.[98] Dworkin could have said that every interpreter has a conception of the community's conception of fairness, but I really do not understand that to be anything other than a pointless iteration.[99] At the end of the day, within the community there can only be individual competing conceptions of *the* concept of fairness.[100]

The interpreter, therefore, must test settled decisions against his or her own conception of fairness, but because (as Dworkin so powerfully argued) one cannot apply an idea of fairness that one does not, at least provisionally, believe is true, the conception of fairness used by the interpreter will simply reflect his or her own

ber of the group has "different conceptions of fairness." Dworkin, *TRS*, at 135 (emphasis added).

[98]   Ibid., at 55: "[W]hen people assert normative rules, even in the case of conventional morality, they typically assert rules that differ in scope or in detail, or in any event, *that would differ if each person articulated his rule in further detail*" (emphasis added).

[99]   There is a similar ambiguity in *Law's Empire*. In the *McLoughlin* example, after Hercules has determined that two of six possible legal principles "fit" the law of emotional distress, he is supposed to choose between the two on the basis of "substantive political morality." Dworkin, *Empire*, at 248. At this point, according to Dworkin, Hercules' interpretation of "best light" "will depend . . . not only on his beliefs about which of these principles is superior as a matter of abstract justice but also which should be followed, as a matter of political fairness, in a community whose members have the moral convictions his citizens have." Ibid., at 249. First, it is unclear, for the reasons offered *supra*, what Dworkin meant by contrasting Hercules' conception of the substantive political morality of emotional distress with that of the community's. Second, if the institutional history supports either principle, what would be the reason for giving any weight to a principle that instantiates the conception of political morality that is, in Hercules' opinion, wrong? Third, if Hercules were actually to balance his conception of political morality against the community's, what would be his test for determining whether the community's conception was a mistake (i.e., how would he choose between the two)?

[100]   Ibid., at 71; see also Dworkin, *TRS*, at 126 ("if we wish to use the concept of a community morality in political theory, we must acknowledge conflicts within that morality as well"). This is not to suggest that each person's conception is necessarily different from another's. Everyone could happen to share the same conception of fairness. For example, they all could believe that Bentham was correct. The point is that each thinks that fairness "is" Bentham's utilitarianism because they think Bentham was objectively right about fairness, not because they were able to apply some empirical test for identifying the meaning of fairness, such as looking up the word *fairness* in a dictionary. Ibid., at 135.

sincerely held and carefully examined beliefs about justice.[101] But then Richards was right: If what counts as a mistake is any decision that contradicts the interpreter's political morality, then no novel doctrine based on the interpreter's political morality will ever be constrained by the criteria of fit, because any case that would contradict that novel doctrine will be declared a mistake according to the interpreter's own theory of mistakes.[102] Larry Alexander made exactly the same point about the fundamental rights approach in general:

> If correct political/moral principles guide our inference from text and precedents to the underlying principles, won't they always guide the inference to themselves? In other words, won't correct political/moral principles always urge their own adoption and never the adoption of (by hypothesis) incorrect political/moral principles, *no matter how well the latter "fit" existing texts and precedents?*[103]

Dworkin could try to repair the theory of mistakes. He could argue that the theory of integrity makes clear in a way that the theory of institutional rights does not that the theory of mistakes is supposed to test the coherence and not just the consistency of settled

---

[101] "[T]he community's morality . . . is not some sum or combination or function of the competing claims of its members; it is rather what each of the competing claims claims to be. When Hercules relies upon his own conception of [morality] . . . he is still relying on his own sense of what the community's morality provides." Ibid., at 128–9 (emphasis supplied).

[102] An example of Dworkin's theory of mistakes in action is Justice Holmes's dissent in *Northern Securities Co. v. United States*, 193 U.S. 197 (1904). The government's case was based, partially, on the fact that the Sherman Act was intended to prevent anticompetitive combinations. Holmes noted that the Sherman Act "says nothing about competition" and then argued that even if the Act's framers had desired to reach such conduct, the Act's framers could not have really intended to reach anticompetitive private arrangements, because that would give it a design based on a patently false social theory. See Spencer Weber Waller, *The Antitrust Philosophy of Justice Holmes*, 18 S. Ill. U.L.J. 283, 290–1 (1993). Thus, despite virtually conclusive evidence that the Sherman Act was designed to regulate and criminalize voluntary anticompetitive agreements, Holmes declared Congress's intent a mistake: "[T]he act of Congress *will* not be construed to mean the universal disintegration of society into single men, each at war with all the rest, or even the prevention of all further combinations for a common end." *Northern Securities*, 193 U.S. at 407 (emphasis added). It is ironic that in antitrust, Holmes – the author of the famous dissent in Lochner – allowed his conception of social relations to dominate his theory of mistakes.

[103] Larry Alexander, *Book Review*, 8 Const. *Commentary* 463, 467 (1991) (reviewing Harry H. Wellington, *Interpreting the Constitution* [1990] and Tribe and Dorf, *On Reading the Constitution* [1991]).

law.[104] But as Raz has argued, this really does not change the problem with the theory of mistakes identified previously, because coherence ends up playing no role in the theory of law as integrity:

> [Dworkin's] is not a coherence explanation of either law or integrity. His position is: the law consists of those principles of justice and fairness and procedural due process which provide the best (i.e. morally best) set of sound principles capable of explaining the legal decisions taken throughout the history of the polity in question. . . . Thus, while coherence may be a by-product of the best theory of law, a preference for coherence is not part of the desiderata by which the best theory is determined.[105]

The implication of Raz's argument is that Dworkin's theory of adjudication still cannot provide a reason from within the theory of fit (or integrity) that explains why and when "the existence of a less than perfect law justifies deviating from what is otherwise morally best."[106]

But why cannot Dworkin reply that under the original theory of mistakes, the interpreter should test putatively mistaken past decisions not against his or her own conception of fairness but against the concept of the "general grounds" of the practice?[107] In the same way that institutional rights must ultimately be determined by reference to the general grounds of a practice, so should we determine the *inverse* of institutional rights (whether a mistake was made in

---

[104]   Dworkin, *Empire* at 219–22. For an example of the coherence test of mistakes, see ibid., at 247: "[Hercules] cannot simply count the number of past decisions that must be conceded to be 'mistakes' on each interpretation. . . . He must take into account not only the numbers of decisions counting for each interpretation, but whether the decisions expressing one principle seem more important or wide-ranging than the decisions expressing the other."

[105]   Joseph Raz, *Ethics in the Public Domain* 305–6 (1994). Larry Alexander and Ken Kress have noted that Dworkin speaks as if the reason integrity requires us to select a morally suboptimal settled principle over a morally optimal novel principle is that integrity reflects the independently valuable constraint of "equality." Larry Alexander and Ken Kress, *Against Legal Principles,* in *Law and Interpretation* 295 (Andrei Marmor, ed., 1995) (citing Larry Alexander, *Striking Back at the Empire: A Brief Survey of Problems in Dworkin's Theory of Law,* 6 *Law and Philosophy* 419, 426–31 [1987]). Alexander and Kress argued that an attempt by Dworkin to use equality as a morally independent criterion of mistake would be a failure, because "each moral theory – each set of moral principles – will generate its own conception of equality. . . . Thus, there cannot be a coherent reason in terms of the true value of equality for ever departing from the requirements of the correct moral theory." Ibid., at 295.

[106]   Ibid., at 291–3.

[107]   This is, I believe, the reason that Dworkin redeployed the argument about fit by using different language in *Law's Empire.*

past determinations of institutional rights). Dworkin essentially said as much when he noted that debates about the conception of law (what institutional rights people have) must take place by reference to the concept of law (the general grounds of the practice):

> I am defending this suggestion about how we might describe our concept of law: for us, legal argument takes place on a plateau of rough consensus that if law exists it provides a justification for the use of collective power against individual citizens or groups. General conceptions of law . . . begin in some broad thesis about whether and why past political decisions do provide such a justification.[108]

The general ground of law – what Dworkin most recently called the preinterpretive "plateau" of consensus – has assumed different forms over the course of Dworkin's writings. He first framed his analysis like this: The general ground (or concept) of law was that "judicial decisions enforce existing political rights,"[109] and the correct conception of law was that "[o]ur constitutional system rests on a particular moral theory, namely, that men have moral rights against the state."[110] The general ground referred to in this analysis is fatally ambiguous, however. If by "political right" Dworkin meant "what is right according to objectively true political morality," then he has merely asserted the strong epistemic natural law view that persons *qua* persons have moral rights that no one, including the state, can violate. By doing this Dworkin collapsed the distinction between institutional rights in law and the general ground of law. If by "political right" Dworkin meant "institutional rights," then he has collapsed his definition of the general ground of law into a definition of the general ground of *any* concept – it is true by definition that the general ground of *every* practice is the ground of that practice's institutional rights. The problem with this second option is that it is hard to see how conception of the concept can involve such rich normative content when the general ground does nothing more than state a conceptual claim about social practices in general.[111]

In later writings, when Dworkin defined the general ground of law, it appears that he embraced the former alternative and in-

---

108 Dworkin, *Empire*, at 108–9.
109 Dworkin, *TRS*, at 87.
110 Ibid., at 147.
111 Dworkin almost certainly intended "political right" to mean the former. In his discussion of whether his conception of institutional rights under the Constitution is superior to rival conceptions, the ultimate test – the job performed by the gen-

cluded within the preinterpretive plateau only those actions by the state that are *morally* justified: "[L]aw . . . provides a justification for the use of collective power against individual citizens or groups."[112] However, when Dworkin expanded upon the meaning of the word *justified* he repeated the same fatal ambiguity seen previously:

> [The preinterpretive concept] of law is different from justice. Justice is a matter of the correct or best theory of moral and political rights. . . . Law is a matter of which supposed rights supply a justification for using or withholding the collective force of the state because they are included in or implied by actual political decisions of the past.[113]

In this passage, Dworkin seemed to be saying that the preinterpretive plateau of law contains only actions by the state that are "justified." A necessary and sometimes sufficient condition of justification is the "actual political decisions of the past." But we know that Dworkin's use of justification as a empirical, nonmoral test collapses into a moral use of the term *justified. Which* group actions are "actual political decisions" as opposed to not-"actual" political decisions? The theory of mistakes tells us that past legal decisions will be excluded if they contradict the interpreter's political morality. This will generate the consequence (again) that the theory of mistakes will expand to exclude all settled legal principles that compare unfavorably with "morally better" albeit less settled legal principles.[114] Why, for example, should Dworkin's hypothetical Nazi judge "Siegfried" find for the plaintiff in a contract case based on a law that denies the usual defenses to a Jewish defendant?[115] If, as Dworkin hypothesized, the law is clear, then the plaintiff has a right to win (although the judge may still exercise a moral duty by lying) because apparently there are institutional rights based on past political decisions that justify the plaintiff's victory.[116] But I have

eral ground – turns out to be which conception better protects the moral rights men have. See ibid., at 131–5.

[112] Dworkin, *Empire,* at 109.

[113] Ibid., at 97.

[114] Raz, *Ethics in the Public Domain,* at 287. Thus, the theory of mistakes, when used in the process of determining the content of the preinterpretive plateau of law, requires the courts to ask, "Should we adopt what would have been morally the best outcome . . . or should we follow [settled legal principle], which may lead to an otherwise less than ideal solution" from the perspective of morality? See ibid., at 289.

[115] Dworkin, *Empire,* at 106.

[116] Ibid.

shown this argument to be false: Consistent (some might say merci-less) application of the theory of mistakes would show that the set-tled legal principles which support the defendant's putative institu-tional right fail the test of fit/integrity. But this is identical to Fuller's and Dyzenhaus's Almost Strong Epistemic Natural Law arguments.

Dworkin could respond that Siegfried must inform his theory of mistakes with the normative content of "justification" fixed by past political decisions: "[O]ur reasons for supposing that [the plaintiff] has legal rights are quite special – they depend on the idea that peo-ple should be protected in relying and planning on law even in wicked places – and they survive rather than depend on our inter-pretive judgments of the system as a whole."[117] In other words, Dworkin's theory of "naturalism" is a method that needs an "ac-tual" political act to launch the specification of a conception of the concept of "justified collective power."[118] But this assumes that we would know the "actual" political act if we saw it – that is, we need an epistemic theory that tells us how we know which of the many political acts that some people claim underwrite the concept of "jus-tified collective power" is actually *the* actual act. Dworkin might have meant to include in the group of "actual" political decisions all or some nonlegal political decisions, such as the acts of legislatures or constitutional conventions.

There are two problems with this proposal. First, why should Siegfried treat with greater deference the events that led to a settled practice of denying Jews contract defenses just because the practice was the product of legislation as opposed to the accretion of com-mon law precedent?[119] As Dyzenhaus argued with regard to South Africa, there was no reason for a South African "Siegfried" to treat

---

[117]   Ibid.

[118]   This is not to suggest that Dworkin is in any way a relativist: He clearly be-lieves that some conceptions of the concept of justified state force are not richly inter-pretable (like Nazism) while other conceptions are very rich (like the U.S. Constitu-tion or the common law). See ibid., at 106–7.

[119]   It is important to remember that in his earlier discussions of the theory of mistakes Dworkin emphatically denied that there is a significant difference between judicial interpretations of legal rights and other political acts that "create" legal rights: "a precedent is the *report* of an earlier political decision; the very fact of that decision, *as a piece of political history,* provides some reason for deciding other cases in a similar way in the future." Dworkin, *TRS,* at 113 (emphasis added).

clear and carefully drafted racist laws any differently from the racist interpretations of the common law urged by racist lawyers.[120] Second, even if we could satisfy ourselves that a necessary condition of an "actual" political decision is that it is a nonlegal political decision, how do we know whether a controversial decision that looks and feels like a "political" decision is an "actual" political decision? Political decisions, even more so than legal decisions, do not come with easily identified features that place them into some "natural kind" of "actual" political decisions. The set of "actual" political decisions must be defined by a test that distinguishes between "actual" and merely putative political decisions. If the test is the system's own rules for identifying political decisions, then we have just pushed the problem up one level. Obviously, the same reasons that support Siegfried's belief that the precedent cited by the plaintiff is a mistake should be applied to the legislation under which the precedent was established. One might think that Siegfried has taken his job of testing the plaintiff's claim of institutional right against the concept of "justified collective power" a bit too seriously. But why?

As we have seen, the answer cannot be because there is something epistemically special about political decisions.[121] Dworkin, in fact, rejected the claim that political decisions resulting from democratic processes are epistemically significant. In *Taking Rights Seriously* Dworkin asked why a legal system should enforce the results

---

[120]   Dyzenhaus, *Hard Cases in Wicked Legal Systems*, at 252–4. Dyzenhaus based his argument on a legal system in which there are a mixed collection of putatively "actual" political decisions to which an interpreter could refer. Dyzenhaus did not suggest that his argument turns on an empirical measure of the number or frequency of the putative "actual" political decisions that would allow a sincere interpreter to know which set of putative "actual" political decisions were really the "actual" political decisions of the system (and which, conversely, were mistakes), but I imagine that he would agree with Dworkin that the answer to this epistemic problem would have to be approached, as in the *McLoughlin* example, through an evaluation of the "importantness" or "fundamentalness" of the rival sets of putative "actual" political decisions. See *supra* note 99.

[121]   It is important to remember that I am not challenging Dworkin's argument that the best account of political legitimacy is the theory of "associative obligations" based on the political ideal of integrity. See Dworkin, *Empire,* at 206–15. I am raising an epistemic question: Assuming that a judge or a citizen believes (rightly or wrongly) that he or she owes a duty to obey the laws of his or her legal system, can Dworkin's theory of fit/integrity help the judge or citizen answer the question: "Is 'x' a law in my legal system?"

of democratic procedures if the results were unjust.[122] Dworkin noted that *if* democracy means political decision by majoritarianism, then "we should have to rephrase our question to ask why we should have democracy" to resolve "unsettled" political issues.[123] But this argument, regardless of its merit as a critique of democracy, reproduces the same ambiguity identified previously: Even if a judge or citizen adopted the view that "unsettled" political issues should not be decided exclusively by democracy, how does he or she *know* when an issue has been settled?[124] The question of how one knows when to abandon democracy was mercifully dropped by Dworkin in *Freedom's Law*; in this latest version of his argument, he rejected the counterfactual introduced in *Taking Rights Seriously* and argued instead that democracy does not mean political decision by majoritarianism.[125] According to Dworkin, democracy cannot be based on the "majoritarian premise" because majoritarianism is only contingently related to the "defining aim of democracy . . . [which is] that collective decisions be made by political institutions whose structure, composition, and practices treat all members of the community, as individuals, with equal concern and respect."[126] If we reject the majoritarian premise, we must believe that:

> Democracy means government subject to conditions – we might call these the "democratic" conditions – of equal status for all citizens. When majoritarian institutions provide and respect the democratic conditions, then the verdicts of these institutions should be accepted by everyone for that reason. But when they do not, or when their pro-

---

[122] "The argument from democracy is not an argument to which we are committed by our words or our past. We must accept it, if at all, on the strength of its own logic." Dworkin, *TRS*, at 141.

[123] Ibid.

[124] Furthermore, because every political decision (including foundational ones) were "unsettled" before they became decisions, it is hard to see why settled political decisions are, in theory, not subject to the same analysis.

[125] See Dworkin, *Freedom's Law*, at 15–19. This argument bears some affinity to recent "republican" arguments made by Michelman and Sunstein. See, for example, Frank Michelman, *Law's Republic*, 97 *Yale L.J.* 1493 (1988) and Cass Sunstein, *Beyond the Republican Revival*, 97 *Yale L.J.* 1539 (1988). For a careful analysis distinguishing republican arguments from justice-seeking arguments, see Sager, *The Incorrigible Constitution*, at 915–24.

[126] Dworkin, *Freedom's Law*, at 17.

vision or respect is defective, there can be no objection, *in the name of democracy,* to other procedures that protect and respect them better.[127]

I am not concerned in this chapter with whether Dworkin's conception of democracy is better than competing conceptions. I am interested instead in the relationship between Dworkin's conception of democracy and his theory of mistakes. It should be clear that, from the perspective of a Dworkinian citizen, anyone living in a democracy would be wrong to construct a conception of "justified collective power" that was inconsistent with the theory of legitimate majoritarianism (unless that interpreter could propose a theory of democracy that was a better interpretation than Dworkin's). From this step, it is not difficult to further conclude that, from the perspective of a Dworkinian citizen, the test for an "actual" political decision in one's legal system would treat a political decision that was inconsistent with legitimate majoritarianism as either a "mistake" (if it was "settled") or simply as an expression of private (perhaps even revolutionary) sentiment. I fail to see how this result differs at all from the Almost Strong Epistemic Natural Law view that I earlier attributed to Fuller and Dyzenhaus.

Finally, what about Siegfried? Unlike the Dworkinian citizen living in a democracy, he is not required to conclude that the test for an "actual" political decision is the rich standard reflected by legitimate majoritarianism. One might think that this is the line that keeps Almost Strong Epistemic Natural Law from collapsing into strong natural law: At least Dworkin could argue that the single but crucial existence condition denoting when justice is the source of supreme law in a legal system is an "actual" political decision by a democracy to "be" a democracy. But Dworkin's first argument against the privileging of democracy suggests that he cannot avail himself of *any* positivist existence conditions. Recall that Dworkin noted that *if* democracy means political decision by majoritarianism, then "we should have to rephrase our question to ask why we should have democracy" to resolve "unsettled" political issues.[128] It seems reasonable to assume that if a society makes a political decision to instantiate an illegitimate majoritarianism instead of a legitimate majoritarianism, its "settled" political decision should be subject to a theory of mistakes based upon legitimate majoritarianism

---

[127] Ibid. (emphasis added).
[128] Dworkin, *TRS,* at 141.

regardless of whether it also stated in the same political decision that the system it was adopting was intended to be a *legitimate* form of majoritarianism. Why then, should Dworkin's question about democracy be restricted to just democracies? Why shouldn't a Dworkinian ask about any legal system in which he or she is asked to identify the law, "*If* [political decision procedure *x*] means political decision by anything less than legitimate majoritarianism, then why should we have [political decision procedure *x*] to resolve unsettled political issues?"[129]

To conclude this section, then, Richards was right: Dworkin is a strong (albeit confused) natural lawyer. The interpretation of institutional rights in a legal system ultimately relies upon a normatively loaded identification of a preinterpretive concept of law. Upon Dworkin's plateau stand *only* those acts of collective power that can be explained in terms of the interpreter's conception of institutional rights. Obviously, not all of these actions will turn out to be *valid* institutional rights. I suggest, however, that all of them will turn out to be interpretable *only* according to a theory of institutional rights that turns out to be a strong natural law theory. Thus, said Richards, Dworkin manipulated his account of law so that "the pea of morality" is always found beneath the "shell of a given political system."[130] The reason our institutional rights under the Constitution resemble the moral rights we would have under the interpreter's conception of the best political morality is that the "concept" of law with which he or she begins includes only those acts of collective power that are required by the best political morality, are consistent with the best political morality, or are recognizable as mistakes because they contradict the best political morality.[131]

The only problem for Richards is that his argument against Dworkin turns out to be a Pyrrhic victory. The same arguments that revealed Dworkin to be a strong natural lawyer can be used to show that Richards's methodological natural law, as well as other Weak Epistemic Natural Law theories, is a form of strong natural law too.

---

[129] This is the implication, I believe, of Michelman's "always under law" thesis. See Michelman, *Always Under Law?*

[130] Richards, *Taking TRS Seriously*, at 1298 n81.

[131] Thus, the reason why our institutional rights under the Constitution resemble the moral rights we would have under Dworkin's theory of equal concern and respect is that the interpreter of the law must use the best (i.e., Dworkin's) conception of political morality to interpret the institution of law.

Dworkin's theory of "naturalism" collapsed into natural law because it could not sustain the distinction between the "natural" preinterpretive concept of law as "justified collective power" and the non-"natural" conception of "justified collective power" as those acts required by political morality under the constraint of fit as determined by the theory of mistakes. Because the definition of fit relies on moral principles for its application, and an interpreter's conception of the concept of law is ultimately defined through reference to the constraint of fit, the concept of law is ultimately defined through reference to moral principles. Dworkin's troubles began when he tried to find a nonmoral basis for "justification" in his concept of law. He could not, not because one cannot conceive of such nonmoral meanings but because none were consistent with his idea of how fit operates in his theory of adjudication. If fit is based on moral principles, and every historical event upon which justification can be based must "fit," then one's test for justification will have a moral foundation. But Dworkin tried to give his test for fit an empirical foundation: He originally thought that the interpreter should use the *community's concept* of fairness/political morality to test putatively mistaken decisions. Dworkin had to abandon this appeal to the empirical because, as I argued previously, moral conceptions must be perspectival. If Dworkin did not have to base his test for fit upon a perspectival conception, it is possible that he would have been able to revert to some test for fit that did not simply reproduce the interpreter's conception of justified collective force.

Richards accepted Dworkin's analysis of the distinction between moral concepts and conceptions.[132] This distinction, which was borrowed from Rawls,[133] is widely accepted, and it contains the key to understanding why Richards and other fundamental rights theorists cannot escape Dworkin's fate. In Richards's theory, each interpreter's conception of legal rights under the Constitution is based on an initial constitutional act that relies upon, to use Dworkin's phrase, some "actual" political decision to identify a conception of legal rights. The initial constitutional act is not subjected to the test of fit, because that political decision (the Constitution's ratification) is presumed to be the original positive event presupposed by Weak Epistemic Natural Law theory. But the concept of the Constitution

---

[132] Richards, *Moral Criticism of Law*, at 52–3, 92–3.
[133] Rawls, *A Theory of Justice*, at 5.

is more than a formal claim of supreme power (if it were only that, it would be identical to the Not Very Strong Epistemic Natural Law of the unwritten constitution view). According to Weak Epistemic Natural Law theory, the act of ratification entrenches through an "actual" political decision a specific conception of the concept of legal rights. It does this through the specification of a *summum bonum*; for example, in Richards's theory it is autonomy.[134] Because the posited conception of institutional rights under the Constitution has moral content, its test for fit (one assumes it must have a test for fit) will use moral terms.[135] But, we might ask, as we asked of Dworkin, if the conception of institutional rights under the Constitution has a theory of mistakes, at what point does that theory of mistakes stop testing past legal and political decisions? Clearly, Richards imagined the theory of mistakes to be very far-ranging, because the institutional rights under the Constitution are coextensive with the rights guaranteed under Rawls's principle of equal liberty, or whichever conception of contractarian moral theory the particular interpreter believes is objectively true.[136] Such a theory of our institutional rights would include a radical revision of our constitutional jurisprudence, including the determination that some well-established doctrines were mistakes.[137] Thus, if Richards's theory of mistakes were applied vigorously, it would revise decades if not centuries of past Supreme Court decisions concerning the permissibility of state and federal legislation, as well as repudiate settled doctrine concerning the duties of the state under the Constitution.[138] But then, we might further inquire, if the theory of mistakes

---

[134] Richards, *Commercial Sex and the Rights of the Person* at 1228–31 (1979); Richards, *Sexual Autonomy and the Constitutional Right to Privacy,* at 970–2.

[135] See, for example, Richards, *Taking TRS Seriously,* at 1296.

[136] See Richards, *Sexual Autonomy,* at 965–74.

[137] For example, Richards would simply rewrite constitutional obscenity law, reversing *Roth v. United States,* 354 U.S. 476 (1957) (upholding federal statute prohibiting any person from mailing an "obscene" publication), and mooting *Miller v. California,* 413 U.S. 15 (1973) (setting out test for obscenity). Richards would completely change the doctrinal foundation of the right to privacy (basing it on the "principle of love as a civil liberty") and would reverse *San Antonio Independent School District v. Rodriguez,* 411 U.S. 1 (1973) (federal constitution does not require states to provide equal educational funding), because it violates Rawls's principle of distributive justice. Richards, *Moral Criticism of Law,* at 69–70, 155–7.

[138] I do not mean to invoke *stare decisis* as an independent virtue or suggest that either Richards or Dworkin does so either. Rather, I want to stress that Richards's theory reveals openly what Dworkin tried to obscure: that the fundamental rights methodology shared by the two of them has no tolerance for what Dworkin called "mistakes."

can require the courts to recognize that past *legislative* action and in-action were "mistakes," why could it not reach further and require a citizen to recognize that specific putatively "actual" acts of the constitutional convention itself were mistakes? After all, as Dworkin conceded, it is not sufficient to say that the Constitution was ratified by a political decision, or even a putatively democratic political decision – the argument from democracy itself is valid only if it passes the test posed by the theory of mistakes.[139]

The Weak Epistemic Natural Lawyer's answer must be something like this: The theory of mistakes can revise any part of the political history of the institution in which it sits *except* those political decisions that specified the *summum bonum* that generated the theory of mistakes itself (i.e., the founding moment). But this objection trades on two ambiguities. First, the theory of mistakes, when applied to the founding, is not revising the *fact* that the legal system was founded; it is determining whether a putative political decision is *actually* part of the legal system, in the same way it might review putative precedents and putative political decisions that resulted in regrettable mistakes within the legal system. It might seem odd to say that we must challenge the normative significance of the founding in order to respect its normative significance, but, as a matter of practice, it is no more odd than challenging others' deeply held and carefully considered moral conceptions in order to respect their commitment to the moral concepts they have (mistakenly) attempted to interpret.[140] When we argue with others that they have misapplied a concept that they claim to embrace, we are not deny-

---

[139]   In fact, it is quite unlikely that the best theory of justice will support a practical conclusion about the validity of a political act based on an argument from pure majoritarianism. Rawls's theory does not endorse any form of purely majoritarian democratic theory. See Rawls, *Theory of Justice,* at 228. See also Murphy, *Ordering of Constitutional Values,* at 729 (constitutional justice cannot be majoritarian). Furthermore, it should be uncontroversial that "super majority" voting rules, such as those used in amending procedures, are merely variations on the argument from pure majoritarianism.

[140]   Michelman made this point with reference to constitutional amendments: "Constitutional democrats (those who are earnest about democracy) attribute higher lawmaking to 'The People Themselves,' conceived as *self*-governing; and it's precisely *because* they do so that they cannot conceive higher lawmaking either as total revolution or as writing on a clean slate." Michelman, *Why Constitutionalism?,* at 302 (footnote omitted). If an interpreter can sincerely challenge the conception of self-government instantiated through one form of higher law making (amending), why can't he or she raise the same challenge about the other form of higher law making (ratification)?

ing their loyalty to the concept. On the contrary, we take it so seriously that we intervene to help them achieve what they truly desire, although they may be unable to recognize that their conception is in fact inferior to our conception.[141]

Second, while the conception of institutional rights that generates the theory of mistakes may have been launched *by* a political decision, the moral principles entailed by that conception must be independent of the sort of reasons one would use to identify the political decision that launched the conception of institutional rights. This disjunction between the nonmoral identification of the *summum bonum* and the moral content of the *summum bonum* is supposed to be the chief virtue of Weak Epistemic Natural Law, and the reason why it is not strong natural law. Under the *summum bonum* view, the existence of an empirical condition (ratification) is the reason why moral principles (a conception of justice) become the supreme source of institutional rights. The epistemic utility of the empirical reason is based on its independence from moral reasons. Within its own sphere, an empirical fact can guide action, just as the moral principles specified by the *summum bonum* guide action (by creating rights and duties) in their own sphere. But just as moral principles cannot provide the existence conditions for the "founding" of a legal system (that would be strong natural law), empirical facts cannot play a role in the determination, under the theory of mistakes, of whether any political decision was "actual" or putative.[142] But then the Weak Epistemic Natural Lawyer must take the bitter with the sweet: Having introduced moral principles into an institution, he or she cannot arbitrarily cabin them, even if they would operate to review the very set of events that were the means by which they were given institutional effect.

If this argument is correct, then it must be true that, regardless of the positive origins of a legal system's founding, a legal system that

---

[141]   See, for example, George, *Individual Rights, Collective Interests, Public Law and American Politics,* at 257–8 (serious disagreement over moral choice may be rooted in great mutual respect).

[142]   This dichotomy of reasons parallels Duncan Kennedy's distinction between formality and substantive rationality. See Duncan Kennedy, *Legal Formality,* 2 J. Legal. Stud. 351, 363–4 (1973). Raz would disagree with this model because he believes that the sort of empirical reason discussed in this chapter – ratification – may be a "protected reason": a combination of a reason to perform an act (the specification of supreme law) and an "exclusionary reason" not to act for certain reasons (not to take moral reasons into account in the specification of supreme law). See Raz, *Practical Reasons and Norms,* at 191.

posits a *summum bonum* as the foundation of its institutional rights must accept that every political decision, including the founding positive acts, must be interpreted according to the interpreter's own conception of that *summum bonum*. This argument therefore proves that Richards would behave just like a strong natural lawyer were he to encounter a legal system that posited a moral concept as the foundation of its institutional rights (such as the U.S. Constitution as understood by Richards). Thus, at its very minimum, Weak Epistemic Natural Law theory collapses into strong natural law theory after the interpreter concludes that the founders posited a *summum bonum* as the source of the legal system's institutional rights.[143]

6.4. DOES THE FUNDAMENTAL RIGHTS THEORIST HAVE AN EPISTEMIC THEORY OF LAW?

The problem posed by the collapse of Weak Epistemic Natural Law into strong natural law is that it is not clear how a fundamental rights theorist can identify true propositions of constitutional law without accepting natural law. The problem is not, as some conservative legal scholars might frame it, that the theorist (or, more important, a judge or citizen) would be left without constraints to interpret the constitution according to his or her own political views.[144] My concern is different: If a citizen sincerely desires to follow *the* Constitution, how can he or she know whether any given proposition is really law, as opposed to either a novel but nonlegal interpretation of the Constitution, or a mistaken, albeit settled, interpretation of the Constitution? This is an epistemic question, and, when it is raised sincerely, it may reflect no greater political agenda than a wish to follow the law. I concluded previously that Dworkin and Richards have no answer to this question except to collapse the test for law with the test for justice. I will briefly review two contempo-

---

[143] Therefore, the distinction "collapses" because, as we have seen earlier, the incorporation of moral principle is a one-way street. Once incorporated, "justified collective power" becomes the test for *all* questions of collective power: Any question that *can* be tested from the perspective of moral principle *must* be tested from that perspective. The fact that the test of moral principle was identified through a nonmoral test (such as whether a certain political action occurred) cannot be used as a reason to limit the scope of the test of moral principle.

[144] This is the "countermajoritarian difficulty" that brought the legal process scholars to the impasse that prompted Judge Wright's article. See Wright, *Professor Bickel*, at 769.

rary justice-seeking theorists to see whether they can answer the epistemic question any better than Dworkin or Richards.

Barber has argued that the political decision to ratify the Constitution established justice as the *summum bonum* because the supremacy clause commanded that "the Constitution would be authoritative as a conception of . . . the good society."[145] From this Barber drew two further conclusions: first, that the Constitution's means are always "derivative" from its end,[146] and second, that by its own command, the Constitution ceases to be authoritative if "we" determine at any time that the Constitution fails to "conform to our present conception of the best norms by which we might govern ourselves."[147] Barber needs a theory of mistakes for the following reason: If, as Barber says, the Constitution's subjects must recognize it as "a *working* instrument of justice" (and not an ideal instrument), then there must be some way of knowing whether one of the Constitution's imperfect "means" is actually part of the Constitution.[148] But according to Barber's theory of mistakes, a constitutional means that fails to promote the interpreter's conception of the good society as well as a practical real-world alternative must be a mistake unless the interpreter believes that retaining the suboptimal means serves his or her conception of justice.[149] Unless Barber had a reason based in justice for distinguishing between suboptimal means and suboptimal means that are "really" optimal from a constitutional perspective, his theory of mistakes simply collapses the epistemic test for constitutional law into a problem of practical political philosophy. This is true even when the interpreter might conclude that a portion of the Constitution or even the Constitution itself no longer serves the end of justice.[150] If the set of mistakes the interpreter is forced to set aside as mistakes is so large that the Constitution would be thrown into incoherence or impotency, then at this point an interpreter may have an independent duty rooted directly in justice to use "constitutionalist" (but not constitutional)

---

[145] Barber, *On What the Constitution Means*, at 57.
[146] Ibid.
[147] Eisgruber, *Justice and the Text*, at 13 (citing Barber, *On What the Constitution Means*, at 57). It is unclear whether "we" means the interpreter or a group of people observed by the interpreter.
[148] See Barber, *Justice-Seeking Constitutionalism*, at 42 (emphasis added).
[149] See Barber, *Constitution of Judicial Power*, at 64.
[150] See ibid., at 207–8.

reasoning to "reinstate" the conditions under which obeying the Constitution could be possible.[151]

Michelman's most recent arguments concerning constitutional democracy have elements that are similar to those of other fundamental rights theorists discussed in this chapter.[152] Although he may have been tempted by the process-perfecting aspects of republicanism,[153] Michelman has tried to show that every (democratic) constitution has to specify a conception of justice as its source of supreme law in order for the constitution to claim justified authority.[154] I will show that Michelman purchased this ersatz form of strong natural law at the cost of losing whatever epistemic test for law his republican theory of law may have had. Michelman argued that a democracy must specify some "principles [that] will stand as fundamental – central, definitive, constitutive – for the political order in question."[155] In exactly the same way prescribed by the *summum bonum* view of the Weak Epistemic Natural Law theory, a "constitutionist culture" erects a "prescriptive proposition" that justifies the collective power of the state.[156] Michelman identified two reasons why "People legislating a constitution" would attempt to fix a principle of justice through a political decision.[157] The first is that all law making is always under some other higher law.[158] This is because law, which is the use of collective force, must be justified, and it can be justified only by reference to "some preexisting, publicly ascertainable . . . standard of right or good."[159] But, as Michelman noted, why would someone demanding justification accept a higher law that was in fact the creation of someone else's political decision (regardless of how old the decision)? This is where the second reason comes into play. A higher law, being law, must be "laid down" *by someone* even if it incorporates a "standard of right or good" and it must be addressed to someone.[160] But for law to be cre-

---

[151]   See Barber, *Justice-Seeking Constitutionalism*, at 44.
[152]   See Michelman, *Can Constitutional Democrats Be Legal Positivists?*; Michelman, *Always Under Law?*
[153]   See Sager, *The Incorrigible Constitution*, at 923.
[154]   See Michelman, *Always Under Law?*, at 238.
[155]   Ibid.
[156]   See Michelman, *Why Constitutionalism?*, at 299.
[157]   See Michelman, ibid., at 301.
[158]   Michelman, *Always Under Law?*, at 230.
[159]   Michelman, *Always Under Law?*, at 233 (Michelman seemed to agree entirely with Dworkin on the concept of law).
[160]   See Michelman, *Always Under Law?*, at 233–41.

ated and addressed, there must be a People recognizable to themselves both as author of the law and its addressee.[161] Hence the logic of the Constitution as higher law: "[A] population's conception of itself as self-governing, as legislating law to itself, depends on its sense of its members as, in their higher lawmaking acts, commonly and constantly inspired by and aspiring to some distinct regulative idea of political justice and right . . . an idea that itself has sprung from the politics of the self-same self-governing People."[162]

The epistemic problem with Michelman's extraordinary attempt to reconcile popular sovereignty and the fundamental rights approach is that the historical event which specifies the conception of justice that justifies all subsequent law making has an entirely formal status. Unlike Richards, who tried to avoid this conclusion, Michelman embraced this feature of his theory, but the epistemic problem still remains. His theory of mistakes must naturally follow from his concept of law, which is *justifiable* (under higher law) state power. Michelman's interpreter, in order to determine whether a settled doctrine or political decision is law or merely a mistake, will therefore apply a test that relies on his or her interpretation of his or her legal system's higher law. If that higher law were fixed by a historical fact, the interpreter would have an empirical reason for believing that a given moral concept had been selected. But Michelman explicitly stated that higher law, from the perspective of those under the law, is never knowable by empirical reason; it must be *justified* under "higher law n+1."[163] So, from the point of view of the interpreter, being faithful to higher law means engaging in justification "all the way up," which really means testing higher law "all the way up."[164] Functionally speaking, Michelman's interpreter must act like a strong natural lawyer.

6.5. THE INSATIABILITY OF JUSTICE AND MONISTIC PRACTICAL REASON

The reason so many fundamental rights theories turn out to be strong natural law theories is not that they made a simple mistake

---

[161] See ibid., at 240–1.
[162] Ibid., at 241.
[163] Ibid., at 230.
[164] Ibid. Michelman uses the phrase "law-all-the-way-up" to explain the "always under law" thesis. See ibid., at 230.

somewhere in their arguments that can be corrected by changing a single assumption or premise. Nor is the collapse of Weak Epistemic Natural Law into strong natural law a novel but limited problem found only in jurisprudence. The collapse of the fundamental rights approach through its own theory of fit has analogs throughout the whole field of practical reasoning.

The problem with the incorporation of justice as a *summum bonum* (whether it is autonomy, equal concern and respect, or human dignity) is that justice is *insatiable*. Justice, once set into motion, cannot be limited except by a value that can override justice itself.[165] It is not clear what sort of value can, from the perspective of justice, trump justice, which is exactly why moral reasoning has proven so alluring to political and legal philosophers. If it is true that justice conceives of itself as dominant over all other values, then it is easy to see why every reason for action, including reasons to treat past political decisions as law, will be suborned to justice.[166] Ultimately, each interpreter subjects every competing reason for action in a legal system – including others' moral principles – to his or her own theory of mistakes, ensuring, as a result, that the resulting interpretation of the legal right in question reflects the principles of justice the interpreter believes are objectively true.

Justice is insatiable because practical reasoning in which justice is the ultimate value is not interpretive. This is because justice is not an interpretive concept in the Dworkinian sense. In saying this, I recognize that Dworkin has claimed just the opposite.[167] But Dworkin's claim is odd, in that he qualified it in a way which makes it clear that for him, justice is interpretive in name only. Immedi-

---

[165] "Once loosed, the idea of Equality is not easily cabined." Archibald Cox, *Foreword: Constitutional Adjudication and the Promotion of Human Rights*, 80 Harv. L. Rev. 91, 91 (1966). It is hard to avoid the conclusion that, within systems of practical reasoning, justice is insatiable. Finnis's idea of "practical reasonableness," for example, assumes that any human action can be evaluated in light of whether it is entailed by one of the "basic requirements" that are the means by which the "basic goods" are achieved. See Finnis, *Natural Law and Natural Rights*, at 127. As Robert George pointed out, we should be able to observe a human action and "[trace] a chain of practical reasoning back to its ultimate term" – for example, a basic good. George, *Recent Criticism of Natural Law Theory*, at 1393. To put it differently, moral reasoning is not a form of practical reasoning that allows for what Raz called "content-independent reasons," in which "there is no direct connection between the reason and he action for which it is a reason." Raz, *Morality of Freedom*, at 35.

[166] Larry Alexander made the same point when he said that "moral theory is imperialistic." Larry Alexander, *Impossible*, 72 Denv. U. L. Rev. 1007, 1008 (1995).

[167] See Dworkin, *Empire*, at 73.

ately after stating that justice is, like other social practices, an interpretive concept, he noted that it is interpretive in a way that makes
it "more complex and interesting" than other social practices such
as etiquette, because people who employ the concept of justice
claim that it has "a more global or transcendental authority" than
social practices like etiquette:

> The leeways of interpretation are accordingly much more relaxed: a
> theory of justice is not required to provide a good fit with the political
> or social practices of any particular community, *but only with the most
> abstract and elemental convictions of each interpreter.*[168]

But of course, as we saw previously, a criterion of fit that is rooted
in each interpreter's own conception of the concept in question is a
criterion that is so "loose" that it does not really exist. Just as the
idea of the *community's* conception of fairness collapsed into nothing less than each interpreter's conception of fairness, so too must
the search for the community's conception of justice (which we
would have to define in order to provide a criterion of fit) collapse
into a full-blown search for the "best" meaning of justice.

It should neither surprise nor disturb us to discover that for
Dworkin, justice is all "best light." A familiar assumption of moral
philosophy is that the theorist is supposed to check his or her claims
constantly and to accept whatever conclusions survive the test of
moral reasoning. Thus, although Dworkin was right to suggest that
interpretation involves two axes, "best light" and "fit," he was
wrong to think that a theory of law can be justice seeking and still
retain the structure of an interpretive theory.

The problem of insatiability is not unique to the fundamental
rights approach or to epistemic natural law. It is a problem which
arises in any system of practical reasoning that is what we might
call monistic. Normative systems are either *monistic* or *mixed.*[169] A

---

[168] Ibid., at 73 n20 (emphasis added). I am grateful to John Goldberg for pointing
this footnote out to me.

[169] Cass Sunstein used the concept of monism to draw a similar distinction:
"Human morality recognizes irreducibly diverse goods, which cannot be subsumed
under a single 'master' value. The same is true for the moral values reflected in the
law. . . . It would be absurd to try to organize legal judgments through a single conception of value." Cass Sunstein, *General Propositions and Concrete Cases (With Special
Reference to Affirmative Action and Free Speech),* 31 *Wake Forest L. Rev.* 369, 381 (1996)
(citations omitted) and see Cass Sunstein, *Incompletely Theorized Agreements,* 108
Harv. L. Rev. 1733, 1748 (1995) (on monistic reasoning in law). On the other hand,
Sunstein and I do not agree on the proper description of the best alternative to

monistic system of reason is characterized by the commensurability of the reasons one has for making the choices one makes. Monism is marked by more than the existence of ordinal preferences; it assumes not only that the choices one makes can be ranked but also that one's reasons are comparable along a common metric. In a mixed system, the set of reasons upon which one bases one's choices is simply incommensurable: There is no metric upon which one could evaluate or measure the reasons that underlie an ordinal preference structure.

It is easy to see why insatiable normative concepts lead to monistic systems of reason. We saw previously that norm N is insatiable if every norm in system S is measured against and revised under a theory of mistakes premised on N. From this it follows that N will govern every relevant decision point in S unless one of two circumstances arises.[170] First, N may not govern decision making if there was an error in the decision makers' reasoning and N was not applied when it should have been. Second, N may not govern if N was not applied because it was trumped by another norm (~N) that requires a different result from the result that would have been required under N. In the first instance, the result, which was reached through means that were *in fact* not rooted in N, may still be accepted in S *if* N itself requires that the fact of whether the result was achieved through means not rooted in N remain undetected and hence uncorrected. For example, it may turn out that the cost of identifying errors in S is very high, and so a person making decisions in conformity with N may have a reason to accept an occasional lapse in N-based decision making in order to ensure the maximum conformity to N overall.[171] But this is simply N governing its

monism. A system of normative practical reasoning that could produce an "incompletely theorized agreement" is not necessarily a "mixed" system of reasoning. Sunstein rejected monism because he thought that fully theorized judgment was a theoretical and practical impossibility. See Cass Sunstein, *Legal Reasoning and Political Conflict* 44 (1996). I do not think that monism is impossible in moral reasoning (on the contrary, I suspect it is all too possible); I simply think that monistic systems of practical reasoning cannot be sources of law. See Joseph Raz, *The Relevance of Coherence,* in *Ethics in the Public Domain: Essays in the Morality of Law and Politics* 261 (1994).

[170] See, for example, discussion of Dworkin's analysis of precedent in the *MacPherson* case in section 6.3.

[171] An example of this phenomenon is what Bernard Williams called the "'gas bill' model" of utilitarianism, which occurs when "the cost to an enterprise of interfering with a fixed process for handling transactions and halting a given item is greater than loss which is indeed incurred on that item." Bernard Williams, *A Critique of Utilitarianism,* in *Utilitarianism: For & Against* 126 (J.J.C. Smart and Bernard

scope of application by specifying not only when it should be applied but also when errors in its application should be ignored. N governs in either case.

Second, N may not govern if we have a reason to adopt ~N and allow ~N to govern the selection within the choice set. That is, unlike the first source of non–N-based decision making, which was the result of the result of the accidental failure of the decision maker to apply N, the source of non–N-based decision making is a deliberate choice to apply ~N. The justification for decision making governed by ~N is not a decision to ignore the possibility of a non–N-based decision but, in this one instance, explicitly to allow another norm to trump N. To the extent one thought that one saw genuine cases of the second instance in S, one might be tempted to argue that, unlike in the case of error, non–N-based decision making resulting from the deliberate rejection of N proves that although N is insatiable, S is not monistic, because decision making in S would be based on plural, or mixed, ultimate norms. But there are no genuine cases of the second instance where N is insatiable. If ~N is simply the antithesis of N, it could not survive the test of fit, because it would clearly be detected as a mistake under N. If ~N is a norm that diverges from N in order to promote the ultimate realization of N, then it is simply an episode of the first source of submaximality, where divergence was not chosen but tolerated. In either case N either eliminates ~N or governs its adoption. Thus, ~N is not an ultimate norm in S and S is a monistic system of reason.[172]

Whether or not it is possible to have mixed systems of practical reasoning in *morality* is an open question on which this chapter

---

Williams, eds., 1973). Larry Sager seemed to rely upon a version of this argument to explain why episodes of injustice must be tolerated by a justice-seeking constitution. See Lawrence G. Sager, *Justice in Plain Clothes: Reflections on the Thinness of Constitutional Law*, Nw. U. L. Rev. 410, 419 (1993) (citing Lawrence G. Sager, *Fair Measure: The Legal Status of Underenforced Constitutional Norms*, 91 Harv. L. Rev. 1212 [1978]).

[172] Schauer's criticism of "rule-sensitive particularism" is quite similar to my characterization of monism. The rule-sensitive particularist values rules that prohibit direct consideration of his or her ultimate ends if and only if those rules ensure that the particularist's ultimate ends will be achieved. Schauer argued that because not only the content of a rule but also its application is governed by the decision maker's ultimate ends, under rule-sensitive particularism "everything" about a rule, including whether or not it will promote the decision maker's ultimate ends, "is open for consideration by [the] decision maker." But see Gerald Postema, *Positivism, I Presume . . . Comments in Schauer's "Rules and the Rule of Law"* 14 Harv. J.L. & Pub. Policy 797, 813–17 (1991) (arguing that Schauer's own form of "presumptive positivism" is identical to rule-sensitive particularism).

takes no view.[173] On the other hand, I do think that we can draw a tentative sketch of what a mixed system of practical reasoning in law might look like. In Rawls's "practice conception of rules," for example, there is strict separation between the content of a norm (N) and the content of the norms that are instantiated by the practice that authorized N's adoption (~N).[174] Under the practice conception, a rule-utilitarian could not ask, at any given episode of promising, whether it was maximal to remain committed to the practice of promising. Because "the point of the practice [of promising] is to abdicate one's title to act in accordance with utilitarian and prudential considerations," the question is not available in the course of practical reasoning about the promise.[175] Where a given practice is a *mixed* form of practical reasoning, each person recognizes that some rules "necessarily [involve] the abdication of full liberty to act on utilitarian and prudential grounds."[176]

Rawls drew two implications from the practice conception of rules: first, that there is no necessary relationship between the justification one has for obeying N and ~N. That is not to say, Rawls explicitly cautioned, that one necessarily has a reason for obeying either N or ~N.[177] It is to say, however, that if a person is asked to explain why he obeys N, "his explanation or defense lies in referring the questioner *to the practice*" itself, and not to ~N.[178] It is also to say, second, that maintaining the separateness of N and ~N is a necessary element of maintaining a system of practical reason in which there is a "division of labor" between the source of a rule and the rule appliers – in other words, where the rule of law exists. According to Rawls,

---

[173] It is possible that Rawls's rejection of utilitarianism in favor of the theory of "justice as fairness" reflected his concession to the inevitability of monism in moral theory and his best attempt to describe a monistic moral theory based on justice. See Rawls, *A Theory of Justice,* at 27–33. It is also likely that his move toward a concept of justice that is "political not metaphysical" reflected his recognition of the problems with the monism of his 1971 approach. Rawls noted that the latest version of his theory of justice has the advantage of being "partially comprehensive," in contrast to "a doctrine [which] is fully comprehensive [because] it covers all recognized values and virtues within one rather precisely articulated system." John Rawls, *Political Liberalism* 152 n17 (1993).

[174] See John Rawls, *Two Concepts of Rules,* in *Theories of Ethics* 144 (Phillipa Foot, ed., 1967).

[175] Ibid., at 155.

[176] Ibid., at 162.

[177] Ibid., at 169.

[178] Ibid., at 165 (emphasis added).

On the practice conception, if one holds an office defined by [N or ~N] then questions regarding one's actions in this office are settled by reference to the rules which define [N or ~N]. If one seeks to question these rules, then one's office undergoes a fundamental change: one then assumes the office of one empowered to change and criticize the rules. . . . The summary conception does away with the distinction of offices and the various forms of argument appropriate to each. *On that conception there is one office and so no offices at all.*[179]

Although Rawls was discussing morality, his use of the word *office* was felicitous. The consequence of the fundamental rights approach is ultimately the collapse of law into morality: In Dworkinian terms, law becomes all best light and no fit. One feature of this collapse is the loss of any distinction between types of political authority.[180] As we saw earlier in this chapter, Weak Epistemic Natural Law subjects political decisions to the same test of fit as judicial decisions. The collapse of "office," as Rawls put it, is a necessary feature of monistic systems of practical reasoning, and his foregoing description of the collapse of the summary conception of rules in moral theory could just as easily be applied to our earlier discussion of the collapse of the fundamental rights approach into strong natural law.

6.6. CONCLUSION

I asserted at the beginning of section 6.5 that an insatiable concept, once set into motion, is not easily cabined, and I have shown that this problem with insatiability is a persistent problem in many forms of practical reasoning.[181] In this chapter I have not argued against monistic theories of practical reasoning. My goal has been simply to bring into sharper focus the relationship between the fundamental rights school and monistic legal theory. Someone might want to embrace monism in law and morality – one could be a de-

---

[179] Ibid., at 166 (emphasis added).

[180] Kant, like Rawls, was worried that the pursuit of justice, if mishandled, would make law impossible. That is why he linked his deontological moral philosophy to legal positivism. See Jeremy Waldron, *Kant's Legal Positivism*, 109 *Harv. L. Rev.* 1535 (1996).

[181] I have given illustrations from law and moral philosophy, but I could have given other examples as well. For example, the problem of insatiability and monism is the subject of "the theory of second best" in economics. See R. G. Lipsey and R. U. Lancaster, *The General Theory of Second Best*, 24 *Rev. Econ. Stud.* 11 (1956); James A. Henderson Jr., *Extending the Boundaries of Strict Products Liability: Implications of the Theory of Second Best*, 128 *U. Pa. L. Rev.* 1036, 1036–8 (1980).

fender of both strong natural law and act-utilitarianism. But the past thirty years have seen a steady pull away from monism in practical reasoning, and the point of this chapter has been to show that it will be difficult for the fundamental rights theorist to repudiate monism. This chapter goes no further than proving that the fundamental rights approach reproduces the monism of strong epistemic natural law and that the monism found in both is an inevitable consequence of the insatiability of justice. In so concluding, I am not prejudging the question of whether we should resist monism in law, but I am making clear the monistic consequences of viewing law as the instantiation of an insatiable norm.

On the other hand, I also have argued that we can build upon the somewhat pessimistic conclusions of this chapter. Rawls's practice conception of rules points toward the direction that legal theorists will want to go if they hope to describe a mixed theory of law that takes justice seriously.[182] It is important to note that unlike certain alternatives to the fundamental rights approach, a mixed theory of law does not in any way abandon the possibility of moral concepts' playing an important role in the content of both constitutions and legislation. What the practice conception grapples with, and what any mixed conception of practical reasoning must confront, is the tendency of moral concepts to act insatiably within any given system of practical reasoning. But as I hope I have demonstrated, the phenomena of insatiability and monism are not unique to legal theory, and they reflect a dilemma commonly found in practical reasoning. I believe that it may be possible to develop a theory of law that borrows the core ideas of the practice conception of rules and adapts them to jurisprudence. Such a theory would explain how it is that a legal system can build moral norms (such as justice) into its constitution and yet entrench a theory of fit that is independent of the constitution's moral norms. Therefore, the arguments I have offered about the problems of insatiability support the view that constitutional interpretation has to be based on some form of legal positivism.

---

[182] Hart's "social rule theory" bears an uncanny resemblance to Rawls's practice conception of rules. See Hart, *The Concept of Law*, at 77–91; see Dworkin, *TRS*, at 48–51 (on Hart's social rule theory). Interestingly, Hart redescribed the social rule theory as "the practice theory of rules" in the Postscript to the second edition of *The Concept of Law* but did not explicitly draw a connection between his choice of language and Rawls's 1955 article.

Chapter 7

New Legal Positivism
and the Incorporation of Morality

Weak Epistemic Natural Law collapses into strong epistemic natural law because once the ground of law is morality, no nonmoral reason can cabin it. For some conservative legal process scholars, such as Bickel, Bork, and Wechsler, the insatiability of justice was not a problem, because, as we saw in Chapter 5, they did not believe that morality could be objective, and therefore did not think that moral reasoning was anything other than the expression of subjective preference. For these theorists, all law could do was capture the personal preferences of its framers. Hence, adjudication was the application of the original intentions of a law's framers to a set of facts.

If the only positivist reaction to the fundamental rights approach were the originalism of Bickel, Bork, and Wechsler, then the final chapter of legal positivism in the United States would have been a story of a decline into irrelevancy, with the final scene being, perhaps, the defeat of Robert Bork's nomination to the Supreme Court in 1987. Since the late 1980s, originalism has lost much of its influence both in the academy and among the public.

Legal positivism has generated another, much more powerful response to the fundamental rights approach that is rooted in neither moral skepticism nor originalism. This modern form of positivism, which I will call the "New Legal Positivism," has been propounded by a group of scholars in the United States, Canada, and England in reaction to the fundamental rights approach championed by Ronald Dworkin.[1] As we saw in Chapter 6, Dworkin's contribution to the constitutional theory of fundamental rights was a part of his

---

[1] To some extent, the New Legal Positivists are continuing the debate begun by H.L.A. Hart and Fuller.

larger jurisprudential program of epistemic natural law. Unlike other fundamental rights theorists, who came of age by attacking legal process, Dworkin developed his Weak Epistemic Natural Law argument by directly attacking legal positivism itself. Beginning in the mid-1960s, Dworkin began to focus his energies on H.L.A. Hart's account of positivism.[2] Dworkin's critique, while original and subtle, nonetheless picked up where Fuller had left off: at the point of proving that Hart's theory of law was wrong because it denied that there was a necessary connection between law and morality. The New Legal Positivists – partially in reaction to Dworkin – have defended Hart's legacy by insisting on the separation of law and morality, and they have done so without subscribing to the moral skepticism and originalism that marked the conservative legal process school. I will argue in this chapter that the New Positivists have developed a theory of law that is consistent with the original legal process school, and that the politically liberal ambitions of Hart and Sacks are well served by this new form of positivism. New Legal Positivism provides a vision of what Hart and Sacks's positivism could look like once the mistakes of the conservative legal process generation are stripped away and repudiated.

New Legal Positivism developed in three stages. First, there was the "founding," which took place not even in America, but in England, through the publication of H.L.A. Hart's *The Concept of Law.* Hart set out the essential principles of the New Positivism, and much of the conflict among subsequent New Positivists has been over the proper interpretation of his legacy. The second stage was the critique of Hart's positivism by Dworkin. Dworkin was a critical player in the development of New Legal Positivism, because his restatement of Hart's theory – for no other purpose than to criticize it – has been very influential among Hart's later defenders. The final stage, which began in the early 1970s and is still unfolding, involves efforts by New Positivists to answer Dworkin and refine Hart's work. The third stage is marked by the emergence of two

---

[2] Although Dworkin's first sustained critique of Hart's positivism was *The Model of Rules,* 35 *U. Chi. L. Rev.* 14 (1967), Dworkin had already begun to develop his antipositivist views in *Judicial Discretion,* 60 *J. Phil.* 624 (1963); *Wasserstrom: The Judicial Decision,* 74 *Ethics* 47 (1964) (reprinted as *Does Law Have a Function? A Comment on the Two-Level Theory of Decision,* 74 *Yale L.J.* 640 [1965]); *Philosophy, Morality and Law – Observations Prompted by Professor Fuller's Novel Claim,* 113 *U. Pa. L. Rev.* 668 (1965); *The Elusive Morality of Law,* 10 *Vand. L. Rev.* 631 (1965). See Stephen Guest, *Ronald Dworkin* 2–6 (1991).

dominant trends. On the one hand, there are those who focus upon Hart's conceptual separation of law and morality and argue that Hart acknowledged that in some legal systems morality could be a condition of legality. This view has come to be known as incorporationism or inclusive legal positivism.[3] On the other hand, there are those who defend Hart's conceptual separation of law and morality and argue that Hart did not think (or should not have thought, if he did) that morality could ever be a condition of legality. This view has come to be known as exclusive legal positivism.[4]

7.2. FROM RULES TO PRINCIPLES: HART, DWORKIN, AND THE DEFENSE OF HART

As we saw in Chapter 2, Classical Legal Positivism was characterized by three fundamental principles: the separability thesis, the command theory of law, and the sources thesis. I argued in Chapter 4 that in addition to rejecting formalism's cramped view of legal reasoning, Hart and Sacks had also rejected the command theory of law in favor of a view similar to Hart's social rule theory. In this way, Hart and Sacks paralleled H.L.A. Hart's critique of classical positivism. In *The Concept of Law,* Hart argued that Austin's idea that law had to be an expression of a human "will" introduced many confusions into legal positivism and fatally weakened it as a theory of law for modern societies like those of England or the United States. According to the critique set out in *The Concept of Law,* Austin's theory was deficient for three reasons. First, Hart argued that it simply is not true that citizens view a law as nothing more than a command accompanied by a sanction.[5] Austin confused obedience (being obliged to act) with obligation (having an

---

[3] See Jules Coleman, "Authority and Reason" in *The Authority of Law: Essays on Legal Positivism* (Robert George, ed., 1996) (on incorporationism) (hereafter *AR*) and Wil J. Waluchow, *Inclusive Legal Positivism* (1994) (on inclusive legal positivism). Incorporationism has also been called "negative positivism" by Schauer, although this use of the term should not be confused with Coleman's use of the same expression for very different purposes. Compare Frederick Schauer, *Playing by the Rules: A Philosophical Examination of Rule-Based Decision Making in Law and Life* 197 (1991) (hereafter *Rules*) with Jules L. Coleman, *Negative and Positive Positivism* 11 *J. Legal Stud.* 139, 141 (1982), reprinted in Jules L. Coleman, *Markets, Morals, and the Law* (1988). Hart himself characterized the incorporationist position as "soft positivism" in his Postscript and suggested that he was quite sympathetic with the approach. See H.L.A. Hart, *The Concept of Law* 250 (2d ed., 1994) (hereafter *CL*).

[4] See Coleman, *AR*, at 288 and Waluchow, *Inclusive Legal Positivism*, at 82–3.

[5] See *CL*, at 22–5.

obligation to act) and therefore could not explain the existence of law even in the absence of sanction.[6] Second, Hart argued that not all laws are commands. Austin believed that every law had to limit the liberty of its subject by telling the subject what he or she could not do (proscription) or must do (prescription). As Hart noted, while Austin's model captured the core of criminal law, it failed to capture the many power-conferring rules found in modern private law and public law. For example, the law of wills expands liberty by enabling private parties to create new relationships through law; similarly, where the law confers legislative or regulatory powers, the liberty of private citizens is not obviously limited.[7] Finally, Hart argued that Austin was wrong to picture law as the will of a person or group. Austin's sovereign was that person (or persons) whose "orders the great majority of the society habitually obey and who does not obey any other person or persons."[8] Hart argued that by conflating law with a flesh-and-blood entity, Austin's theory became entangled in the small but fatal fact that while humans are mortal, laws are not. For example, it is obvious that laws remain valid and in force after the sovereign who wrote them dies or leaves office.[9] Similarly, where one tries to apply Austin's test to a modern democracy, one finds that it is impossible to ascertain exactly who is the population to whom obedience is directed without reference to at least some of the rules that the sovereign is alleged to have commanded.[10]

In response to each of these criticisms of Austin, Hart offered a correction. First, Hart argued that law following is distinguished from simple obedience because law followers adopt a certain attitude toward law called the "internal point of view." The internal point of view sets Hart apart from Austin, because Hart believes that one can adopt only the internal point of view with regard to rules, as opposed to mere commands.[11] Furthermore, one has an internal point of view if one follows a rule not out of prudence or habit but because one believes that the rule itself provides a reason for doing what the rule says, as evidenced by the fact that one be-

---

[6] See ibid., at 83–6.
[7] See ibid., at 36–8.
[8] See ibid., at 50.
[9] See ibid., at 51–8.
[10] See ibid., at 74–8.
[11] See ibid., at 85.

lieves that failure to conform to the rule is a reason to criticize a nonconforming actor.[12]

Second, Hart argued that if modern legal systems are built out of rules, not commands, then legal positivism must explain how different rules are created, changed, and identified. Hart built on the insight that law both limits and expands liberty and argued that rules that limit liberty are "primary" rules, whereas rules that confer powers are "secondary" rules.[13] There are three types of secondary rules. There are rules that confer the power to change primary rules. Hart includes in this category the rules of legislation and the powers of private law making ("the making of wills, contracts, transfers of property . . .").[14] There are rules that confer the power to adjudicate primary rules. These rules determine whether "a primary rule has been broken."[15] But the most important type of secondary rule is the "rule of recognition." This rule sets out the conditions that must be satisfied by a norm if it is to count as a primary rule.[16]

Third, Hart argued that if law is based on citizens' adopting the internal point of view toward the primary and secondary rules of their community, the law is the rules actually in force at a given time, and not the will of a person or group of people. Obviously the secondary rules that confer power to change laws recognize certain persons as occupying legislative offices, and the secondary rules that confer power to adjudicate recognize certain persons as occupying judicial offices, but in neither case is the law the will of the people occupying those offices, even though the wills of those officers certainly affect the operation of the law.[17]

Hart's three modifications of Austin's command theory led naturally to his social rule theory. A social rule is "a convergent social practice and a shared critical or reflective attitude towards that practice."[18] The rule of recognition is a convergent social practice about which legal officials share a reflective or critical attitude. In other words, it is a social rule. Thus, Hart's reformulation of the

---

[12] See ibid., at 90.
[13] See ibid., at 94.
[14] See ibid., at 96.
[15] Ibid., at 97.
[16] See ibid., at 94–5. As Coleman and Leiter note, unlike the other two secondary rules, the rule of recognition is not a power-conferring rule. See Jules L. Coleman and Brian Leiter, *Legal Positivism*, in *A Companion to Philosophy of Law and Legal Theory* 245 (Dennis Patterson, ed., 1996).
[17] *CL*, at 144–5.
[18] Coleman, *AR*, at 294.

positivist test for law replaced the command theory with the social rule theory. However, we should note that Hart's rejection of Austin left intact the separability thesis and the sources thesis. Dworkin felt that Hart had failed to address the core problem with positivism. Dworkin argued that the rejection of the command theory could not save positivism, because Hart's continued commitment to the separability thesis and the sources thesis rendered his entire theory unacceptable. Dworkin took one of Hart's main achievements – replacing commands with rules – and turned it against Hart by arguing that the "model of rules" was inconsistent with how judges view adjudication in modern society.

Dworkin's argument had four parts. First, he observed that when judges decide cases, they invoke principles and not just rules. A principle is different from a rule in that rules are applied in an "all or nothing fashion," whereas principles have "weight." From this Dworkin concluded that whereas valid legal rules cannot conflict in a legal system, valid principles can conflict, and they often do.[19] Second, Dworkin argued that Hart's rule of recognition cannot recognize principles. According to Hart, the *rule* of recognition set out the validity conditions for a legal system's primary *rules.* Dworkin argued that Hart's use of a restrictive term like *rules* (as opposed to *rules* and *principles* or just *norms*) was no accident. "Validity is an all or nothing concept, appropriate for rules, but inconsistent with a principle's dimension of weight."[20] Because the rule of recognition sets out conditions of *validity,* Dworkin concluded that even if Hart had been tempted to expand the scope of the rule of recognition to include principles, he would not have been able to do so.

Third, Dworkin argued that Hart was wrong to endorse the separability thesis. Dworkin drew this conclusion by showing that some of the principles which Hart had ignored were necessarily moral principles. How could Dworkin move from the claim that law includes "principles *and* rules" to the conclusion that law must include moral principles? As we saw in Chapter 6, Dworkin has a very particular view of adjudication. The point of "law" is that it provides a "general" or "adequate" justification for the "exercise of coercive power by the state."[21] Only a political morality that reflects "principles of justice, fairness, and procedural due pro-

[19] See Ronald Dworkin, *Taking Rights Seriously* 26 (1977) (hereafter *TRS*).
[20] Ibid., at 41.
[21] See Ronald Dworkin, *Law's Empire* 139, 190 (1986) (hereafter *Empire*).

cess" can provide that justification.[22] Hence, for Dworkin, the principles of political morality invoked by judges "are accorded the status of law."[23]

Fourth, and finally, Dworkin argued that Hart was wrong to conclude that judges exercised discretion.[24] Dworkin assumed that Hart's argument for judicial discretion was a consequence of Hart's commitment to the model of rules.[25] According to Dworkin, "arguments of principle justify a political decision by showing that the decision respects or secures some group or individual *right*."[26] Dworkin's use of the word "right" in his early theory had a double meaning. First, it suggested a connection with the argument made just prior to this one – that legal decisions based on principle were based on morality. Second, Dworkin explicitly argued that because legal principles "secured" political rights, in every case where a legal principle is at stake (which means every case) one of the two sides has a "right" to win.[27] Judges, it turns out, never have discretion because in fact the law is a "seamless" web of principle: Every legal rule is actually underwritten by legal principle; hence, the law never has gaps and never runs out.[28]

As Hart noted in his Postscript to the second edition of *The Concept of Law*, he never intended to suggest in 1961 that the law consisted only of rules or that the rule of recognition could not provide validity conditions for principles.[29] Nonetheless, Dworkin's critique of Hart's "model of rules" seemed, for a while, to pose a powerful rebuttal of positivism and provided another reason for lawyers to

---

[22] See ibid., at 225.

[23] See David Lyons, *Principles, Positivism and Legal Theory*, 87 *Yale L. J.* 415, 428 (1977) (hereafter *Principles*).

[24] By *discretion* Dworkin meant "strong" discretion: The law applier is "simply not bound by standards set by the authority in question" or "is not controlled by a standard furnished by the particular authority we have in mind when we raise the question of discretion." Dworkin, *TRS*, at 32–3. Hart and Sacks meant much the same thing when they used the term *discretion*. According to their theory of noncontinuous discretion, however, the scope of questions subject to a judge's "strong" discretion was always constrained by law.

[25] In fact, it is just as likely that Hart's views on discretion were rooted in his views on language. See Hart, *Positivism and the Separation of Law and Morals*, at 607–11, on the difference between core and penumbral meaning in language and its consequences for law.

[26] Dworkin, *TRS*, at 82.

[27] See ibid., at 89 and Dworkin, *Empire*, 152.

[28] See Dworkin, *TRS*, at 155 and Waluchow, *Inclusive Legal Positivism*, at 43 (according to Dworkin, legal principles "are as much law as the rules they support").

[29] See Hart, *CL*, at 259–61.

take the fundamental rights school seriously. The defense of Hart against Dworkin's attack marked the beginning of the last stage in the development of New Legal Positivism. Between 1972 and 1977, a number of articles appeared which made the fundamental point that nothing that Hart had written excluded principles from the positivist's analysis of the law. In rapid succession, three authors made the same argument, each with a slightly different emphasis.

Joseph Raz argued in *Legal Principles and the Limits of Law* that although there is a logical distinction between rules and principles, that fact in no way entails that the rule of recognition must be abandoned. Raz argued that there is no necessary relationship between the amount of discretion present in a legal system and the absence or presence of rules: A legal system may have a rule that limits discretion, while another legal system may have a principle that confers and guides discretion.[30] Furthermore, argued Raz, there is no reason to believe that the rule of recognition cannot set out validity conditions for a principle.[31] Principles may be enacted in a constitution or statute, or recognized because they enjoy a requisite degree of institutional support, as in the common law.[32] Nothing about the features of a principle that distinguish it logically from a rule makes principles immune from validation under a master rule of recognition. According to Raz, Dworkin's real argument with Hart is not that the rule of recognition cannot recognize principles in the same way that it recognizes rules, but that the criterion of legality upon which the rule of recognition relies cannot even adequately explain how rules are recognized. According to Dworkin, "institutional support" is inadequate to establish the validity of a rule *or* a principle. But then, replied Raz, Dworkin's real argument is simply that social facts can never provide the conditions of legality. According to Raz, Dworkin's rejection of the possibility of social facts' providing the validity conditions for either rules or principles is simply a rejection of the idea of the rule of recognition.[33]

David Lyons argued in *Principles, Positivism and Legal Theory* that Dworkin fallaciously assumed that legal principles eliminate inde-

---

[30] See Joseph Raz, *Legal Principles and the Limits of Law*, 81 *Yale L. J.* 823, 845–7 (1972) (hereafter *Legal Principles*).
[31] "Legal principles may be valid in precisely the same way that rules are." Ibid., at 852.
[32] See ibid., at 852.
[33] See ibid., at 853.

terminacy in a legal system. Like Raz, Lyons noted that just as there is no reason to assume that a "system of hard and fast rules" could not "yield determinate answers to all questions that arise under them," there is no reason to assume that legal principles necessarily eliminate judicial discretion.[34] Lyons noted that Dworkin's real argument could not have been that the model of rules is false because it precommits the positivist to the view that judges always have discretion, but rather that the model of rules is false simply because the rule of recognition cannot include legal principles.[35] According to Dworkin, a rule of recognition cannot condition legality upon a test of "content" as opposed to "pedigree." According to Lyons, Dworkin's reasons for believing this may have been based on the way Hart described the rule of recognition, or it may have been based on Dworkin's assumption that, if a rule operates in an "all or nothing fashion," it must provide a test that can be conclusively satisfied, as opposed to a test that may be satisfied by partial "weight."[36] Because moral principles condition legality on the basis of conformity with their normative content, they cannot be part of the rule of recognition; but rules, which condition legality upon the satisfaction of empirical criteria, may be part of the rule of recognition. Lyons argued that nothing in Hart's theory of the rule of recognition says that legality must be conditioned on pedigree alone. All the positivist must say is that the existence of the rule of recognition is determined by the social fact of official practice, not that the content of the rule of recognition must restrict itself "to criteria that themselves incorporate such social facts about accepted practices."[37] Therefore the rule of recognition can include legal principles.

Philip Soper, in *Legal Theory and the Obligation of a Judge: The Hart/Dworkin Dispute*, argued that Dworkin was wrong to think that just because the content of a principle cannot be "listed exhaustively" (like the content of a rule) the rule of recognition cannot include principles. Soper noted that Dworkin was right to point out that there is a difference between rules and principles: "a standard

---

[34] See Lyons, *Principles*, at 422.

[35] See ibid., at 421–2. Whether judges always have discretion is an important question that positivists might ultimately have to answer, but it cannot be answered through a comparison of the comparative features of rules and principles.

[36] See ibid., at 418.

[37] Ibid., at 425.

is a rule, however vague, if it embraces a limited range of principles and policies that are taken to be *exclusively* relevant."[38] But, like Raz and Lyons, Soper argued that this difference between principles and rules was irrelevant to Dworkin's argument against Hart. Dworkin took the fact that principles "are too controversial, numerous, and changing" to be captured under a single test as proof that the rule of recognition could not include principles.[39] But, as Soper argued, it is not obvious why the fact that positivism's "master test" cannot identify in advance, or comprehensively, all the laws of a legal system proves that positivism's master test is impossible. Soper suggested that the real reason why Dworkin felt that the rule of recognition could not capture certain legal standards (whether rules or principles) is not that they are controversial, numerous, or changing but that they are incapable, in theory, of ever being validated by reference to a social rule. According to Dworkin, the standards that "bind judges" are inherently normative in that the duty to recognize rights (what Dworkin originally called the "doctrine of political responsibility") is based not upon custom or practice but on morality.[40] Dworkin's argument was, therefore, that Hart was wrong not because he said that the rule of recognition included only rules, but that he was wrong because it turns out that the rule of recognition contains only principles. Soper's answer to Dworkin's argument was a little different from either Raz's or Lyons's. Rather than defend the compatibility of legal principles and social fact, or challenge the claim that legal principles could not have moral content, Soper questioned Dworkin's strict dichotomy between moral and social content. According to Soper the "obligations of the judge" are based on neither custom nor morality but on "translegal" principles that simply are part of "the concept of 'rationality' or 'judging'" in the same way that the rules for proper scientific induction are part of the concept of rationality in science.[41] So even if Dworkin was correct that the rule of recognition cannot base

[38] E. Philip Soper, *Legal Theory and the Obligation of a Judge: The Hart/Dworkin Dispute*, 75 *Mich. L. Rev.* 473, 481–3 (1977) (hereafter *Legal Theory*).

[39] Ibid., at 484.

[40] See ibid., at 491–2.

[41] Ibid., at 490–3. If Soper's "translegal" principles of law are necessary features of any legal system, then they might be a version of the "morality of law" position adopted by Fuller. The difference, of course, is that Soper does not claim that the presence of the translegal principles necessarily produces substantively moral outcomes (or is inconsistent with substantively immoral outcomes).

legality on social fact alone, he still did not prove that legal principles must condition legality on morality.

7.3. NONINCORPORATIONISM

The first group of responses to Dworkin agreed on two things: Positivism was not committed to the model of rules and positivism was committed to the rule of recognition. This agreement concealed an important ambiguity. When Raz claimed that "legal principles may be valid in precisely the same way rules are," he meant to limit legal principles to those principles that, like legal rules, could be validated by their pedigree. Because, for Raz, this seemed to include all the legal principles he felt Hart's theory needed to address, in his eyes his response was a complete rebuttal to Dworkin. Lyons and Soper, on the other hand, meant something very different when they argued that the rule of recognition can include principles as well as rules. They meant that a rule of recognition can include *moral* principles in the standards that set out the conditions of legality. For Raz, any differences there might be between legal rules and legal principles were not very interesting, because both are social standards that can be identified by their pedigree.[42] For Lyons and Soper, any differences there might be between legal rules and legal principles were not very interesting, because the rule of recognition can include a test that conditions legality on either the pedigree or morality. Between these two groups of positivists there was a deep divide – not over whether the rule of recognition could include principles as well as rules but over whether the rule of recognition could make morality a condition of legality. Raz's view would come to be identified with nonincorporationism, and Lyons's and Soper's with incorporationism.

Raz's version of nonincorporationism is based on his interpretation of "sources thesis": "A jurisprudential theory is acceptable only if its tests for identifying the content of the law and determining its existence depend exclusively on facts of human behavior capable of being described in value-neutral terms and applied without resort to moral argument."[43] Notice that the "tests" to which Raz referred may include either rules or principles; all that matters is that the satisfaction of conditions of which are set out by the tests cannot depend on moral argument. That is not to say, Raz stressed, that legal

[42] See Joseph Raz, *Practical Reason and Norms* 49 (2d ed., 1990).
[43] Joseph Raz, *The Authority of Law* 40 (1979) (hereafter *AL*).

norms may not also be moral norms: "moral views . . . [can] become social norms in the community . . . no [positivist] has ever denied that some social norms can be legal norms as well."[44] The nonincorporationist simply demands that there must be a social fact associated with the moral norm that satisfies the criteria of legality in the rule of recognition.[45]

Raz had two arguments for the sources thesis. The first is a functional argument, in that Raz thought that the sources thesis captures a truth about how law functions in everyday life. According to Raz, "the sources of a law are those facts by virtue of which it is valid and which identify its content."[46] This can include both formal and informal sources, ranging from Acts of Parliament to interpretive materials like treatises and custom. But the emphasis is on the word *fact*. A source must be something that can be validated without resort to moral argument. What would be the reason for this? According to Raz, *if* the function of law is to facilitate "various patterns of forbearance, co-operation, and co-ordination" in society, *then* law must "[provide] publicly ascertainable ways of guiding behavior and regulating aspects of social life."[47] The "publicly ascertainable" standards cannot be based on morality because then each subject would justify "non-conformity by challenging the justification of the standard."[48] Raz noted that Hart "more than anyone" emphasized this point – after all, the move from Austin's command theory to the social rule theory presupposes that the law can be identified without even the aid of a sovereign's threat.[49]

In order to illustrate the argument from function, Raz offered the image of a system in which the courts are not bound by any rules or precedents. Although not permitted to decide in an arbitrary fashion, these judges are entitled to "make that decision which seems best to them in the circumstances."[50] Raz argued that we would not recognize this as a legal system, because every legal system must

---

[44] Raz, *Legal Principles,* at 848.

[45] See Raz, *Authority, Law, and Morality* in *Ethics in the Public Domain: Essays in the Morality of Law and Politics* 235 (1994) (hereafter *ALM*). Thus, for example, Raz thought that the nonincorporationist can easily explain how certain moral norms, such as the equality provision found in the Canadian Charter or the equal protection clause found in the U.S. Constitution, can be recognized under a rule of recognition. Ibid., at 233.

[46] Raz, *AL,* at 48.

[47] Ibid., at 50–1.

[48] Ibid., at 52.

[49] See ibid., at 51.

[50] Ibid., at 112. It is important to note that this example captures a system close

have limits; a legal system of absolute discretion is unrecognizable to us.[51] Raz next drew a connection between our resistance to the idea of absolute judicial discretion and the sources thesis: "If the courts do not have absolute discretion to act on whichever standard seems to them best, this can only be because they are bound to follow some standards *even if they do not regard them as best*."[52] According to Raz, the only way to guide discretion is to ensure that it is never based upon the interpretation of moral principle.

Raz's second argument is based on his claim that the law must be capable of bearing practical authority. Raz noted that there may be reasons unrelated to the law's capacity to bear authority which produce the consequence that a given legal system in fact lacks authority. But if the law can bear authority, then it must by necessity exhibit the features of a practical authority. A practical authority "mediate[s] between people and the right reasons which apply to them, so that the authority judges and pronounces what they ought to do according to right reason."[53] Raz called this "the service conception of authority." Two additional features flow from the service conception of authority. We can assume that the reasons upon which the authority bases its directives are the same as the sort of reasons that the subjects of the authority themselves consider relevant to solving the dispute at hand.[54] Yet the reason that the authority gives for action to its subjects preempts and displaces the original reasons the subjects had for action: "[T]he mediating role of authority cannot be carried out if its subjects do not guide their actions by its instructions instead of by the reasons on which they are supposed to depend."[55] According to Raz, the features of a practical authority place constraints on the rule of recognition that in turn entails the sources thesis.

The sources thesis is entailed by the service conception of authority because the subjects of authority will need an objective, noncontroversial device to alert them to the substance of the authority's outcome. If, in order to obey the authority, the subjects had to de-

---

[51]   Ibid., at 115; and see Raz, *Practical Reason and Norms,* at 139–40.
[52]   Raz, *AL,* at 115 (emphasis added).
[53]   Raz, *ALM* 214 (emphasis removed).
[54]   Ibid., at 212.
[55]   Ibid., at 215. As Perry pointed out, the preemption thesis reintroduces the concept of the "exclusionary reason," which Raz first introduced in *Practical Reason and Norms.* Stephen R. Perry, *Judicial Obligation, Precedent and the Common Law,* 7 Oxford J. Leg. Stud. 215, 229 (1987) (hereafter *Judicial Obligation*).

pend on the sorts of reasons that they had asked the authority to choose among, the whole point of having an authority would be lost. The authority's decision "is serviceable only if it can be identified by means other than the considerations the weight and of outcome of which it was meant to settle."[56] Legal authority is serviceable if it is reflected in sources that require "little more than knowledge of English (including technical legal English)" such as legislation, judicial decisions, and custom.[57] Like the functional argument discussed previously, the argument from authority assumes that any moral language introduced into the rule of recognition makes its conditions of legality uselessly subjective and inherently indeterminate.

Nonincorporationism has been applied vigorously to American law by Frederick Schauer. I say this even though Schauer has been careful to distinguish himself from Raz. Schauer admitted that he is sympathetic to Raz but insisted that nowhere in his writings has he ever adopted the position that as a conceptual matter, nonincorporationism is true "in *any* community," as opposed to just the United States and "most other modern communities."[58] I will argue that there are so many affinities between Schauer's and Raz's arguments that it makes sense (at least for the purposes of this book) to compare the common features of their nonincorporationism with the arguments of the incorporationists. Furthermore, even under Schauer's own caveat, it seems fair to link him with Raz. Because many incorporationists think that the United States has a rule of recognition that incorporates morality, Schauer's claim that the American rule of recognition is nonincorporationist suggests that he has a picture of positivism very similar to Raz's.[59]

According to Schauer, there is a close affinity between positivism and "rule-based decisionmaking." Like Raz, Schauer did not think that there is any important difference between rules and principles. For Schauer, the important distinction in practical reasoning is between "particularism" and decision making by "entrenched generalization." According to Schauer, every rule is an attempt to gener-

---

[56]   Raz, *ALM*, at 219.
[57]   See ibid., at 221.
[58]   Frederick Schauer, *Rules and the Rule of Law*, 14 Harv. J.L. & Pub. Pol'y 645, 670 n49 (1991) (hereafter *RRL*).
[59]   See Schauer, *Rules*, at 202–3 (arguing that American common law system can be best explained as a form of "presumptive positivism" as opposed to incorporationism); Schauer, *RRL*, at 678–9 (same).

alize about what people ought to do in the future under certain circumstances in order to achieve some desired state of affairs. Schauer called the state of affairs that the rule is designed to achieve the rule's justification.[60] Because it is impossible ever to frame a prescriptive generalization that will fit perfectly the ends that it was designed to achieve, every rule, no matter how vague or open-ended it is, will be either under- or overinclusive relative to its purpose or justification. It is important to see that this feature – the ineliminable gap between a prescriptive generalization and its justification – is a feature of all norms, regardless of whether they are called rules or principles.[61]

Therefore, according to Schauer, every rule has the potential to fall short of its justification, and eventually all rules do. Someone engaged in practical reasoning can respond to this fact in one of two ways. One choice is to revise the content of the rule every time one discovers that it has fallen out of step with its justification. Schauer called this approach particularism. Particularism treats norms as "rules of thumb." A rule of thumb is not a rule at all, because it is continuously malleable and is therefore always "defeasible in the service of [its] generating justifications."[62] Under the second approach, the rules are treated as if they were *entrenched*. When a rule is entrenched, a decision maker may not reformulate that rule even if he or she knows that applying the rule will produce the "'wrong' result ... from the perspective of the justification undergirding the ... rule."[63] Every rule or principle, if it has the qualities of a

---

[60] See Schauer, *Rules*, at 1–52.

[61] Schauer calls all norms rules for reasons peculiar to his theory. See ibid., at 12–14.

[62] Frederick Schauer, *Rules, the Rule of Law, and the Constitution*, 6 Const. Commentary 69, 75–6 (1989). See also Frederick Schauer, *Formalism* 97 Yale L.J. 509, 534 (1988): "The view that rules should be interpreted to allow their purposes to trump their language in fact collapses the distinction between a rule and a reason, *and thus loses the very concept of a rule.*"

[63] Schauer, *RRL*, at 649. This form of decision making treats rules as "sticky" and therefore as a potential source of frustration to the decision maker. See Schauer, *Rules*, at 87. Schauer conceded that decision making is rarely a pure case of one or the other model and that the two models represent ideal points, at the end of a continuum. Thus, decision making in the real world will reflect a blend of particularism and entrenchment. Schauer distinguished decision-making systems that *blend* particularism and entrenchment from another position, which posits a third form of decision making called "rule-sensitive particularism." Rule-sensitive particularism requires the decision maker to reformulate the rule whenever it is over- or underinclusive, but only after the decision maker has balanced the "value of having a rule" against the gain accruing from reformulation. While Schauer recognized the logical

"real rule," must, by definition, constrain those to whom it has been addressed. As Schauer argued, "the absence of continuous malleability . . . is the feature that is both a necessary and sufficient condition for the exercise of rule-based decisionmaking."[64] Therefore, every rule of recognition, if it is really a rule, must constrain its subjects from revising it in light of their discovery that it fails to achieve its purpose or justification. Schauer did not claim that every legal system must be entirely rule-based. While he suggested that such a legal system might be possible, he thought that it would be unattractive.[65] Different decision-making systems will have different degrees of ruleness, depending on what goals or aims the system's designers have in mind. Schauer's point was that the idea of entrenchment is a necessary feature of a legal rule.[66]

Despite Schauer's statements that he did not want to enter into the debate between incorporationism and nonincorporationism, he was certain that only nonincorporationism has any connection with his account of rule-based decision making.[67] Like Raz, Schauer be-

possibility of rule-sensitive particularism, he thought that the same reasons that would lead a decision maker to forbear from treating rules as continuously malleable would apply equally to a decision maker who sought to determine, on a case-by-case basis, whether to reformulate a rule. See Schauer, *Rules,* at 97–9; Schauer, *RRL,* at 649–50. Gerald Postema argued that there is no difference between rule-sensitive particularism and Schauer's rule-based decision making in its "presumptive" form. See Gerald Postema, *Positivism, I Presume? . . . Comments on Schauer's "Rules and the Rule of Law,"* 14 Harv. J.L. & Pub. Pol'y 797, 813–17 (1991).

    [64] Schauer, *Rules,* at 84.

    [65] See Schauer, *Formalism,* at 536.

    [66] Schauer thought that American legal reasoning is a form of "presumptive positivism." In a system of presumptive positivism, rules exist and have force, but decision makers are allowed to act on nonpedigreed reasons when some "extreme" factor intrudes that signals to the decision maker that she should put aside the rule. See Schauer, *RRL,* at 677. Schauer distinguished presumptive positivism from "rule-sensitive particularism," which, like rule-utilitarianism, takes the view that the decision maker should make each decision on an "all things considered basis." See Frederick Schauer, *The Rules of Jurisprudence: A Reply,* 14 Harv. J.L. & Pub. Pol'y 839, 845 (1991) (denying that, in practice, presumptive positivism is extensionally equivalent to rule-sensitive particularism). Ironically, Schauer's argument against rule-sensitive particularism is the mirror image of Postema's argument against presumptive positivism.

Presumptive positivism, if it is a real alternative, represents an important way in which Schauer and Raz are different. Schauer was drawn to the idea that a decision maker can "peek behind" a rule without destroying the rule because he did not have as strict a conception of exclusionary reasons as Raz. According to Schauer, Raz failed to recognize that a reason can have exclusionary force and yet be overridden (Schauer called this "exclusionary weight"). See Schauer, *Rules,* at 90–1.

    [67] Ibid., at 198; see also Schauer, *RRL,* at 666 n41 (if incorporationism is the correct account of positivism, "then so much the worse for positivism," because it can-

lieved that "any version of positivism" must adopt the sources thesis.[68] Like Raz, he thought that incorporationism would erroneously allow the rule of recognition to include a rule that gave complete discretion to a law applier. According to Schauer, a rule of recognition that did not "demarcate [a] community's law from its morality" would be no different from a 'rule' that said take "as law the *ad hoc* decisions of one person."[69] Schauer, like Raz, thought that a legal system in which moral norms were incorporated into rule of recognition is really a system of pure discretion.

Schauer's reasons for rejecting incorporationism are slightly different from Raz's. Unlike Raz, Schauer did not directly reject the idea that the rule of recognition can condition legality upon a moral norm. Schauer's argument was simply that under incorporationism, the rule of recognition will be particularistic. Legal reasoning must be a form of entrenched decision making because a legal decision maker "constrained to take account of only a limited set of rules [will] on occasion make decisions other than those that she would have made were she not so restricted."[70] Schauer argued that where the test for law relies – even in part – on morality, decision making cannot be restricted to an entrenched set of norms but will be particularistic because the decision maker will revise his or her decision in light of the justification or purpose of the legal system. Decision making based on moral norms would have to allow particularism because the application of moral norms demands the application and balancing of "the full array of a society's moral, social, and political principles."[71] Incorporationism would allow decision making on an "all things considered" basis, hence it would envision a legal system without rule-based decision making.[72]

According to Schauer, the only way to avoid the trap of particularism is to limit legal decision making to "pedigreed" norms: "Both the idea of a rule and the idea of positivism as a limited set of norms entail some extensional divergence between the set of results

---

not explain what the theory of rule-based decision making explains, which "is how a limited set of pedigreeable materials appears to dominate the legal consciousness"); Anthony J. Sebok, *Is the Rule of Recognition a Rule?*, 72 *Notre Dame L. Rev.* 1539, 1549–50 (1997) (on Schauer's rejection of incorporationism).

[68] See Schauer, *Formalism*, at 536 n81.
[69] See Schauer, *Rules*, at 198.
[70] Schauer, *RRL*, at 667.
[71] Ibid., at 669.
[72] See Schauer, *Rules*, at 201.

indicated by a set of pedigreeable rules" and the rest of society's norms.[73] Schauer, like Raz, believed that legal rules must be identifiable by their pedigree, not their moral content. What Raz called the sources thesis, Schauer called the "limited domain thesis": that the rule of recognition contains a set of "limited and pedigreeable set of norms" that is distinct and separate from "the nonpedigreed set of norms then accepted within a society."[74]

We can now sum up the similarities between Raz's and Schauer's arguments for nonincorporationism. For Schauer, a decision maker who referred back to the justification of a norm would not be treating the norm like a rule. This parallels Raz's argument that a decision maker who referred back to the dependent reasons upon which a judgment was based would not be treating the judgment as authoritative.[75] Schauer's account of rule-based decision making sounds just like Raz's preemption thesis.[76] Furthermore, both Schauer and Raz argued that their conceptual account of law is attractive because each paints law in a more modest or self-effacing light than incorporationism. According to Raz, his argument that legal reasons preempt the other first-order reasons for action "does not express the immense power of authorities . . . [r]ather it reflects their limited role."[77] This is because all a legal authority does is "reflect dependent reasons in situations where they are better placed to do so."[78] Schauer argued that rules "serve the cause of decisional or personal modesty . . . [because] rules can cause the individual decisionmaker to submerge her own judgment of what the best result ought to be and of who ought to make that determination."[79]

---

[73] Schauer, *RRL,* at 667.

[74] See ibid., at 666.

[75] In fact, at times Raz's characterization of the preemption thesis sounds just like Schauer's argument for rule-based decision making: "Thus norms [i.e., exclusionary rules] have a relative independence from the reasons which justify them. In order to know that the norm is valid we must know that there are reasons which justify it. But we need not know what these reasons are in order to apply the norm correctly to the majority of cases. . . . It prevails in virtue of being an exclusionary reason." Raz, *Practical Reason and Norms,* at 79.

[76] "Rules *block* consideration of the full array of reasons that bear upon a particular decision in two different ways. First, they exclude from consideration reasons that might have been available had the decisionmaker not been constrained by a rule. Second, the rule itself becomes a reason for decision." Schauer, *Formalism,* at 537.

[77] Raz, *ALM,* at 215.

[78] Ibid., at 215.

[79] Schauer, *RRL,* at 689–90. See also Schauer, *Formalism,* at 543. In fact, Schauer explicitly connected his claim about rules and judicial modesty to Raz's arguments

Schauer argued that this conception of legal positivism asks the law applier to adopt a form of "role morality" in which he or she "does not engage in some (or all) of the moral reasoning that would be engaged in by the best all-things-considered moral reasoner not constrained by the responsibilities of role."[80] Role morality has many social advantages, and "if one denies legal positivism, then one must deny role morality."[81] Raz made a similar argument when he explained how to understand normative statements made from "a legal point of view."[82] Raz pointed out that it is quite possible that people "make normative statements from a point of view which they do not necessarily adopt."[83] A meat eater could tell a vegetarian about a dish that contained meat "you should not eat that dish" without believing that the vegetarian really has a reason to refrain from eating the dish. Like Schauer's legal actor who submerges his or her judgment, Raz's meat eater, by adopting vegetarianism as an authoritative norm, acts modestly even as he or she issues commands.

The argument from "modesty" helps us understand who are the subjects of the rule of recognition in nonincorporationism. As both Raz and Schauer noted, legal systems typically have norm-creating and norm-applying institutions.[84] Of course, the difference between these two "institutions" is functional, not physical; sometimes the same person can apply the law as well as create it, as when a judge follows precedent in one case and exercises discretion in another. The focus of the sources thesis or the limited domain theory is the law-applying institution: "Of legal systems it can be said that every act by a public official which is the performance of a duty or an exercise of a regulative power is generally regarded as a law-applying

---

for authority. See Schauer *RRL*, at 690 n87 (citing Raz, *The Morality of Freedom*, at 38–69 and Raz, *Practical Reason and Norms*, at 36–48).

[80] Frederick Schauer, *Constitutional Positivism*, 25 *Conn. L. Rev.* 797, 810 (1993) (citing David Luban, *Lawyers and Justice* 104–47 [1988]).

[81] Schauer, *Constitutional Positivism*, at 827. Therefore, for Schauer the question of law always is, when and how should the law constrain an actor to a role? The answer is one of institutional design: "In a world of non-ideal decisionmakers, therefore, one should calculate the virtues of ruleness based not only on an assessment of the costs of errors of under- and over-inclusion, but also on an assessment of the incidence and consequences of those errors that are more likely when decisionmakers are not constrained by rules." Schauer, *RRL*, at 685.

[82] See Raz, *Practical Reason and Norms*, at 174–7.

[83] Ibid., at 177.

[84] Raz noted that norm-creating institutions are prevalent in modern legal systems but not a necessary feature of a legal system. See Raz, *AL*, at 105.

act." Both Raz and Schauer described the full range of law-applying actors as the proper subject of the rule of recognition – police officers, elected representatives, bureaucrats, and finally judges.[85] Of this large set of law appliers Raz distinguished the law enforcers from "primary" law-applying organs. A law-enforcing institution merely brings about the state of affairs demanded by the application of the law (such as the seizing of a suspect or the sale of property to pay off a debt).[86] A primary law-applying organ "is concerned with the authoritative determination of normative situations in accordance with pre-existing norms."[87] A typical example of this sort of organ is a court, although as we noted, other public officials can, to varying degrees, possess primary law-applying power. As Raz pointed out, primary law appliers are very special kinds of authorities. By definition, because they are *applying* the law, they must be treating the law as an authority – that is, as a preemptive reason for their action (their judgment). But they are not applying the law to themselves; they are applying it to others. Even so, the primary law appliers are still subject to authority; they are not authorities themselves.[88] Therefore, the primary law-applying organs must regard the rule of recognition as a preemptive reason or an entrenched generalization.[89] Otherwise, the law could be nothing more than the discretion of the judge, which would mean a complete collapse of the law-making and law-applying functions. To avoid this collapse, the rule of recognition must speak to the primary law-applying organs through "social facts which can be established without resort to moral argument."[90]

Raz's and Schauer's arguments for nonincorporationism are complementary halves of each other. Raz's sources thesis came to the conclusion that the law must be based on a subset of the norms in society (Schauer's limited domain thesis) because the entire set of social norms would include moral norms. A moral norm cannot be a condition of legality because it cannot bear practical authority.

---

[85] See Raz, *AL*, at 107, and Schauer, *Rules, The Rule of Law, and the Constitution*, at 78–9.

[86] See Raz, *AL*, at 108.

[87] Ibid.

[88] Except in the sense that they are experts in a technical field. In this sense, they are authorities in the same way that an engineer is an authority. But this is not the sense that Raz or Schauer intends.

[89] See Raz, *ALM*, at 231.

[90] Ibid.

Schauer's limited domain thesis came to the conclusion that the law cannot be based on moral norms (Raz's sources thesis) because the application of a moral norm would require the consideration of all social norms in legal decision making. "All things considered" decision making is wholly particularistic, and a wholly particularistic system of decision making is not rule-based. Raz feared "all things considered" reasoning because it entailed moral norms; Schauer feared moral norms because they entailed "all things considered" reasoning.

7.4. INCORPORATIONISM

Incorporationism holds that moral principles may be part of the conditions of legality set out in the rule of recognition. Something like incorporationism motivated Lyons's response to Dworkin.[91] In 1982 Jules Coleman offered a clear statement of the incorporationist position, and since 1982 Coleman has developed his views by self-consciously contrasting himself with Raz and Schauer.[92] Incorporationism is built out of two claims: the "negative" claim that there is no necessary connection between law and morality, and the "positive" claim that the authority of the rule of recognition is a matter of social convention.[93] Incorporationism, therefore, clearly denies the truth of natural law theory, provides an account of the authority of law, and provides an analysis of what it means for something to be a rule of recognition. The difference between incorporationism and nonincorporationism is that the latter places restrictions on the content of the rule of recognition, whereas the former does not. Coleman offered two arguments for why the nonincorporationists are wrong to place limits on the content of the rule of recognition.

First, Coleman argued that there is no reason for positivism to restrict the rule of recognition to pedigree standards of legality. Coleman asked why someone who embraced the separability thesis could not endorse a rule of recognition that relied on nonpedigreed standards, such as moral norms.[94] The separability thesis does not

---

[91] See Lyons, *Principles*. Rolf Sartorious made much the same argument in the early 1970s. See Rolf Sartorious, *Social Policy and Judicial Legislation*, 8 *Amer. Phil. Q.* 151 (1971).

[92] See Coleman, *Negative and Positive Positivism*; Coleman, *AR*; Jules L. Coleman, *Rules and Social Facts* 14 *Harv. J.L. & Pub. Pol'y* 703 (1991) (hereafter *RSF*).

[93] See Coleman, *RSF*, at 717; Coleman, *Negative and Positive Positivism*, at 148.

[94] See Coleman, *RSF*, at 719.

bar this possibility, because the separability thesis says only that the rule of recognition does not necessarily contain nonpedigreed standards, not that it could never contain them. Raz's functional argument was that it is the job of law to provide readily ascertainable, public standards by which people could noncontroversially know their primary duties. If the rule of recognition contained a controversial condition of legality (like a moral norm), then it could not fulfill its function. Coleman's response to Raz's argument from function was to challenge Raz's picture of the rule of recognition's function. As noted in Chapter 6, Coleman thought that a rule of recognition can have a semantic or epistemic function.[95] Coleman noted that Hart distinguished between two types of epistemic functions: validation and identification. The rule of recognition serves a validation function when it "enable[s] relevant officials to judge the validity of official actions."[96] The rule of recognition serves an identifying function when it helps ordinary citizens determine "which of the community's norms [are] binding on them."[97] According to Coleman, Raz basically argued that if the rule of recognition identifies law according to its content as opposed to its pedigree, then it will fail in its identifying function, because "a content-based rule of recognition will fail adequately to provide the information ordinary citizens need."[98]

Coleman's first argument in response was that "contentful" standards of legality can be identified by their pedigrees. A moral principle could be incorporated into the rule of recognition by the fact that it is cited in the preamble to legislation, or is cited in judicial decisions.[99] But Coleman's response was not completely responsive, because the point of Raz's argument is not that the rule of recognition cannot attempt to incorporate contentful standards but that in doing so, it would fail to serve its identifying function, because the adoption of a contentful standard into the rule of recognition could not guarantee that it could be used by an ordinary citizen to determine his or her legal duties. Coleman had a response to this: It may be the case that certain contentful standards simply are shared so broadly that there is no controversy among the citizenry

---

[95] He has also added a third function, the "metaphysical," but we will not take up that issue here. See Coleman, *AR*, at 291.

[96] Ibid.

[97] Ibid.

[98] Ibid., at 292; and see Coleman, *RSF*, at 720.

[99] See Coleman, *AR*, at 292.

about how to apply the standard.[100] But this begs the question, because it is clear that in the case of many moral norms, their application *is* controversial. Coleman's real argument is that the controversy among citizens surrounding the meaning of contentful standards is irrelevant to the successful functioning of the rule of recognition. Raz (and maybe Hart) simply was wrong about the rule of recognition serving an identification function. The rule of recognition is "fundamentally" a validation rule.[101] The rule of recognition is directed toward legal officials, not citizens. The rule of recognition does not identify primary duties – it is not used to identify when a citizen ought to act or forbear from some action. The rule of recognition validates the actions of other legal officials – for example, it tells when an act of Parliament or a lower court decision is law.[102] The legal officials must agree, of course, on the identification *of* the rule of recognition, but that is not the same thing as saying that the rule of recognition has an identifying function. Nothing that has been said so far about the potentially controversial nature of contentful standards prevents legal officials from using contentful standards when they validate other legal officials' actions: "That a rule of recognition may be controversial in its instantiations, however, does not entail that judges disagree about what the rule is. They disagree, perhaps, only about what it requires. In that case they do not disagree about what the validation standard is, only about what it validates."[103] Coleman concluded that because the rule of recognition does not serve an identifying function for either legal officials or citizens, Raz's argument from function fails.[104]

---

[100] See Coleman, *RSF,* at 720.

[101] See Coleman, *AR,* at 292.

[102] See ibid., at 293. Coleman, in his essay with Brian Leiter on legal positivism, argued that Hart's original dichotomy between primary and secondary rules really is a trichotomy. The secondary rules that create the power to legislate and adjudicate are not like the secondary rule of recognition, because the former are power-conferring rules but the latter is not: "Hart really believes that there are three kinds of legal rules: those that obligate, those that [enable,] and the rule of recognition that sets out validity conditions." Coleman and Leiter, *Legal Positivism,* at 245.

[103] Ibid., at 252.

[104] David Lyons argued that Raz's argument from function really is an argument from political theory. Lyons suggested that Raz thought that the rule of recognition cannot include contentful norms because society would break up if individuals used moral argument in adjudication. Individuals would "break the law in hopes of avoiding the legal consequences by 'challenging the justification of the standard.'" David Lyons, *Moral Aspects of Legal Theory,* in *Midwest Studies in Philosophy* VII 245

Coleman made a similar argument against Schauer's argument for the limited domain thesis. The limited domain thesis says that "the law must be only a part of [a] community's stock of norms."[105] As with his argument against Raz's argument from function, Coleman argued that the limited domain thesis is not entailed by the separability thesis. Coleman noted that Schauer believed that the claim that law is a social fact entails the pedigree constraint, and Schauer believed that the same reasons that demand the pedigree constraint demand the limited domain thesis. The pedigree constraint states that the test of legality under the rule of recognition must be a matter of simple, uncontroversial, and empirically verifiable fact.[106] But as we saw in the preceding paragraphs, the epistemic function of the rule of recognition does not demand the sort of "epistemic adequacy" that can be satisfied only by a noncontentful norm. As long as the legal officials can identify the rule of recognition, it is no challenge to its epistemic adequacy that there is disagreement as to its valid instantiations.[107] Schauer thought that the set of "hard facts" denoted by the pedigree constraint could play the role of entrenched generalizations in a rule-based system of legal reasoning.[108] But if, as Coleman showed, there is no reason to distinguish between contentful and noncontentful norms on the basis of epistemic adequacy, then the limited domain thesis has to stand on its own argument. Schauer's argument is simply that *if* the rule of recognition is a rule, and every rule is extensionally divergent from some set of norms that would better promote its purpose, *then* the rule of recognition cannot include all of a "community's stock of norms."[109] In other words, the rule of recognition cannot be particularistic. Coleman asked why. If legal officials test the validity of law particularistically *because* the criterion of legality in the rule of recognition requires them to do so, and the criterion is epistemically adequate, both the separability thesis and the social rule theory are satisfied. There is nothing about positivism that prohibits the contingent (and somewhat unlikely) overlap between the set of

---

(Peter A. French, Theodore E. Uehling Jr., and Howard K. Wettstein, eds., 1982). Raz denied that this was ever his argument. See Raz, *ALM*, at 235.

[105]   Coleman, *RSF*, at 723.

[106]   Ibid., at 718.

[107]   See ibid., at 720–2.

[108]   The phrase "hard facts" is Coleman's. See Coleman, *Negative and Positive Positivism*, at 149.

[109]   Coleman, *RSF*, at 723.

norms identified by a society's test of legality and that society's entire set of norms.

Second, Coleman argued that the law's claim to be a practical authority does not restrict the rule of recognition to criteria that tests only a norm's social source, not its substance or moral merits.[110] According to Raz, an authoritative conclusion has to be ascertainable without reference to the dependent reasons that the authority was supposed to consider in drawing its conclusion. If a judge is to determine whether a norm against murder is valid law, the rule of recognition is supposed to provide a second-order reason for adopting the norm, even though it is likely that the judge would have adopted the norm on the basis of his or her own first-order, dependent reasons. Coleman, who was sympathetic to Raz's account of authority in law, did not think that incorporationism "requires uncovering a norm's underlying justificatory reasons."[111] This is because not every moral value in a rule of recognition will necessarily be relevant to the considerations that underlie every norm in a legal system. Coleman offered the following example: Imagine a legal system that restricts legality to only those laws that do not violate "fairness." A judge who had to determine the validity of a law that prohibited murder would not have to "look to the underlying moral reasons for having a prohibition against certain intentional killings."[112] According to Coleman, the judge would have to test the enactment against other moral values, such as values relating to the form and manner of enactment, and other issues of "fairness," but those values do not relate to the first-order reasons the judge might have for thinking that a law against murder was a good thing.[113] So a rule of recognition that incorporated a nonsocial source such as a moral value into its criteria of legality could still provide a second-order reason for action.[114]

---

[110] Coleman, *AR*, at 305; Coleman and Leiter, *Legal Positivism*, at 256–7. Schauer did not think that law must necessarily be capable of being a practical authority, and therefore he did not follow Raz in taking up this argument. See, for example, Frederick Schauer, *Positivism Through Thick and Thin* (Address at a Conference on the Works of Jules Coleman, October 14, 1996); Frederick Schauer, *Fuller's Internal Point of View*, 13 *L. & Phil.* 285 (1994).

[111] Coleman, *AR*, at 306.

[112] Ibid., at 307.

[113] See Coleman, *AR*, at 307; and see Coleman and Leiter, *Legal Positivism*, at 356.

[114] See Coleman, *AR*, at 307; and see Waluchow, *Inclusive Legal Positivism*, at 139–40.

Coleman also argued that it would be a mistake to rely covertly upon the argument for the pedigree constraint in trying to make an argument for the sources thesis. At times we speak of law's being an authority for *citizens*. One might argue, therefore, that in order to be an authority, the law must be easily discernible. In other words, unless the rule of recognition is objective and noncontroversial, it will fail to function as a second-order reason for action for the general populace.[115] Coleman noted that this really is just the epistemic function argument again, and it fails for the same reasons it failed before.[116] First, the rule of recognition is a validation rule, not an identification rule. Second, it will be recalled that the rule of recognition is addressed to legal officials, not to citizens. Ordinary citizens, if they ever think about the law, do not refer to the rule of recognition when they try to determine the primary rules that impose duties upon them. Citizens very often utilize a variety of *identification rules* to determine their legal duties, but there is no reason to assume that the citizens' identification rules resemble the rule of recognition.[117] One might think that the main feature of an identification rule would be that it was a reliable indicator of the primary rules in society. For example, a very useful identification rule in a complex legal system like modern America's is "To determine what your primary duties are, ask a lawyer." It is possible, therefore, that in a modern constitutional democracy the most useful identification rules do not incorporate moral language, while the rule of recognition does. In that case, the sources thesis would be a constraint on the rules that citizens use to determine their obligations, but not on the rule that legal officials use to determine legal validity. An incorporationist rule of recognition could be a second-order reason for action for judges while a nonincorporationist rule of identification could be a second-order reason for action for citizens.[118]

Finally, Stephen Perry raised an argument against nonincorporationism related to Coleman's critique of the argument of the sources thesis. If, as Raz argued, judges are to treat social sources as authoritative conclusions, then judicial precedent must have the same preemptive force as legislation.[119] As Perry showed, although courts do treat precedents as second-order reasons for action, contrary to

---

[115] See Coleman, *AR,* at 307.
[116] See Coleman and Leiter, *Legal Positivism,* at 257.
[117] See Coleman, *AR,* at 308; Coleman and Leiter, *Legal Positivism,* at 258.
[118] This is a possibility Coleman acknowledged. See Coleman, *AR,* at 308.
[119] See Perry, *Judicial Obligation,* at 232.

Raz's characterization of practical authority, courts do not treat them as exclusionary reasons.[120] Courts typically look to the reasons underlying a precedent in the course of determining its application. Perry therefore argued that common law precedents "cannot be regarded as being instances of Raz's central case of exclusionary rules, which are rules that possess a relatively large measure of independence from their justifying reasons."[121] This is not to say that precedents are not second-order reasons for action, just that second-order reasons for action may still permit some consideration of first-order reasons. A court is bound by precedent unless it is "satisfied that the collective weight of the reasons supporting the opposite result is of greater strength, to some degree, than the weight which would otherwise be required to reach that result on the ordinary balance of reasons."[122] Accordingly, the rule of recognition in common law systems sometimes determines the validity of judicial decisions by directly applying the sort of values the decisions were meant authoritatively to determine. This does not make law any less of a practical authority, because Perry insists that common law judges are guided by second-order reasons for action, and are not simply legislating.[123] But it does show that the demand that the law bear practical authority does not force a positivist to restrict the rule of recognition to social sources, because moral norms can provide second-order reasons for action.

To conclude this section, then, the incorporationists seemed to have successfully argued that neither of the commitments that they share with the nonincorporationists requires that the rule of recognition exclude moral values from the criteria of legality. Hart clearly agreed. In his Postscript to *The Concept of Law,* he stated that he never intended to endorse "plain fact positivism," in which "the identification of law must consist only of historical facts."[124] Hart said that if by "pedigree" we mean only historical facts "which con-

---

[120] See ibid., at 235–6.
[121] Ibid., at 239.
[122] Ibid., at 222.
[123] Perry called his characterization of the role of second-order reasoning in common law systems the "strong Burkean conception of precedent": "[P]revious judicial reliance upon the set of principles for which a given proposition stands does not exclude action upon a subsequently reconsidered balance of reasons, but is simply deemed, in effect, to confer a somewhat greater weight upon those principles than they would otherwise have received when reconsideration occurs." Ibid., at 239.
[124] Hart, *CL,* at 247.

cern law-creation and adoption," then he is not a plain fact positivist, because he clearly believes that the rule of recognition in the United States (for example) explicitly adopts substantive constraints on the content of legislation.[125] Although Hart never said so explicitly, Dworkin's characterization of "plain fact" positivism was really the same as Raz's pedigree constraint on the rule of recognition.[126] Hart's reasons for rejecting the pedigree constraint (whether Dworkin's or Raz's) were slightly different from Coleman's, however. Hart conceded that the incorporation of morality into the rule of recognition would make it a less reliable tool for the identification of the law.[127] Rather than argue that the rule of recognition does not have an identification function, Hart argued that the rule of recognition's identification function is a matter of degree. Hence, a rule of recognition that is less ascertainable than another might still provide an adequate test for law: "[T]he exclusion of all uncertainty at whatever costs in other values is not a goal which I have ever envisaged for the rule of recognition . . . a margin of uncertainty should be tolerated, and indeed welcomed in the case of many legal rules. . . ."[128] Hart concluded that the criteria of legality may be contentful because as long as the rule of recognition fulfills some part of its identification function, it is fulfilling its function.

7.5. INCORPORATIONISM AND
THE PROBLEM OF INSATIABILITY

An incorporationist can show why the rule of recognition may be controversial in its instantiations and yet still be epistemically adequate. He or she can show why the rule of recognition may require judges to make normative judgments and yet still be a practical authority. In both arguments part of the incorporationist's argument turns on showing that the normativity of a moral value does not interfere with other features it may possess that enable it to be a criterion of legality. So, for example, Coleman proved that the fact that a moral norm may be less ascertainable than a social fact is irrelevant to the question of whether the norm could be used to validate the acts of other legal officials. And Coleman also proved that the fact

---

[125] See ibid., at 250.
[126] See Coleman, *AR*, at 290.
[127] See Hart, *CL*, at 251.
[128] Ibid., at 251–2.

that a criterion of legality based on a moral value may require a law applier to engage in moral reasoning is irrelevant to the question of whether it could be a second-order reason for action for legal officials. These sorts of arguments against nonincorporationism fall under what might be called the "no difference thesis": that it makes no difference to the operation of the rule of recognition whether a criterion of legality is a moral value or a nonmoral fact.

Raz and Schauer have one remaining argument that challenges the "no difference thesis." They claimed that morality is different from other criteria of legality because any attempt to incorporate a moral value into a rule of recognition results in the illegitimate introduction of additional moral values into the law applier's reasoning. These additional values are illegitimate because they were not originally part of the rule of recognition; hence the law applier ceases to act in his or her capacity as a law-applying organ and becomes a law-creating organ. Rather than promote modesty and "role morality," incorporationism promotes a form of judicial usurpation.[129] That is why the pedigree constraint and the sources thesis are needed – unless the criteria of legality are tethered to noncontentful facts, law-applying organs will illegitimately engage in law creation. It is important to note that this argument is not based on a concern that a rule of recognition which incorporated morality would be difficult to ascertain, or that it would require judges to consider first-order reasons for action. The argument is, rather, that moral values cannot be cabined – that once one moral value becomes part of the rule of recognition, more follow. Of course, this is a version of the insatiability argument I made against Dworkin in Chapter 6. Raz and Schauer claimed, in effect, that it works as well against Coleman and Hart as it does against the fundamental rights theorists. It is important to see why the nonincorporationists might say this and why they would be wrong.

The pedigree constraint was designed to establish what Raz called the "limits of law." Contrary to the incorporationist, who thought that whether law and morality are extensionally divergent

---

[129] Schauer thought that only if a rule applier is limited to a set of norms smaller than all the norms in society can there be differentiation among roles in a legal system. This is clear from Schauer's argument connecting rule-based decision making and what he calls "role differentiation": "Only when there is role differentiation, *and always when there is role differentiation,* will [rules] be an essential component of the process of differentiation, of the process of allocating decisionmaking power." Schauer, *RRL,* at 686.

is a contingent matter, Raz thought that the law must have limits because the law cannot "contain all the justifiable standards (moral or other) nor does it necessarily comprise all social rules and conventions."[130] Schauer thought the same thing: "positivism is about normative systems smaller than and distinguishable from the entire normative universe."[131] The limits of law thesis presupposes that there must be a way to describe the point at which the extensional divergence between legal norms and moral norms occurs. On the other hand, incorporationism cannot "provide an adequate criterion for separating legal references to morality . . . from cases of judicial discretion, in which the judge, by resorting to moral considerations, is changing the law."[132] Unless such a criterion can be described, the incorporationist must conclude that "all social norms are automatically . . . binding as law" and therefore violate the demands of the limits of law.[133]

As we saw previously, the incorporationist can argue that positivism is compatible with a rule of recognition that was contingently coextensive with "all" the norms of its society. But the insatiability argument focuses on a different point. Raz and Schauer believed that because the incorporationist cannot provide a test that identifies *which* moral values are in the rule of recognition (and which are not), the law applier will always act as if *all* of society's moral values are in the rule of recognition whenever a moral value is part of the rule of recognition. Why did the nonincorporationists think this?

Raz thought that the incorporationist is committed to saying that "all that is derivable from the law (with the help of other true premises) is law."[134] Hence, the incorporationist thinks that "all the moral consequences of a legal rule are part of the law."[135] There are two steps to Raz's argument. First, Raz equated "all the moral consequences of a legal rule" with "all of society's moral values." This equation is not obvious. It may be possible that the moral consequences of a rule against murder, for example, may be only a subset of all the moral values in a society. It is not clear, for example, what the values implicated in a rule against murder have to do with issues of economic equality. Second, Raz claimed that the incorpora-

---

[130] Raz, *AL*, at 45.
[131] Schauer, *Rules*, at 199.
[132] Raz, *AL*, at 47.
[133] Raz, *Legal Principles*, at 849.
[134] Raz, *ALM*, at 229.
[135] Ibid., at 230.

tionists made the mistake of equating "being entailed by the source-based law" with "being endorsed by the sources of law."[136] Raz's argument is that because the rule of recognition is the expression of an authority's belief or opinion, it cannot be interpreted to be an endorsement of all of the conclusions it logically entails.[137] That may be true enough, but the incorporationist needs to claim only that the rule of recognition can be interpreted to be an endorsement of *some* of the conclusions it logically entails. Hart suggested as much when he distinguished between core and penumbral meaning.[138] Raz himself noted that while he rejected the claim that authorities command all that is entailed by what they say, authorities "can and do direct and guide by implication."[139] Raz had to say the latter because he rejected originalism. Raz, unlike Bickel or Bork, thought it incoherent to believe that the only way to interpret the Eighth Amendment of the U.S. Constitution is to say that its meaning "is determined by the thoughts actually entertained by the lawmakers when making the law."[140] He argued, instead, that the authors of the Eighth Amendment could have had the concrete intention that their words be interpreted according to whatever rule of interpretation was required by the legal system's rule of recognition.[141] The content of the rule of interpretation and the ultimate results it generates would vary from legal system to legal system, but what would not change is that "the character of the rules for imputing intentions and directives to the legal authorities is a matter of fact and not a moral issue."[142] Because the rules of interpretation of moral language are themselves matters of convention, the rule of recogni-

[136]   Ibid., at 231.
[137]   Raz argued that when the rule of recognition includes sources that do not have single identifiable (or even natural) authors, the rule of recognition will establish a convention that provides when certain sources will be treated as the product of authorial intent. See ibid., at 236.
[138]   See Hart, *Positivism and the Separation of Law and Morals*, at 607.
[139]   Raz, *ALM*, at 230. This argument was in response to David Lyons's claim that Raz's nonincorporationism is based on an "explicit content thesis." See Lyons, *Moral Aspects of Legal Theory*, at 237.
[140]   Raz, *ALM*, at 232. Unlike Bickel or Bork, Raz has not evidenced any moral skepticism: He rejected the idea that nonincorporationism "[presupposes] a non-naturalist ethical position." Raz, *ALM*, at 235. For a more complete picture of Raz's own form of liberalism, see Joseph Raz, *The Morality of Freedom* (1986).
[141]   See Raz, *ALM*, at 233. In the case of the U.S. Constitution, it is probable that the original framers thought their words should not be interpreted through the method of originalism. See H. Jefferson Powell, *The Original Understanding of Original Intent*, 98 Harv. L. Rev. 885 (1985).
[142]   Raz, *ALM*, at 233.

tion's moral implications are distinguished by a nonmoral fact from the rule's moral entailments. Raz's argument has to have been, therefore, that in the absence of a convention for the interpretation of moral language, a judge would have no way of limiting the set of moral implications entailed by that language. Conversely, where a judge uses a rule of interpretation in tandem with moral language, the rule of recognition is not incorporating a moral value, because the law applier is not interested in what the moral concept denoted by the moral language *really* means; the law applier is interested in what the concept *conventionally* means.[143]

Schauer thought that the rule of recognition cannot incorporate a moral value because if it does then the judge will apply the law based on an "all things considered" judgment.[144] Thus, he thought that if the rule of recognition incorporates *a* moral value, it incorporates "the full set of society's principles."[145] As I noted previously in the discussion of Raz, it is not obvious why moral values should behave insatiably in the rule of recognition. Schauer's answer was rooted in his theory of rules. For Schauer, every rule or principle has a justification or goal. If the rule applier is allowed to revise the content of the rule in light of the rule's original goal, then the rule applier will inevitably be led through an endless series of revisions:

> [T]he potential tension between the general goal and its concretized instantiation exists at every level. At one level, the tension is between language and purpose; at the next, it is between that purpose and the deep purpose lying behind it; at the next, between the deep purpose and an even deeper purpose, and so on. When we decide that purpose must not be frustrated by its instantiation, we embark upon a potentially *infinite regress* in which all forms of concretization are defeasible.[146]

---

[143] "A law has a source if its contents and existence can be determined without using moral arguments (*but allowing for arguments about people's moral views and intentions, which are necessary for interpretation, for example*)." Raz, *AL,* at 47 (emphasis added).

[144] See Schauer, *Rules,* at 199. I agree with Coleman that by "all things considered" judgment, Schauer meant that "in a particular case, a judge should reach the result that is best, all things considered." Coleman, *RSF,* at 712.

[145] Schauer, *RRL,* at 669.

[146] Schuaer, *Formalism,* at 534. Schauer made a similar argument in the case of the First Amendment. He argued that if one viewed the First Amendment as incorporating a moral value, one would be obliged to view the First Amendment as incorporating the entire stock of society's norms. This is because no matter which norm one adopts to explain the First Amendment, there could always be a deeper and more general norm to explain the first norm: "[W]hat is the relationship, for exam-

In the case of common law precedent, for example, Schauer argued that if the rule of recognition is seen as incorporating a nonpedigreed moral value, then a judge attempting to determine the holding of a given case will be plunged into an infinite regress until he or she ultimately decides the case on the basis of the "non limited set of social norms."[147]

Schauer noted that the incorporationist might want to argue that the inclusion of a nonpedigreeable value would cabin the judge to just the one value, not "the full totality of social factors."[148] Schauer argued that the cabining is an illusion. If the nonpedigreeable value is part of the law because it possesses the feature of morality, then other nonpedigreeable values that also possess the feature of morality are parts of the law, too. If the law's point or purpose is to secure some state of affairs *because* that state of affairs is warranted by morality, then the criterion of legality for that law is morality. Like Raz, Schauer was assuming that every moral value is potentially entailed by any law with a moral goal. Schauer, in fact, had a reason for making this assumption. He argued that every time a judge considers a nonpedigreeable norm, he or she is implicitly (or perhaps explicitly) considering the entire "universe of judicially usable social propositions."[149] This is because "if positive law is always capable of being set aside in the name of nonpedigreed values, then even a decision not to set aside the positive law involves a decision, *en passant*, that the positive law is consistent with those larger values."[150] By extension, a decision not to set aside one set of larger values must involve a decision that they are consistent with an even larger set of values, and so on, until the decision maker ultimately is deciding whether to set aside the positive law on the basis of an "all things considered" judgment about what ought to be done in that situation.

How can the incorporationist respond to the insatiability argument? It should be obvious that it is simply not responsive for the incorporationist to say, as Coleman did, that nothing in positivism

---

ple, of a 'public deliberation' justification for the First Amendment to the 'democracy' justification that might lie behind *it*?" Schauer, *RRL*, at 683 n78.

[147] Schauer, *RRL*, at 671.

[148] Ibid., at 670.

[149] Frederick Schauer, *Is the Common Law Law?*, 77 *Calif. L. Rev.* 455, 466 (1989) (reviewing Melvin A. Eisenberg, *The Nature of the Common Law* [1988]).

[150] Schauer, *Rules*, at 201.

prevents that "the law in a particular community be unlimited."[151] This argument, while probably correct, is beside the point. The target of Raz's and Schauer's insatiability argument was not a rule of recognition that explicitly incorporates all the community's stock of moral norms into the law (e.g., x is law iff x is what one should do, all things considered). They each had reasons for doubting that a decision-making system based on such a rule would be a legal system, and we have looked at those arguments already. Their primary target was a rule of recognition that incorporates *a* moral value but not *all* moral or social values. An example of this sort of "limited" incorporation is the following rule: "no norm can count as part of the community's law if it violates fairness."[152] Raz's and Schauer's arguments were that although this rule of recognition is supposed to incorporate only one aspect of morality, it will inevitably incorporate all of morality, thereby converting a "limited incorporationist" rule of recognition into a rule that incorporates society's complete stock of norms.

We have already seen that Coleman had two responses to the insatiability argument. First, as he noted in his argument against Raz's argument from function, the fact that the correct application of a moral value may be controversial does not mean that a judge is applying an open-ended set of moral values when using that moral value to validate official acts. For example, the fact that the application of the word *fairness* may be controversial does not mean that each judge is not actually testing the validity of the law against the moral value of fairness, as opposed to justice, or equality, or what would be best "all things considered."[153] According to Coleman, the ability of legal officials to converge around *certain* moral principles (such as fairness) is quite separate from the unnecessary and unlikely demand that they agree on what those moral principles require.[154] Therefore, the fact that the concept of fairness may have a potentially broad set of logical entailments or might require the judge to take into account a wide range of social values does not challenge the incorporationist claim that every judge can and does refer to certain aspects of morality like fairness when he or she validates some legal act. Second, as we saw in Coleman's rebuttal to

[151] Coleman, *RSF*, at 724.
[152] Coleman, *AR*, at 306.
[153] Ibid., at 296.
[154] Ibid., at 295–6.

Raz's argument about practical authority, the *aspects of morality* that a judge would use to determine whether a law was fair are not the same as the "aspects" of morality that would justify the law. In the example he offered, Coleman noted that the first-order reasons a judge might have for thinking that someone ought not intentionally take human life except under certain conditions are very different from the first-order reasons the judge might have for believing that a law against murder is fair.[155] For this argument to work, the aspect of morality denoted as "fairness" cannot turn out simply to be the same as the aspect of morality that would motivate a law against murder: There must be some way of applying the latter without collapsing it into an "all things considered" judgment that incorporates the former. Coleman asserted that there is no reason to assume that such a collapse must occur: An "inquiry into fairness does not lead inevitably to the moral or other reasons that would justify the [law] in the first place."[156]

The incorporationist's argument against the insatiability thesis relies on the claim that a decision maker can apply an "aspect" of morality such as fairness without engaging in a broader "all things considered" judgment. I think that the incorporationist can make this claim about moral values, but it is not obvious and will require additional argument. The problem is this: As we have seen in Chapter 6, moral reasoning *is* insatiable. Conscientious decision makers applying a moral value must test and revise each and every step of their practical reasoning against the theory of morality they believe is true. That theory may be simple or complex, consequentialist, deontological, intuitionist, or any one of a variety of approaches, but it will ultimately answer the same question: What ought to be done, "all things considered"? This is a commonplace point, and it is easily illustrated within the context of Coleman's own example. He claimed that in order to determine whether a law against murder is "fair" we would not have to examine the reasons that would justify "a prohibition against certain forms of intentional killing."[157] Coleman seemed to think that "fairness" is a feature of just "the form and manner of enactment" of a law."[158] But this is not obviously correct. Fairness might involve the point or purpose of the law, and

---

155   Ibid., at 307.
156   Ibid., at 306.
157   Ibid., at 307.
158   Ibid.

not just how the point or purpose was realized. In Coleman's example, fairness may require an examination of precisely those considerations that one would use to determine which forms of intentional killing the law will prohibit. For example, a feminist might argue that the substance of a murder statute must take into account the unfair treatment of women by society in general and by the police more specifically. Under this account, a murder statute that did not expand the definition of "self-defense" to include women who killed their sleeping batterers would not be fair, even if the form and manner of enactment were impeccable.[159]

That any one aspect of morality is connected to other aspects of the moral theory of which it is an aspect is a problem that is quite familiar to students of constitutional law. The entire debate over the proper interpretation of the due process clause of the Fourteenth Amendment illustrates how difficult it is to make *a priori* distinctions between one aspect of morality (for example, "due" process) and other aspects of morality, such as equality, liberty, and privacy.[160] As Justice Harlan noted, the due process clause "is not a series of isolated points pricked out in terms of the taking of property; the freedom of speech, press, and religion; the right to keep and bear arms; the freedom from unreasonable searches and seizures; and so on . . . [i]t is a rational continuum."[161] It does not take much argument, or a very sophisticated political philosophy, to see that each of these aspects of morality may affect the others, and that from the perspective of moral judgment, each must be reconciled with the others under the umbrella of a theory of justice. This is not because the language of morals is indeterminate. Waluchow argued that although terms like *equality* and *liberty* are more open-textured than words like *vehicle* and *radio*, they nonetheless "admit of deter-

---

[159] See generally *Self-Defense and Relations of Domination: Moral and Legal Perspectives on Battered Women Who Kill, A Symposium* 57 U. Pitt. L. Rev. (1996), and especially Anthony J. Sebok, *Does an Objective Theory of Self-Defense Demand Too Much?*, 57 U. Pitt. L. Rev. 725, 753–6 (1996) (arguing that definition of terms like *imminent* should reflect unequal distribution of risk as a result of institutional sexism).

[160] Paul Brest has argued that no matter which moral value a rule of recognition actually tries to identify, that value can always be "manipulated" to reach an ever-widening set of new problems. See Paul Brest, *The Fundamental Rights Controversy: The Essential Contradictions of Normative Constitutional Scholarship*, 90 Yale L.J. 1063, 1083–5 (1981). I agree with Brest that the insatiability of morality is a problem for constitutional law; I just don't agree that it is an insoluble problem.

[161] *Poe v. Ullman*, 367 U.S. 497, 543 (1961) (Harlan, J., dissenting).

minate meaning."[162] Raz and Schauer were quite comfortable saying that the words *equality* and *liberty* have determinate meaning;
what they might have pointed out, however, is that each legal official determines the meaning of different moral terms according to
the theory of morality he or she endorses. The argument from insatiability does not rely on the open texture of moral language but on
the monistic and quite determinate nature of moral reasoning. Neither utilitarians nor Rawlsians think that the answer to the question
"Does law *x* violate fairness" is necessarily indeterminate; nor
would they think that the answer to the question "Does law *x* violate equality" is necessarily indeterminate. But both utilitarians and
Rawlsians would say that the answer to either question ought to be
determined through the same method – the theory of morality he or
she endorses (which, of course, they disagree upon). So nothing in
this argument turns on an appeal to the open texture of moral language; if anything, the argument gets its force from the fact that it
recognizes that because moral reasoning can be determinate, it can
be far-reaching in its scope.

Confronted with the insatiability argument, the incorporationist
could go in two directions. One strategy is to admit that Raz and
Schauer (and Dworkin) are correct, and that every rule of recognition which incorporates a moral value commits the law applier to
making judgments based upon the moral theory he or she thinks is
best, all things considered. It will be recalled that Coleman argued
that a rule of recognition which explicitly incorporates an "all
things considered" criterion of legality could be a legal system, and
so this strategy is available to the incorporationist. This approach is
descriptively identical to strong natural law.[163] The incorporationist, then, is free to say that every rule of recognition which incorporates a moral value is really incorporating all of justice. This
would not make the incorporationist a natural lawyer – after all, it
may simply be a contingent fact that every rule of recognition that
incorporates a moral value is coextensive with justice.[164] An important reason to resist this solution is that it would conflict with the
general consensus among positivists that no modern legal system
has completely incorporated all of morality or justice into its rule of

---

[162] See Waluchow, *Inclusive Legal Positivism*, at 159.
[163] "Suppose the clause in the rule of recognition states: The law is whatever is
morally correct." Coleman, *Negative and Positive Positivism*, at 156.
[164] Coleman, *RSF*, at 724.

recognition. Modern legal systems, such as those of the United States, Canada, and England, have adopted "limited incorporationist" rules of recognition. They are written in a form similar to Coleman's example: x is a law iff x satisfies an *aspect* of morality. The incorporationist, if he or she wants to take seriously these legal systems, must find a way to resist the conclusion that every rule of recognition which incorporates an aspect of morality incorporates all of morality.

The second direction the incorporationist could go is to argue that the reason legal officials can treat moral values like "fairness" or "equality" as aspects of morality is that there are rules of interpretation which determine what role moral reasoning will play in the application of these values. A simple legal system – one that explicitly embraces a monistic test of legality – would not need a rule of interpretation *in* its rule of recognition. The rule of recognition that "the law is whatever is morally correct" or that "whatever Dworkin says is law" tells the law applier to adopt a simple norm as his or her test for validity.[165] While the two rules may be very different in the degree of controversy that may accompany the application of the single norm each contains, there could be complete agreement among the relevant legal officials over what each rule says. That was the lesson of Coleman's distinction between the identity and validation functions of the rule of recognition.

Now imagine that a rule of recognition possesses more than one norm. For example, the rule is "a legislative enactment can be valid only if it meets the demands of fairness."[166] This rule is complex in the following way: It has at least two parts. First, a law applier must be able to identify when an official act is a "legislative enactment" (or authorized under a "legislative enactment"). Second, a law applier must be able to identify "fairness" among all the moral values that make up the theory of morality of which it is an aspect. Satisfying both parts of the rule like this is something that law appliers do all the time; but we should notice *how* they do it. In the foregoing example of the complex rule, the law applier determines that a putatively legislative act is actually a legislative act because it satisfies certain criteria. That may seem simple, but of course it is not: It involves not only the ability to count votes in a legislative session but also the ability to determine when certain qualifications have been

---

[165] See Coleman, *Negative and Positive Positivism,* at 156; Coleman, *AR,* at 293.
[166] See Coleman, *AR,* at 306.

met. The conception of a "valid enactment" has no *a priori* status; it is determined by a social rule that tells legal officials when something is to be treated, for purely conventional reasons, as a legal fact. Hart called this sort of social rule a secondary "rule of change."[167] Coleman and Leiter argued that either the rules of change are validated by the rule of recognition, in which case they are not social rules, or they are part of the rule of recognition, in which case they do not serve an identification function.[168] It seems to me that Hart's view was that rules of change were part of the rule of recognition *and* served an identification function.[169] This comports with our experience of complex rules of recognition. If the rule tells a legal official that an enactment is law *if* it is fair, then the rule of recognition presupposes that a certain legal fact – the "enactment" – will be identified by the legal official and then tested against fairness. The result of this multistep process will be an answer to the question "Is an official act valid?" (i.e., is an arrest/ obligation under this law valid?), but only after the legal official charged with determining validity also determines the identity of certain legal facts (e.g., was this law signed by the queen in Parliament?). The same ineliminable need for the rule of recognition to include rules of identity explains how complex rules of recognition incorporate legal facts such as the holdings in precedents. A rule of recognition which says that a precedent is law *if* it is fair presupposes that a certain legal fact – the precedent's holding – will be identified by the legal officials and then tested against fairness. Even more so than with legislation, the rule of recognition will have to include a set of social rules that tell when putative holdings are really holdings. Whereas legal systems often try to codify the rule of change, rules of "adjudication" are mostly conventional, in that their presence in the legal system is based on nothing more than "a convergent social practice and a shared critical or reflective attitude" among legal officials.[170]

We therefore see that although simple rules of recognition do not serve an identification function, complex rules of recognition do

---

[167] See Hart, *CL,* at 95.

[168] See Coleman and Leiter, *Legal Positivism,* at 245.

[169] "Plainly, there will be a very close connection between the rules of change and the rules of recognition: for where the former exists the latter will necessarily incorporate a reference to legislation as an identifying feature of the rules. . . ." Hart, *CL,* at 96 (emphasis added).

[170] Coleman, *AR,* at 294.

serve as rules of identification for legal officials even as they serve as rules of validity as well. This point was nicely illustrated by Kent Greenawalt's discussion of the rule of recognition in the United States. Greenawalt argued that, as an initial matter, it would be a mistake to say that most of the written Constitution is part of the rule of recognition in the United States.[171] The amending clause (Article V) is part of the rule of recognition because it is the supreme criterion of legality, but the Fourteenth Amendment is not because legal officials refer to criteria like the amending clause to determine that the Fourteenth Amendment is part of the Constitution.[172] If the rule of recognition were simply the amending clause, then one could conceivably argue that the United States' rule of recognition served only a validation function. But Greenawalt thought that the rule of recognition for the United States must include much more than just the supreme criterion of legality. He noted that the amending clause must be supplemented by "standards of interpretation" that enable legal officials to apply the amending clause and the norms identified by the amending clause. So, for example, the rule of recognition includes standards of interpretation for statutes, common law precedent, state constitutions, and the constitutional language itself.[173] These standards of interpretation are, nonetheless, social rules.

Imagine that an appellate judge is asked to validate an official act taken under Article III involving the application of a substantive tort doctrine by a federal district court judge in a diversity case. The amending clause, which can point the law applier toward a whole host of rules authorized through the Judiciary Act of 1789, will not be an effective validity rule unless the judge can identify binding substantive state law precedent.[174] The rule of recognition in the United States must include an interpretive rule that tells judges how to do the latter. That rule of interpretation will be a social rule: Judicial practice concerning the identification of state common law precedent will converge around it, and judges will criticize those

[171] Kent Greenawalt, *The Rule of Recognition and the Constitution*, 85 *Mich. L. Rev.* 621, 643 (1987).

[172] See ibid., at 643. The rule of recognition, if it were just the amending clause, would be: "whatever the Constitution contains that is not itself enacted according to another part of the Constitution." Ibid., at 637.

[173] See ibid., at 659.

[174] See ibid., at 648–9.

who reject it as the way to identify state common law precedent. This is exactly what Hart had in mind when he described how interpretive rules may be incorporated into the rule of recognition. He noted that "the rule of recognition is treated in my book as resting on a conventional form of judicial consensus. That it does so rest seems quite clear at least in English and American law for surely an English judge's reason for treating Parliament's legislation (or an American judge's reason for treating the Constitution) as a source of law having supremacy over other sources includes the fact that his judicial colleagues concur in this as their predecessors have done."[175]

7.6. INCORPORATIONISM AND IDENTIFICATION

Once we realize that complex rules of recognition serve an identification function for legal officials, the problem of insatiability becomes quite manageable for the incorporationist. Let us return to the example of a complex rule of recognition from the preceding example. We saw how rules of interpretation (about statutes) would help legal officials identify the legal facts called "enactments." The second half of the rule demands that we test the enactment against "fairness." Just as an enactment can be identified only through the application of a rule of interpretation that is part of the rule of recognition, the same can be said of "fairness." *Fairness* in the legal context does not mean "what ought to be done, all things considered." Like the word *enactment, fairness* does not have an *a priori* legal meaning, even if it does have a determinate but contested meaning to the Rawlsian and the utilitarian. Hart argued that under the English and American legal systems the rule of interpretation concerning legislative supremacy often directs a judge to identify a legal fact notwithstanding the judge's own convictions. We should assume that there are rules of interpretation concerning moral values that also direct a judge to identify the "legal" meaning of words like *fairness*, notwithstanding the judge's conviction of what fairness *really* means, all things considered.

Thus, a judge who applied the rule of recognition in the foregoing example to an official act in which someone was convicted for a certain form of intentional killing would have to identify "fairness" in his or her legal system. To do this the judge would have to look to

---

[175] Hart, *CL*, at 267.

the rule of recognition for the rules of interpretation. Just as with the rules of interpretation concerning the identity of legislative enactments, there will be rules of interpretation that will tell the judge how to identify fairness. The actual set of rules of interpretation will vary from legal system to legal system. They may direct the law applier to consult a variety of sources, ranging from the original intent of the framers of the enactment, the legislative materials they left behind, the dictionary meaning of the word in question, the current popular understanding of the word, or the judge's own view of what should be done, all things considered. The one thing the rule of interpretation cannot do is tell the rule applier to determine the fairness by asking *only* "what justice would require, all things considered." This would convert a complex rule of recognition into a simple rule of recognition.

The limitations of using morality as an interpretive rule is something that both Greenawalt and Perry noted in their discussion of complex rules of recognition. Greenawalt, for example, observed that the American rule of recognition would require a judge to interpret the phrase *search and seizure* in a manner that balances the rule of interpretation "fairness (in police searches) means what is fair according to the best moral theory" with other rules of interpretation, such as "fairness means what a clear line of precedents says it means" or "fairness means what a clear line of precedents says it means in cases not involving new technologies."[176] Perry noted that the "strong Burkean model," which he believed characterizes the common law system, recognizes that a judge must use reasons independent of justice in the course of identifying moral values in the law.[177] Unlike Raz, who argued that judges may never use first-order reasons to identify the law, Perry, as we saw previously, argued that judges may examine the first-order reasons the rule of recognition was designed to settle. But Perry's views on the revisability of the rule of recognition are compatible with – in fact presuppose – rules of interpretation of the sort discussed previously. This is because under the strong Burkean conception a judge cannot simply decide according to what "he now thinks is correct" but must balance his or her conclusion against a range of factors, including "the position in the judicial hierarchy of the courts that have relied upon the [competing] proposition in the past, the num-

---

[176] Greenawalt, *Rule of Recognition and the Constitution*, at 656–67.
[177] See Perry, *Judicial Obligation*, at 222.

ber of times that it had been relied upon, and the age of the relevant precedents."[178] The point of this argument is not to approve of the particular mix of interpretive rules that Greenawalt and Perry claimed to have found in the rules of recognition that they analyze. Greenawalt and Perry simply illustrate my point that if a rule of recognition includes a rule of interpretation that asks the judge to make an "all things considered" judgment about what justice would require fairness to mean, that rule will necessarily be balanced against other rules of interpretation.

It should be clear that the rules of interpretation used by the judge to identify fairness may produce highly controversial results, and that there may be more disagreement among judges who engage in the task of identifying fairness than if the same judges were trying to identify whether an official act was an enactment. But that is not evidence of the value "fairness" acting insatiably, but a consequence of the fact that some legal concepts are more vague than others.[179] If, as Hart argued, vagueness is not fatal to the rule of recognition serving its identification function, a rule of interpretation could be a social rule even if its application were controversial:

> It is true that a rule of recognition containing such an interpretive criterion could not, for reasons discussed [previously,] secure the degree of certainty in identifying the law which according to Dworkin a positivist would wish. None the less, to show that the interpretive test criterion was part of a conventional pattern of law-recognition would still be a good theoretical explanation of its legal status.[180]

The fact that the same rule of interpretation can be used to identify many different conceptions of fairness does not mean that a rule of recognition such as "a legislative enactment can be valid only if it meets the demands of fairness" is so unascertainable as to be use-

---

[178] Ibid., at 240–1. It is clear from Perry's discussion that he conceived of common law reasoning as a blend of "all things considered" moral judgment and precedent, but there is no reason why the blend should be restricted to just two sources of interpretation. His own example of the identification of the standards of liability in negligence suggests that a common law system could also require judges to take other sources into account, such as public attitudes about what is "reasonable" conduct that the judge him- or herself does not believe would bring about the best result, "all things considered." See, for example, Perry's rejection of Dworkin's view that the point of adjudication is the development of the "soundest" theory of law that can be developed for a jurisdiction. See Perry, *Judicial Obligation*, at 255 n133.

[179] See Hart, *CL*, at 251.

[180] Ibid., at 265–6.

less. Obviously, if the rule of recognition depends on two concepts, and one of them (fairness) is the product of a combination of elements including but not limited to what the judge thinks fairness, from the perspective of justice, means, judges will disagree both in the application *and* the identification of fairness. But agreement in the *identification* of fairness may not be an important element of the rule of recognition, because what the judge should do if there is disagreement will depend on the rule of recognition itself. While it is true that there must be agreement among the relevant legal officials as to the identification of the rule of recognition, as Hart noted, there can be far less agreement among the legal officials over the identity of the legal concepts upon which the rule of recognition relies, such as "enactment" or "fairness." If there is great disagreement over the identity of a concept such as "fairness," then the rule of recognition must have a rule that tells law appliers what to do in the face of that controversy. The rule may tell rule appliers to ignore the fact that other law appliers have identified different conceptions of fairness, or it may tell them to defer to another law applier in certain circumstances. As Coleman pointed out, "existence of controversy [in the rule of recognition] does not preclude the existence of conformity of practice in resolving it."[181]

This review of the role that rules of interpretation play in the identification of different elements of complex rules of recognition gives us a better understanding of how judges can have strong discretion in legal systems that incorporate moral values. Hart argued that even cases which involve the application of moral values might require judicial discretion. Of some cases involving the identification of a moral value Hart said, "[S]uch cases are not merely 'hard cases,' controversial in the sense that reasonable and informed lawyers may disagree about which answer is legally correct, but the law in such cases is fundamentally *incomplete*: it provides *no* answer to the question at issue in such cases."[182]

One might think that if the law incorporates a moral value, such as fairness, the theory of morality of which fairness is an aspect will always be able to "complete" the law.[183] But if it is true that the rule

---

[181] Coleman, *Negative and Positive Positivism*, at 161.

[182] Hart, *CL*, at 252.

[183] See Coleman and Leiter, *Legal Positivism*, at 251: "By allowing moral principles to count as law . . . the number of occasions on which a judge will face a case without the benefit of guiding or controlling legal standards will decrease significantly. . . . At some point it may be reduced to an insignificant fraction of the total

of recognition in complex legal systems never permits an incorporated moral value to act insatiably, then it is hard to see how the need for strong discretion is eliminated just because one criterion of legality is an aspect of morality. Returning to our previous example, it is always possible that after the judge applies a rule of interpretation that takes into account his or her own views of what fairness requires, precedent, and other concerns independent of the judge's own view of justice, he or she might believe that there is no answer, based in the rule of recognition, to the question "Is this enactment fair?" This result could occur if the norms applied by the judge in the course of identifying fairness are incomplete or indeterminate. It could be the case that there is no agreement among the relevant legal officials about the scope and weight of various rules of interpretation in this area of the law, and there is no agreement about what to do when the rules of interpretation are incomplete. An inconclusive legal result is perfectly consistent with the judge's being able to state without hesitation what ought to be done in the case before him or her if the only thing that mattered was what justice said fairness required. The proper response by the judge if faced with an inconclusive legal result is not to determine that the legal meaning of fairness is simply what justice requires. No rule of interpretation authorizes the judge to do that. Similarly, it would not be proper for the judge to determine that the legal meaning of fairness is what the author of the enactment originally meant it to be. No rule of interpretation authorized the judge to do that, either. And yet the judge must do something, because the rule of recognition clearly says that he or she must decide whether the official act being presented is valid or invalid. In that case, the judge has strong discretion – she must produce an answer to the question of whether the enactment is fair, even though, technically speaking, there is no legal answer to that question. The significance of the judge's act of discretion will vary according to the rule of recognition's own rules of interpretation. In common law systems the rule of recognition usually includes a rule that allows other legal officials to treat the decision arrived at by the judge as a legal fact that can affect the ap-

number of cases litigated." On the other hand, Coleman and Leiter also acknowledged that if Hart's theory of language were correct, then the incorporation of moral values could *increase* the number of occasions on which a law applier had to exercise discretion because the language in which moral values is expressed is especially susceptible to the core/penumbra phenomenon.

plication of the rule of interpretation in subsequent decisions.[184] Code systems may not have this rule, leaving judicial discretion no precedential force.

7.7. CONCLUSION

New Legal Positivism has taught us that the law can incorporate principles as well as rules. The fundamental rights school argued that the law can incorporate moral principles only if it adopts some form of weak epistemic natural law. The question with which New Legal Positivists have tried to grapple is whether the fundamental rights school is correct. The nonincorporationists agreed with the fundamental rights school. They agreed because they thought that there is no escape from the insatiability thesis. The incorporationists, I have argued, assumed that the challenge of the insatiability thesis can be met but they never exactly say how. In this chapter I have attempted to construct an answer on behalf of the incorporationists. I have used the resources available to me from the arguments of Coleman, Greenawalt, and Perry, although I recognize that my reconstruction of the incorporationist position diverges from their work in fundamental ways. Let us review how far my arguments have taken us from the original incorporationist position.

First of all, I have argued that complex rules of recognition have an identification as well as a validation function. This is because the rules of recognition of modern legal systems usually condition the validity of the acts of inferior legal officials upon the joint satisfaction of certain conditions. Those conditions, such as "enactment" or "fairness," must be *identified* by the legal official applying rules of interpretation contained in the rule of recognition. Not only do I think that it must be the case that complex rules of recognition serve an identification function, but it seems clear to me that Hart thought so, too.

---

[184] If the judge's reasons for a decision can be explained in a way that extends the rule of interpretation, his or her rationale for the decision can become part of the rule of recognition if it becomes a social rule. Of course, the rule of recognition cannot make the judge's act of discretion part of its own complex of rules of interpretation. If the legal officials in fact converge around the novel rule of interpretation, then it becomes part of the rule of recognition. For example, one could argue that this is how Justice Stone's equal protection analysis in footnote 4 of *Carolene Products* or California's "market share liability" rule became part of the American rule of recognition. See, for example, *United States v. Carolene Products Co.*, 304 U.S. 144 (1938) and *Sindell v. Abbott Laboratories*, 36 Cal. 3d 588 (1980).

Second, a complex rule of recognition cannot incorporate "all of society's moral values." Coleman's example – a law that incorporated fairness but not all of justice – suggests that he should agree with me, but elsewhere he stated that there is no reason why a rule of recognition could not incorporate morality "completely."[185] Perhaps he would agree with me that *complex* rules of recognition cannot incorporate all of morality. The reason why a complex rule of recognition could not incorporate morality "completely" is not, as Raz and Schauer argued, that a rule of recognition which asked law appliers to engage in substantive moral reasoning would be the same as a system of *ad hoc* decision making where law makers usurp law appliers. It is because the rule, being a complex of elements, offers the possibility that there are some legal valid outcomes which are determined not by their justice, but by another element. If legal validity can be determined by a factor unrelated to justice, some legally valid outcomes may be unjust. But this is just another way of saying that if a rule of recognition requires the law applier to identify a concept that is an aspect of morality (as opposed to the moral theory of which that concept is an aspect), then legal validity under that rule of recognition is not coextensive with the moral theory of which that concept is an aspect.

None of what I have argued excludes the possibility that a simple rule of recognition could still incorporate "all of morality." Raz and Schauer are committed to saying that the criterion of legality in a simple rule of recognition must have a social source. We have canvassed their reasons for the sources thesis and the limited domain thesis and, except for the insatiability thesis, have found them wanting. But the insatiability thesis poses no threat to a rule of recognition of the form, "x is law iff x satisfies all of morality." The insatiability thesis is an argument about the collapse or failure of the rule of recognition to perform its epistemic function – specifically, its identification function. The argument of the insatiability thesis is not that a rule of recognition which contains moral values fails in its identification function because it is difficult for citizens to ascertain the identity of the law. That is the argument from function, and I reject it. The insatiability thesis says that because a law applier cannot distinguish an aspect of morality from the moral theory of which it is an aspect, a rule of recognition cannot incorporate

---

[185] See Coleman, *RSF,* at 723.

just one aspect of morality without rules of identification that are not themselves conditioned on morality. But in the case of a simple rule of recognition, the law applier is not attempting to identify an aspect of morality but is really trying to apply morality – all of it – to the case before him or her. There is no problem with morality acting insatiably, because the criterion of legality *is* morality. There is no failure to distinguish between morality and an aspect of morality, because the law applier has not been asked to do any distinguishing. The law applier has been asked to apply morality, and nothing less.

I therefore agree with Coleman that a rule of recognition may incorporate all of morality. My amendment to this claim is, however, that all such rules of recognition must be simple. This leads me to my third point. I am not sure if the incorporationist should be very interested in simple rules of recognition, because no modern legal system has ever had one. Certainly none of the legal systems that the incorporationists discuss – those of the United States, England, Canada, or the nations of western Europe – possess simple rules of recognition. That being the case, it seems to me that we cannot do without the sources thesis so easily. Coleman argued that if Raz's sources thesis is wrong, then positivism imposes no constraint on the content of the rule of recognition. The criterion of legality can be anything, including all of morality. If there is no necessary constraint on the content of the rule of recognition, then there can be no thesis about the "sources" of the criteria of legality other than the tautological statement that they are sources if they provide the content of the rule of recognition's criterion of legality. So New Legal Positivism might differ from classical positivism not only in its rejection of deductive legal reasoning and replacement of the command theory with the social rule theory but also in the abandonment of the idea that positivism can be identified by the way it characterizes sources of law.

I argued in Chapter 2 that classical legal positivism restricted the content of the rule of recognition to the will of the sovereign. This was an obvious consequence of the command theory. Hart noted that once the positivist abandons the command thesis in favor of the social rule theory, the range of sources that can make up the rule of recognition expands as well. "In a modern legal system where there are a variety of 'sources' of law, the rule of recognition is correspondingly more complex: the criteria for identifying the law are multiple and commonly include a written constitution, enactment by a legislature, and judicial precedents."[186] Following Hart, I have argued that positivism does place limits on the content of the rule of recognition, at least with regard to the complex rule of recognition. Of course, this does not mean that I agree with Raz's definition of the "strong" sources thesis – that legality must "depend exclusively on facts of human behaviour capable of being described in value-neutral terms, and applied without resort to moral argument."[187] The sources thesis I urge (for complex rules of recognition) is that the criteria of legality can be based on any value that is itself capable of being identified by a social rule. Thus, just as the concept of "fairness," when it is understood to be an aspect of morality, may be part of a complex rule of recognition, "fairness," when it is understood as a judgment about what one ought to do, "all things considered," may not be the only part of a complex rule of recognition. The sources thesis, as I understand it, does no more than insist that the concepts that make up the rule of recognition be interpreted according to the rule of recognition, and not the other way around.

New Legal Positivism, as first articulated by Hart, and later developed by the incorporationists, is a worthy heir to the legal process school. As we saw in Chapter 4, Hart and Sacks, like H.L.A. Hart, rejected the command theory in favor of something like the social rule thesis, and they accepted the separability thesis. I want to conclude this chapter by arguing that Hart and Sacks's idea that law is a system of "general directive arrangements" closely resembles the revised sources thesis that is implicit in the concept of a complex rule of recognition. I argued in Chapter 4 that Hart and Sacks's embrace of positivism was motivated by their belief that the function of law was to determine how practical reason would be exercised by the state. Hart and Sacks viewed adjudication as the application of reason under very specific conditions. Those conditions served to cabin the scope of the principles that the law applier was authorized to apply. This process of reasoning through constraints imposed by law is what Hart and Sacks called reasoned elaboration. Reasoned elaboration clearly takes place in the context of the sort of complex rule of recognition I have been discussing in this chapter. In order for law appliers to engage in the reasoned elaboration of a statute, common law doctrine, or a command of an administrative agency, they must consult a wide range of rules of interpre-

---

[186] Hart, *CL*, at 101.
[187] Raz, *AL*, at 39–40.

tation that will tell them not only what counts as an enactment or administrative decision but also what counts as "fair" or "reasonable" in their particular legal system. The rules could apply to a rich and diverse range of sources, but the identification of each source, in the end, will depend on a rule of interpretation in the rule of recognition. This is what makes the rule of recognition directive as well as authoritative. A rule of recognition that authorized a legal official to do what was best, all things considered, might be a practical authority, but it is not directive. The sort of legal systems with which Hart and Sacks were concerned had to have rules of recognition that were both authoritative and directive. In other words, they were concerned with complex rules of recognition.

New Legal Positivism, as I present it in this chapter, can explain one feature of reasoned elaboration that Hart and Sacks failed adequately to explain or defend. The conservative legal process scholars forced upon Hart and Sacks's theory a skeptical view of morality that turned legal process into a crude form of originalism. The only alternative to this view of legal process was the fundamental rights school, which, as I argued in Chapter 6, rejected the separability thesis. New Legal Positivism shows us how reasoned elaboration of moral principles can occur without collapsing into the moral wasteland of neutral principles or the moral quicksand of fundamental rights. Hart and Sacks assumed that the reasoned elaboration of moral principles was not different in kind from the reasoned elaboration of other standards, such as "reasonable care" in tort law or "unfair competition" in trade law.[188] They argued that in both sorts of cases the adjudicator, whether a judge interpreting common law or an administrator interpreting an agency directive, has to engage in noncontinuing discretion.[189] Noncontinuing discretion is the constraint of "strong" discretion, not its elimination. It is what happens when there is law, but the law commands the law applier to reason from principle. Hart and Sacks viewed noncontinuous discretion as the *elaboration* of a value within constraints set out by law. As I noted in Chapter 4, they argued that an "inchoate" law (such as the command that a judge prohibit competition that is "unfair") did not grant a judge the power to engage in an "all things

---

[188] See Henry M. Hart and Albert M. Sacks, *The Legal Process: Basic Problems in the Making and Application of Law* 1309–10 (William Eskridge Jr. and Philip Frickey, eds., 1994).
[189] Ibid., at 143.

considered judgment." For Hart and Sacks, an inchoate law – which they saw as one of the most important innovations of the new administrative state – was a delegation to the judge of the task of identifying a value (like fairness) through the exercise of reason cabined by law.[190] We can now see that the phenomenon of noncontinuous discretion is made possible by the structure of the complex rule of recognition. Like Coleman, Hart and Sacks assumed that the elaboration of a moral principle in a modern legal system could be cabined so that the principle did not incorporate the entire moral theory of which it was an aspect. Rules of interpretation show us how the cabining of moral reasoning can occur in complex rules of recognition. The rule of recognition itself determines how the moral concept is to be elaborated. These rules of interpretation, being part of the rule of recognition, are themselves social rules. Thus, moral principles can be part of noncontinuous discretion without the rule of recognition collapsing into a grant of continuous discretion.

[190]   See section 4.4.

Index

319